Goodbye Forever
miscellaneous memoirs of an English Lama
volume three

Goodbye Forever

miscellaneous memoirs of an English Lama

volume three

Ngakpa Chögyam

Aro Books WORLDWIDE

2023

Aro Books WORLDWIDE,
PO Box 111, 5 Court Close
Cardiff, Wales, CF14 1JR

© 2023 Ngakpa Chögyam

All rights reserved. No part of this book may be reproduced in any form or by any means electronic or mechanical, including photocopying, recording, or by any information storage and retrieval system, without permission in writing from the publisher.

First Edition 2023

ISBN: 978-1-898185-66-6 (paperback)
ISBN: 978-1-898185-67-3 (ePub)

For further information about Aro Books WORLDWIDE please see http://aro-books-worldwide.org/

To obtain copies of all our publications please visit https://www.lulu.com/spotlight/arobooksworldwide

contents

Introduction

Part One – *the theatre of visions*		1
1	*the black wrathful mother*	3
2	*saints and madmen*	17
3	*Jétsunma*	31
4	*mChöd rTen*	45
5	*dancing in colour*	57
Part Two – *the king of realised activity*		71
6	*Mahasiddha Karma Gyalpo*	73
7	*Zorro*	91
8	*a British army rifle*	105
9	*brug pa kun legs*	133
10	*convivial vicar of Vajrayana*	147
11	*many corpses*	157
12	*chaotic humour*	171
13	*perchance to dream*	179
14	*mantra hurling assembly*	197
15	*miraculous mistresses*	205
16	*Charong Drüpchen*	223
17	*ma-dzé da-gyüd*	235
Part Three – *nothing to know other than knowingness*		247
18	*dön'dré*	249
19	*perfect, just as it is*	269
20	*awareness*	281
21	*hitting the essence*	295
22	*Johnny Gurkha*	299
23	*homeward bound*	311
Appendices		321
I	*gTértöns and gTérma*	323
II	*the inner tantras*	341
III	*A Descriptive History of the Rig'dzinpas and Rig'dzinmas of the Great Secret Mantra Vehicle*	347
Glossary		357

Introduction

Pel Drukdraling Foundation

08 December 2022

Ngak'chang Rinpoche—*writing as Ngakpa Chögyam*—is the incarnation of gTértön Aro Yeshé, the son and heir of Khyungchen Aro Lingma (1886–1923). Ngak'chang Rinpoche is a meditation master, author, poet, artist, musician, and vocalist. Kyabjé Düdjom Rinpoche, Jig'drèl Yeshé Dorje, recognised him as the lineage holder of Aro gTér Nyingma Vajrayana teaching in 1971, when Ngak'chang Rinpoche was nineteen years old.

He underwent a period of intensive training in Vajrayana practice and meditation, with Kyabjé Düdjom Rinpoche Jig'drèl Yeshé Dorje and Kyabjé Künzang Dorje Rinpoche. They gave him the unbroken lineage of Dzogchen teachings which are appropriate to practise in modern Western and European countries. They gave him detailed advice on: *becoming a Lama in the West; working with his own students; finding a sangyum*; and, *revealing the Aro gTér*.

Ngak'chang Rinpoche also underwent training in Düd'jom gTér Mahayoga studies with Ngakpa Yeshé Dorje and came to know his wife Jétsunma Khandro Ten'dzin Drölkar – an advanced Dzogchen yogini and disciple of Kyabjé Künzang Dorje Rinpoche. Hence, they both underwent training in Dzogchen with Künzang Dorje Rinpoche – and are still good friends up to the present. Ngak'chang Rinpoche then returned to Britain via Afghanistan to give Nyingma teachings in the West.

Ngak'chang Rinpoche's fascinating book *Goodbye Forever* – Volume III illuminates the numerous Dzogchen practices and teachings he received from Kyabjé Düd'jom Rinpoche, Kyabjé Künzang Dorje Rinpoche – and many great Dzogchen masters. This account is interwoven with the period of training in Illustration at Bristol Art School during his twenties – from which he gained a 1st Class honours degree.

We thus take this especial privilege to urge different readers at various levels of experience to study this exceptionally extraordinary book. It offers clear indications which can be applied throughout one's life as a Vajrayana practitioner.

Khar-trül Wangchuk Rig'dzin Rinpoche (PhD)
Resident Lama – Drala Jong Aro gTér Nyingma Vajrayana Centre, Britain
Executive Director – Pel Drukdraling Foundation, Bhutan
Fullbright Scholar – Wheaton College, USA

HE Trülku Ugyen Dro'dül Thinley Kunkyab Rinpoche
President – Pel Drukdraling Foundation, Bhutan, Incarnation of gTértön Drukdra Dorje Rinpoche

Pel Drukdraling Foundation, Thimphu, Bhutan

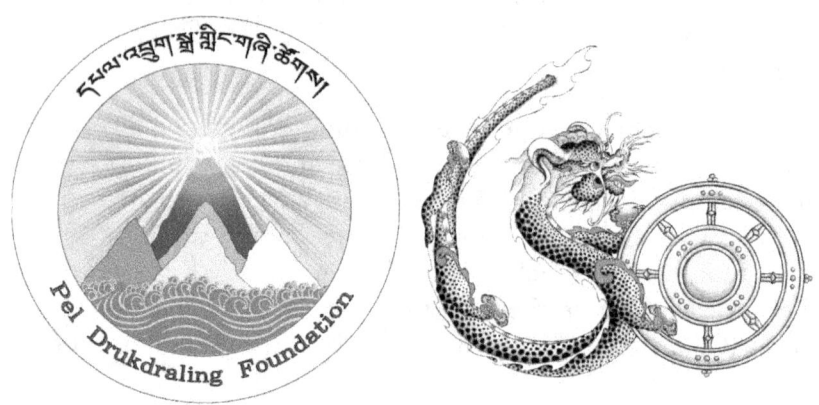

དཔལ་འབྲུག་རྒྱལ་ཁབ་ཀྱི་གཞི་རྟེན།
PelDrukdraling Foundation

PDF/EDO/December/2022/037   08 December 2022

Introduction to *Goodbye Forever* – Volume III

Ngak'chang Rinpoche—*writing as Ngakpa Chögyam*—is the incarnation of gTértön Aro Yeshé, the son and heir of Khyungchen Aro Lingma (1886—1923). Ngak'chang Rinpoche is a meditation master, author, poet, artist, musician, and vocalist. Kyabjé Düd'jom Rinpoche, Jig'drèl Yeshé Dorje recognised him as the lineage holder of Aro gTér Nyingma Vajrayana teaching in 1971, when Ngak'chang Rinpoche was nineteen years old.

He underwent a period of intensive training in Vajrayana practice and meditation, with Kyabjé Düd'jom Rinpoche Jig'drèl Yeshé Dorje and Kyabjé Künzang Dorje Rinpoche. They give him the unbroken lineage of Dzogchen teachings which is appropriate to practise in modern western and European countries. They gave him detailed advice on: *becoming a Lama in the West; working with his own students; finding a sangyum*; and, *revealing the Aro gTér*.

Ngak'chang Rinpoche also underwent training in Düd'jom gTér Mahayoga studies with Ngakpa Yeshé Dorje and came to know his wife Jétsunma Khandro Ten'dzin Drölkar — an advanced Dzogchen yogini and disciple of Kyabjé Künzang Dorje Rinpoche. Hence, they both underwent training in Dzogchen with Künzang Dorje Rinpoche — and are still good friends up to the present. Ngak'chang Rinpoche then returned to Britain via Afghanistan to give Nyingma teachings in the West.

Ngak'chang Rinpoche's fascinating book *Goodbye Forever* – Volume III illuminates the numerous Dzogchen practices and teachings he received from Kyabjé Düd'jom Rinpoche, Kyabjé Künzang Dorje Rinpoche — and many great Dzogchen masters. This account is interwoven with the period of training in Illustration at Bristol Art school during his twenties — from which he gained a 1ˢᵗ Class honours degree.

We thus take this especial privilege to urge different readers at various levels of experience to study this exceptionally extraordinary book. It offers clear indications which can be applied throughout one's life as a Vajrayana practitioner.

Khar-trül Wangchuk Rig'dzin Rinpoche (PhD)
Resident Lama – Drala Jong Aro gTér Nyingma Vajrayana Centre, Britain
Executive Director – Pel Drukdraling Foundation, Bhutan
Fulbright Scholar – Wheaton College, USA

HE Trülku Ugyèn Dru'dul Thinley Rimkyab Rinpoche
President – Pel Drukdraling Foundation, Bhutan
Incarnation of gTértön Drukdra Dorje Rinpoche

part one

the theatre of visions

One hundred thousand galaxies gathered in display. A great expanse in which all appearances are completely contained. The illusory display of boundless sky-dancing ladies whose self-radiant wisdom destroys all outer, inner and secret demons. Obsession, aggression, and torpid indifference are overpowered by the astounding splendour of their laughter. From *Tröma's Strong Laughter* – the Düd'jom gTér Drüpthab[1] of Tröma Nakmo[2], the Black Wrathful Khandro.

Repeated returns to the Himalayas were interrupted only by the necessity of earning the wherewithal to return to the Himalayas. Fortunately, these working periods enabled me to avoid the Monsoon season in which the heat and humidity were not optimal with regard to health. I worked on building sites, roadworks, and—when lucky—I found truck driving jobs.

I customarily visited Ngakpa Yeshé Dorje[3] and Khandro Ten'dzin Drölkar[4] first, as they always knew whether Kyabjé Düd'jom Rinpoche was in Bodhanath[5] or not. There was also the poetry of replicating my first journey to the Himalayas in 1971.

There was the sense in which I would continue in this way for the rest of my life – apart from the fact that I'd get too old to hod bricks. Long distance truck-driving would take me into my middle age – but I had no way of knowing whether this kind of work would always be available. I gave these thoughts no weight. Being in my early twenties, I was not living my life with long-term comfort and security in mind. That was not an option for a young ngakpa. What was 'caution' vis-à-vis old age when '… *one hundred thousand galaxies were gathered in display. A great expanse in which all appearances were completely contained.*'? I imagine I was not unique, in acting as if I'd be young in perpetuity.

1 *sGrub thab* / སྒྲུབ་ཐབ / *sadhana*.
2 *khro ma nag mo* / ཁྲོ་མ་ནག་མོ / *Khrodha Kali*.
3 *sNags pa ye shes rDo rJe* / སྔགས་པ་ཡེ་ཤེས་རྡོ་རྗེ
4 *mKha' 'gro bsTan 'dzin sGrol dKar* / མཁའ་འགྲོ་བསྟན་འཛིན་སྒྲོལ་དཀར
5 Seven miles from the city of Kathmandu.

1

the black wrathful mother

"*Past-mind no longer exists. Future-mind is not yet present. Whatever arises in the moment is indecipherable because it cannot be translated by thought without converting it into thought. Let thoughts of past and future settle in the present moment – and, in that moment, simply experience what is naturally there.*" Kyabjé Düd'jom Rinpoche Jig'drèl Yeshé Dorje

Arriving in Delhi on Afghan Air, it was the hour-of-day at which I should have been waking up subsequent to a good night's sleep. I was bleary. I pushed through, as was my custom – and before long, I felt quite alert. I spent a day in Old Delhi reading – and browsing the two Tibetan antique shops in the Red Fort. That was also my custom. Eventually I caught the overnight train from Old Delhi Station to Pathankot and—counter to expectations—I managed to replace the sleep I had missed. I slept soundly, the noise of a few thoroughgoing stertorians[1] notwithstanding.

I dreamt. I was in a room somewhere. I didn't recognise the room. I was talking with Ron Larkin and Steve Bruce[2]. They were Levi'ed from shoulder to ankle, as was our style at the end of the 1960s. Ron had an apple in his hand, as he often did. Steve rested his right index finger against the side of his nose, as he often did. We'd just come in on the end of a conversation – and Ron was saying *"So"* with a huge grin *"yer went to Tibet after all. Always knew yer would."* That was the entirety of the dream. It was brief yet vivid. I wanted to get back to sleep again to tell them all about it – but it was gone. Goodbye forever. The dream was not to return. Why did I want to return to an illusion? Maybe it was because Ron and Steve had seemed so real. Be that as it may – it was the antithesis of *a dream of clarity*. I found myself disappointed with my inability to distinguish reality and illusion. I hoped there would come a time when I would cease to dream-create phantasmagoria.

---

1   Author's neologism based on *stertor* from Latin 'stertere' to snore – first used in 1804.
2   Two prominent members of the *Savage Cabbage Blues Band* for which Ngak'chang Rinpoche had been the vocalist (1966–1970). Ron Larkin played lead and Steve Bruce played bass. The drummer was Jack Hackman. See volume II of *an odd boy* by Doc Togden.

Then, two buses. Pathankot—*via Lower Dharamsala—Dharamsala—Upper Dharamsala*—finally to arrive in McLeod Ganj[3]. The road kept climbing – likewise ebullience. Sky segued from brown to blue as the altitude increased. Temperature steadily dropped. Perfection manifested incrementally. I alighted from the bus in a place I knew as well as I knew my hometown – or better, because Farnham had changed and kept changing. How strange to feel such security in a remote foreign destination.

I will not describe delving the wonders of the Himalayan Antiquities Emporia in the Red Fort in Old Delhi – or the overnight train journey. It was little different from what is described in the previous volume. The emporium brimmed with objects – and there were always those pieces which caught my attention. As always, I dwelt wordlessly on my relationship with them. What was the nature of appreciation? I didn't indulge fantasies about having owned them in a previous life – merely because I found them beguiling. It was a pleasure to peruse them nonetheless. I purchased a small and rather plain brass shrine box in which to keep tokens I had been given by Kyabjé Düd'jom Rinpoche and Dilgo Khyentsé Rinpoche. It would polish splendidly.

It was not the adventure it had been in 1971. I'd been nineteen years old then – and that *elderly teenager* seemed so young to me now. Adulthood arrives in increments – with each increment feeling like adulthood. At fourteen I was in an *adult relationship* with Anelie Mandelbaum – a 22-year-old Swiss au pair[4]. At sixteen I was professionally adult – on stage with the Savage Cabbage Blues Band. At seventeen I weathered the deaths of my two best friends – along with the loss of Lindie Dale. At eighteen I went to Art School – and, although I was legally adult, it felt little different from how I was in previous years.

---

3 A common mistake is to use the name 'Dharamsala' for McLeod Ganj. The town of Dharamsala is actually below the town of Upper Dharamsala – which is below McLeod Ganj. This may be a deliberate obfuscation of the fact that McLeod Ganj was the name of a British Army Hill Station in the days of the British Raj.
4 Anelie Mandelbaum had been a Swiss au pair girl temporally living in Farnham. See: *Goodbye Forever*—Volume I—chapters 7 and 8—Ngakpa Chögyam—Aro Books worldwide—2020; and *an odd boy*—Volume I—chapter 9—Doc Togden—Aro Books worldwide—2011.

the black wrathful mother

At nineteen I set out for the Himalayas – and four years later, I'd completed the Düd'jom gTérsar ngöndros[5].

At the age of 23 I'd been awarded a 1st Class Honours degree in Illustration. Beyond that… what? Was I now an adult? I presumed so – but how would I feel about that after another few years had passed? What did adulthood mean? Responsibility, reliability, integrity, decency, honour? Yes, I could realistically confirm that. Independence, self-determination, self-sufficiency, autonomy… Yes, more-or-less – but emotional maturity? That was perhaps, still in question. I was not immature – but I was still rather susceptible to unlikely romances. It was fine to be open and unreserved – but foolish to fall in love with every lady who turned her headlights on me, full beam.

Self-determination was easy enough with *culinary* temptation. I could easily be sensible with my dietary concerns – but with ladies all sense of self-preservation evaporated. The usual order in life is that *males are the predators* – and so ladies have to have the intelligence which enables them not to act unwisely. They know how to say *'I like you as a friend – but…'* That was something that I was going to have to develop if I was to fulfil Kyabjé Düd'jom Rinpoche's prediction concerning finding a sangyum[6]. Maybe all I had to do was keep that thought in mind when ladies turned their headlights on me. There was something hypnotic about that – and I was always so charmed that I always said 'yes'. I'd fall in love with anyone at the drop of a hat. That had to stop.

That this journey to the Himalayas was not *the adventure it was when I was nineteen*, is not entirely accurate. The Himalayas are *always* an adventure. If anything, this expedition was stranger than the first, inasmuch as familiarity and unfamiliarity jostled at unlikely times.

---

5 *bDud 'joms gTer gSar sNgon 'gro* / བདུད་འཇོམས་གཏེར་གསར་སྔོན་འགྲོ་ – *Preliminary Practices of the New Treasures of Dud'jom*. The longer ngöndro by Düd'jom Rinpoche is *The Chariot Path of Union* – sung jug lam-gyi shing-ta (*zung 'jug lam gyi shing rTa* / ཟུང་འཇུག་ལམ་གྱི་ཤིང་ཏ་) revealed by Dud'jom Lingpa (*bDud 'joms gLing pa* / བདུད་འཇོམས་གླིང་པ་ / 1835–1904) as part of the pure vision cycle *Dag-nang Yeshé Drawa, The Wisdom Net of Pure Vision*. The Mind incarnation of Dud'jom Lingpa—Düd'jom Jig'drèl Yeshé Dorje (1904–1987)—expanded and clarified the text.

6 *gSang yum* / གསང་ཡུམ་ / *guhyakalatrata* – literally 'secret mother', but meaning *consort, religious wife*.

Time had passed. I'd experienced wonder, weirdness, and woe. In terms of wonder, I'd spoken personally with the 16th Gyalwa Karmapa – and received transmission of Formless Mahamudra[7]. He'd given me what felt like a degree course in two private interviews. He had told in detail of the 25 Siddhas of Chimphu[8]. He had given me the empowerments of Dorje Tröllö[9] and Dorje Bérnakchen[10] from the gTérma of Yong-gé Min'gyür Dorje[11]. In terms of the weirdness of the time, it would serve nothing to itemise it. Likewise with woe.

Everything was easier than it had been on the first trip. I knew exactly how everything would unfold. Ngakpa Yeshé Dorje and Khandro Ten'dzin Drölkar would not unaccountably be 'somewhere else' – as could easily have been the case. I knew this because I'd received various letters from friends in McLeod Ganj who had given me a detailed picture of the situation. Ngakpa Yeshé Dorje and Khandro Ten'dzin Drölkar were expecting me – and, what is more, they wanted me to come to them directly on arrival.

---

7   Formless Mahamudra—chag chen nam 'mèd (*phyag chen rNam 'med* / ཕྱག་ཆེན་རྣམ་འབྲེད་) —comprises of the Najor Zhi (*rNal 'byor bZhi* / རྣལ་འབྱོར་བཞི) – the four yogas: 1. Tsé gCig (*rTse gCig* / རྩེ་གཅིག་) – one pointedness; 2. Trodral (*sPros bral* / སྤྲོས་བྲལ་) – non-elaboration or lacking complexity; 3. Ro-gÇig (*ro gCig* / རོ་གཅིག་) – one taste; and 4. Gom'mèd (*sGom 'med* / སྒོམ་འབྲེད་) – non-meditation. Formless Mahamudra is also known as Naked Mahamudra (chag chen gÇér thong / *phyag chen gCer mThong* / ཕྱག་ཆེན་གཅེར་མཐོང་).

8   25 Siddhas of Chimphu—je wang nyer nga (*rJe 'bangs nyer lNga* / རྗེ་འབངས་ཉེར་ལྔ་)—were the 25 disciples of Guru Rinpoche all of whom attained realisation. There are several lists – and when added together it is evident that there were as many as 31. There were also 25 female disciples – and others in other lists. The full number may be closer to 300.

9   *rDo rJe gro lod* / རྡོ་རྗེ་གྲོ་ལོད་ – one of the Eight Manifestations of Guru Rinpoche riding upon a pregnant tigress. He assumed this manifestation in Paro Taktsang in Bhutan in order to bring the transdimensional beings under his control. There are thirteen different places called Taktsang (Tiger's Nest) at which Guru Rinpoche manifested in the terrifying wrathful form of wisdom chaos.

10 *rDo rJe ber nag chen* / རྡོ་རྗེ་བེར་ནག་ཆེན་ – the great black cloaked protector; a form of Nagpo Chenpo (*nag po chen po* / ནག་པོ་ཆེན་པོ་ / *Mahakala*).

11 *yongs dGe mi 'gyur rDo rJe* / ཡོངས་དགེ་མི་འགྱུར་རྡོ་རྗེ་ / 1628–1708 – a Nyingma gTértön and a close student of Karma Chag-mé, the 10th Karmapa Chöying Dorje, and Surmang Trungpa Kun-ga Namgyal (*zur mang drung pa kun dGa' rNam rGyal* / ཟུར་མང་དྲུང་པ་ཀུན་ དགའ་རྣམ་རྒྱལ་) the 4th Surmang Trungpa. His most illustrious students included the 11th Karmapa, the 8th Tai Situ, Kunkhyen Chökyi Jung-né, and gTértön Könchok Dorje.

Sônam Wangdü was there outside Nowrojee's Store[12]. He had arranged to meet me – and accompany me to Ngakpa Yeshé Dorje and Khandro Ten'dzin Drölkar's collection of connected huts. He was to translate, as he had translated previously.

That's what I was expecting – and that is exactly what happened. A journey sans disappointment. A journey sans confusion or surprise. Mystery however, was always present – purely in the texture of being with Ngakpa Yeshé Dorje and Khandro Ten'dzin Drölkar.

Jétsunma[13] Khandro Ten'dzin Drölkar was always luminous in her being. She had a way of looking at me which was hard to describe: affectionate curiosity; sympathetic inquisitiveness; benevolent absorption; effusive attention – there are no exact words that I can attribute to what I saw. She could remain motionless in a statuesque manner for surprising lengths of time – and then, when she moved, it was never possible to detect the moment when her change of posture commenced. She was almost transparent. It was not that I could see through her – but she posed no obstacle to anything. It was as if she were part of everything that I could see. She was non-separate from her surroundings – as if she was an apparition who was connaturally becoming tangible. Then she'd ask me questions which were couched as statements:

"Dzogchen."

"Yes, every day for one or two hours."

"Mi lam."

"Every night."

Then followed a list which included various aspects of Dzogchen-related practice such as the breathing exercises of rTsa rLung, the practice of the 'jig rTen drug[14] and others.

---

12 *Nowrojee & Son General Merchants* (1860–August 2020) sold newspapers, magazines, confectionary such as *Blue Bird* toffees; cigarettes such as *Passing Show, Craven A*, and *Number Ten Virginia*; beer, wine, and occasionally *Southern Comfort* whiskey liqueur. The wooden shop displayed advertising posters from the British Raj and antiques, such as a *Petromax* 835 *Special* – a German hanging-wick lamp.
13 *rJe bTsun ma* / རྗེ་བཙུན་མ་ – means 'Lady', as in the female of 'Lord'.
14 *'jig rTen drug* / འཇིག་རྟེན་དྲུག་ / *khams drug* / ཁམས་དྲུག་ – the Dzogchen practice of the Six Lokas, or experiential domains of duality.

With each subject she mentioned, I confirmed that I'd practised consistently. She beamed at me *"Yag-po dug [15]—yag-po dug—thug-ché ché [16]."*

Ngakpa Yeshé Dorje asked *"Düd'jom ngöndro completing?"*

"Yes. The four ngöndros are now completed – the Shorter, the Longer, the Khandro Thugthig, and the Tröma ngöndro."

"Ya-tsan[17]! Good!" in Tibetan and English, holding up two fists and shaking them with joy.

He asked if I'd had time to make gTorma[18] and I told him that I had made quite a few gTorma over the three years – especially in retreat. I explained that my retreats had only been a week in duration because of Art School and working in the Summers – but that I'd spent over a month each year in retreat. Khandro Ten'dzin Drölkar was concerned with my Anuyoga and Dzogchen practice and Ngakpa Yeshé Dorje with my Mahayoga practice.

Then it was time for giving presents. I delved into my 100-litre rucksack and pulled out a pair of Frye's cavalry boots[19] for Ngakpa Yeshé Dorje and a pair of Scarpa[20] Italian mountaineering boots for Khandro Ten'dzin Drölkar. This is what each had wanted when I'd asked them what they'd like from the West in 1971.

---

15 *yag po 'dug* / ཡག་པོ་འདུག་ – this is good.
16 *thugs rJe che* / ཐུགས་རྗེ་ཆེ་ – thank you.
17 *ya mTshan* / ཡ་མཚན་ – amazement.
18 *gTor ma* / གཏོར་མ་ / *balingta* – a three-dimensional strewing-oblation profferment, either edible or nonedible; sculpted objects ceremonially presented to a yidam (*yi dam* / ཡི་དམ་ – awareness being, meditational deity) or protector for diverse purposes connected with rites of amenity and attainment.
19 The Frye Company—founded by John Frye in 1863—is the oldest American shoe company. During the 1960s Frye made custom boots for Bing Crosby, Jerry Lewis, Barbra Streisand, Bette Midler, Stan Laurel and Oliver Hardy, Liza Minnelli, Carole King, Gene Autry, and President Richard Nixon. They introduced the Harness Boot in the 1960s, inspired by the Union Cavalry boot.
20 Scarpa was founded by Lord Rupert Edward Cecil Guinness and Luigi Parisotto. Luigi Parisotto, a highly skilled boot maker, was hired in 1938 by Lord Rupert Edward Cecil Guinness, second Earl of Iveagh. Together they gathered the most talented craftsmen in leather work.

Khandro Ten'dzin Drölkar often hiked to sacred places of Guru Rinpoche and Yeshé Tsogyel[21] and wanted something more robust than was available for women in India. I'd described mountaineering boots – and she'd said they sounded ideal.

Ngakpa Yeshé Dorje wanted a boot that was more comfortable than a Tibetan boot – and without a fabric strap at the top. These straps always came undone – and he found them a nuisance. I also found them a nuisance and eventually devised my own fastening system which employed a buckle and a canvas strap[22]. It seemed that there were no alternative boots to be had in India – and so he was well pleased with what I brought. He was, in fact, far more than well pleased. It was wonderful to see the look of sheer glee on his face. He kept gazing at them and caressing them. Khandro Ten'dzin Drölkar smiled and nodded to me – indicating that she had observed how unusually pleased her husband was with his new boots. I'd looked for the best footwear available – as my gratitude for their having sent me to Kyabjé Düd'jom Rinpoche Jig'drèl Yeshé Dorje was immense. It was the very least I could do to show my appreciation.

In 1971, I had sought the help of a local cordwainer in Upper Dharamsala. He had come with me to see Ngakpa Yeshé Dorje and Khandro Ten'dzin Drölkar – and had measured their feet. He had made interesting drawings of their feet. He got them to stand on sheets of paper – and then he had drawn around their feet with his pencil at different angles so that each foot had three different base profiles. He then measured their insteps and their ankles – and provided me with the measurements. The cobbler seemed extremely happy in the execution of his profession and absolutely refused payment. He told me that it was his honour to be of service. I then took these measurements home and obtained boots which seemed to come as close to the measurements as was feasible.

---

21 Khandro Chenmo Yeshé Tsogyel (*mKha' 'gro chen mo ye shes mTsho rGyal* / མཁའ་འགྲོ་ཆེན་མོ་ཡེ་ཤེས་མཚོ་རྒྱལ).
22 Ngak'chang Rinpoche eventually designed a leather robe boot based on the Tibetan boot – but which had a riding heel. It was made by Vogel's Boots of New York and adopted by many of those who Ngak'chang Rinpoche and Khandro Déchen ordained.

Ngakpa Yeshé Dorje and Khandro Ten'dzin Drölkar tried on the boots and were delighted with them. I was relieved. I'd been slightly anxious about the fit – and was therefore as elated as they were. Everything had worked out. Maybe everything else would work out. Anything was possible. I was certainly functioning within comprehensible Himalayan socio-religious parameters – so there was no obstacle to anything in that sphere of existence.

One day when Ngakpa Yeshé Dorje was away—discussing his potential new Gompa[23] with the Dalai Lama[24]—I was able to spend time with Khandro Ten'dzin Drölkar on her own. Sônam Wangdü was free to translate – and so I asked Khandro Ten'dzin Drölkar whether she would speak a little on the practice of the 'jig rTen drug. She was happy to do so – and it was wonderful to hear her teach. Up to that point Ngakpa Yeshé Dorje had been the one to teach whilst Khandro Ten'dzin Drölkar sat with me listening.

"You are 'jig rTen drug from Kyabjé Düd'jom Rinpoche receiving. Many different versions. The one I am knowing – from my Tsawa'i Lama coming: from Kyabjé Karma Gyalpo Rinpoche[25]. Five emotions having – and when each is rising then there is one realm becoming. If much angriness and nothing is transformed then hell vision developing. But where hell? Where hell finding? Hell, nowhere finding – but with anger cause, hell existing. Self-created suffering vision then existing. Every day accumulating dualistic vision causes. In this moment no hell-realm or god-realm vision having. Mainly, precious human condition having. This precious human vision dimension – this realm of vision is where Vajrayana practising possible.

---

23 *dGon pa* / དགོན་པ་
24 A grant was given to Ngakpa Yeshé Dorje through the auspices of the Dalai Lama to build a Lhakhang complex for the practice of the Kagyèd (*bKa' brGyad* / བཀའ་བརྒྱད་) the 8 Nyingma Hérukas from the lineage of 5th Dalai Lama. This was named Zilnön Kagyèd Ling (*zil gNon bKa' brGyad* / ཟིལ་གནོན་བཀའ་བརྒྱད་) and built in the late 1970s. It was formally empowered by Kyabjé Trülshik Rinpoche Ngawang Chökyi Lodrö (*'khrul zhig ngag dbang chos kyi blo gros* / འཁྲུལ་ཞིག་ངག་དབང་ཆོས་ཀྱི་བློ་གྲོས་ / 1924–2011) the incarnation of gTértön Trülshik Do-ngak Lingpa who revealed the Dzogchen Yangti Nakpo cycle. He was first based on the northern slopes of Mount Everest in Rongpuk Gompa (*affiliated to Mindröl Ling*). He was a heart son of Kyabjé Düd'jom Rinpoche Jig'drèl Yeshé Dorje and Dilgo Khyentsé Rinpoche.
25 Karma Gyalpo Rinpoche is Künzang Dorje Rinpoche. I did not know until years later that Khandro Ten'dzin Drölkar and I had the same Tsawa'i Lama. Düd'jom Rinpoche had told me I was never to mention Künzang Dorje Rinpoche to anyone.

"But this precious human vision – this exhausted becoming. Then dying. Then bardo²⁶ experiencing. After bardo of existence, karma potentiality according to strongest causes driving. When directly knowing chö-nyid ngön-sum²⁷ then not necessary karma following. Then possibility always incarnation somewhere where there Dzogchen finding. Then free from rigid duality. Then nondual realisation possibility. But not all people having – because they always karma potentiality following, and they never 'causes' transforming."

Khandro Ten'dzin Drölkar then gave a detailed description of the practice with each locus – and how the visualisation accorded with the recitation of the syllables Om, A'a: and Hung. Her explanations were extremely thorough. At their conclusion she smiled at me *"Method you are already knowing from Kyabjé Düd'jom Rinpoche – so maybe no need for me saying."*

Sônam Wangdü and Khandro Ten'dzin Drölkar exchanged a few words and then we wandered back to McLeod Ganj. On the track back to the village Sônam Wangdü told me that Khandro Ten'dzin Drölkar had asked him to explain to me that I should not mention to anyone that she had given any teaching – as it could cause problems for her. I assured him that, of course, I would never mention it to anyone – but I was never in the habit of chattering about teachings or practices in any case. I asked him—tentatively—what sort of problems there could be? Sônam didn't answer for some dozen paces – but then said *"Tibetan women not so free like west. More free than India and Nepal – but still, not so free. Young Tibetans different coming – but older Tibetans still like Tibet living."*

I felt moved to ask whether this would apply to Ngakpa Yeshé Dorje – but had the sense that I'd already ventured into a delicate area. Sônam Wangdü was evidently a little embarrassed. I valued him as a friend – and asked nothing further. I had the sense however that it might be wise not even to mention this discussion to Ngakpa Yeshé Dorje. I sometimes made the mistake of seeing Tibetans as being *almost the same as western people* – albeit more straightforward and cheerful. They were surprisingly au fait with modern electronic technology in comparison with the average Indian – but they were still to some extent time travellers from Mediæval Tibet. There was, of course, much which was valuable about Mediæval Tibet.

---

26 *bar do* / བར་དོ་ – intermediate state.
27 *chos nyid mNgon sum* / ཆོས་ཉིད་མངོན་སུམ་ / *manifest dharmata* – the appearance of actual reality; direct perception of essential nature of reality.

There was much which was valuable about the modern west. There was much which was valuable about the synthesis of the cultures which were unravelling in different ways in different places.

Chögyam Trungpa Rinpoche had certainly dove headlong into western culture without losing anything of the essence of Vajrayana. The question was: What would *Ngakpa Chögyam* do? I couldn't dive into my own culture, as if it were entirely new to me – so how was I to attempt what Chögyam Trungpa Rinpoche had accomplished. I could certainly look for what was wholesome in western culture. I relished Baroque and Classical Music. I relished Blues, Shakespeare, Albrecht Dürer, Hieronymus Bosch, Bruegel, and the Surrealist painters. Maybe that was a good start. There was much that was wonderful in western culture – and it was often neglected by those who looked to the East. One thing was certain: the status of women would figure prominently in anything with which I was involved. I was supposed to teach at some point in the future – and, if a sangha ever evolved around me, I would make a point of giving women every encouragement in terms of ordination. My sangyum —whomsoever she might turn out to be—would never be secondary to me. I would not challenge the mores in the Himalayas – but Britain was another matter. Besides which, we had a Queen. We'd had Queens in the past. Queen Elizabeth the 1st had been a powerful woman – as had Queen Victoria. Our current Queen was a highly resilient, circumspect woman – and so there was every hope that Vajrayana in the West could be a scenario where *gender* was not a lop-sided equation.

I went to see Ngakpa Yeshé Dorje and Khandro Ten'dzin Drölkar in the period leading up to leaving for Nepal – and received many teachings on the practice of Tröma Nakmo.

"This text" Ngakpa Yeshé Dorje smiled *"Tröma's Strong Laughter. By splendour overpowering. So beginning."* He looked down at his text for some minutes before commencing – then suddenly and in an unusually powerful tone of voice, he launched into the text.

"A hundred thousand galaxies gathered as great expanse. All appearances completely inside contained. **Phat**:[28] *Boundless khandros; illusory display; self-radiance wisdom – these are all outer, inner and secret demons* [29] *destroying.* **Phat—Phat—Phat**: *Then… mother Sang-gyé Khandro, central. She is uncontrived activity of chö-ying knowing. So attraction, aversion, and indifference she is overpowering in astounding splendour – and in ku-sum expanse dissipating by* **Phat** *sounding. Then mother Dorje Khandro from East coming and astounding splendour of uncontrived activity —as mirror wisdom—aggression demons overpowering.* **Phat—Phat—Phat**: *Then mother Rinchen Khandro from South coming – and uncontrived activity equanimity wisdom, arrogance demons – she is with astounding splendour overpowering.* **Phat—Phat—Phat**: *Then mother Lé-kyi Khandro from North coming and uncontrived self-accomplished wisdom activity paranoia with astounding splendour overpowering.* **Phat—Phat—Phat**:"

Ngakpa Yeshé Dorje looked up from his text after a moment of silence *"Lama, Sang-gyé, Chö, and Gendün Kyab su che; ku-sum Khandro, Five Great Element Mothers – all demons overpowering, all element entities overpowering. All sa bDag overpowering – all tamed by astounding splendour transmission of Khandro Yeshé Tsogyel. Righteous! All good increasing."*

We sat in silence for a moment – before Ngakpa Yeshé Dorje remarked *"Like this you practising – then all good coming. Now – Pure Vision Red Feast."*

It was not so easy to write it all as it was spoken and I sometimes had to request a pause so that I could check what I had written. Sônam Wangdü always seemed content with what he heard back and only occasionally checked with Ngakpa Yeshé Dorje. Sometimes Sônam Wangdü had to plead for a pause in order to translate – and this always made Ngakpa Yeshé Dorje laugh.

"Yah… so…" Ngakpa Yeshé Dorje continued at astounding speed *"Retinue of obedient protector demons of existence and mamos come here and consume the profferments. Delight in the red feast of flesh and blood. Severance in basic space terminates conditions of demonic disease.*

---

28 *phat* / ཕཊ྄ – disperse into beginningless space! Combination of **pha** – beyond; and **t** (reversed) – cutting.

29 Chi dag ta'i rudra (*phyi bDag lTa'i ru dra* / ཕྱི་བདག་ལྟའི་རུ་ད྄ར་) – the outer rudra of viewing in terms of gross self-referencing. Nang dag ta'i rudra (*nang bDag lTa'i ru dra* / ནང་བདག་ལྟའི་རུ་ད྄ར་) – the inner rudra of viewing in terms of self-referencing. Sang-wa dag ta'i rudra (*gSang ba bDag lTa'i ru dra* / གསང་བ་བདག་ལྟའི་རུ་ད྄ར་) – the innermost 'secret rudra' of viewing in terms of self-referencing.

"Bestow the supreme and ordinary siddhis. Phat—Phat—Phat. The emotions arising from obsession, aggression, and indifference; the effects of sickness, errors, obscurations; the habituated tendencies; the physical body of flesh and blood – all these are fed to the sky-dwelling khandro above one's head. Her retinue of protectors and demons of existence consume everything without leaving a morsel.

"Then, finally…" Ngakpa Yeshé Dorje concluded *"All guests delight in the red feast of flesh and blood. Yah! Basic Space severs conditions of disease and demons – and khandros then supreme and ordinary siddhis bestowing. Phat—Phat—Phat. Emotions of outer and inner clinging – and all that comes from it: sickness, demons, errors, obscurations and habits, along with the material body of flesh and blood. All these are fed to the earth-dwelling khandro below and her retinue.* "Everything is consumed without leaving a morsel. It is proffered with the first Phat. Obtained with the second Phat. Then with the third Phat – everyone and everything everywhere is satisfied by the one taste of ecstasy and emptiness. Finally: the profferment; the one who proffers; and those who receive what is proffered become one in sensation in nonduality. Enter the womb of the innately pure basis of reality. Rest in the radiance of the indestructible dorje."

This is just a section taken from my note book of the time – and, of course, I had to have it all checked when I was in Nepal. The final version—with mantras—is not publishable, as it is a category of material that should only be made available to those who have received transmission of Tröma Nakmo. I give it here as an illustrative vignette of being fabulously assailed with symbolism. At times it was so dense that it caused me to disappear into a pristine panoply of perfect perplexity – in which confusion somehow failed to be an obstacle. I realised that I didn't have to understand in order to *understand*. It was as if I was flying through space observing galaxies unfolding out of primal zero.

Coming to this understanding took me back to my childhood – or rather, the early period of my existence in which Khyungchen Aro Lingma manifested in my room or in my dreams. All else from my childhood seemed vague – as if it had happened to a character in a book I'd read. When Khyungchen Aro Lingma appeared, I'd be left knowing something – but I'd have no words for *what* I knew. This *knowingness* is there in the torrent of language I transcribe. This knowingness is always simply there. All I had to do was reconnect with it – or fail to get in the way of reconnecting with it. It was the same knowingness which I experienced as an infant, as a child – and later, less frequently as a teenager. Now—in my twenties—however, this sense of knowingness was returning.

It was most apparent in the presence of Kyabjé Düd'jom Rinpoche – but it was also here in the explanations I was receiving on the Tröma Nakmo drüpthab.

2

saints and madmen

Ngakpa Yeshé Dorje was to leave for Southern India at the end of the week. There was a drought. He had been called upon to facilitate rain. I had witnessed him stopping the rain on several occasions – and only once was there a situation in which he was not entirely successful, and the torrential rain gave way to a drizzle. I remember one occasion when the Dalai Lama was performing a large public ceremony in McLeod Ganj. I attended it with Ngakpa Yeshé Dorje, Khandro Ten'dzin Drölkar, and their children. The entire Tibetan population of the area was there – as well as Indians and Injis of assorted nationalities. I'd never seen so many people – other than at the Bath Jazz and Blues Festival in 1970[1].

We had been standing sheltered by trees – but the rain had increased. The sky was as dark as a daytime sky could be without looking like night. I wondered what Ngakpa Yeshé Dorje would do. I wondered if the Dalai Lama had to request him directly to stop the rain – or whether he would just command the cessation of precipitation of his own volition. Suddenly he shook his head and exclaimed a rather displeased *"Yah!"* He untied the kangling[2] from his shamthab[3] sash and reached in his bag for his drilbu[4] and gÇod damaru[5]. He began to ring the drilbu in time with his gÇod damaru and chanted some lines with frequent exclamation of the syllable 'Phat'. Then he began to chant mantra *'Om A'a: Hung Chakra Bendzra Bendzra Thum Thum Chil Chil Hung Hung Phat Phat Naga Radza Phat.'*[6] After a few recitations, he gestured to me to join him. This was simple, as I knew the syllables from other practices. We recited for some five minutes. Then he blew his kangling in the four cardinal directions.

---

1 The Bath Jazz and Blues Festival featured Johnny Winter, Frank Zappa, Canned Heat, John Mayall, Dr John, Colosseum, and many others.
2 *rKang gLing* / རྐང་གླིང་ – trumpet made from a human femoral bone – mainly employed in the practice of gÇod (*gCod* / གཅོད་).
3 *sham thabs* / ཤམ་ཐབས་ – a pleated skirt tied at the waist with a sash.
4 *dril bu* / དྲིལ་བུ་ / *ghanta* – bell.
5 *gCod rNga* / གཅོད་རྔ་
6 The mantra is given here because it was not deemed secret. Everyone there could hear it quite clearly.

He repeated this three times – and, by the third repetition, the rain had stopped. The sky cleared – and after ten minutes there was a blue sky and sunshine. *"O yah [7]! char-gÇodpa! [8]"* he beamed at me. Needless to say, I took this all in good fun. Ngakpa Yeshé Dorje was a great exponent of positive reinforcement. He had absolute success with me – because I always responded with enthusiasm in terms of effort.

I had no idea *what* he had done or *how* he had accomplished it. I was as delighted to have witnessed this siddhi of rain-stopping as I was on previous occasions – but I had no strong wish to enter training to gain that capacity. If I was to teach – I wanted to teach people *how to be happy*. Not that 'happiness' is the goal of Buddhism – but neither is misery; especially unnecessary misery. As I saw it, we were surrounded by immense wealth – simply through having senses. If people could learn to value what was freely available through the senses – then kindness would prevail and poverty would disappear. That seemed a tall enough order, as it was – without gaining control of the environment. People in the West seemed addicted to making themselves miserable for no apparent reason. It often occurred to me that *'khorwa [9] was bad – but* we *made it worse*. Sickness, old age, and death notwithstanding – life *could* be far more pleasurable than people allowed it to be. War was *not* an absolute requirement of life on Earth. People *could* be kind, generous, and open minded. How hard could that be? If anything motivated me, it was to help people understand that the *dog-eat-dog* policy led to misery for everyone. There was enough and plenty for everyone – just not enough for everyone's greed. There were people who were wealthy enough to have extremely expensive copies made of their jewellery. They'd then keep their jewellery in a safe – and wear the reproductions. This was an example of the insanity that made 'khorwa worse than it had to be.

An interesting aspect of Ngakpa Yeshé Dorje's *miraculous* feat, was that no one looked surprised. It was obvious that the Tibetans in the audience saw what he had done as normal. That is what weather makers did. If— back in Bristol—a plumber had come to fix some problem, no one would have seen it as a miracle. That is the rôle of a plumber – and, although their work requires expertise, it causes no sense of wonderment. In McLeod Ganj on that day – it was no different.

---

7   Few people seemed to realise that 'o yah' is Tibetan – and spelled *'ong yag* / ཨོང་ཡག.
8   *char gCod pa* / ཆར་གཅོད་པ – rain-stopping practitioner.
9   *'khor ba* / འཁོར་བ / *samsara* – cyclic perception and cyclic experience.

Ngakpa Yeshé Dorje expected no applause or praise. He had simply carried out a duty. The Dalai Lama's ceremony should not be marred by rain. It wasn't. The splendidly professional *tantric plumber* had fulfilled his obligation.

The sound of a kangling is impossible to forget. There is nothing else like it. On that occasion the sound seemed to pierce the rain. Rain usually dampens the way in which sound carries – because the sound waves are interrupted. On this occasion however the sound of the kangling was audible everywhere in the vicinity. It was not because it was particularly loud or piercing in itself. The kangling makes an unusual sound—not like any other trumpet-instrument—but that alone does not account for the way in which it defied the laws of nature.

The next place on the agenda for Ngakpa Yeshé Dorje in his rôle as char-gÇodpa was Bylakuppe[10], Southern India. That was a place I would never visit – due to the heat. I have to avoid excessive heat because I tend to lose consciousness at unlikely times when the temperature rises beyond a certain point. I collapsed in Lucknow[11] in a queue waiting to get my sleeping-berth ticket for Delhi. I was lucky to have had Tibetan friends with me who were able to grab the items I dropped – such as my money and passport. They bundled me onto the train just in time, I failed to get a sleeping-berth and had to lie on the floor until one became vacant. That was one of the low points of travel in India.

After he left McLeod Ganj, I would not see Ngakpa Yeshé Dorje again on that particular sojourn in the Himalayas – so he decided to take me with him on his last rounds of chir-dog[12] in the area. I was to carry the implements.

---

10 Bylakuppe is in Karnataka and home to several Tibetan settlements established in 1961 and 1969. It is the second largest Tibetan settlement in the world outside Tibet.
11 Lucknow is the capital of Uttar Pradesh. It is a multicultural city which flourished culturally and artistically during the Nawab period (18th–19th centuries).
12 *phyir bzLog* / ཕྱིར་བཟློག – exorcism.

Goodbye Forever

There were our dorje[13] and drilbu sets; our skull damarus[14]; gÇod drums; and phurbas[15]. These were standard for practice – but for exorcism many other implements were required. There were rolmo[16] and a large stick drum[17]. There were many vajra weapons: hammer, axe, spear, sword, dagger, knife, lance, and various others[18].

On other occasions he'd needed the help of two people to carry everything, but my experience as a hoddie came in useful – along with a 100-litre rucksack with straps for external pouches. It made Khandro Ten'dzin Drölkar laugh with delight when—eventually—she watched me load myself to the point at which I resembled a burdened yak. She expressed great surprise that I could actually walk thus laden.

Before then however – there was much to learn. It all happened quite rapidly. At first, I was simply to accompany Ngakpa Yeshé Dorje. Then everything shifted. I was to participate. This involved three *dawn-to-late-night* days of intense preparation in which I had to absorb many different ritual procedures at an alarming rate. To others it may not have been alarming – but to me it was almost overwhelming.

---

13 *rDo rJe* / རྡོ་རྗེ / *vajra* – thunderbolt sceptre.
14 Skull damaru – thöd nga (*thod rNga* / ཐོད་རྔ) or go-ru nga (*mGo rus rNga* / མགོ་རུས་རྔ). It is made from a male and female human calvarium, cut above the ears. Internally they are inscribed with male and female yidam mantras. The skins are cured by burying them with copper; mineral salts, and herbal formulations for a few weeks. These are then stretched and applied to the two sides, giving the skins a mottled green or blue appearance. From the 1960s diaspora, they were made up to the late 1980s in India and Nepal. India and Nepal however, are no longer a source – export being banned, due to criminal acquisition of human bone.
15 *phur ba* / ཕུར་བ / *kila or kilaya* – thunderbolt nail: the three bladed dagger of emptiness which stabs attraction, aversion, and indifference.
16 *rol mo* / རོལ་མོ – large wrathful cymbals with hemispherical bosses. Rolmo bupchal (*rol mo sBub chal* / རོལ་མོ་སྦུབ་ཆལ) – extremely large wrathful cymbals.
17 Stick drum – lag nga (*lag rNga* / ལག་རྔ).
18 Other implements: grigug (*gri gug* / གྲི་གུག) – a hooked knife with a curved blade; dri-dre (*gri 'dre* / གྲི་འདྲེ) – demon knife; sor (*bSor* / བསོར) – spear; tsé dreng wa (*rTse sGreng ba* / རྩེ་སྒྲེང་བ) – scimitar; ma dung (*mDa' mDung* / མདའ་མདུང) – arrow-spear; sèl shing (*gSal shing* / གསལ་ཤིང) – impalement stake; tri kang (*kring kang* / ཀྲིང་ཀང) forked spear; te'ü dung (*sTe'u mDung* / སྟེའུ་མདུང) – axe-lance; ta-ri (*sTa ri* / སྟ་རི) – hatchet; tog tsé (*tog tse* / ཏོག་ཙེ) – mattock; ral-dri (*ral gri* / རལ་གྲི) – sword; dPa'wo chag (*dPa' bo lCags* / དཔའ་བོ་ལྕགས) – hero's whip; dung-wa (*rDung ba* / རྡུང་བ) – cudgel; towa (*tho ba* / ཐོ་བ) – hammer; tholum (*tho lum* / ཐོ་ལུམ) – iron ball; zorwa (*zor ba* / ཟོར་བ) – sickle; shurma (*shur ma* / ཤུར་མ) – pike; and, chag drog (*lCags sGrog* / ལྕགས་སྒྲོག) – shackles.

I cautioned Ngakpa Yeshé Dorje—as best I could within the bounds of Vajrayana courtesy—that I was slow. I *could* learn a great deal – but only in a great deal of time. I was somewhat trepidatious with regard to making mistakes – but he laughed and waved away the possibility. As far as he was concerned, I was protected by the trans-dimensional influence of Kyabjé Düd'jom Rinpoche – so nothing could go wrong. Expressed in that way, I agreed. Nothing would go wrong.

Sônam Wangdü was enlisted to transcribe sections of the text in phonetic so that I could chant what was most essential – along with Ngakpa Yeshé Dorje. There was no time for translation – but it was deemed not to be vital that I understood what I was chanting. I found that idea peculiar at first – but then concluded that if Ngakpa Yeshé Dorje was confident of the procedure, then so was I. After all, it was a Düd'jom gTér text – and, for me, that carried the weight of Kyabjé Düd'jom Rinpoche. A fleeting notion crossed my mind – and Ngakpa Yeshé Dorje nodded, seemingly pleased that I'd overcome my anxiety. He never found out what made me smile. It was a farcical scenario in which I found myself in Paris having agreed to play a part in the play *Tartuffe*[19] by Molière. I had to memorise —and speak—French that I could not understand. The limit of my French was a series of words and expressions I'd learnt at Art School – along with '*Laissez le bon temps rouler*' [20] which I was accustomed to use on stage when I performed Blues. The farcical scenario was short lived – but it served to make me relax with the high intensity education I was receiving about ritual procedures. The easiest of these procedures was making gTorma. I was used to that from the practice of Tröma – and so there at least I had some proficiency. I also had my Art School background – and so Ngakpa Yeshé Dorje invariably expressed pleasure in witnessing my level of sculptural finesse.

It never occurred to me to say *'Rinpoche, I'd rather not do this.'* It never occurred to me to explain that I wasn't naturally drawn to exorcism, sorcery, or other such magical procedures. I was a ngakpa – but not because I wanted to become a thaumaturge. I was simply a noncelibate Nyingma ordainee.

19 Tartuffe, ou l'Imposteur (*The Impostor*), first performed in 1664, is a farce by Molière. The characters: Tartuffe, Elmire, and Orgon are amongst the most noteworthy classical theatre rôles. Jean-Baptiste Poquelin (1622–1673) stage name Molière was a French playwright, actor, and poet, regarded as one of the greatest writers in the French language. His works include tragi-comedies, comedies, and farces.
20 '*Laissez le bon temps rouler*' is Louisiana French *Blues patois* for '*Let the good times roll*'.

It was not until later that I discovered that there were three branches of the gö kar chang lo'i dé[21]: Black, Multicoloured, and White[22].

The Black Ngakpas were those like Ngakpa Yeshé Dorje. They specialised in the Outer Tantras and Mahayoga – in terms of rituals. They were often healers, weather makers, exorcists, or astrologers. Ngakpa Yeshé Dorje was also a gÇodpa and practitioner of Kyabjé Düd'jom Rinpoche's Tröma Nakmo drüpthab. Ngakpa Yeshé Dorje was not an astrologer – but he majored in the other fields of expertise. Black Ngakpas are sometimes referred to as 'village ngakpas' – but this is a misleading derogatory term. There *are* village ngakpas – and some do only possess a limited range of skills. Some spend little time in retreat. Ngakpa Yeshé Dorje however, had completed several long solitary retreats – and therefore he bridged the Black and Multicoloured wings of practice. The same was true of all those Black Ngakpas I met.

I never met a village ngakpa in all my years in the Himalayas. The closest I came to meeting a village ngakpa was Ngakpa Dawa, who was an itinerant herbalist. He spent his life walking between Leh[23] in Ladakh and the Tibetan villages in the Kangra District of Himachal Pradesh. He gathered herbs and minerals as he walked – and stayed in certain villages on his journey to make medicines. I once travelled with him into Chamba, Lahaul, and Spiti[24] – which lay over the ridge from Triund[25], the place where I spent three-month and six-month periods in solitary retreat. It was wonderful to travel with him and observe the way in which he knew the land. There were special places for herbs and minerals and he only collected enough to make the quantity of medicine he knew was going to be needed on his travels.

21 *gos dKar lCang lo'i sDe* / གོས་དཀར་ལྕང་ལོའི་སྡེ་ – white raiment and uncut hair series (category or class).
22 Black gö kar chang lo: Nagpo'i Ngak'phang (*nag po'i sNgags 'phang* / ནག་པོའི་སྔགས་འཕང་); multicoloured gö kar chang lo: Tra-chol lé'i Ngak'phang (*khra chol le'i sNgags 'phang* / ཁྲ་ཆོལ་ལེའི་སྔགས་འཕང་); white gö kar chang lo: Karpo'i Ngak'phang (*dKar po'i sNgags 'phang* / དཀར་པོའི་སྔགས་འཕང་).
23 Leh is the largest town in Ladakh in India. Leh Palace, the former residence of the royal family of Ladakh, was built in the same style and at about the same time as the Potala in Tibet. Leh is at an altitude of over 11,000 feet.
24 The Lahaul and Spiti district in Himachal Pradesh consists of the two formerly separate Tibetan areas Garzha (*gar zha* / གར་ཞ་) and Spiti (Chi-ti / *sPyi ti* / སྤྱི་ཏི་). It is the least densely populated area of India.
25 Triund is high in the foothills of Dhauladhar mountains at the height of 8,000 feet.

He was a doctor – so he treated people as he travelled and they were always happy to give him food and shelter. He never charged for his services – but some people gave him money when they could afford to do so. It seemed entirely irrelevant to him whether he was paid or not – he simply needed shelter and sustenance. As for clothing – this was given to him from time-to-time as-and-when he needed it. He left his heavier warmer clothes at certain homes en route – and had his life calculated so perfectly that it appeared almost as if it were a walking holiday. Ngakpa Dawa provided me with some wonderful rilbu[26] to support meditation in long retreats. He gave me others[27] which were for the purification of the rLung and the subtle channels. It seemed that he was often in McLeod Ganj in the Spring – and was wonderfully kind in discovering where I was.

The Multicoloured Ngakpas were those whose practice was primarily Mahayoga and Anuyoga. They engaged in long retreats. They specialised in the practice of drüpthab and in the inner yogas[28]. The Multicoloured Ngakpas had a far higher level of education. They were—unlike the Black Ngakpas—well versed in Vajrayana in terms of teaching and giving elaborate empowerments. They were invariably trained in all the Vajrayana Arts.

The White Ngakpas were primarily Dzogchen practitioners. They did not tend to engage in long retreats because they employed everyday life as retreat. They *were* educated in terms of Vajrayana ritual – but regarded ritual as a secondary practice. It became clear to me that what felt natural —and what suited my disposition—was the path of the White Ngakpa.

---

26 *ril bu* / རིལ་བུ་ – medical pills.
27 Ngödrüp rilbu (*dNgos grub ril bu* / དངོས་གྲུབ་རིལ་བུ་) – siddhi pills; Chhi'mèd rilbu (*'chi 'med ril bu* / འཆི་མེད་རིལ་བུ་) – long-life pills; and, 'ja'lü ril bu (*'ja' lus ril bu* / འཇའ་ལུས་རིལ་བུ་) – rainbow light pills, prepared from Black Naga Devil lu-dud nagpo (*kLu bDud nag po* / ཀླུ་བདུད་ནག་པོ་ / codonopsis / bonnet bell-flower).
28 Naro chö drug (*na ro chos drug* ན་རོ་ཆོས་དྲུག་); nigu chö drug (*nig u chos drug* / ནི་གུ་ཆོས་དྲུག་ / *saddharma*) – the six yogas of Naropa or the six yogas of Niguma: 1. gTummo (*gTum mo* / གཏུམ་མོ་ / *candali*) – spatial heat; 2. gyü-lü (*sGyu lus* / སྒྱུ་ལུས་ / *Smayakaya*) – illusory body; 3. mi-lam (*rMi lam* / རྨི་ལམ་ / *vapnadarsana*) – dream-path / dream yoga; 4. 'ö-Sel (*'od gSal* / འོད་གསལ་ / *prabhasvara*) – clear light luminosity; 5. 'pho-wa (*'pho ba* / འཕོ་བ་ / *samkranti*) – transference of consciousness; and 6. Bardo (*bar do* / བར་དོ་ / *antarabhava*) – intermediate states. There is also Drong'jug (*grongs 'jug* / གྲོངས་འཇུག་) – transference of consciousness to someone or some animal who has just died. This however was lost when Marpa's son died. It is however held to exist in a few small gTérma lineages.

When that became clear to me – I was both relieved and uncomfortable. I was uncomfortable about the idea because I could not see myself being capable of *employing everyday life as retreat* – but it *was* what I wanted. It was not because I could only set out on *the most exalted path*. There were those who only wanted the highest and rarest – but that made no sense to me. It was the magic of the everyday world—the mystery of quotidian reality—which motivated me. It was the indivisibility of sacred and secular that I found far more exciting than sorcery.

I recalled Peter Adams at Netherfield School. He'd aspired to be an Olympic runner. I'd espied him running in Farnham Park on numerous occasions during the time I was at Art School in Farnham. Always running. Never time to stop and talk. Just an acknowledgement of my greeting as he ran. He was determined. He was absolutely committed – but he never came close. He never came close, even in British events. His body simply wouldn't provide the speed he tried to reach. I remembered feeling sad for him. All that *effort*. All that *time*. All that *hardship*. One can try one's best in life and fail. Maybe he accepted the negation of his aspiration with good grace. Maybe he enjoyed the attempt. I will probably never know – but *that* was likely to be *me*, in terms of wishing to be a White Ngakpa.

Fortunately, there were no *Ati-yoga Olympics* – and I could spend my life failing without wasting my life. The path was self-rewarding. At that point in time however – I simply knew that *silent sitting* had primacy. This was what I had initially discussed with Düd'jom Rinpoche in 1971 – and although he instructed me to complete ngöndro, it was presented as a means to an end. I was to teach—at some point in the future—and so I needed a firm foundation.

In the event of it being misunderstood—with regard to Mahayoga ritual — I *always* heartily enjoyed whatever I learnt with Ngakpa Yeshé Dorje. Nothing was irksome. I saw it all as valuable. It was simply not reflective of what I saw as the pattern of *the rest of my life*. So, I knuckled down to learning the mudras and mantras. Most of the time when Ngakpa Yeshé Dorje would be chanting, I would be reciting mantra – but then I'd have to come in at his cue, to recite with him. I made myself a pé-cha style text on long strips of paper – writing out the phonetic along with the Tibetan U-chen and Romanised transliteration. At some later point I'd translate it with the help of my Chandra Das Tibetan-English Dictionary – and have it checked by whichever Düd'jom gTér Lama I could find.

There were three families which he had to visit to perform chir-dog. This was new to me. I knew about it – but it was not part of my curriculum as Düd'jom Rinpoche had defined it. It was not part of my own life-plan either, in terms of what I wanted to do. I did not see myself as a being within the Shamanic wing of Vajrayana – but I considered everything which Ngakpa Yeshé Dorje had to teach as being valuable in terms of experience. I doubted that I would ever perform chir-dog again in any other context – but I considered the widening of my experience to be worthwhile in itself. I was generally open to learning anything in terms of Vajrayana – and so I absorbed what I could of Ngakpa Yeshé Dorje's explanation of what we were about to undertake. I never learned the entire ritual – but I learnt enough to participate as his assistant.

So, the day arrived and—laden like a yak—I followed Ngakpa Yeshé Dorje down the hill. The weight was fine at first and I smiled about the fact that my strength was useful. It was not long however before I realised that I'd overestimated my capacity. I was strong – but not strong enough for the work in hand. Was I to admit defeat? No, that was not likely. I'd said I could do it and so I had to carry through. It was too late to find helpers – and we were expected. I clenched my teeth and pressed on. I was Molière's Imposter as a Black Ngakpa – so the least I could do was to be an authentic Samson or Hercules. I always was more brawn than brain. These words made me smile – which made my burden lighter.

The ordeal was over in less time than I imagined – and soon I heaved the rucksack off my back. Walking without it on my back was at first almost like levitation and I was not entirely clear that my feet were touching the ground. I found that amusing – and Ngakpa Yeshé Dorje responded to my expression of pleasure with a resounding *"O yah! Drüpthob! Yagpo dug—yagpo dug—yagpo dug!"* That was somehow hilarious – and even more hilarious, was the idea that this mirth was a precursor to exorcism.

A friend had once inveigled me into seeing *The Exorcist* [29] with her – and, although I had no interest in horror movies, I obliged. I disappointed her, by not being horrified.

---

29 The Exorcist was a 1973 horror film directed by William Friedkin and written for the screen by William Peter Blatty, based on his 1971 novel. The film follows the demonic possession of a young girl and her mother's attempt to rescue her through an exorcism by two Roman Catholic priests. The film was popular – but some viewers experienced adverse physical reactions. Several cities attempted to ban it or prevent children from attending.

Goodbye Forever

I found the movie rather silly and unconvincingly acted. Apart from that, I would have needed to have believed in the theological / diabolical theory behind the film for it to have had any effect on me. The idea of 'the Devil' and the 'God' who created him *(yet seemed unable to control him)* was antithetical to my world view.

I remembered the mood which the movie attempted to inculcate – but it bore no resemblance whatsoever to what was taking place with Ngakpa Yeshé Dorje in McLeod Ganj. It was more of a pleasant social visit at first. The family seemed quite at peace and reasonably cheerful. The late middle-aged gentleman who required the exorcism was somewhat quiet and withdrawn – but apart from that he looked relatively normal. The family might have been slightly apprehensive about the Inji who Ngakpa Yeshé Dorje had in tow – ngakpa robes notwithstanding. When I placed my dorje, drilbu, and skull damaru in front of me on the çog-tsé[30] they'd provided however – they smiled and all seemed well. There was one young girl there—perhaps in her early teens—who could speak reasonable English. She translated a little—unrequested—and I thanked her for it. She told me that they were all astonished by the weight I'd carried. It took two of the menfolk to bring my rucksack into the house and they thought I must have special powers to shoulder such a burden. I tried to explain that I'd worked on building sites – but this did nothing to dispel their wonder.

Tea was about to be poured for me. Ngakpa Yeshé Dorje waved his hand —shook his head—and laughed *"Chu tangmo."* [31] Their eyes widened. There was some excited speech and the young girl giggled. *"They are saying 'Only saint*[32] *and madman* [33] *cold water drinking.' Is Tibetan proverb."* So, which was I? Or which of the two options seemed more likely to the gathering. *"Tell your family"* I laughed *"That I'm neither – I'm just an Englishman and drinking cold water is quite normal for us."*

That seemed to be the funniest thing they'd ever heard. After that, everyone relaxed and I was accepted as a viable human being.

---

30 *çog tse* / ཅོག་ཙེ – small practice table.
31 *chu grang mo* / ཆུ་གྲང་མོ་ – cold water.
32 Saint – kyebu chenpo (*sKyes bu chen po* / སྐྱེས་བུ་ཆེན་པོ་ / *satpurusha*)
33 Madman – myönpa (*sMyon pa* / སྨྱོན་པ་).

Once Ngakpa Yeshé Dorje had drunk his tea he placed his Dorje Zahorma hat[34] on his head and passed one over for me to wear. Fortunately, our head size must have been the same and it must have appeared as if I was used to wearing such a hat. This was taken as the sign that the ceremony was beginning and everyone sat quietly observing us. At various points amulets were tied to the arms of the gentleman with the malady – and finally a band was wrapped around his head with the amulet in the middle of his forehead.

Ngakpa Yeshé Dorje indicated where I was to chant with him, by pointing whatever object he had in his hand in my direction and turning his head toward me. He'd speak the few syllables of the first line – then begin again so that I could chant with him. The rest of the time I chanted a series of mantras at a whisper that—although barely audible— was perceived by the family. Everything proceeded perfectly smoothly – as if Ngakpa Yeshé Dorje was in the habit of being accompanied by an Inji ngakpa. It surprised me later to learn that he'd never attempted it previously. The other thing which surprised me was the point in the ceremony where he opened a bag and drew out a strange leathern object. It was a bat. He whirled the bat around his head shouting various forceful syllables. He cued me to recite with him – and so, knowing the syllables, I gave voice to them. He smiled at my volume and at the surprised faces of the family. Maybe I was a sMyon p after all. Seeing him smile they accepted that I'd not exceeded my remit. The bat didn't smell that wonderful and a fragment of it flew off and struck the young girl in the ear – but she was obviously not hurt and found it funny. I smiled at her. She giggled.

Then came the section in which I was required to pass Ngakpa Yeshé Dorje implements. The first were the phurba and vajra hammer. Apart from the phurba these weapons were mainly handmade – cut with tinsnips from vegetable oil cans. They were coloured with bright enamel paints. The heavier weapons were either brass or iron – the iron weapons being the older. Each one was carefully wrapped in deep red cloth which was obviously quite old and had seen much use. It was apparently bu-ré – Bhutanese spider-silk, like our ngakpa shawls.

---

34 *rDo rJe za hor ma* / [Tibetan] or *rig'dzin chi-wa* (*rig 'dzin sPyi zhwa* [Tibetan]) – the general Nyingma Lama's hat. For empowerments the lotus hat of Ögyen is worn – Ögyen pé-wa (*o rGyan pad zhwa* / [Tibetan]).

Unwrapping each weapon and passing it to him was a strange experience – an unexpectedly strange experience. Each weapon seemed to become heavier as it was unwrapped. Their temperature changed, not greatly – but enough to feel a slight warmth developing in them. Then as they were passed back to me to stow – I noticed they were warmer than they were before I had passed them to Ngakpa Yeshé Dorje. I considered for a moment that he might have had rather hot hands – but decided that this could not account for it. There were then experiences which were probably imagination or hallucinations – but there seemed to be a halo effect which surrounded the weapons. It was not constant however – and so I was never really certain whether I was seeing it or not. Before I could work out the nature of this phantasmagoria it all ended rather abruptly when I was called on to play the large stick-drum as Ngakpa Yeshé Dorje played rolmo.

The rolmo woke me out of whatever day-dream state I'd entered and suddenly I was in an ordinary room – ordinary that is, as Tibetan shantytown shacks go. The sound of the rolmo however, did what they always did. As those hemispherical bosses passed each other, it was almost as if the left and right hemispheres of my brain were following suit. Then the chanting with gÇod damaru and bell. Then with skull drum and bell. Then it concluded and we sat in silence for somewhat less than 20 seconds before conversation broke out. The family thanked Ngakpa Yeshé Dorje. They thanked me too. They gave us both envelopes. I knew what these contained. They contained money. I later gave my envelope to Ngakpa Yeshé Dorje. It was mortifying for me to accept money, under what I felt to be false pretences. Ngakpa Yeshé Dorje could not really understand my reticence – but accepted my envelope without demur.

There was a rather jolly atmosphere at the end of the ceremony and the family looked at me with what seemed to be affection. No, this was nothing at all like *The Exorcist*. This was real. It was real in every way. The gentleman perked up by the end of the ceremony and thanked Ngakpa Yeshé Dorje. His eyes looked alive whereas before his eyes had looked flat, or dead – or simply lacking any sparkle. He didn't suddenly become a bon vivant – but he became part of his family again.

We partook of a meal together. Ngakpa Yeshé Dorje had requested momos[35]—knowing my partiality for them—and Khandro Ten'dzin Drölkar came to join us. She didn't usually do this – but she told me that she thought it would be good in view of the fact that my time was running out in McLeod Ganj and we never knew when we might see each other again. There could be obstacles to us meeting – and so we should make sure that we made full use of the time we had. This seemed to carry some meaning below the surface – but I had no idea what it was. I put it down to my imagination and let it go – but it returned every once in a while. There were always obstacles – and no one could guarantee that they would always be in the same part of the world at the same time.

Khandro Ten'dzin Drölkar however knew that I always returned to McLeod Ganj in October. It would therefore have been simple for her to have met me on every visit – if such had been her wish. Maybe what she had said, was simply something that people said in Tibetan culture – but nonetheless there was the atmosphere in which I had heard her words. I was not a sensitive type and never went in for reading hidden meanings into people's words. There was however, something different about what Khandro Ten'dzin Drölkar had expressed. A friend with a life-threatening disease might say *'I hope you'd never miss me too much if, by some chance, I wasn't around.'* A reply could then be offered *'Are you planning on emigrating?'* The answer would be *'No – nothing like that. I was wondering, that's all.'* That was how it felt. I knew that I would have to ask Khandro Ten'dzin Drölkar if I wanted to know – but, as usual, it seemed rude to probe. It was an uncomfortable feeling. I really would have to let it go.

---

35 *mog mog* / མོག་མོག — Tibetan fried or steamed pasties with a meat or (*modern*) vegetable filling.

3

Jétsunma

Ngakpa Yeshé Dorje had left for Bylakuppe – and I spent the rest of my days in McLeod Ganj with Jétsunma Khandro Ten'dzin Drölkar This proved to be an astonishing revelation. It became evident that Khandro Ten'dzin Drölkar was a profoundly accomplished Lama.

Sônam Wangdü was happy to translate – and on the first day I asked Khandro Ten'dzin Drölkar if she would be so kind as to tell me about the Düd'jom gTér from her own experience. She was a little reticent at first – but after consideration she said *"In everyday way, I am not teachings speaking – but you are my dearest close friend, so always I must be answer giving."*

She then gave a discourse which sounded as if she was utterly familiar with teaching. This was wonderful – but how was I suddenly Khandro Ten'dzin Drölkar's *'dearest close friend'*? It was as if Her Majesty Queen Elizabeth had telephoned me and spoken to me as if I was one of the family. It was a shock. It was a joyous shock – but a shock nonetheless. Khandro Ten'dzin Drölkar must have detected my wide-eyed astonishment – because she laughed *"All good coming."* She uncurled the elephant ear flap of my waistcoat which had somehow bent inwards – almost like a mother adjusting her son's tie before school in the morning. *"Thug-jé-ché"* I thanked her in Tibetan.

"Düd'jom Tröma ngöndro." PAUSE *"This from Düd'jom gTér-sar lineage coming."*

The word gTér-sar means new treasures. They are highly effective and profound. Their goal is the nondual state. Tröma Nakmo is a mind gTérma transmitted by Guru Rinpoche and received by Kyabjé Düd'jom Rinpoche. Tröma Nakmo is one of the three primordial wisdom khandros of the universe. The other two are Dorje Phagmo and Küntuzangmo[1]. Küntuzangmo is the Chö-ku[2]. Dorje Phagmo is the Long-ku. Tröma Nakmo is the Trülku.

Guru Rinpoche concealed many texts which were later discovered at the times prophesied by the gTértöns indicated.

---

1   *kun tu bZang mo* / ཀུན་ཏུ་བཟང་མོ་
2   *chos sKu* / ཆོས་སྐུ་ / *dharmakaya* – the sphere of unconditioned potentiality.

Goodbye Forever

One such gTértön was Düd'jom Lingpa[3], who discovered the Düd'jom gTér in the 19th century. It contains hundreds of texts and 22 volumes of teachings. Düd'jom Lingpa stated that these teachings were particularly profound, effective, and applicable for this time. Over thirteen of his disciples attained rainbow body[4] by following this gTérma – and countless others attained the state of Rig'dzin[5].

The Düd'jom gTér-sar lineage comes to us directly from Guru Rinpoche through Düd'jom Lingpa to Düd'jom Jig'drèl Yeshé Dorje[6]. Just like his predecessor, Kyabjé Düd'jom Rinpoche was a gTértön who revealed over 23 volumes. Kyabjé Düd'jom Rinpoche's previous incarnations have included many of the greatest masters, naljorpas[7], and scholars[8] in the history of Himalayan Buddhism. Among them are Nuden Dorje Chang[9], Shariputra[10], Saraha[11], Chölon kLu'jom[12], Hungkara[13], Khye'u-chung Lotsa[14] and Drènpa Yeshé Drakpa[15].

---

3 *bDud 'joms gLing pa* / བདུད་འཇོམས་གླིང་པ་—Cha-kong gTértön (*lCags sKong gTer sTon* / ལྕགས་ སྐོང་གཏེར་སྟོན་)—(1835–1904). In 1858, at the age of 23, Dud'jom Lingpa left Sér Valley for Mar-do Tashi Chöling – where he took residence under the patronage of the Gili family. In 1860, Düd'jom Lingpa revealed—from the escarpment of Ba-ter—a prophetic guide (kha chang – *kha byang* / ཁ་བྱང་)—which contained instructions as to how and when he should discover gTérma cycles. He then revealed a major gong gTér (*dGongs gTer* / དགོངས་གཏེར་) from Ngala Tak-tse in Sér Valley. He discovered altogether 20 volumes of gTérma as well as Sa gTér (*sa gTer* / ས་གཏེར་), earth gTérma – physical religious objects.
4 'Ja'lü (*ja' lus* / འཇའ་ལུས་) – dissolution of the body at death into the essence of the elements, as coloured light.
5 Rig'dzin (*rig 'dzin* / རིག་འཛིན་ / *vidyadhara*) means awareness holder. The Sanskrit term vidyadhara refers to either 1. one who has gained siddhis through accomplishment (Vajrayana tantric literature); or 2. a magical winged being (Sutric literature).
6 *bDud 'joms jigs bral ye shes rDo rJe* / བདུད་འཇོམས་འཇིགས་བྲལ་ཡེ་ཤེས་རྡོ་རྗེ་ / 10th *of June* 1904 – 17th *of January* 1987.
7 *rNal 'byor pa* / རྣལ་འབྱོར་པ་ / *yogi or yogin* – practitioner of Vajrayana yogas such as the Six Yogas of Naropa and Niguma.
8 Scholar – Kun-khyen (*kun mKhyen* / ཀུན་མཁྱེན་).
9 *nus lDan rDo rJe chang* / ནུས་ལྡན་རྡོ་རྗེ་ཆང་
10 Shariputra / Sharibu (*sha ribu* / *sha' ri'i' bu* / ཤུ་རིའི་བུ་)
11 Saraha (da'nün / *mDa' bsNun* / མདའ་བསྣུན་)
12 *chos longs kLu 'joms* / ཆོས་ལོངས་ཀླུ་འཇོམས་
13 Hungkara (Hungchenkara / Hung-dzé) (*hung ka ra* / ཧཱུྃ་ཀ་ར་ / *hung chen ka ra* / ཧཱུྃ་ཆེན་ཀ་ར་ / *hung mDzad* / ཧཱུྃ་མཛད་)
14 Khye'u-chung Lotsawa (*khye 'u chung lo tsa' ba* / ཁྱེའུ་ཆུང་ལོ་ཙཱ་བ་).
15 *dran pa ye shes grags pa* / དྲན་པ་ཡེ་ཤེས་གྲགས་པ་

"Guru Rinpoche prophesying anyone who vajra connection and unbroken vows with Kyabjé Düd'jom Rinpoche having, is directly Zangdogpalri [16] travelling." Khandro Ten'dzin Drölkar smiled *"Anyone just seeing or voice-hearing from Kyabjé Düd'jom Rinpoche is liberated and will not bardo [17] frightened coming."*

The goal of these practices is to diminish the dualistic derangements[18] of self-inflicted anguish, hindrances, and debility – as well as to avoid inner and outer calamities. Tröma practice also empowers the recognition and development of wisdom and ability. All beings have potential for nondual awakening. The Düd'jom gTér-sar teachings are direct, vibrant, and fresh. This lineage is impeccable, and unimpaired by broken vows.

All beings are Buddhas by nature – but obstacles, debasement, and deleterious conceptualisation obscure that nature. It is as if the brilliance of the sun were occluded by penumbra. Without a skilled diamond cutter, a diamond is mere rock. The benedictions of the great masters together with dedication in meditation are the diamond cutter. This means the ability to cut dualistic derangement. By practising with devoted dedication, one can attain the nondual state in one life.

We are Tröma practitioners. We apply the *Dzogchen space treasury of the nature of phenomena* to achieve realisation in one life – so we need qualities which differentiate us from those who waste their time. We require undiscriminating love and compassion for beings. We require pure perception. We require genuine affection for our vajra brothers and sisters. We require diligence in accumulating mantra recitations.

---

16 *zangs mDog dPal ri* / ཟངས་མདོག་དཔལ་རི – the Copper-coloured Mountain is the dimension of Guru Rinpoche. Kyabjé Düd'jom Rinpoche said *"Guru Rinpoche manifested the inconceivable Palace of Lotus Light, and presides there with emanations in each of the eight continents of the rakshasas, giving teachings like the Eight Great Methods of Attainment of the Kagyèd."*

17 Liberation on hearing—bardo (*bar do* / བར་དོ)—is the intermediate phase between lives, and the Bardro Thödröl (*bar do thos grol* / བར་དོ་ཐོས་གྲོལ) is liberation on hearing in the Bardo. There are other means of liberation such as: Thongdrol (*mThong grol* / མཐོང་གྲོལ) – liberation through seeing; Nyongdröl (*nyong grol* / མྱོང་གྲོལ) – liberation on tasting; Takdröl (*bTags grol* / བཏགས་གྲོལ) – liberation on touching or wearing; and, Drèndröl (*dran grol* / དྲན་གྲོལ) – liberation on recollection or ideation.

18 Five dualistic derangements – nyon mongpa dug nga (*nyon mongs pa dug lNga* / ཉོན་མོངས་པ་དུག་ལྔ): 1. obduracy, arrogance, territorialism; 2. aversion, aggression, militancy; 3. obsession, fixation, fascination; 4. paranoia, envy, jealousy, protectiveness; and, 5. indifference, unresponsiveness, oblivious torpor.

We require confidence in our Lamas and yidams[19]. This will make us conscientious in practising uninterruptedly – without discrimination between *this* and *that*. We should also develop especially strong confidence that our Lamas are Buddhas – not merely prodigiously kind people with superior qualities. With this view meditation practice increases like the waxing moon.

Tröma Nakmo is the essence of the buddhas of the ten directions and three times. Tröma Nakmo is an uncontrived meditation—beyond normal spiritual conventions—in which all phenomena spontaneously appear as the yidams of the essential nature.

"Outer container of world and inner essence of beings. This is dKyil'khor [20] of Küntuzangmo's Great Palace 'og-Min [21], charnel ground of revelling in great secret, great bliss phenomena. On lotus of uncontrived wisdom – awareness in form Tröma Nakmo arising."

Surrounding *Tröma Nakmo*—on an eight-petaled lotus, in the four cardinal directions—are the four khandros of the four wisdoms. In the intermediate directions are the activity khandros of the four immeasurables[22]. Surrounding them are the four female Hérukas on a four-spoked wheel. This represents cutting-off dualistic existence with wrathful nondual activity as an expression of the space of chö-nyid. In the outer environs are hosts of arrogant lords of appearance who unceasingly manifest their power.

---

19 *yi dam* / ཡི་དམ་ – meditational deity: the nondual anthropomorphic form employed for self-identification in visualisation practises of Tantra.
20 *dKyil 'khor* / དཀྱིལ་འཁོར་ / *mandala* – centre and periphery.
21 (*og min* / འོག་མིན་ / *Akanistha* – means literally 'not below' i.e. above all. The name is used to refer to different dimensions, which are the highest, in relation to specific criteria. Longchenpa speaks of three 'og-Min in relation to the three spheres of being.
22 Four Immeasurables: equanimity, loving kindness, compassion, and joy. *Equanimity* is the wish to be free from preference and prejudice; to know things simply as they are; to experience the world knowing one is simply existent; and, to perceive the nature of whatever arises. *Loving kindness* is the wish for all to be happy, well, and at peace; to be open to whatever presents itself; to experience the world—as one is encountered by it—to be what it actually is; and to welcome whatever arises. *Compassion* is the wish to free all from suffering, harm, and disturbance; to accept life circumstances as they are; to experience natural acceptance for all beings; and to serve whatever needs arise for others. *Joy* is to enjoy the activities of life; to enjoy phenomena simply as they are; to experience the joy of reality in terms of whatever is accomplished; and to know how to respond in relation to whatever arises.

Then there are the four powerful protectors who guard the doors against mistaken cognition. One must visualise them completely. Cultivate certainty that the kyil'khor is the Mirror Wisdom[23], Equanimous Wisdom[24], Discerning Wisdom[25], and Self-Accomplishing Wisdom[26].

"You must trülku Tröma Nakmo becoming" Khandro Ten'dzin Drölkar explained. *"Then eight-sided amethyst heart-centre, inside visualising. Then in heart centre – on lotus and sun throne, is longku Dorje Phagmo. She is bright red – and grigug cleaver holding. She is skull-bowl and khatvangha holding. On Dorje Phagmo head's crown: squealing sow's head visualising. Her body naked, adorned with six bone ornaments. Feet dancing posture. In space of red wisdom fire she is revelling. At your heart-centre – then moon throne appearing and Küntuzangmo manifesting. Bright white, naked-sitting. In her Heart's middle – sun throne appearing with blue syllable Hung. This is all abilities and qualities of all buddhas. Surrounding syllable Hung, there is mantra garland of blazing beryl [27] —fine as with a single hair written—anti-clockwise going. Light rays all qualities radiating. Obscurations all destroyed."*

Khandro Ten'dzin Drölkar then went on into great detail about every aspect of the practice and I filled most of my notebook with her explanations. It was astonishing because she did not refer to notes. It was evident that she was seeing it all as she spoke.

---

23 Mirror wisdom – mélong tabu'i yeshé (*me long lTa bu'i ye shes* / མེ་ལོང་ལྟ་བུའི་ཡེ་ཤེས་ / *adarsajnana*)
24 Equality Wisdom – nyam-nyid yeshé (*mNyam nyid ye shes* / མཉམ་ཉིད་ཡེ་ཤེས་ / *samatajnana*)
25 Discerning Wisdom – so-sor thogpa'i yeshé (*so sor rTog pa'i ye shes* / སོ་སོར་རྟོག་པའི་ཡེ་ཤེས་ / *pratyaveksanajnana*)
26 All-accomplishing wisdom – ja-wa drup-pa'i yeshé (*bya ba grub pa'i ye shes* / བྱ་བ་གྲུབ་པའི་ཡེ་ཤེས་ / *krtyanusthanajnana*). The fifth of the five aspects of primordial awareness—Yeshé Nga (*ye shes lNga* / ཡེ་ཤེས་ལྔ་)—is Space Wisdom – chö-kyi ying-kyi yeshé (*chos kyi dByings kyi ye shes* / ཆོས་ཀྱི་དབྱིངས་ཀྱི་ཡེ་ཤེས་ / *dharmadhatujnana*)
27 Beryl—(mechung shel / *me 'byung shel* / མེ་འབྱུང་ཤེལ་)—is a mineral composed of beryllium aluminium silicate. Common varieties of beryl include emerald and aquamarine. Naturally occurring, hexagonal crystals of beryl can measure up to eight yards – but terminated crystals are rare. Pure beryl is colourless – but it is frequently tinted by impurities which give it tinges of green, blue, yellow, pink, and red.

"Tröma Nakmo mantra – all sounds like bees when nest disturbed. All appearances much shaking and vibrating. When mantra reciting, syllables rising and anti-clockwise spinning. Accomplishment mantra reciting – always in awareness abiding." PAUSE *"Yah – now talking all finishing. Now together we chang[28] drinking."*

We sat in a warm glow of contentment. Everything felt complete. All that was required was to enjoy the colour and ambiance of the room. Khandro Ten'dzin Drölkar fetched glasses and poured out chang. After a few sips—sampled in serene silence—she asked me what boots I wore in England. I told her I mainly wore western boots. Some people called them 'Cowboy boots' – but a wide variety of people wore them including horse ranchers. I also had a pair of tall lace-up boots which were late 1800s style western riding boots. She asked me to describe the western boots. I did so – right down to the multicoloured stitchwork patterns of flames on the shafts and the pale brown lizard-hide of the foot part of the boot. She was intrigued and said that if I ever saw a pair which would fit Ngakpa Yeshé Dorje—which didn't cost too much—that he'd very much enjoy wearing them. I said I'd see what I could find – but that they were not that easy to find in Britain. However, I'd leave no stone unturned. There was a US Air Force base near Reading—which was close to where I lived—and American clothing often turned up in second hand shops around that area. That was where I found all my western boots. On this delightful note I decided I'd better turn in for the night. It had become quite late.

I took the track down to the village of McLeod Ganj and climbed the short rise to my hut which overlooked the ramshackle settlement. I grinned at the intense purity of the stars. The lights which shone could have been oil lamps – and many of them were, because electricity was not in common supply. What electric light existed only gave a yellow glow. It struck me that I could be anywhere in any century.

That was the last normally understandable thought I had. What followed was incomprehensible inasmuch as it was not a dream – or if it was, it occurred whilst walking. There was a faint radiance high up in front of me. Snow on the peaks of mountains. That in itself was not unusual for Himachal Pradesh – but these were not of that range. These mountains were in the Tibetan borderlands with Bhutan – and it was not entirely Ngakpa Chögyam who was noticing them.

---

28 *chang* / ཆང་ – barley beer.

There was some distant sense that Ngakpa Chögyam was there – but Aro Yeshé[29] was also there as a strong element of the same context. The sense of Ngakpa Chögyam was dwindling and that didn't seem to be a cause of anxiety – as it maybe should have been. I was on my way to a group of tents in a defile. There were lights burning within the tents and as I approached, they grew brighter to the eye. A gap occurred in the sequence of events and suddenly I was inside the tent. Two young ladies sat together to one side. We had evidently been sitting there for a period of time. One young lady—the younger of the two—was singing. She seemed to fluctuate in appearance between someone I remembered from childhood to someone with whom I had recently become acquainted. The two faces were similar and so it was not possible to fully understand which was which and why the change occurred. The words of the song were Tibetan – and it was as if I understood the meaning without understanding the words. This conundrum only became evident when I awoke in my hut in the morning – having no memory of the process by which I came to be there. I tried to remember the song – but to no avail. Only the melody lingered and soon that evaporated into the daylight atmosphere of McLeod Ganj. My robes were not where I usually left them and they were folded in a different manner.

After breakfast, as I sat with Khandro Ten'dzin Drölkar, I told her about the hallucination—or daydream—or whatever it was. She did not seem surprised. She simply nodded her head and told me that experiences of this kind were not uncommon. She said that most people had the idea that time proceeded in one direction – and that it only travelled forwards. She said this was relative time – not ultimate time. Ultimate time was not constrained by a forward sequential direction. Anything—and anyone—at any time – could be anywhere. Before Sônam translated this for me – he apologised. He told me that he *would* translate – but that he did not understand what Khandro Ten'dzin Drölkar had said. What she had said was translatable as words but he did not comprehend the meaning of the sentences. I nodded *"That is fine with me Sônam – just say it word for word in English and I'll make sense of it in any way I can. I'll be happy to hear it, however it comes across."*

---

29 gTértön Aro Yeshé (*gTer sTon A ro ye shes* / གཏེར་སྟོན་ཨ་རོ་ཡེ་ཤེས་ / 1911–1951) – the author's previous incarnation.

Whilst Sônam began translating – it made perfect sense. Later however, I realised that the paradigm which Khandro Ten'dzin Drölkar had presented was not entirely unlike something Albert Einstein might have said – or maybe some later physicist. I'd heard about such things. Books had been written about the new paradigms in physics[30]. I'd not read them – but people had explained aspects of them to me. What Khandro Ten'dzin Drölkar had explained had similar implications.

I had experiences in dreams and visions when I was a child, when I'd become someone else. I'd had a dream in Exeter where I was in a tent with the sisters Jomo A-yé Khandro and Jomo A-shé Khandro – and part of the night in which that dream had occurred, was not a dream. I had seen different phases of the moon on the same night.

I'd asked Khandro Ten'dzin Drölkar if it were possible to go too far into the past dimension and get lost there – but it made her laugh. She told me that I could only be lost if I didn't know where I was – or if I wanted to be somewhere else and didn't know how to find my way back. She then asked me whether I was worried that I would never find my way back to England again. I told her the thought had never occurred to me. She asked me whether I'd been concerned about finding my way back to McLeod Ganj the previous night – when I was in Tibet. Again, I told her the thought hadn't occurred. Did I need to know who I was? Did I need to know whether I was Ngakpa Chögyam or Aro Yeshé? I answered *"No… it had been irrelevant."* And that was true – it really didn't matter who was there. It all made sense at the time, sitting with Khandro Ten'dzin Drölkar. Later however, it all seemed rather strange – as if the discussion with Khandro Ten'dzin Drölkar had been a dream. Sônam had been there to tell me that it hadn't been a dream – so I let the subject permeate my gestalt without trying to convert it into a conveniently conventional theory of reality.

---

30 In 1961 Eugene Wigner wrote *Remarks on the Mind-body Question* in which he suggested that a conscious observer played a fundamental role in quantum mechanics. His paper served as inspiration for later mystical works by others. He later rejected the role of consciousness in quantum mechanics. In the 1970s various authors—such as Arthur Koestler, Lawrence LeShan—began to interpret quantum physics. Fritjof Capra wrote *The Tao of Physics: An Exploration of the Parallels Between Modern Physics and Eastern Mysticism* in 1975. Gary Zukav wrote *The Dancing Wu Li Masters* in 1979. These books—although now regarded as fanciful—contained enough factual material to cause serious questioning.

On my next meeting with Khandro Ten'dzin Drölkar it occurred to me that this was a wonderful opportunity to request teachings from her and so I asked her whether she would be so kind as to speak to me concerning Lama'i Naljor. She smiled *"Chögyam no need my words hearing. But because you are close friend and always so kind, I some words saying – but all these things you are already too well knowing."*

Khandro Ten'dzin Drölkar wrapped her gö kar chang lo shawl around her. *"No one…"* she commenced *"nondual state finding – without profoundly Lama'i Naljor practising. Lama'i Naljor must be powerful without any conflict. Then transmission of Lama's instant awareness receiving. Without the Lama, there is no Buddha. This rare chance occurring. Mind-to-mind transmission of realisation only arising – from promises to Lama keeping. Mind must primed and receptive. Like this Chögyam sitting. Like always. Like silence sitting. Like always. This I am seeing. Always Chögyam-mind of loyalty to Kyabjé Düd'jom Rinpoche having."*

Khandro Ten'dzin Drölkar explained transmission could occur both in formal empowerments and in teachings. It could also occur unexpectedly. There were many accounts of people experiencing powerful glimpses of nonduality when they were *shocked* by their Lamas. The most famous of these accounts was that of Mahasiddha Tilopa slapping Naropa in the face with his sandal. Tilopa had started out as a scholar – but he completely followed Tilopa's instructions no matter how bizarre they were. So, after years of study and practice Naropa enquired as to when nondual realisation might dawn. *"Oh – it's nondual realisation wanting. Why not before asking?"* At that moment Tilopa suddenly slapped Naropa in the face with his sandal. This was the moment of informal symbolic transmission in which Naropa was introduced to *the nature of Mind*.

Khandro Ten'dzin Drölkar laughed at this point *"This maybe Kyabjé Düd'jom Rinpoche never same doing – but with Drüpchen* [31] *Karma Gyalpo this always possible."* Drüpchen Karma Gyalpo was, Khandro Ten'dzin Drölkar explained, a most wrathful Lama.

Karma Gyalpo Rinpoche had a student at one time. He was said to be a tulku – but he showed no obvious qualities. One day Karma Gyalpo went for a walk with the young tulku. When they reached the top of a hill – the young tulku laid out his shawl as a seat for Karma Gyalpo Rinpoche. Karma Gyalpo seated himself and handed the young tulku his boots.

---

[31] *grub thob chen po* / གྲུབ་ཐོབ་ཆེན་པོ་ / *mahasiddha.*

"Very fine boots like ones you for my husband bringing." As the young tulku placed the boots on a rock where he thought they would be safe, one tilted over and was about to fall. The young tulku lunged to prevent the boot from falling – and in that moment Karma Gyalpo Rinpoche seized the other boot and struck the young tulku's head with the heel of the boot. Khandro Ten'dzin Drölkar laughed uproariously about this. *"Young tulku much dazed – but shock transmission* nature of Mind *giving."* After that there was no scholastic dissertation which was above or beyond the young tulku's comprehension.

For most people, transmission evolves progressively rather than in a single moment. Each time teachings are heard; their meaning becomes more naturally present in how reality is perceived. Each time one meets with the Lama – openness to living the view develops. The manner in which obstacles are constructed from conceptual patterning becomes increasingly apparent. The Lama provides the methods for disassembling dualistic constructions. Every time the Lama's methods are employed, conviction is strengthened and appreciation of the Lama's realisation increases. It becomes obvious that reliance on the Lama is like reliance on a parachute. The notion of cutting the parachute cords to escape from the parachute would not enter one's mind. Authentic devotion is the same.

"Outside same appearing. Inside mind expansive becoming. Identity-clinging into nondual nature reality dissolving. From first nondual realisation of Lama seeing…" the translator had difficulty at this point *"Lama is… impenetrable… penetrating…"* I nodded to convey that I had understood. *"Suddenly mind-to-mind transmission – words not necessary."*

At that moment my eyes fell on the boots which I had given to Ngakpa Yeshé Dorje. They had been polished as boots can only be polished in India. They shone like glass. Khandro Ten'dzin Drölkar observed that I had noticed the boots and laughed *"O yah, husband too much liking. Now like 'ö-Sèl shining."*

I asked Khandro Ten'dzin Drölkar about her life – as there was still time before I had to leave. She smiled *"Yah—still time having—but not much saying. My life not special"* and began her account.

She was born in the Rongshal area of Tibet – close to the Nepalese border. Rongshal is near to Lapchi, the area where Milarépa stayed for a long time.

She grew up in Rongshal—a village strongly associated with Milarépa—and lived there until she was sixteen years old.

I asked Khandro Ten'dzin Drölkar about her previous lives – but she shook her head. *"Other lives as child remembering – but now forgetting. Always Vajrayana interested."*

She said that her father didn't live with her family. He was drafted into the Tibetan army. He divorced her mother and went to Lhasa. She never saw him again. She lived with her mother – supported by her uncle. When her mother died, her uncle wanted her to marry – but she had no interest in that prospect. She decided it would be good to evade the pressure to marry – and set out for Zarhombu where Trülshig Rinpoche's gompa was situated. At that time Trülshig Rinpoche was her root teacher. She received many teachings from him and practised intensely until she was 24 years old. During that time, she received the entire cycle of the Mindröl-ling Southern gTérma. Trülshig Rinpoche was an excellent Lama and enabled her to enter solitary retreat. He gave her and her retreatant group frequent personal teachings. After the retreat she undertook an examination in which she gained a successful result. After this she completed a three-to-four month retreat every year – practising Dorje Phurba, Dorje Tröllö, and Hayagriva. Once she completed these practices, she began practising Dzogchen men-ngag-dé[32] and Dzogchen Thöd-gal[33].

In response to this I said that I was surprised she was not well known as a Lama. *"Yah"* she smiled *"Many women Lamas in Tibet – but not famous and only small sanghas having. Sé-ra Khandro, famous female gTértön – Chatral Rinpoche's Lama."*

---

32 *rDzogs chen man ngag sDe* / རྫོགས་ཆེན་མན་ངག་སྡེ་ / *upadesavarga*.
33 *rDzogs chen thod rGal* / རྫོགས་ཆེན་ཐོད་རྒལ་ – the rainbow body practice which involves dark retreat (Mun-tsam (*mun mTshams* / མུན་མཚམས་), having previously engaged in sky gazing Dark retreat is conducted in total darkness, in which vision is experienced beyond the limits of internal and external separation. The practice engages the subtle body of spatial channels, winds, and essences to generate a spontaneous flow of luminous rainbow-spheres which gradually expand in size and complexity – through which one recognizes the nature of Mind in the physical continuum. Thöd-gal (*thod rGal* / ཐོད་རྒལ་) means direct vision. It is also translated as: direct crossing; simultaneous passing; instantaneous directness; crossing in one leap; and passing over the summit. Thöd-gal comprises four visions (thöd-gal gyi nangwa zhi / *thod rGal gyi sNang ba bZhi* / ཐོད་རྒལ་གྱི་སྣང་བ་བཞི་) – Manifest Chö-nyid, Heightened Experience, Summit Awareness, and Exhaustion of Limitations.

At 25 she met and married Ngakpa Tséring Thöndrüp, the eldest son of Lama Pasang Rinpoche – but they were separated by the Chinese invasion. She fled to Nepal when she learned that Ngakpa Tséring Thöndrüp was dead. After that her life became difficult. She went to a refugee camp where she worked making carpets. She had not known that she was pregnant when she escaped from Tibet – which resulted in her being alone with her daughter. Nonetheless she continued her practices in the mornings and evenings whilst nursing her daughter. In 1970 she left Nepal and went to McLeod Ganj in India, where she met Ngakpa Yeshé Dorje. They married and went to receive the entire Düd'jom gTér transmissions from Kyabjé Düd'jom Rinpoche Jig'drèl Yeshé Dorje.

Somehow Khandro Ten'dzin Drölkar's profound dissertation was only enhanced by its termination in laughter. It was simple. It was perfect. There was nothing else to know.

So, time moved. It moved in a manner almost entirely *other* from the way it moved in England. It was slow as it proceeded – but once a phase had elapsed it seemed to have passed with surprising rapidity. 'Slow' was not what it usually meant – there was no sense of the tedium which usually accompanies time passing slowly. 'Rapid' was not what it usually meant either – because there was no sense of failure in accounting for every moment.

I was not in McLeod Ganj and Forsyth Bazaar for more than three weeks – but it felt like a lifetime until it was over. Then—suddenly—the day of my departure for Nepal arrived and it was as if my sojourn had only been a few days. I did not want to go – yet I was eager to leave, in order to see Kyabjé Düd'jom Rinpoche again. I was eager to get to Nepal—to Bodhanath—but I was somewhat less eager to be travelling.

The journey across India was something of an ordeal – but I found that it was not the ordeal it once had been. A journey is what it is: a series of moments. One can rest in those moments—simply experiencing the colour and sound of the moment—and nothing else is required. The sense of *knowingness* in those moments—when I could simply allow moments to be what they were—was spacious. In that *spaciousness* it didn't really matter what discomfort there might be – because I found that it did not have to define my experience, even in the moment. Maybe I'd gained some maturity. Maybe I'd lost my adolescent anxiety about being a lone traveller in a slightly bewildering environment.

Everything worked well. I arrived at the Nepalese border without undue complications. It was not as hot or humid as it had been in 1971. I grinned at myself for toying with the notion of being a seasoned traveller. I had no idea how it would feel to be seasoned – apart from being free of the need to run a list of trivial complaints through my head. There *were* causes for complaint – but I'd come to see them as foolish. It would have been good to have flown to Kathmandu from Delhi – but that was for the independently wealthy. I'd met wealthy people who travelled by aeroplane. Amusingly, they thought I travelled by bus and train out of choice – and I said nothing to dissuade them of the idea. The notion of claiming relative poverty seemed somehow ungracious. I had no desire to make anyone feel uncomfortable in having the financial wherewithal which I lacked. I've never begrudged anyone their wealth – on the basis that I would definitely have enjoyed it, if I'd had it bestowed upon me by affluent forebears.

I didn't realise it at the time – but when I look back, I feel grateful that my time in the Himalayas was not owed to privilege. I don't say this on the basis of social politics. I don't wish to present myself as a working-class hero. It's more that it gives me the ability to tell people they can do almost anything they wish to do – as long as they're determined. Standing on one's own feet is, perhaps, a *working-class value* – and if so, it is a value which I am content to own. I have known people who were receiving allowances from their parents when they were in their fifties. I would not deride them for it – but I would not wish to remain a child in that way. To be an adult—for me—is to be self-supporting, self-reliant, self-sufficient, and self-determined.

Wherever I was, I knew that I'd put myself there. That doesn't mean that I didn't consider myself lucky. It doesn't mean that I wasn't grateful to those who helped me. My gratitude to Düd'jom Rinpoche was boundless and remains boundless. I was glad however, that I'd paid my own way. There was a sense of fundamental reality. I wasn't privileged – but I had no sense of being underprivileged either. In whatever way I was *inauthentic* – at least in this respect, what I'd done was indisputably genuine. I'd set out from England and arrived in Bodhanath where Düd'jom Rinpoche resided – and I'd accomplished it on the money I'd earned working on building sites.

Suddenly—after nine days travelling—there I was. A mystery – but a mystery solidly founded on reality.

4

mChod rTen

1975 – Bodhanath, Nepal. The ancient environs of the Great Chörten[1] – now a place as familiar as Farnham, my hometown in England. Both places had changed—unsurprisingly—but Farnham had become emotionally unfamiliar. Shops had changed hands. Inevitably, that happens. Change had occurred in increments through my childhood – but not in a way which changed the feeling of the town. One change which irredeemably altered Farnham was the demolition of lovely Georgian houses to build a one-way system. That ripped the heart out of the little town. It was as if a painting by John Vicat Cole[2] had been morphed with an ungainly amateur attempt at Cubism. I ended up visiting Farnham rarely – not even when I visited my mother. It was just another English town.

I'd not realised the one taste of *allure* and *ordure* in terms of architecture. I conjured up those words at the time – and wondered whether I'd ever rid myself of strongly worded censure. Of course, there wasn't the force of expression that once animated such words. Now it was merely the domain of word play. There was no temptation to rant about it. The words were *almost* empty. Still, the barbaric destruction of history saddened me when I thought about it. There was life in the history of buildings which made them living structures for living people. The Art School had sold off the beautiful Georgian house which was the original Art School established by Lieutenant-Colonel John Luard[3] in 1866.

---

1. *mChod rTen* / མཆོད་རྟེན་ / *stupa*.
2. John Vicat Cole (1903–1975) was a painter and stained-glass designer, born in London the son of artist Rex Vicat Cole. John Vicat Cole exhibited at the Royal Academy and the Paris Salon.
3. Lieutenant-Colonel John Luard (1790–1875) was a British Army officer and author of *History of the Dress of the British Soldier*. He was a talented artist and veteran of Waterloo. He retired to Farnham in 1860 and lived in Castle Street until his death.

The spectre of Allen Ginsberg's reference to Moloch[4] came to mind:

> *Moloch whose mind is pure machinery! Moloch whose blood is running money! Moloch whose fingers are ten armies! Moloch whose breast is a cannibal dynamo! Moloch whose ear is a smoking tomb!*

Bodhanath had an ancient history – but that history was only alive in the moment for those who understood its significance. It had a living pulse which I always recognised – even though I only lived there for a month at a time. There was always the question of leaving Nepal to acquire a new visa – but once I returned, it was as if I'd never left. Düd'jom Rinpoche greeted me each time I arrived as if I had seen him the day before, rather than consequent to a journey to Delhi to obtain a new visa. My absences seemed invisible. It made my presence feel like a seamless continuum.

There is a text 'The History of the Great Chörten of Bodhanath[5]'. In Tibetan, it is called Chörten Chenpo Jarung Khashor-gyi Lo-gyü Tho-pé Dröwa[6]. The history was written by Guru Rinpoche – and revealed by Lhatsun Ngönmo, who re-concealed it. It was then re-discovered by Ngak'chang Sakya Zangpo in the 16th century.

The chörten is cared for by the lineage of the Chini Lamas. The first Chini Lama—Ta'ipo Shing—was a Nyingma Lama from China. Ta'ipo Shing settled in Bodhanath after going there on pilgrimage. In 1853, at the end of a war with China, the Nepalese King, Jung Bahadur[7], invited Ta'ipo Shing to the palace to translate at the peace discussions. In recognition of his services, he was appointed as the Governor of Bodhanath and the Lama authority in charge of taking care of the chörten. This made Bodhanath a small kingdom within Nepal – almost like a separate country. The community was entirely Tibetan up to the end of the 1980s.

---

4   Moloch is a Canaanite god appearing in the Hebrew Bible, in the book of Leviticus. Moloch, figuratively, refers to that which demands costly sacrifice. Appearances in literature: *Paradise Lost* by John Milton (1667); *Salammbô* by Gustave Flaubert (1862); and *Howl* by Allen Ginsberg (1955–6).
5   See: *Legend of the Great Stupa and Life Story of the Lotus Born Guru*—Keith Dowman— Dharma Books, Berkeley, California—1973.
6   mChod rTen chen po bya rung kha shor gyi lo rGyus thos pas grol ba / མཆོད་རྟེན་ཆེན་པོ་བྱ་རུང་ཁ་ཤོར་གྱི་ ལོ་རྒྱུས་ཐོས་པས་གྲོལ་བ. Ja-rung Kashor means 'Having Given Permission to Start Building'.
7   Jung Bahadur Kunwar Ranaji, GCB, GCSI was born in 1817 to the Kunwar family. He was a Khas Chhetri, ruler of Nepal and founder of the Rana Regime in Nepal.

The authority of the Chini Lamas increased because they were consuls for the Tibetan Government and all Tibetans travelling to India through Nepal had to have their papers stamped by the Chini Lama. When Ta'i-po Shing died, his incarnation was Sang-gyé Dorje. The next incarnation was Sônam Dorje[8] – and I met him in 1971, when he was visiting with Kyabjé Düd'jom Rinpoche.

The Chini Lama's power was reduced by the Chinese occupation of Tibet in 1951 – as he had no longer a rôle as a Tibetan consul in Nepal. His authority was also reduced by the Hindu authorities who confiscated the surrounding lands of the Chörten in order to raise revenue from pilgrims. Although Nepal is both a Buddhist and Hindu country – the Hindu community have come to own most of the land because the Kings have always been Hindu. This is not a good situation for the Tibetan refugees as they have no political status in Nepal – and now Bodhanath (their small country-within-a-country) is just another part of Nepal. By the time Sônam Dorje Rinpoche died in 1982, his authority had been reduced to almost nothing.

As Nyingmas the Chini Lamas were all ngakpas – and each one married a Sherpa girl. The Sherpas are Tibetan people who live in the northern part of Nepal. 'Sherpa'[9] means 'Eastern People' in Tibetan. Since the death of the 3rd Chini Lama the Chörten has been governed by his descendants, and the families of his disciples who live in the area. It is one of the largest chörtens in the world. Bodhanath is one of the most important Vajrayana Buddhist sites in the Kathmandu Valley.

The chörten has another name: Yambu Chörten Chenpo. Yambu is what Kathmandu is called in Tibetan – and Chörten Chenpo means 'great chörten'. The chörten has an interesting history which explains this strange name. The Buddha prior to Shakyamuni Buddha was Kasyapa Buddha. When Kasyapa Buddha died, an old woman with four sons buried him at the place where the chörten now stands. Before starting the work of building the chörten, she asked the King of Nepal for permission to start building. At that time, the foundations had already been finished – and everyone who saw it was amazed at the size it was going to be.

---

8   bSod nams rDo rJe / བསོད་ནམས་རྡོ་རྗེ / 1886–1982.
9   shar pa / ཤར་པ – Easterner.

The courtiers of the King said *"If such a poor old woman was allowed to complete such a stupendous building – we would have to build a temple as huge as a mountain."* They asked the King to refuse permission – but the King said that he had concluded the permission-order for the old woman and that Kings must not go back on their word. The chörten was therefore permitted – and gained the name 'Having Given Permission to Start Building'.

Gazing at it on my arrival, I felt that I had permission to start living the life I most wanted to live – and, Amji Pema Dorjee (*sic*) and Yeshi Khadro (*sic*) were the delightful people who had made that life highly commodious. I lodged with them in a large apartment which served as their medical surgery. They were Tibetan doctors – and I had known Yeshi Khadro since 1971 when she was a student at the Tibetan Astro-Medical School[10] in McLeod Ganj in Himachal Pradesh. She had arranged a room for me with her aunt, Amala Norga, the local *chang lady*. I had been introduced to Yeshi Khadro by the 'Tibetan Friendship Group' which I had discovered through the British Buddhist Society. She had been my pen-friend – and thus, when I arrived in India in 1971, I became assimilated immediately into the Tibetan community. There'd been no need for the usual run-up to making friends and gaining acceptance. I'd been a *known person* before my arrival – and was immediately on friendly terms with the medical students. I ate dinner with them every evening, and I'd learned to use chopsticks extremely quickly – mainly by virtue of wanting to eat my meal before it froze to the plate.

It was Amji Pema Dorjee and Amji Yeshi Khadro who'd first helped me find Karma Lama[11] – the translator who would help me in receiving teaching and personal instruction from Kyabjé Düd'jom Rinpoche. It had been a little difficult unravelling the English of the monks who translated for me and I'd wanted to find someone who would be a little easier to comprehend – especially as the teachings I was receiving were highly subtle. He was wary of translating for me at first because he was not well versed in Buddhist terminology.

10 The Tibetan Astro-Medical School—Men-tsi Khang (*bod kyi sMan rTsis khang* / བོད་ཀྱི་སྨན་རྩིས་ཁང་)—was inaugurated by Dr Yeshé Dhönden, doctor/teacher of the medicine department, and Dukhorwa Lodrö Gyamtso, teacher of the astrology department.
11 Karma Lama was not a Lama (*bLa ma* / བླ་མ་ / *guru*) – Lama was his surname. Lama as a surname is quite common amongst the Newari Buddhists indigenous to Nepal.

I explained to him however that there was no need to translate the Vajrayana technical terms – he could leave those in Tibetan, as I understood them all. Once this was explained he was entirely happy to translate for me.

Karma Lama was a splendid fellow. He rode a 500cc motorcycle and was the proprietor of a Tibetan antiques emporium near the Royal Palace in Kathmandu. He had a great interest in Blues and we traded expertise. He translated for me – and I fed his fascination by relating my previous life as a Bluesman. The old version of me was obviously not quite as dead as I'd imagined – and I told him just about everything I knew. I knew quite a lot and he never tired of plying me with questions about Muddy Waters, Buddy Guy, Little Walter, Howling Wolf, and the Chicago Blues scene. It was strange that I could spend evenings talking with Karma Lama about Blues – and yet, had no way of conversing with most western Vajrayana students I met. They all seemed to have some kind of agenda – and a spiritual point of view to which mine seemed entirely tangential. That would not have been a problem for me—because I can agree to differ— but for them, it did not seem viable. Most of the western Vajrayana students I met were utterly convinced of their own points of view – and *agreeing to differ* seemed anathema to them.

This was the unlikely environment in which a startling event occurred – and one which would change my future life in ways that were impossible even to consider at the time. Dreams of Khyungchen Aro Lingma had occurred over the three years in Bristol – but they increased as soon as I met Kyabjé Düd'jom Rinpoche again. The dreams had become increasingly vivid and increasingly informational – but not in the sense that the information could be explained in any linear fashion. What came across to me was that *a point in time* was approaching.

I was sitting in meditation for longer periods of time to intensify my preparation for the practices of 'ö-Sel and mi-lam. I had no idea how unusual my situation was. Being able to spend so much time with Düd'jom Rinpoche was a rare privilege. He was immensely kind and dealt with my experience of silent sitting directly – answering every question I had. I had plenty. I studied with Düd'jom Rinpoche whenever I could – and whatever he taught me was always of immense value. My time with Düd'jom Rinpoche however was drawing to a close in terms of being with him every day.

I did not recognise it at first – but as my month in Nepal progressed day-by-day, the number of interruptions to our discussions increased.

The call on Kyabjé Düd'jom Rinpoche's time as the Head of the Nyingma Tradition had been increasing over the previous year and I had been highly fortunate to have arrived in a period which was atypical. Düd'jom Rinpoche still wanted me to be there with him every day – but I could see that I was not always a welcome presence for every official visitor. I asked whether I should stay away but Düd'jom Rinpoche would not hear of it. He told me that it was important for me to be there – and in any case, there would soon come a point at which he would give me instructions. The day on which I would receive instructions for the future was nine days away because certain possibilities had to be investigated. I was on the edge of a great mystery.

The day finally arrived and Düd'jom Rinpoche told me that he had dwelt on the possibilities. He foresaw that Dilgo Khyentsé Rinpoche's time would become as absorbed as his. He had considered sending me to Bhutan to study – but it would have been beyond my financial means.

Düd'jom Rinpoche was my Tsawa'i Lama – but it soon became apparent that our time together had almost run its course. It was no longer 1971. It was now 1975. I had met Düd'jom Rinpoche in 1971 – and if I had gone back in 1972 rather than going to Bristol Art School, everything would have been different. Düd'jom Rinpoche however, had told me that it was important that I went to Art School and obtained a degree – as I would need the proper western qualifications in order to live in the West without too many difficulties. Moreover – I would learn things at Art School which would be of great value to me in later life. Düd'jom Rinpoche's advice was—of course—perfect. My time at Bristol Art School was extremely valuable – and enabled me to augment my studies of Tibetan thangka painting.

The three years which had elapsed whilst I was at Bristol Art School however, had seen the burthen of responsibility grow – with respect to Düd'jom Rinpoche's rôle as Head of the Nyingma Tradition. He no longer had the time he once had – and, after giving me what time he could, he told me that he would have to find a Lama who had sufficient time to work with me personally.

"This matter – some weeks I am considering. There is one Lama I am deciding. He is very well Chögyam suiting. His name Künzang Dorje – and time always having. He, Dzogchen men-ngag-dé master and whatever needed teaching and transmissions giving. Künzang Dorje—very—completely qualified in Dzogchen – also rTsa rLung and Mahayoga. Nothing Vajrayana that he is not knowing."

Düd'jom Rinpoche had considered several different Lamas: Kyabjé Chatral Rinpoche; Dung-sé Thrin-lé Norbu Rinpoche[12] and Chag'düd Tulku Rinpoche. The first he decided was unsuitable in respect of my personality. We would not suit each other. The second two were in the USA and I could not easily travel there. He finally concluded that the best Lama for me would be Künzang Dorje Rinpoche. His only reservation was that Künzang Dorje Rinpoche was known to be a wrathful Lama – and so, wondered how it would be for me.

I'd heard of 'wrathful Lamas' – and was far from immune to the 'romance' which could be ascribed to studying with such a fabulous being. Düd'jom Rinpoche had looked concerned when describing Künzang Dorje Rinpoche as being wrathful – and asked me whether I could venture into such a potentially challenging situation. The adage *'Fools rush in where angels fear to tread'* passed through my mind.

By virtue of my *Easy Rider* motorcycle – I was almost a *Hells Angel*. I therefore immediately chose to be a fool. I rushed in. *"If Künzang Dorje Rinpoche is the Lama you recommend, Rinpoche – then he is the Lama with whom I shall study."*

---

12 Kyabjé Dung-sé Thrin-lé Norbu Rinpoche (*phrin las nor bu* / ཕྲིན་ལས་ནོར་བུ / 1931–2011) was the elder son of Kyabjé Düd'jom Rinpoche Jig'drèl Yeshé Dorje and was the father of Dung-sé Garab Rinpoche and Dzongsar Khyentsé Rinpoche. He was the incarnation of Tulku Dri'mèd 'ö-Zér, one of seven sons of Düd'jom Lingpa – and an emanation of Longchenpa. His wife was Sangyum Jamyang Chödrön (*jam dbyang chos sgron* / འཇམ་དབྱངས་ཆོས་སྒྲོན). They had seven children, three daughters and four sons: Sémo Kèlsang Chödrön, Dzongsar Khyentsé Norbu Rinpoche (*rDzong gSar mKhyen brTse nor bu rin po che* / རྫོང་གསར་མཁྱེན་བརྩེ་ནོར་བུ་རིན་པོ་ཆེ / b. 1961), Srémo Yeshé dPal'dzom, Garab Dorje Rinpoche (དགའ་རབ་རྡོ་རྗེ་རིན་པོ་ཆེ། / b. 1967), Jampal Dorje Rinpoche'(*dGa' rab rDo rJe rin po che* / འཇམ་དཔལ་རྡོ་རྗེ་རིན་པོ་ཆེ / b. 1968), Srémo Pema Chö-kyi (*sras mo pad ma chos sKyid* / སྲས་མོ་པད་མ་ཆོས་སྐྱིད / b. 1976) and Dung-sé Ögyen Namgyal. Sé Rinpoche (Dung-sé Gyanata Rinpoche) the son of Garab Dorje Rinpoche was confirmed by Kyabjé DoDrüpchen Rinpoche as the incarnation of Dung-sé Thrin-lé Norbu Rinpoche in 2015.

As soon as I agreed however, he laughed heartily *'O yah! This I am knowing before question asking! Chögyam much brave—much fierce—like Golok!*[13]*"* Then he told me about a saying which was known in Lhasa, which ran *'Even if you're on your deathbed – if you hear that someone from Golok is approaching, you should get up immediately and run away.'* This adage caused me to laugh a little too loudly and Düd'jom Rinpoche joined me – which made the laughter continue for an unusual length of time.

Once our laughter had abated, Düd'jom Rinpoche said *"Then… before Bodhanath leaving, I am letter for Künzang Dorje writing and saying he—must—Chögyam teaching."* He laughed *"Never before Inji teaching giving, so maybe not—strong joy, for him—but for you, this perfect."* Düd'jom Rinpoche smiled and nodded *"I am also knowing – Künzang Dorje, later, very joyful coming. O yah – this I am knowing."*

This then – was my future.

I was naturally saddened that I would no longer be able to spend as much time with Düd'jom Rinpoche – but he assured me he would always be my Lama, and we would still be able to meet from time to time. In fact – he said *"You naturally back to Bodhanath coming and Düd'jom seeing, after you Künzang Dorje time spending. I must 'Chögyam relationship with Künzang Dorje' – all detail knowing."*

I was extremely happy to hear this. It meant that my relationship with Düd'jom Rinpoche would continue – there would still be times when I could go to see him. *"Main teaching"* he explained *"you from Künzang Dorje needing is Dzogchen men-ngag-dé. You will this teaching too well understanding – because you silent sitting many years practising. But also, transmission needing. This vital. Direct introduction – nature of Mind is—without individual preparation—happening not possible. Preparation always highly individual. You must Bodhanath staying until I am Künzang Dorje finding.*

---

13 *mGo log* / མགོ་ལོག — a region of Tibet known for brigandry and feuding tribes. The Golok were renowned in Tibet and China as ferocious warriors who rejected Tibetan and Chinese control. No external power either Tibet or China was able to subdue them. In ancient times they were ruled by a Queen—an embodied protectress—whose lineal power passed from mother to daughter. A Golok nomad in 1908 was reported to have stated *"We Golok—from ancient times—obeyed none but our own traditions."* (*The A-mNye Ma-Chen Range and Adjacent Regions*—Joseph Rock—1956). A folk song, transcribed in 1951, asserts *'Against the orders of the Dalai Lama, I rebel. Against China I rebel. We make our own laws.' Journey among the Tibetan Nomads*—Namkhai Norbu—Library of Tibetan Works and Archives—1997.

"I must letters writing. Künzang Dorje not easy finding. Always place-to-place travelling. Never anyone telling where next going. I must be finding out where staying. Then you must quickly-going – before he is again moving."

This sounded rather remarkable. I'd not imagined that such Lamas still existed. Künzang Dorje Rinpoche sounded like Drukpa Künlegs[14] or one of the Myon Hérukas[15] – the *realised madmen* or *realised madwomen* of Himalayan Buddhism. I was still sad to be leaving Düd'jom Rinpoche – but sadness was now shimmering together with some kind of insane excitement. I'd thought that my time in the Himalayas was to have had no relation to adventure – but here I was on the brink of the most extraordinary adventure I could imagine.

"You are in Bodhanath nothing saying. To Karma Lama you also nothing saying." On this occasion a Nyingma monk was translating for me. *"Künzang Dorje Rinpoche you must with no one discussing."* Kyabjé Düd'jom Rinpoche said quite pointedly. I was not even to tell Ngakpa Yeshé Dorje. Then he smiled *"Relax and serene staying – alone remaining, best. Too much imitation-Dharma people listening, tired and heavy making. With Dharma-hardened people talking – life wasting. Time valuable. Time precious. It is good no argument discussion with Dharma-hardened people having. You quiet keeping and happy like always. When 1971 coming you are like this – and still like this. It is good you always same like this remaining. Always same interest and devotion to Vajrayana having. Some western people very good—but others often changing—too much changing. When 1971 coming, these ngakpa robes giving – and this time you still wearing. You have other robes now also – but these you wear today are the same?"*

14 *'brug pa kun legs* / འབྲུག་པ་ཀུན་ལེགས་ / 1455–1529—the Madman of the Dragons (*'brug sMyon kun dGa' legs pa* / འབྲུག་སྨྱོན་ཀུན་དགའ་ལེགས་པ་)—was a mahasiddha poet. After training in Ralung, he taught in Bhutan and established Chhi'mèd Lhakhang in 1499. Known for anarchic methods of facilitating realisation, his life inspired the practice of phallus paintings in Bhutan – and placing phallic effigies on rooftops to avert maledictive affliction. Renowned in Bhutan as the mahasiddha of fertility – women from across the world visit Chhi'mèd Lhakhang to seek his inspired sanction. His gompa is resplendent with wine bottles – and contains a wood and ivory phallus from which inspirational connection can be bestowed by the incumbent sacristan.

15 *sMyon he ru ka* / སྨྱོན་ཧེ་རུ་ཀ་ / *avadhuta*. There is no entirely good translation. Keith Dowman employed 'divine madman' others employ 'crazy saint' or 'crazy wisdom master'. Dung-sé Thrin-lé Norbu Rinpoche employs 'wisdom eccentric' and this is probably the best translation. sMyon means mad or crazy. Héruka is Sanskrit, and the Tibetan equivalent is trak'thung (*khrag 'thung* / ཁྲག་འཐུང་) which means *blood drinker* – one who drinks the hot blood of delusion and transforms it into wisdom. Trak'thung can also mean *one who drinks from a human skull bowl*.

"Yes Rinpoche. Whenever I come to see you, I wear the same robes as I wore in 1971 because these are the robes you gave me – when I had them made here in Bodhanath."

Kyabjé Düd'jom Rinpoche smiled and nodded *"Yah… maybe always wearing – but one day worn out. This not mattering. Every robe wearing, I am giving. Not necessary worrying. Many new robe making needing before dying."* PAUSE *"You warmer robe for snow having? Too cold McLeod Ganj and Tso Pema in Winter becoming."*

"Yes Rinpoche – I have a woollen to-nga [16] *waistcoat which I had made in England."*

"Showing possible?"

"No, Rinpoche. I left it in McLeod Ganj with Ngakpa Yeshé Dorje and Khandro Ten'dzin Drölkar because I thought a woollen to-nga would be too hot for Bodhanath."

"Yah, wool very good – but no need this to-nga seeing. You also ngakpa zen needing – but no gö kar chang lo zen from Bhutan coming Bodhanath this time. Maybe later."

And so, the days went by. I saw Kyabjé Düd'jom Rinpoche a little less but he still gave me his time generously and showered seemingly endless kindness on me. To witness him smile at me, was worth a trip to Nepal – without anything else having to happen. This obviously describes me as some kind of simpering devotee – but that would be to mistake the situation and to mistake Kyabjé Düd'jom Rinpoche. I'm sure that a 'cello player could describe a meeting with Pablo Casals in a similar way. One of the reasons western students didn't like me was because I couldn't simper on cue – and because I didn't hold everything in reverence without question. I didn't find India and Nepal blissful. I didn't warm to Eastern toilets. I didn't revile the West – and I didn't conform in many ways to what was expected of a person in my situation.

When western students got to hear that I was spending time with Düd'jom Rinpoche they wanted to ply me with questions about it – and were hostile in response to being told that such discussions were private between a student and Lama. *They* knew *that* as well as I did – but it seemed many of them felt they had some special right to interrogate me. In the end I remained entirely silent unless someone I'd never seen before said hello.

16 *sTod sNgags* / སྟོད་སྔགས་.

There were friendly people around—I wouldn't want to paint too bleak a picture—and when I chanced upon them, I was merry enough.

One day Düd'jom Rinpoche sent a message through to Amji Pema Dorjee and Amji Yeshi Khadro's surgery saying that he needed to see me straight away. I left immediately and Düd'jom Rinpoche laughed when I arrived because of my alarming haste. He'd hardly sent for me before I arrived on his doorstep. No one was there to translate as Karma Lama would have to arrive from Kathmandu. Düd'jom Rinpoche indicated that I should simply sit and wait.

Someone arrived with a few bottles of Sprite. I sat there sipping it – quietly observing, as unobtrusively as I could, whilst Düd'jom Rinpoche read a text. He occasionally looked up at me and smiled.

After an hour Karma Lama arrived and Düd'jom Rinpoche picked up a letter which had been sitting in front of him. *"This letter"* he smiled *"I am writing to Künzang Dorje Rinpoche. He will Tso Pema in January. So you must be that time going."* PAUSE *"Before this – you must back McLeod Ganj going. There you must more with Yeshé Dorje and Khandro Ten'dzin Drölkar studying – because they are with Tröma Nakmo helping. This they main practising – but Khandro Ten'dzin Drölkar also Dzogchen practising. You good translator who Nyingma teachings well knowing?"*

"Yes, Rinpoche—Sônam Wangdü from the Tibetan Medical Centre—he speaks good English and comes from a Nyingma family. He doesn't always know the English for specialised Vajrayana terms but he doesn't need to translate those for me – so it works out very well."

"O yah—good—this system I am liking. Like Karma Lama, you Vajrayana language knowing and Sônam Wangdü other words translating."

I nodded and Düd'jom Rinpoche passed me the letter. *"This letter everything explaining. I am Künzang Dorje—you are my student telling—and that he must all necessary teachings and transmissions giving."*

I carefully wrapped the letter in a white scarf – and placed it between two books in my bag. We talked for a while. Soon lunch appeared. We ate together – and then it was time for me to leave. I was instructed to leave for McLeod Ganj within a few days – but not to tell anyone apart from my hosts that I was leaving.

They were to tell no one where I had gone – and I was to leave Bodhanath early in the morning so that only the local people would see me leave. I almost asked Kyabjé Düd'jom Rinpoche why there was need for such secrecy – but, it didn't feel right to question his instruction. I didn't know how to ask without making it sound as if I considered these precautions unnecessary.

5

dancing in colour

After nine days of the standard unpleasantness—travelling across the Northern India industrial belt—I arrived in McLeod Ganj feeling as if I could sleep for a month. Ama la Norga's son, Phüntsog Wangdü, had found me a place to stay fairly quickly and I was asleep an hour after I moved in.

Far from the month of sleep I felt I needed – I awoke the next morning feeling as right as rain, albeit with a rat peering at me from the side of the bed. It observed my eyes opening – and readjusted its posture slightly. I was most amused. *"Good morning, noble creature"* I declared in a vaguely theatrical Shakespearian manner. It appeared to nod at me. I reached in my bag and placed a piece of Tibetan muffin on the floor. The rat scurried toward it—devoured it voraciously—and disappeared. This was a good start to the day. I rearranged myself. I sat up. The hut was pleasant enough—just bare-board walls and a tin roof—and it was dry. The roof seemed sound enough to keep out the rain – but I'd discover the accuracy of my estimation when the winter rains hit.

Ablutions in McLeod Ganj at that time were accommodated in a manner not dissimilar to a campsite. The toilets and taps were under cover – but only just. Washing was a chilly affair in the winter. After my morning wash I hastened to regain heat in the restaurant on the corner of the main drag – just up from the Chörten. I ordered coffee, boiled eggs, and Tibetan muffins – and soon I felt equipped to walk up to Forsyth Bazaar to see Ngakpa Yeshé Dorje and Khandro Ten'dzin Drölkar. I'd not contact Sônam Wangdü 'til such time as I knew when I'd really require his translation services.

I strode forth feeling highly cheerful. I was always happy to be back in whichever Tibetan settlement it was – and had a sense of the rightness of my situation. I was following Düd'jom Rinpoche's instructions and I knew exactly where I was. I had lived in McLeod Ganj often enough to feel like a resident. The Kharadhanda Road may as well have been the Gloucester Road in Bristol – and in the winter sunshine it seemed entirely perfect.

As I walked, it occurred to me that there'd been another Ngakpa Chögyam. He'd studied at Bristol Art School. He'd travelled to Samŷe Ling in Scotland and met Gyalwa Karmapa. He'd left for India and now he'd lived in the Himalayas for several months. Was it only months? It felt like a year – but not in any arduous sense. It hadn't been like a prison sentence, in which—I presumed—the days passed like weeks. The days *had* passed like weeks – but they had been delightful, fascinating, and—above all—profound. I was living the life I'd wanted to live. I'd planned to do what I was doing. I was doing it – and it was what I had expected it to be. There were the somewhat odious western 'dharmites' of course. I remembered to wish them well and happy. They were nothing to grumble about in comparison with the immense privilege of having spent time with Düd'jom Rinpoche.

I hadn't been expecting utopia in every aspect of my sojourn – and in any case I felt sympathy for the dharmites, when I considered their situation with appropriate circumspection. We were all conditioned. We were *all* mired in duality – and, just because their duality appeared different from mine, gave me no right to judge them, even with mild severity. I simply wished they were more amiable and less free with their opinions. I had plenty of opinions, of course – but I kept them to myself when I felt they would be unwelcome.

I arrived at Ngakpa Yeshé Dorje's house sooner than I'd expected. As usual, I'd been spotted at a distance. Ngakpa Yeshé Dorje and Khandro Ten'dzin Drölkar came out to see me—full of smiles—and it wasn't long before I was ensconced with them. Khandro Ten'dzin Drölkar had already sent for someone at the Children's Village who'd translate, and so I was able to tell them the plan as had been laid out by Düd'jom Rinpoche. They were both very pleased indeed that I'd been able to spend so much time with Düd'jom Rinpoche – and understood only too well that his time was now very much taken up with his rôle as the Head of the Nyingma Tradition. They were surprised in fact, that I'd had as much time with him as I recounted. I explained that I was going on to study at the Nyingma Gompa in Tso Pema. Ngakpa Yeshé Dorje nodded and said *"Kyabjé Düd'jom Rinpoche always best knowing. Never in anything mistake making. Always perfect instruction giving. Before Tso Pema going, Tröma Nakmo teaching – and you must time spending mantra reciting and short gÇod from text practising. Maybe in English writing so chanting and meaning knowing?"*

"Yes, Rinpoche – Sônam la can help me with that. I know Tibetan script well enough to anglicise it – and then he can check and give me the meaning where I don't understand it."

He asked me whether I had been able to get the Tröma Nakmo text. I pulled it from my bag.

"*Ya-tsan!*" he laughed and affirmed in English *"Very good! Very good! Very good!"* – then in Tibetan *"Now all things doing!"*

He then stood up and beckoned Khandro Ten'dzin Drölkar to follow him. They went rummaging in the shrine room and returned with a Zha-nak[1] costume *"This, you need making."*

There was a fearful quantity of brocade in that costume and my immediate thought was that it would use up too much of my money. Brocade was expensive – and this costume would represent too much of my remaining funds. That was no problem however – as it could be made in plain coloured cottons in the five colours. Ngakpa Yeshé Dorje said it wouldn't look good – but he understood that my finances were tight. "*Yah…*" he laughed "*… maybe everyone must be pure vision having – then brocade seeing.*"

"They'd need pure vision with me in any case Rinpoche – because I'm just an Inji ngakpa after all."

Ngakpa Yeshé Dorje shook his head *"Inji ngakpa—Tibetan ngakpa—what difference coming? Good dancer is good dancer. If well learning – all well coming."*

I returned to McLeod Ganj with the Zha-nak robes, to look up the tailor who would make up a set for me. They needed to be made for a taller thinner person – and so I had to be measured. Then the tailor told me how much fabric I had to buy of each colour. The tailor was not over the moon about making the costume in plain coloured cottons – but said that if it was just for practice and Ngakpa Yeshé Dorje was alright with it, he'd make it for me. The next day I wandered down to Upper Dharamsala and found an excellent fabric store where they had some extremely fine tightly woven cotton poplin. It was fairly heavy—almost like cotton drill—but without the same stiffness. It would drape well and —although not silk brocade—it would prove a fair alternative.

1   *zhwa nag* / ཞྭ་ནག — Black Hat. The Black Hat dance is often performed on the eve of Losar (*lo gSar* / ལོ་གསར་), the Tibetan new year.

I bought cotton fabric of the five colours, and black – because that was the original formulation according to Kyabjé Künzang Dorje Rinpoche. The main body of the robe was black – and then it had bands of the five colours in the sleeves and other sections.

Whilst I was waiting for the Zha-nak robes to be made I signed on for a class at Gangchen Kyishong – the Library of Tibetan Works and Archives[2]. Geshé Ngawang Dhargye was teaching there at the time and gave an excellent course on Madhyamaka. Some people wondered why a Nyingma ngakpa should want to study with a Gélug Geshé – to which I replied that I'd come to India to study Dharma. I knew there were differences between schools – but as long as I was clear what the differences were, there was always something valuable to be learnt. That seemed acceptable – but I remained an object of suspicion as far as I could tell. The western students saw little reason to converse with me – and I obliged them by not attempting to inveigle myself into their society. I smiled—probably more often than strictly necessary—and always bid everyone a cheery greeting. Then—as suddenly as I had appeared—I left. My Zha-nak robes were completed and it was time to return to Ngakpa Yeshé Dorje's place. I arranged a time with Sônam Wangdü and set out with both sets of Zha-nak robes – Ngakpa Yeshé Dorje's set and my new set.

I had not thought to explore the world of Mahayoga ritual – but I was also far from averse to learning anything I could in terms of Vajrayana. This was a wonderful opportunity – and Düd'jom Rinpoche had sent me to learn whatever I could of the Tröma Nakmo cycle of practices from Ngakpa Yeshé Dorje. I showed my new Zha-nak robes to him and he admitted that they had turned out better than he had expected. He said that he liked the brightness and vividness of the colours and that I had chosen well. He admitted to being a little concerned as to what the other ngakpas would think of my down-market Zha-nak robes – but thought they would pass muster. He thought he'd have to loan me his robes even though they would have been too short – but decided that these plain ones would look fine on me.

2 Library of Tibetan Works and Archives—Gangchen Kyishong (*gangs chen sKyid gShongs* / གངས་ཅན་སྐྱིད་གཤོངས་)—was established in 1970 for Tibetan Buddhist studies – as a resource for scholars, researchers, and students. Its aims were to: preserve Tibetan culture; acquire, preserve, and conserve books; provide reading materials and reference services; and, provide and publish bibliographies. It also serves as a repository for Tibetan artefacts, statues, thangkas, and photographs.

I suggested I could get some machine embroidery on them in Nepal – and I agreed to taking that forward at my earliest opportunity.

Ngakpa Yeshé Dorje was keen for me to start right in – so we both put on the Zha-nak costumes. I was grateful not to have to wear the hat for the practice sessions because it was not exactly comfortable. He went through the first set of movements and I asked if they could be broken down a little more so that I could build up the sequences by increments. This was accepted with amusement. I had to explain that I could learn most things if approached slowly enough. I wasn't the world's brightest specimen – but I would apply myself with diligence. Standing on one leg proved both difficult and surprisingly taxing – but once I'd got the idea of keeping the leg flexed it became much easier. The dance was extraordinary in many ways and I found myself enjoying the process. Once I started to enjoy the movements they came more easily and naturally and the more I improved the more Ngakpa Yeshé Dorje smiled *"O yah – now great gar'cham* [3] *master becoming!"*

I was glad he was pleased with my progress – but I was far from competent. When I watched Ngakpa Yeshé Dorje dance, it was clear that —even though he was over twice my age—he was the epitome of fluency in movement. Still it was the first day - and by the end of it even I felt as if I'd got somewhere in my efforts. Ngakpa Yeshé Dorje explained what the movements meant. The Zha-nak gar'cham was a dance of exorcism which banished negativity – and the dancer's steps pounded dualistic confusion under foot. The motivation involved was to liberate all beings from their various derangements. I was moved to see yet another example of how the Arts were employed within Vajrayana as a means of realising the nature of existence. Dance and costume were not merely entertainment – they were a vital means of communicating and transforming the ways in which natural joy is corrupted.

I remembered being something of a dancer when I was 14. It had been what had attracted the attention of Anelie Mandelbaum, the 22-year-old Swiss au pair girl who'd become my ladyfriend. She'd assumed I was older than I was – and I said nothing to alter her ideas about that. I'd reached my full adult height at 12 and my voice had broken some years before.

---

3 *gar'cham* / གར་འཆམ་ – ritual dance.

At fourteen I sported a moustache of sorts – which placed me more-or-less where I was supposed to be. On stage at the age of sixteen, I was a walker – and never stood still when I sang. Later when I took up back-up bass for the Savage Cabbage Blues Band, I still walked around in the improvisation sections – so I was used to using my body.

When it came to gar'cham however – I was aware that this helped very little. The music was not music as it would normally be understood – it was sound. There was rhythm – but the rhythm had nothing to do with music. It was unearthly. I loved the sounds of the Vajrayana orchestra – but they defied all categories. I have often tried to describe the sound of the rolmo cymbals – but have never been able to verbally assemble the astonishingly contradictory aspects of their overall timbre. They are thick heavy cymbals—almost crude in their weightiness—but they have a delicacy that *spins* out of their deep tones which is rich with dynamic overtones and harmonics. There's also the sensation of hearing them. When the two hemispherical bosses pass each other, it is as if the left and right hemispheres of the brain are subtly teased apart. They do nothing to assist the balance of the dancer until the dancer *enters into* the disorientation they produce. Paradox. Then there's the drum. The drum is fairly simple – but adds weight to the deep note of the rolmos.

After several days of dancing, Sônam Wangdü no longer had to be present. I knew the steps and simply had to repeat them. At first Ngakpa Yeshé Dorje played rolmo and Khandro Ten'dzin Drölkar played the drum – but when I'd got it down, they left me to it. I danced in silence every day – stopping only for meals. Khandro Ten'dzin Drölkar would call me in to lunch with a merry smile and after dinner in the evening I'd walk back to my hut – sometimes performing a few dance steps on the way.

One day – an assorted group of ngakpas arrived and fortunately Sônam Wangdü was there to translate. Ngakpa Yeshé Dorje had sent a message to him. Some of the ngakpas wore full gö kar chang lo robes and some simply wore maroon or black chubas[4]. All had uncut hair and all had earrings of one sort or another.

---

4   The black chuba was one of Kyabjé Künzang Dorje Rinpoche modes of dress. It symbolised his mode as a phurba master – one accomplished in the rites of Dorje Phurba (*Vajrakilaya*).

One of the ngakpas had a fine set of dung-kyi a-long [5] and I enquired where they could be found – but he'd got his in Tibet. There were none to be found in India – unless I could find someone to make them for me. Bodhanath in Nepal was probably the best place.

Ngakpa Yeshé Dorje said *"Kyabjé Düd'jom Rinpoche will know where dung-kyi a-long making – but very difficult now because many not this skill having."*

"Should I try to have some made, Rinpoche?"

"O yah – and for me also making" Ngakpa Yeshé Dorje grinned.

"I'll organise that as soon as I get back to Bodhanath. That'll be just before I go home to England – so I will have to post them to you from Nepal."

Ngakpa Yeshé Dorje shook his head *"No… then stealing possible. Just bringing – when you next time to McLeod Ganj coming."* And so it was arranged.

The next day brought the occasion for which I had been practising and the gathered ngakpas were somehow intrigued—partially amused—to see how the Inji ngakpa would dance. I appeared in my dance costume at the appointed time. I'd changed into it 'round the back of the house and they greeted me with a variety of cheerful sounds. I'd been informed that I'd be given my cue at a certain point in the proceedings. I was to dance until the concluding cue was given and then go and change back into my regular robes.

I sat on a box at one end of the shrine room and the proceeding commenced. I remembered sitting in on a nine day session back in 1971 and even recognised some of the same faces. I wrote about that event and how it hit me at the time.

> *There were about a dozen of the most fearsome ngakpas I'd ever seen. Fearsome wasn't the right word – but what other word was there? Awesome? No, that would have been clichéd – and awful has been afflicted with negative associations. The best I could manage was to say that they were from another time and another place.*

---

5   dung kyi A long / དུང་གྱི་ཨ་ལོང་ – conch shell earrings. The best have a spiral carved out of their centres – but most are simple hoops. The dung-kyi a-long are part of the gö kar chang lo dress. They were common in Tibet but rarely seen after the exodus.

> *It felt as if I'd slipped sideways through time to a place where 'supernormal' was as normal as a Belisha beacon [6] on a zebra crossing.*

Be that as it may, the box was rickety and I wondered how long it would support my weight before spilling me ignominiously onto the floor. I didn't let the thought disturb me overmuch. It would either collapse or not – and thinking about it would serve no purpose. My main aim was to keep a close eye on Ngakpa Yeshé Dorje. He would raise his dorje and make three circling movements with it – and that was to be my cue to stand and prepare to commence the Zha-nak dance. This first cue would be followed by a more definite cue to dance – but I'd have to be on my feet ready to start as soon as the rolmos clashed.

Why is it that *awaited cues* always arrive more suddenly than you'd imagine? It caught me slightly unawares even though my mind had not wandered. Maybe it was simply that I felt partially hypnotised by the Vajrayana orchestra. I raised my knee immediately – but felt as if I could have been half a second earlier because no sooner had I made the first move than the rolmos and drum cut in and I began the gyrations. Once I was a few steps into the dance I relaxed and it all flowed quite comfortably. Then— suddenly—there was the final cue to stop and return to my seat. I'd been all set to dance for far longer and it was almost disappointing to bring the dance to a halt. The rites went through a phase that followed the dance and at the next cue I rose and left the shrine room in a series of swirls that landed me at the entrance – facing inwards as planned. I backed out of the shrine room and went to the back of the house. My regular robes were sitting where I'd left them. Khandro Ten'dzin Drölkar met me with a glass of Sprite. She found it highly amusing to come upon me in my underpants and left with a giggle. I downed the Sprite in a few gulps as I was monstrously thirsty. By the time I was back in my robes Khandro Ten'dzin Drölkar appeared again with another glass. She must have known how thirsty I would be after the dance and I made as many appreciative noises as I could in my rudimentary Tibetan.

---

6 A Belisha beacon was an amber-coloured globe lamp on a tall black and white pole, marking pedestrian crossings of streets in Britain. It was named after Leslie Hore-Belisha (1893–1957), the Minister of Transport. He added beacons to pedestrian crossings, marked by large metal studs in the road surface in 1934. These crossings were later painted in black and white stripes and became known as zebra crossings.

After a suitable break from my exertions—prompted by Khandro Ten'dzin Drölkar—I re-entered the shrine room. The rites were concluded and we all ate dinner together. The ngakpas were all very funny in their appreciation of my dance and made all sorts of swirling gestures with their hands in imitation of my dance – accompanied by exclamations of *"Yag-po dug!"* at which I grinned like an idiot. What a *fine* day that had been!

I walked back to my hut feeling both exhilarated and tired. I left the gar'cham robes at Ngakpa Yeshé Dorje's place – and that's where they'd remain until I passed that way again after my time with Kyabjé Künzang Dorje Rinpoche. Then I'd take them to Nepal and have someone machine embroider them with the appropriate motifs. I wondered if I'd ever be called upon to dance again – and decided that I'd welcome the opportunity whenever it arose. I'd have to practise from time to time just to make sure that I was always ready.

The days went by extremely pleasantly. I learned how to make the Tröma Nakmo gTormas in all their varieties – and I learnt many other ritual procedures. Ngakpa Yeshé Dorje was a master ritualist and his knowledge of Mahayoga was exhaustive. I asked what he knew of Dzogchen men-ngag-dé – but he admitted this was not the field of his expertise. He knew some things but he did not feel qualified to speak on the subject. Khandro Ten'dzin Drölkar was familiar with Dzogchen – but I could tell that she didn't wish to hold forth when her husband had declined to comment.

Khandro Ten'dzin Drölkar was a highly advanced practitioner. I later discovered that she was highly respected by Kyabjé Düd'jom Rinpoche and his son Dung-sé Thrin-lé Norbu Rinpoche. She had completed dark retreats and was thoroughly qualified to teach Dzogchen Thöd-gal – the practice which led to 'ja'lü. It was not that Khandro Ten'dzin Drölkar was humble – or not humble in the sense that she was doing anything deliberate to appear humble. She was simply disinterested in status. She had no self-concept. She had nothing to prove and nothing to hide. She was happy to give me teachings when Ngakpa Yeshé Dorje was away – and there seemed no limit to what she knew. In the few days which led up to my departure for Tso Pema I had the opportunity to ask Khandro Ten'dzin Drölkar questions concerning Dzogchen.

Khandro Ten'dzin Drölkar explained that Dzogchen was not philosophical doctrine like the Madhyamaka. Dzogchen concerned discovering one's essential condition beyond cultural conditioning and beyond philosophical constructs. Dzogchen meant the primordial nature of each individual. This was utter ordinariness. It was not in any way exotic. The world—just as it was—was perfectly pure. The world did not look different with nondual realisation – but nevertheless, it would be *as if seen for the first time*.

"This is not a good analogy – but could it be analogous to suddenly falling in love with somebody one has known for years?" I asked somewhat delightedly – but suspecting the answer would not be affirmative.

"O yah!" Khandro Ten'dzin Drölkar laughed *"Not same – but like reflection. Good analogy making."*

In the lineage of Dzogchen there have been Lamas of all social classes, including nomads, the nobility, the peasantry, the monastics, the gö kar chang lo'i dé, and lay practitioners. The lay practitioners are those who have received teachings and empowerments – but who have not taken the robe-wearing vows with their special inner and outer commitments.

Khandro Ten'dzin Drölkar said that Dzogchen was not dependent on externals – but neither did it reject externals. Dzogchen wasn't contingent on culture – but neither did it deny culture. It could be practised in any context. This meant, she said, that when I returned to Britain – it was not necessary that I wore robes. I could wear any clothing. I would naturally wear robes where appropriate – but robes did not have to define my inner practice. She said that, in Dzogchen it was important to allow natural awareness to function – and to function within whatever circumstances arose.

With Dzogchen the most important point was to discover the *nature of Mind*. Initially one had to discover the nature of the quotidian frame of reference – the *everyday mind*. If one did not discover the *everyday mind* and its limitations – then attempting to discover the nature of Mind was difficult. It was therefore crucial to understand the basic relative condition of existence in terms of Body, Speech, and Mind.

Jampal Shé-nyèn[7] received transmissions of Dzogchen from Garab Dorje[8]. He divided them into three series: Dzogchen sem-dé[9], Dzogchen long-dé[10], and Dzogchen men-ngag-dé.

Dzogchen sem-dé meant the *series of the nature of Mind*. The *nature of Mind* was the pluripotential dimension of being which could not be characterised – but which gave rise to *that which could be characterised*. One would be introduced to the *nature of Mind* by the Lama in order to have authentic experience of the source of manifest reality. Dzogchen sem-dé went beyond intellect through the nature of intellect itself – and was therefore the series with the most explanations.

Dzogchen long-dé meant *the series of vastness* or *the series of space*. In this system *space* referred to the primordial dimension which served as a base for manifesting practitioners' innate clarity. Unlike Dzogchen sem-dé, Dzogchen long-dé functions through the corporeal dimension – and therefore has far fewer explanations. In Dzogchen long-dé Mind was understood as pervasive throughout the physical body – and therefore no particular emphasis was placed on mind in relation to brain.

Dzogchen men-ngag-dé meant the series of 'no word'. The result of these practices was inherent in their explanation. If one understood the explanation of the practice – then one simultaneously understood the result of the practice. In Dzogchen men-ngag-dé there were simply the practices – and nothing else was required; hence 'no word'.

Garab Dorje, before he attained rainbow body, left the précis of his teachings known as his Three Principles Phrases: *Direct introduction, Remaining without doubt*, and *Continuing congruence with reality*.

Direct introduction occurred when the primordial nature was transmitted immediately by the Lama. The Lama always remains congruent with the primordial nature, and the presence of this nature is communicated to disciples, whatever situation subsists.

Remaining without doubt occurred when—through experiential familiarity—the primordial nature itself has removed all doubt. It is not a decision or an act of faith. It is self-evident.

7   *'jam dPal bShes gNyen* / འཇམ་དཔལ་བཤེས་གཉེན་ / Manjushrimitra.
8   *dGa' rab rDo rJe* / དགའ་རབ་རྡོ་རྗེ་ / Pramodavajra, Prahevajra, Surativajra.
9   *rDzogs chen sems sDe* / རྫོགས་ཆེན་སེམས་སྡེ་ / cittavarga.
10 *rDzogs chen kLong sDe* / རྫོགས་ཆེན་ཀློང་སྡེ་ / abhyantaravarga.

Continuing congruence with reality occurred when disciples continue at all times in returning to the nondual nature of the primordial state, until every experience spontaneously self-liberates in the instant it arises. There is no effort. Nothing hides the authentic nature of the individual. One continues in this gestalt and complete realisation becomes natural in each moment.

"*Düd'jom Rinpoche*" Khandro Ten'dzin Drölkar smiled *"face of rigpa directly introducing.* [11] *Face of naked mind as the rigpa itself he is directly introducing. This is innate primordial wisdom.*

"*Then – without doubt. On one point only, settling* [12]. *Düd'jom Rinpoche stating all phenomena—whatever samsara or nirvana manifesting—these none other than rigpa playing. So complete and direct settling. Nothing else – only resting in rigpa.*

"*Then confidence directly. Arising namtogs liberating* [13]. *Düd'jom Rinpoche saying 'When namtogs recognising – direct confidence in simultaneous arising and dissolving in the space of chö-ku. This unity of rigpa and space."*

Khandro Ten'dzin Drölkar laughed because I was furiously scribbling notes and Sônam was looking entirely bewildered *"Chögyam not Tibetan understanding – but Dzogchen understanding. Sônam Tibetan words understanding – but not Dzogchen meaning."* She then told Sônam that he had translated well because she could see that I had understood what she was saying.

She then said that the *Mirror of the Heart of Dorje Sempa* [14] explained that Dzogchen is *'Great' Completion* because it was the zenith of nondual view, nondual absorption, and nondual comportment. *"Never from natural state moving"* Khandro Ten'dzin Drölkar began. *"Never hindrances in dimension beyond alteration making. Never dimension beyond referentiality leaving. Never dimension beyond obsession leaving. Never dimension of ecstasy beyond communicative disjuncture leaving.*

---

11 Ngo rang thog tu trèd pa (*ngo rang thog tu sPrad pa* / ངོ་རང་ཐོག་ཏུ་སྤྲད་པ་).
12 Thag gÇig thog tu chèd pa (*thag gCig thog tu bCad pa* / ཐག་གཅིག་ཐོག་ཏུ་བཅད་པ་).
13 Deng dröl thog tu cha' ba (*gDeng grol thog tu bCa' ba* / གདེང་གྲོལ་ཐོག་ཏུ་བཅའ་བ་).
14 Mirror of the Heart of Dorje Sempa (*rDo rJe sems dPa' sNying gi me long* / རྡོ་རྗེ་སེམས་དཔའ་སྙིང་གི་མེ་ལོང་) – one of the 17 tantras of Dzogchen men-ngag-dé (*man ngag sDe'i rGyud bCu bDun* / མན་ངག་སྡེའི་རྒྱུད་བཅུ་བདུན་) explains how lamps (*sGron ma* / སྒྲོན་མ་) are the self-display of awareness. It itemises 21 pointing-out instructions appropriate for people with varied predispositions and predilections – with four vital points and practice directives. These 17 Tantras are to be found in Nyingma Gyüdbum (*rNying ma rGyud 'bum* / རྙིང་མ་རྒྱུད་འབུམ་). Dorje Sempa (*rDo rJe sems dPa'* / *Vajrasattva*).

"Dzogchen is nonduality origin and always pervading. Dzogchen is awareness beyond substantial and insubstantial – beyond cause and effect. Dzogchen in equanimity remaining – but dimension of ecstasy and essence not leaving. Dzogchen everywhere without dependence on location existing. Dzogchen essence of everything without word needing or syllable establishing."

Oral transmission, she explained, occurred when the Lama introduced the real nature by explaining through words in ordinary language. This was the reason why Lamas explained different methods and ways of discovering authentic nature for many days. Lamas gave examples, and explicated by the use of the mirror, the faceted crystal, and the crystal sphere. Through showing these symbols, students comprehend the authentic nature and its potentiality. Once these symbols have been explicated – students are prepared to receive direct transmission.

At this point Khandro Ten'dzin Drölkar held up a mélong *"This example."* She sat silently showing me the mirror for some minutes *"Mélong everything manifesting. All forms, shapes, and colours manifesting. Mélong is subject or object no idea having. Mélong always mirror qualities manifesting—always authentic nature remaining—but, through secondary causes, everything else manifesting."* Then she laughed *"Mélong never changing. Marmot or Mahakala manifesting – no difference in mirror coming. Mélong all same reflecting."* PAUSE *"Maybe you are Karma Gyalpo Rinpoche in Tso Pema meeting. He is powerful Drüpchen. If meeting possible – then he is everything most perfectly explaining."* I said that I would enquire after Karma Gyalpo Rinpoche when I got to Tso Pema. After translating these final words, Sônam had to leave. I asked whether I should also leave – but Khandro Ten'dzin Drölkar wanted me to remain and have dinner with her.

Khandro Ten'dzin Drölkar and I sat together in silence for a while after Sônam took his departure. The daylight was beginning to fade. She lit a few kerosene lamps – and their cheerful glow spread across the room in which we sat. The next action she took was to point to her mouth and oscillate her raised hand. I made the same gesture. We both laughed. We both understood the gesture. Her gesture meant *'I can't speak English.'* Mine meant *'I can't speak Tibetan.'* Why this made us laugh is indecipherable. Khandro Ten'dzin Drölkar was quite adept with gestures. She showed me a faceted crystal and pointed at her heart. Then she used her hands to give the impression of light rays moving outward and creating the environment.

Then she showed me a crystal sphere and by the use of her hands she indicated that *what was external* and *what was internal* were inseparable. There was no inside or outside – there was simply the space of manifestation.

Khandro Ten'dzin Drölkar suddenly shifted in mien and told me she had prepared mo-mos. This I understood without need of translation and thanked her enthusiastically, in Tibetan. There was also tsé-cho[15] to accompany the mo-mos. At this level my Tibetan—*minimal and execrable*—was sufficient. After a short time in the kitchen, she brought out the dinner and we ate together and sipped a little chang. We exchanged a few fragmented pieces of information about my time of departure and the length of my stay in Tso Pema – but otherwise we simply smiled at each other.

After a while I decided that it would be polite to take my leave. Khandro Ten'dzin Drölkar stood waving me goodbye until darkness visually divided us.

This was my last meeting with Khandro Ten'dzin Drölkar in that period. I was to leave for Tso Pema the next day. I was to make a pilgrimage. I said nothing of going to study with Künzang Dorje Rinpoche because Kyabjé Düd'jom Rinpoche had told me to tell no one – not even Ngakpa Yeshé Dorje. I felt I *could* have told Khandro Ten'dzin Drölkar—it would have felt 'right'—but I'd made a promise to Kyabjé Düd'jom Rinpoche.

---

15 *tshal cho* / ཚལ་ཆོ་ – vegetable chow-mein (lo-mein in the USA).

part two

the king of realised activity

The word Mahasiddha—Drüpchen—is used to describe the 84 great *nondual realised adepts* of the ancient Indian subcontinent – from as far east as Burma[1] to Afghanistan[2].

The Mahasiddhas were individuals who, through the practice of drüpthab, attained the realisation of siddhi: extrasensory preternatural ability and unrestricted unbounded cogency. They were tantrikas—practitioners of yoga and tantra—and their influence throughout India and the Himalayas is vast. It is expressed in their songs of realisation and hagiographies[3] – many of which have been preserved in Tibet and Bhutan. The Mahasiddhas were the founders of Vajrayana. The Tantric communities of India—between 750 BC and 1150 AD—were guilds of exceptional enquiry in terms of reality. In contradistinction to the Buddhist monastic universities, they were decentralised and dispersed – but they were post-doctoral experiential-laboratories of liberation.

There have continued to be Mahasiddhas – and many have lived within the Vajrayana culture of the Himalayan countries. They are not enumerated as Mahasiddhas, as were their Indian predecessors – but they had and have the same glorious propensities.

Kyabjé Künzang Dorje Rinpoche was one such Mahasiddha. It was a miracle of human possibility that I was able to study one-to-one with Kyabjé Künzang Dorje Rinpoche – and another that the same had been possible with Kyabjé Düd'jom Rinpoche Jig'drèl Yeshé Dorje. The value I place on the time spent with them grows with time – and will continue to grow. I am staggered by my good fortune.

1 Ri-nub (*ri nub* / རི་ནུབ་) – Burma, now called Myanmar.
2 Tak-zig (*sTag gZig* / སྟག་གཟིག་) – including Tajikistan, Kazakhstan, Uzbekistan, Kyrgyzstan, Turkmenistan, and Baluchistan.
3 Hagiography – namthar (*rNam thar* / རྣམ་ཐར་).

6

Mahasiddha Karma Gyalpo

Suddenly—it was always suddenly—I was on the bus to Mandi[1]. My journey is described in *Wisdom Eccentrics*[2] – so I shall not elaborate, apart from saying that it was a journey into the past. However '1950s' McLeod Ganj had been – Mandi was of some earlier period. Tso Pema[3] was older still. The *age* was in the buildings – but also in the daguerreotype atmosphere.

After the usual quasi-gruelling journey, I arrived in Tso Pema. I found fabulous lodgings at the Nyingma Gompa – due to factors of which I was naïvely insensible. I was bearing a letter which introduced me to Kyabjé Künzang Dorje Rinpoche – written by Kyabjé Düd'jom Rinpoche Jig'drèl Yeshé Dorje. This marked me out as prestigiously non-ordinary. I had no idea that this would be the case – although it should have been obvious. Another factor was that I was wearing what was deemed to be an *aristocratic tulku's waistcoat*. This is because it was extremely dark maroon. I'd had it sewn up for me by an old Art College friend in Bristol from a length of woollen fabric I'd bought as a remnant from the John Lewis Department Store[4]. It cost next to nothing – because it was such a short length. I hadn't a clue that a maroon fabric *so* dark—let alone pure wool—was hideously expensive in India. The third factor was I had a rather voluminous beard and Tibetans rarely grow much in the way of a beard. Mahasiddhas—I was told—always had such beards. The fact that every other hippie at that time had a similar beard, didn't seem to register in terms of how I was perceived. I concluded that it was a combination of factors. Be that as it may, I considered myself extremely fortunate in being taken under the wing of Lama Könchog Rinpoche. He made sure I was more at home than I ever imagined I could be, in a place I'd never visited before.

---

1 Mandi (*known as Zahor in Tibetan*) is a town 3,425 feet above sea-level, in Himachal Pradesh; 89 miles north of Simla.
2 *Wisdom Eccentrics*—Ngakpa Chögyam—ARO BOOKS inc—New York—2011.
3 *mTsho pa dMa* / མཚོ་པད྄—Rewalsar Lake—is located on a mountain spur about 15 miles southwest from Mandi and 4,500 feet above sea level.
4 John Lewis is a chain of high-end department stores. The first was opened in Oxford Street, London, in 1864.

I had no idea at the time that Kyabjé Düd'jom Rinpoche had already written to Könchog Rinpoche to inform him of my arrival.

It was too late at that point to go to see Künzang Dorje Rinpoche, so Könchog Rinpoche invited me to dine with him. He asked me if there was anything I liked in particular. I admitted to relishing fried mo-mos and they were duly provided – along with tsé cho-cho. We conversed concerning many different topics. He told me a great deal concerning Dorje Tröllö—his main practice—and explained it was an ideal practice to accompany Dzogchen methods. He had a small Dorje Tröllö shrine room in which he practised. It contained a huge—larger than life—statue of Dorje Tröllö. He invited me to practise with him later in the evening. It is not a simple matter to describe what *that* was like – because it was not like anything I had ever known. It was not that the statue came to life – but it ceased to be a statue. It did not move – but neither was it absolutely static. It did not exactly radiate light – but there was a radiance in the shrine room and the statue of Dorje Tröllö seemed unusually vivid. It had a depth and intensity of colour which made it seem as if I was seeing colours I'd never seen before. It occurred to me that velvet could be like that in comparison to ordinary fabric. Könchog Rinpoche introduced me to the Dorje Tröllö mantra and we vocalised loudly for at least an hour. He played the large rolmo and I kept time with the large gompa drum[5].

I went to see Kyabjé Künzang Dorje Rinpoche the next day with Pema Dorje, my appointed translator. I was pronounced a 'thom yor[6]—an idiot —by the Lama who was to replace Kyabjé Düd'jom Rinpoche as my Tsawa'i Lama. "*What does this 'thom yor want?*" he asked.

Of course, now those words cause me endless amusement and delight. They make Khandro Déchen laugh. Our students find them equally hilarious. They hear about our meeting as a wonderful adventure. They wish they had been there with Künzang Dorje Rinpoche. They wish he'd called them 'thom yor too. They probably don't wish that Künzang Dorje Rinpoche's wrath would bring them to the brink of vomiting or falling unconscious. People watch films about heroic exploits and identify with the hero or heroine.

---

5   Large gompa drum – nga-chen (*rNga chen* / རྔ་ཆེན་).
6   *'thom yor* / འཐོམ་ཡོར་ – idiot.

They fantasise about being the great warrior or the great explorer – but the actual situation is never quite what it is on the screen or in the words of a book. Looking back, of course, I would not have changed anything. It was perfect exactly as it was.

On the day, those words *"What does this 'thom yor want?"* made me utterly wretched. I'd been running downhill in a carefree manner – and suddenly, I fell on my face. I hit the dense unyielding ground of derision. Düd'jom Rinpoche had told me Künzang Dorje Rinpoche was a *wrathful Lama* – but I imagined the *wrath* would be something which would be called forth by my lack of ability to understand, or my being too slow to understand. I'd not expected the wrath quite so immediately. It was a bad beginning— or so it seemed—but, 'thom yor or not, I went back every day. I was shouted at every day – for a week or so, before I gained reprieve.

I find myself at a loss for words when attempting to encapsulate my time with Künzang Dorje Rinpoche in a chapter; it would take a weighty volume – and that has already been written. I had no idea at the time I would write memoirs of my life with regard to Vajrayana – or else what was written in *Wisdom Eccentrics* would have appeared here. There will be some duplication of material – but there is a great deal more to tell than I could have included in the prior book.

Being with Künzang Dorje Rinpoche was like being with Düd'jom Rinpoche in one way – as *spending time in his presence* was all that could ever be required. It was also utterly different – because it was never possible to relax or let my attention slip, even for a moment. I can only compare it to driving far too fast and knowing any error could be terminal.

I should begin by saying he gave me no teachings on Dzogchen men-ngag-dé 'til the end of my sojourn with him was in sight – or rather no overt, obvious, Dzogchen men-ngag-dé teachings. By the end, I realised that my entire time with Künzang Dorje Rinpoche had been the constant transmission of Dzogchen. I simply failed to see it, *as it was happening*.

I had expected Dzogchen men-ngag-dé to be a linear explanation. I had expected to hear explanations concerning *the nature of Mind*. I had expected technical terms. There were almost none – until the end of our time together. Of course, then, technical terms were necessary. Künzang Dorje Rinpoche always gave what was necessary – but, at first, *only* what was necessary. There was no leeway. There was no comfortable or comforting exchange of pleasantries.

It *did* occur later – but at first our communication had more in common with a police investigation in which I was the prime murder suspect.

What Künzang Dorje Rinpoche did in terms of teaching, was to peel me like a prawn or crack me open like a lobster. He often reduced me to a blithering caricature of what I thought I was. Every day I went to see Rinpoche, a misremembered line from Tennyson's 'Charge of the Light Brigade' ran through my thoughts '… *into the valley of death…*'[7] It might have been easier if there had been 600 others with me – but Rinpoche wouldn't have been perturbed; he'd have shouted at the entire gathering – including their horses, saddlery, sabres, and uniforms.

I shall try to explain Künzang Dorje Rinpoche as he appeared at the time. He was 45 years old when we met – but he was somewhat ageless. I took him to be in his thirties because he showed so few signs of age. It's sometimes difficult to tell the age of someone of another ethnic group – but I'd been around Tibetans and had some sense of how they appeared at different ages. He was a mystery to me – because he seemed to stand outside time. He was both old and young. He was almost as western in his appearance as he was Asiatic. He had the kind of face which defies categories. The closest description I can manage is that he looked a little like Errol Flynn. I could imagine him in a pirate movie because he had a swashbuckling mien which I later saw in the Khamba and Golok horsemen who sometimes appeared in Bodhanath.

He was a man who was used to riding horses. He was familiar with living in the mountains. He wasn't a city dweller – but neither was he out-of-place riding trains and buses. He seemed at home wherever he was. I cannot speak of his realisation or compare him with Kyabjé Düd'jom Rinpoche – because such a comparison would be meaningless. How can a boy who's sat on a donkey at a village fête compare two Olympic Gold Medal Equestrians? To say that Künzang Dorje Rinpoche had undoubted devotion for Düd'jom Rinpoche would not necessarily make him the lesser Lama – but I had no way of knowing. All I knew was I loved them both dearly – and in some way they were the same. They were the same even though they were, in some ways, entirely different. Kyabjé Düd'jom Rinpoche was not wrathful – at least never as far as I ever saw.

---

7   '*Half a league, half a league, half a league onward, All in the valley of Death rode the six hundred.*'

He was the epitome of kindness and gentleness – but not because he lacked power. Künzang Dorje Rinpoche was also gentle and kind – but it took longer to experience that. The one who sends you to the surgeon may seem entirely benevolent – but the surgeon cuts you open. The surgeon's knife is, of course, benevolently wielded – but you tend to understand that later. You experience it when you're back on your feet – with a good life ahead of you, rather than the protracted incapacity which would have resulted had you not had the operation. This was the reality of what I experienced.

I thought back to my time with Ngakpa Yeshé Dorje and wondered—at times—why Kyabjé Düd'jom Rinpoche had told me to study Tröma Nakmo with him before going on to see Künzang Dorje Rinpoche. Was it simply because Künzang Dorje Rinpoche would not be in Tso Pema at the time I left Bodhanath? He had known that I had spent time with Ngakpa Yeshé Dorje and Khandro Ten'dzin Drölkar – so maybe it seemed better to him that I was gainfully occupied. My study of Mahayoga ritual was certainly interesting and valuable. What Vajrayana study is ever *not* valuable? It was so different however, from what was ahead of me in Tso Pema. I had, of course, spent time alone with Khandro Ten'dzin Drölkar – and she had given me Dzogchen teachings. Maybe that was why Düd'jom Rinpoche suggested I spend a while in McLeod Ganj. Maybe he had wanted me to discover Khandro Ten'dzin Drölkar myself. Of course, Düd'jom Rinpoche would not have known whether I would gain any time with her on her own. Sometimes the directions of great Lamas have the quality of a game of chess. A pawn moves. One sees it as arbitrary and innocuous. One doesn't know checkmate is nine moves away. It occurred to me later, had Kyabjé Düd'jom Rinpoche told me to *seize the moment* if ever I was on my own with Khandro Ten'dzin Drölkar – it would have skewed my behaviour. It would have skewed my relationship with Ngakpa Yeshé Dorje. I was obviously far better placed not knowing *that which I had no need of knowing*.

In my time with Künzang Dorje Rinpoche there was almost no symbolic activity. When I tell people of that time, they are always vaguely astonished at how different it was from any other kind of study they have known in terms of Vajrayana. It was a period of intense experience. It was a form of learning which had nothing to do with 'learning about'. There was information—certainly—but the main force of what I gained was perceptual. I felt as if my eyes, ears, and every other sense organ had been removed and replaced. I no longer saw or heard in the same way.

I no longer thought in the same way. I'd gained a sense of logic which I'd never known before. I'd always been 'logical' to a certain degree – but I'd never understood patterns as readily. After this time, I could see where people were coming from in their stated convictions. I could follow their systems and comprehend how they reached their conclusions. I didn't become an 'arguer' by virtue of this insight – but I did learn how to be silent when silence was required. I learned how to make statements when they needed to be made – and, even to insist on being heard. It was rare that I ever needed to insist on anything – but I knew I had that capacity, if it was required. I found I spoke less and listened more. I didn't always enjoy what I heard – but I rarely felt the need to express my absence of enjoyment.

Künzang Dorje Rinpoche's system of teaching was to recount narratives of Tibetan Lamas. These were stories which many Lamas told – because they had been handed down through generations. Some of the stories I had heard before – but Künzang Dorje Rinpoche told them with alternative angles and uncommon emphases. Sometimes the details in the stories differed quite markedly. I realised early on there was no story which only had *one version*. There was no *correct version*. Each story was correct – because each time it was told, it was told for a purpose. Unless you measure the pinch of salt which goes into an omelette on a microscale, every omelette will be different. *Lama stories* are methods of imparting information – and so all the stories Künzang Dorje Rinpoche recounted had specific purposes in terms of making me understand *principle* and *function*.

These two factors—*principle* and *function*—existed in everything. There was nothing which could not be understood if one determined the *principle* and *function*. This was a way not only to understand Vajrayana – but each of the nine yanas. It was also a way to understand how other religions worked. It could be applied to philosophy, politics, and even to business. There is no human system which cannot be examined and understood through identifying the *principle* and *function*.

So, Künzang Dorje Rinpoche would relate these Lama stories – and then interrogate me quite ferociously as to what they meant. He would cross-examine me as to the motivation of each character. *'The benefit of all sentient beings'* was strictly out of bounds as an answer. He regarded it as a puerile evasion, the answer of a mealymouthed 'thom yor.

He let me know immediately if I gave a *stock answer* – and after the second day he told me that if I gave another *stock answer*, I would have to leave and never return.

The problem with *stock answers*—he explained—was that they were merely *a series of sounds*. They were words – but they may as well have been meaningless phonemes. I had to show insight – or, at the very least, show I had tried to investigate the mindset which lay behind whatever action it was in the story he told. *Not knowing* was acceptable – but only after I'd expended effort in attempting to understand. My exertions in comprehension therefore had to be open to his scrutiny. I had to explain my process aloud – even though it might lead nowhere. There were essential configurations in terms of Vajrayana and the patterns which deviated from it. The deviations were predictable if one understood the nature of duality and nonduality. Vajrayana was not a subject which could be studied as other fields of knowledge were studied. Vajrayana was reality – and reality explained itself, if one had basic guidelines. Künzang Dorje Rinpoche pointed out that I had received all the basic guidelines – and so all I had to do was apply what I already knew. If I did this, then there would be no mystery about Vajrayana – or anything concerning perception and response.

After a week of this onslaught, I hardly knew who I was. All I knew was that Düd'jom Rinpoche had sent me to Tso Pema to study with Künzang Dorje Rinpoche. Düd'jom Rinpoche had obviously known what was likely to happen. I reassured myself at the end of every horrendous assault on my reality that *all was well*. Düd'jom Rinpoche had sent me with a letter – and Künzang Dorje Rinpoche was to teach me. *That* was all I needed to know. I had some insane sense of assurance that Künzang Dorje Rinpoche meant me well. After a while, I began to gain the impression that he was moving in the direction of not entirely disliking me. I would sometimes catch a fleeting hint of a smile. Sometimes there was a sense of something in his eyes which suggested that I was not as entirely torpid as I felt myself to be in his presence.

Apart from his insisting that I employed my capacity for cognition – there was another factor which made me a 'thom yor. What he wanted from me however, was just too simple for me to see. He just wanted me to be natural. He did not want a *Himalayan Buddhist re-enactor* – even though I was far from the standard variety. I wasn't the type of Inji who adopted Tibetan culture wholesale.

I wasn't consciously *acting a part* – but I was still not *natural*. I was too concerned with being polite. I was stultified with deference. I was debilitatingly anxious with respect to wasting his time with vapid personal ideas and opinions. What he wanted however – was exactly what I thought he would *not* want. It was not *my opinions per se* – but their structure and pattern. He wanted to know how my perception functioned. He was almost a Tibetan anthropologist studying another species who looked human.

He knew very well how Tibetans functioned – but I was the first Inji whom he had ever had the misfortune to teach. He therefore had to investigate – and discover what sort of creature this 'Ngakpa Chögyam' might be. My effort in being the *good Vajrayana Buddhist I thought I was supposed to be* – merely obfuscated *the way in which I perceived*. He wanted to know exactly how the Inji perceived. As soon as I allowed myself to trust the fact that he wanted me to *be myself* – everything began to change. It took a while. I occasionally slipped back into sacerdotal mode – but as the days proceeded, I learned to trust being utterly vulnerable *in the open ground of our being together*.

"*Today Dorje Thegpa speaking – Vajrayana. Nyingma, nine yanas coming – and six are Vajrayana. Kagyüd, Sakya and Gélug four tantras having – but Nyingma six having. This you are knowing – but today detail giving. Three outer tantras in all traditions same. Only inner tantras different in Nyingma.*"

Kyabjé Künzang Dorje Rinpoche explained that the entire scope of the Buddhist teachings was divided differently according to tradition. He said he would not address that which lay outside Himalayan Buddhism other than to say that it was wrong to describe Theravada as Hinayana – because it contained teachings on cultivating loving kindness. He said it was wrong also to describe Ch'an and Zen as being *solely Mahayana*, because these systems contained teachings which were similar to Dzogchen sem-dé – at least as far as lhatong[8] and possibly nyi'mèd[9].

He explained the Kagyüds and Sakyas mainly spoke of Hinayana, Mahayana, and Vajrayana. Gélugs spoke of Hinayana and Mahayana – and then divided Mahayana into exoteric[10] and esoteric[11].

8 *lhag mThong* / ལྷག་མཐོང
9 *gNyis 'med* / གཉིས་འམེད.
10 Exoteric Mahayana – Chi-kor (*phyi sKor* / ཕྱི་སྐོར).
11 Esoteric Mahayana – Nang-kor (*nang sKor* / ནང་སྐོར).

The exoteric Mahayana was the Sutras and the esoteric Mahayana was Tantra. The outcome of this system was to make Vajrayana dependent on Sutrayana. Vajrayana, from this point of view, did not have a unique independent base. This meant that from the point of view of this system – one could not begin with Vajrayana. It also meant Vajrayana had to be congruent with Sutrayana. This was why the Gélug was an entirely monastic school. He explained there were benefits for every way of dividing Buddhism – and these different approaches suited different predispositions and predilections in people. *"For some peoples, Vajrayana too much dangerous."* PAUSE *"Sometimes Vajrayana too much shouting"* he laughed. *"Then Sutrayana preferring possible."*

At this point in our relationship, I was able to laugh as well.

"So... first three Outer Tantras coming. Beginning ja-wa'i gyud [12]. *What are view, meditation and action, you must be knowing. View is phenomena no self-nature having. Phenomena – four limits not coming."*

These four limitations were existence and non-existence – appearances and emptiness.

The view of ja-wa'i gyüd is based on ultimate and relative. In terms of the ultimate, ja-wa'i gyüd speaks of the inseparability of appearances and emptiness – and phenomena being essentially beyond emerging and ceasing from emergence. In terms of the relative, phenomena are viewed as the display of yidams. Ja-wa'i gyüd emphasises purification, ritual ablution, and requirements concerning diet, and clothing. The yidam is regarded as superior to oneself, whereas in subsequent tantras the yidam is seen as the nature of mind.

"All phenomena Kyil'khor of yidams appearing. Meditation same."

The purpose of purification—ablutions and generally heightened cleanliness—according to Künzang Dorje Rinpoche, was based on the nature of transition from Sutrayana to Vajrayana. He explained that Sutrayana emphasised *form* being *emptiness* – but that Vajrayana began from the *emptiness* from which *form* manifested as the *natural energy of reality*.

---

12 *bya ba'i rGyud* / བྱ་བའི་རྒྱུད་ – Kriyatantra.

From the point of view of Sutrayana – there is a great risk at this point in terms of becoming attached to form as a definition of being. Because of this risk of appropriating *form*—and ascribing to it an *enduring signifying quality* that it only possesses in the moment—one has to be punctilious in one's 'perceptual hygiene'.

This was why one visualised the yidam rather than becoming the yidam. To *be* the yidam at this juncture would be fraught with the risk of self-aggrandisement and self-obsession. For this reason, one uses physical form as a method of disciplining perception. This is the reason why one would avoid anything that could be regarded as tainted in any way – even to the extent of abjuring garlic and onions. The existence of what some consider noisome breath should never defile a shrineroom or a thangka hanging on the wall of one's home. Rinpoche pointed out *"We gos dKar lCang lo'i sDe belonging—and Inner Tantras priority having—so we garlic and onion, always eating possible. We all eating and no one bad-smell-nose finding. Inner tantras view – pure-impure idea, transcending.*

"So, with ja-wa'i gyüd oneself in ordinary form seeing. This dam-tsig sem-dPa' [13]. *Yidam then yeshé sem dPa'* [14] *called and in front appearing like King or Queen. Then wisdom receiving from King or Queen. So Action: cleanliness, concentration, fasting and mantra reciting – and path is yidam offerings making. Offering connection coming – like beautiful khandro flowers giving. Beautiful khandro flowers giving – then symbol becoming. "Symbol meaning ka-jor;* [15] *meaning drub-dé ma*[16] *becoming. Then drog dza'* [17] *becoming. So yidam communication like this making."*

Pema Dorje was busy giving me the Tibetan spellings whilst I wrote my notes, in order that I was able to spell everything correctly. I'd explained that writing in phonetics wouldn't enable me to make sense of my notes at a later point – as I could not look up the words in my Chandra Das Tibetan-English dictionary. This dictionary was my prized possession as they were not easy to obtain.

---

13 *gDam tshigs sems dPa'* / ༄༅། – avowed mind hero.
14 *ye shes sems dPa'* / ༄༅། / *jnana sattva*.
15 *kha sByor* / ༄༅། – sexual union, also kissing. Nyi'mèd ka-jor (*gNyis 'med kha sByor* / ༄༅།) – means nondual integration.
16 *sGrub sDe ma* / ༄༅། – consort.
17 *grogs mDza'* / ༄༅། – lover.

The definitions were not always completely accurate – but I kept a notebook of modified translations which were revised on the basis of what I'd learnt from Düd'jom Rinpoche and Künzang Dorje Rinpoche. What I had found was that there were often different meanings for words in the context of Dzogchen.

"So, fruition of result is the attainment of vajra holder of three families [18]: *Buddha-body family,* [19] *lotus-speech family* [20] *and vajra-mind family.* [21] *Fruition also ku-sum* [22] *calling. Then chod-gyüd*[23] *is activity. This also Nyi-ka'i gyud* [24] *twofold tantra – because ja-wa'i gyüd with view of next vehicle practising. Next vehicle naljor gyüd.* [25] *Then, meditation is yidam visualising in front like brother or a good friend. Then wisdom siddhis receiving. O yah – Chögyam too hard working. Much lotsawa writing. Maybe now lunch necessary."*

I'd already started to catch the distant fragrance of mo-mos frying. Rinpoche knew I like fried mo-mos and so we partook of them quite often.

The mo-mos were served. There were glasses of chang which had been freshly made the day before. We ate our meal and then Künzang Dorje Rinpoche said *"England Art study you making."* PAUSE *"This hard work or this easy work?"*

"For me, Rinpoche, it was hard work – but only because I worked hard. For some others it was relatively easy."

"Then difficulty finding Arts writing?"

---

18 Three families – rig-sum dorje 'dzin pa'i sa (*rigs gSum rDo rJe 'dzin pa'i sa* / རིགས་གསུམ་རྡོ་རྗེ་འཛིན་པའི་ས).
19 Buddha-body family – ku-sum dé-zhin sheg pa'i rig (*sKu gSum de bZhin gShegs pa'i rigs* / སྐུ་གསུམ་དེ་བཞིན་གཤེགས་པའི་རིགས).
20 Lotus-speech family – sung padma'i rig (*gSung pad ma'i rigs* / གསུང་པདྨའི་རིགས).
21 Vajra-mind family – thug dorje rig (*thugs rDo rJe rigs* / ཐུགས་རྡོ་རྗེ་རིགས).
22 *sKu gSum* / སྐུ་གསུམ / *trikaya* – the three spheres of being: chö-ku (*chos sKu* / ཆོས་སྐུ / dharmakaya) – the sphere of unconditioned potentiality; long-ku (*longs sKu* / ལོངས་སྐུ / sambhogakaya) – the sphere of nondual appearances; and, trülku (*sPrul sKu* / སྤྲུལ་སྐུ / nirmanakaya) – the sphere of realised manifestation.
23 *sPyod rGyud* / སྤྱོད་རྒྱུད / *Upatantra* – activity tantra.
24 *gNyis ka'i rGyud* / གཉིས་ཀའི་རྒྱུད / *Ubhayatantra*.
25 *rNal 'byor rGyud* / རྣལ་འབྱོར་རྒྱུད / *Yogatantra*.

"No Rinpoche – I found no great difficulty or if I did, the difficulty was only in making everything as perfect as possible. When I said I worked hard – it was more that I worked longer hours than the others. I arrived at the Art School over an hour early and I left when the Art School was closing."

Rinpoche raised his eyebrows *"Long working very good – but why long working?"*

"Well Rinpoche – it was because I saw it as a limited opportunity; limited in time. I only had three years to use the Art School facilities and get my work printed at the expense of the Art School. After leaving Art School I would have to pay for everything myself – including the use of printing presses." PAUSE "To me, it would have been foolish not to have worked as hard and as long as possible." PAUSE "Also… because I worked as hard as I did – I used up far more of the allocated money for student printing. The head of department was quite happy about that – as none of the other students were that interested in having their work printed."

"O yah – like human re-birth. When precious opportunity realising then very much effort making."

"That's why I'm here Rinpoche." PAUSE "Actually that's not true. I'm not here for any other reason than enthusiasm for this situation. I came here because of my devotion to Kyabjé Düd'jom Rinpoche – and now this devotion is also devotion to you." PAUSE "But maybe I shouldn't use the word 'devotion' – because I only use it as a word which is used in Vajrayana. I do not know what other word I would use – but maybe it would just be enthusiasm for the most important situation in which I could engage. When I know what I want – I don't let myself be side-tracked,"

The translator didn't understand the word 'side-tracked' so I had to conjure up alternatives.

"Diverted, distracted, or deterred. It means that I don't follow other interests. I could be interested in many things – and some would merely be entertainments."

"No entertainment liking?"

"Yes, Rinpoche. I can't say that I don't enjoy entertainment – but entertainment can't occupy too much time. So, when I'm here, I'm here. If some high-ranking Lama was visiting Tso Pema and giving an empowerment into something extraordinary – I would not take time away from our time together. I would see that as a distraction." PAUSE "May I tell you a brief story as an example?"

"O yah – story telling. I am enjoying story."

"Well, back in 1971 when I was in McLeod Ganj, Ngakpa Yeshé Dorje and Khandro Ten'dzin Drölkar invited me to attend a nine-day practice of Tröma Nakmo. I attended along with a group of other Injis – but about half way through the nine days, the other Injis left to attend a large ceremony which the Dalai Lama was giving. They were surprised I didn't also leave and tried to explain to me why I should go to the Dalai Lama's ceremony. They had many reasons why it was important and why I would be foolish not to go. I thanked them for the effort to help me but said I had been invited and had accepted the invitation. I said I would consider it rude to leave on the basis there was something better to attend. They then accused me of not respecting the Dalai Lama – and I had to tell them I was not interested in this line of argument. I had no wish to defend myself and had no interest in further discussion of the matter." PAUSE *"So... I could have called it devotion – but I just did what was most important to me."*

Künzang Dorje Rinpoche listened carefully to my account – and at the end he looked at me again in a most loving manner. *"O yah. This devotion. This precious human re-birth recognising. Before I am saying no 'repeated Dharma language' using - no 'repeated answer' giving. This you are not doing – but this now Künzang Dorje saying."* He laughed. *"This too funny."* PAUSE *"Anyway – this, much happy making. So, I am well understanding. Chögyam in Art School – same like Chögyam in McLeod Ganj; same like Chögyam in Bodhanath; same like Chögyam in Tso Pema; same like Chögyam every place."* PAUSE *"Always same like this remaining – and everything accomplishing. Gö kar chang lo in West establishing. No doubt I am having. Chögyam all this accomplishing as Kyabjé Düd'jom Rinpoche asking."*

Yogatantra views phenomena as free from fixed characteristics[26]. Luminosity is inseparable from emptiness[27]. That is absolute truth. Relative truth is understood through realising that chö-nyid and phenomena are perceived as the sphere of the Dorje-ying dKyil'khor[28].

---

26 Free from fixed characteristics – chö tham ché tro-pa'i tshan ma tham-ché dang dralwa (*chos thams cad sPros pa'i mTshan ma thams cad dang bral ba* / ཆོས་ཐམས་ཅད་སྤྲོས་པའི་མཚན་མ་ཐམས་ཅད་དང་བྲལ་བ).

27 Luminosity is inseparable from emptiness – Ö-sel tongpa nyi du ta (*'od gSal sTong pa nyid du lTa* / འོད་གསལ་སྟོང་པ་ཉིད་དུ་ལྟ).

28 Sphere of the Dorje-ying, dKyil'khor Sphere of indestructible space – chö nyid togpa'i jin lab lé dorje ying kyi kyil'khor dKyil'khor (*kun rDzob cir sNang thams cad chos nyid rTogs pa'i byin rLabs las rDo rJe dByings kyi dKyil 'khor* / ཀུན་རྫོབ་ཅིར་སྣང་ཐམས་ཅད་ཆོས་ཉིད་རྟོགས་པའི་བྱིན་རླབས་ལས་རྡོ་རྗེ་དབྱིངས་ཀྱི་དཀྱིལ་འཁོར).

When meditating according to the development phase[29] you are empty of characteristics whilst visualising the yidam externally. You then merge with the yidam – like water being poured into water. During the completion phase[30] of meditating without object you merge perception of phenomena with the nature of that which is beyond characteristics – and remain in that evenness. Phenomena are seen as the play of wisdom manifesting as yidams.

The Action is principally to practise the view of meditation whilst maintaining purity of intention. *"O yah – fruit realisation in three lifetimes coming. Too long. No patience having – we must be one life realisation having."* PAUSE *"O yah… good… but now we must Tso Pema walking."*

I had walked around the lake of Tso Pema several times with Könchog Rinpoche – but never with Künzang Dorje Rinpoche. This came as a surprise – which was in itself a surprise, as surprises were somewhat unsurprising with Künzang Dorje Rinpoche.

We donned our shoes. As I was fastening my laces he looked at me and commented that my boots were good for the mountains – but not for towns. Did I have footwear for towns? Certainly I did. He asked me to describe them and I went through a list in the same way I had explained my western boots to Ngakpa Yeshé Dorje.

"O yah… Ngakpa Yeshé Dorje very much liking. Very—very—much liking – but why he wearing like this in McLeod Ganj? These in McLeod ruining – also not in wet weather good coming. Not warm in cold weather coming. Chögyam mountain boot much better wearing. Khandro Ten'dzin Drölkar same good boot choosing. I am seeing and liking."

"You know Khandro Ten'dzin Drölkar, Rinpoche?" I asked in surprise.

"O yah." Rinpoche narrowed his eyes slightly *"Not… 'thom yor again becoming?"*

I'd realised even as I said it that it was a stupid question. Of course, he knew her – or how would he know her name or see her mountaineering boots.

---

29 Development phase – kyèd rim (bsKyed rim / བསྐྱེད་རིམ).
30 Completion phase – dzog rim (rDzogs rim / རྫོགས་རིམ).

Rinpoche seemed to sense I'd recognised the ridiculousness of my phraseology and continued as if I'd asked him a sensible question.

"Khandro Ten'dzin Drölkar disciple. She maybe 'Karma Gyalpo' name using?"

That was somehow wonderful and made sense of many things.

"Also disciple of Kyabjé Düd'jom Rinpoche and Dung-sé Thrin-lé Norbu Rinpoche. Khandro Ten'dzin Drölkar profound Dzogchen yogini. She dark-retreat many times making. Powerful practitioner."

Suddenly I was sure why Kyabjé Düd'jom Rinpoche had told me to return to McLeod Ganj in the interim before I went to meet Künzang Dorje Rinpoche.

Rinpoche noticed my expression and burst out laughing. He was just like Kyabjé Düd'jom Rinpoche with regard to reading my mind. He could always see me making sense of things – *when* I made sense of things. I suppose the context was fairly transparent. *"O yah! Khandro Ten'dzin Drölkar all things knowing. Dzogchen very well knowing."* Then Rinpoche explained that although Tibetans were extremely proud of their religious culture – they were in many cases in error about their religion. He gave examples – particularly concerning the status of women. He told me Khandro Ten'dzin Drölkar had a high level of experience—more than many male Lamas—but she was never acknowledged as she should be. He said that she was highly respected by Dung-sé Thrin-lé Norbu Rinpoche and also by Kyabjé Düd'jom Rinpoche – but in her marriage she was not really seen as having any spiritual authority. Rinpoche said he had nothing critical to say – but Khandro Ten'dzin Drölkar was Ngakpa Yeshé Dorje's superior. Tibetan culture however did not value women as it should. This was especially the case in respect of Vajrayana. It was, in fact, a breakage of the fourteen root vows of Vajrayana not to respect women.

I told Rinpoche I had in fact received teachings from Khandro Ten'dzin Drölkar on occasions when Ngakpa Yeshé Dorje was not at home. I said I detected the situation to be as he described and felt awkward about it in terms of maintaining pure vision. Rinpoche smiled at me. *"O yah…"* he put his hand gently on my shoulder and said *"Yag po dug."*

We walked in silence for some 20 paces before Rinpoche continued *"You are pure vision having and clear seeing. You will Khandro Ten'dzin Drölkar many many years knowing. "Maybe she one time Nepal living – and your students also meeting. She friend with Sam'phel Déchen* [31] *– and always visiting."* PAUSE *"always much laughing."* Rinpoche chuckled – obviously recalling their laughter. *"Long time good relationship having. Long-time good relationship you also having."*

Rinpoche told me when I established a sangha in the West that all students should be equal – and I should show this by being equal with my sangyum. My students should see my sangyum as being no different from me in terms of devotion. This was a strange concept. Not that I wouldn't want my wife to be regarded as equal. That is exactly what I would want – but the thought of anyone having devotion for *me*, was bizarre. Some sort of modern-day Blues version of devotion toward me might have been plausible, had Ron and Steve not died – and had Savage Cabbage become the next 'super-group'. As it was, I didn't register on the fascination or admiration scale. I felt all I could ever be was someone who provided information.

Düd'jom Rinpoche did not have to provide information to be a Lama and nor did Künzang Dorje Rinpoche. They could merely be there and this would be more than sufficient. I tried to explain these ideas to Künzang Dorje Rinpoche – but he just shook his head and explained it was purposeless to have ideas about what people in the future would either feel or not feel. It was no concern of mine what people might feel. What was important was the lineage of Guru Rinpoche and Yeshé Tsogyel. It was this which flowed through every Nyingma Lama – and there was no value in thinking I was any different. If I had authentic devotion to Guru Rinpoche and Yeshé Tsogyel, then this would be the cause of devotion for me – and for my sangyum.

"Yah… simple – natural. No need complicated making. No need conceptualising. No need 'high' or 'low' thinking. No need 'value' or 'no value' having. No need everything before planning. No need 'later time' understanding." Rinpoche told me I should not waste my time trying to build a scale-model of the future, in the present. Such a scale-model could only appear to make sense in the present. In the future it would probably make no sense at all. It would be like painting a picture of myself as an old man.

---

31 Jomo Sam'phel Déchen (*jo mo bSam 'phel bDe chen* / ཇོ་མོ་བསམ་འཕེལ་བདེ་ཆེན་) – the sangyum of Kyabjé Künzang Dorje Rinpoche.

In order to do this – all I could do would be to look at old men and try to recreate their wrinkles and lines on my face. And who would I choose? A fat man? A thin man? A hirsute man or a bald man? A man who had become blind or a man who still had good vision? A well-dressed man or a badly-dressed man?

All I could do, Rinpoche stressed, was to deal with what could be experienced exactly where I was, at any moment. If he made predictions for my future – there would be no purpose in thinking it might be difficult. Even if there were difficulties – they were simply what I would have to overcome. As a follower of Guru Rinpoche and Yeshé Tsogyel it was my duty to overcome everything. I simply had to face everything. Then, when it came time to die, it would also be simple. Rinpoche said I had the courage for it – and nothing more was required.

Rinpoche made life sound extremely simple and straightforward. I could see that it certainly could be exactly as he explained it. It always was when I was with him. My life made perfect sense when I was with him – and it seemed there was nothing I could not achieve. I simply had to stay with *how it felt* – and not drift into futile doubts.

Then Rinpoche turned everything upside-down and asked me what sort of sangha I could imagine – if I were to build a model of it in the present.

"Well Rinpoche – ideally I'd want everyone to live locally. I'd like to avoid travel if at all possible. I would not want to be on a circuit, travelling to other countries and having students living far away."

Rinpoche grinned at that *"More idea coming?"*

"Yes. I'd like a multi-racial sangha as much as possible – and Bristol is a fairly multi-racial city, so it could happen."

"Old or young?"

"Young."

Rinpoche laughed at this point *"Yah… maybe all 'this way' coming – maybe all 'different way' coming. I travelling thinking—much travelling—and different countries travelling. Maybe old peoples Chögyam students becoming. Maybe different race Chögyam students becoming? Yah… maybe – but one Tibetan maybe Chögyam's student becoming. Maybe more."* PAUSE *"Now what thinking?"*

"I'm thinking I should sing you a song, Rinpoche."

Rinpoche nodded assent and so I launched forth.

"When I was just a little girl, I asked my mother, what will I be. / Will I be pretty? will I be rich? Here's what she said to me. / Que sera, sera – Whatever will be, will be. / The future's not ours to see. / Que sera, sera – What will be, will be. [32]*"*

Rinpoche laughed when it was translated *"This not Blues I am thinking."*

"No Rinpoche – far from it."

"And you are this song liking?"

"No, Rinpoche. I don't like it at all."

"But remembering. Why remembering?"

"Because I write poetry and sing – so the words of songs and their melodies remain in my memory. Then… there's always an occasion where quoting them can be useful. I don't think this song was useful to quote, just funny."

"Why funny?"

"Because it's the kind of song no one would ever imagine me singing – especially to you."

"O yah – kün-né gôd-pa [33]*. Yah – funny. Bad song. 'thom yor song – but not 'thom yor singing."*

Rinpoche at one time thought I was utterly humourless. Then he had questioned me about it and I'd explained that most of my humour was semantically based. I made word plays and puns – and I was often ironic. Whenever Kyabjé Künzang Dorje Rinpoche noticed a certain look in my eye – he would ask *"What kün-né gôd-pa now thinking?"*

Then he continued with his previous vector *"What coming, not fixed. Always possibility changing. Even prediction not certain unless very strong determination having. You must like Ling Gésar becoming. Then all battles winning —all accomplishments having—but first teaching and sangyum finding."* PAUSE *"Tomorrow we must be three inner tantras speaking."*

---

32 Que sera sera—Jay Livingston / Ray Evans—1955.
33 *kun nas dGod pa* / ཀུན་ནས་དགོད་པ་ – irony.

7

Zorro

Clouds had been moving rapidly through the sky – occluding the sun almost stroboscopically. I would not have noticed this in particular – apart from the fact that it made Künzang Dorje Rinpoche flicker—occasionally—almost like an ancient cinema film. I was reminded of Zorro[1] because Künzang Dorje Rinpoche was very much like that old black and white movie hero. Sometimes he could have looked Spanish – and would not have looked out-of-place in some exciting scene where he vanquished three other swordsmen.

Künzang Dorje Rinpoche gave me a broad smile *"Today, Drukpa Künlegs telling. Then great hero seeing."* This was one of those occasions when—like Düd'jom Rinpoche—he read my mind. I decided to ask him – as I didn't really want to remain in a state of imagination about his clairvoyance.

"O yah – swordsman story you seeing, in mind. You are telling, then Künzang Dorje something more saying."

"I was thinking you were like Zorro, Rinpoche" I answered, feeling like an idiot. *"He's a dashing hero who wears a black costume with a cape and rather marvellous hat. He defends the people against tyrants. In the stories, there is a large reward for Zorro's capture. He's too skilful however, for the authorities to catch him – and he delights in humiliating the authorities. Because of this, people call him Zorro – which means 'fox' in Spanish; as the fox is known to be cunning."* PAUSE *"Should I say more Rinpoche?"*

"O yah – good story!"

"Well… Zorro is an acrobat and an expert in weapons. The weapon he employs most frequently is the sword. This is not like the Tibetan sword – it's long and extremely thin, so that it whips and is fast.

---

1   Zorro is a character created by Johnston McCulley. The stories are set during the Spanish California era (1769–1821). Zorro made his debut in the 1919 novel *The Curse of Capistrano*. After the success of the 1920 film adaptation *The Mark of Zorro* starring Douglas Fairbanks, Johnston McCulley wrote more Zorro stories – which amounted to five serialized stories and 57 short stories, the last one appearing in print posthumously in 1959.

Zorro often carves the initial 'Z' on the clothes or property of his defeated adversaries as his sign. He's an accomplished horseman with a large black horse called 'Tornado'. Zorro is secretly the son of a lord and hides his abilities as master swordsman by pretending to be a timid young man who is mainly interested in extravagant clothing."

Künzang Dorje Rinpoche thanked me for my explanation and concluded that he was fairly good with a sword but he wasn't particularly interested in finery when it came to clothes. *"Clothes always clean having and carefully wearing – but brocade not needing. Maybe for empowerment brocade necessary. Chögyam brocade needing when empowerment giving. This important for yidam showing. This also important for understanding. Some people thinking 'no brocade – no Lama' meaning. So, you must one day all things wearing."*

He told me that he was not telling me this story in order to question me – but simply because he had remembered it on waking. I had no need to be questioned any more with regard to these stories.

This is how it was. Drukpa Künlegs was on his way back from A'dzom's chang house, where he'd sat enjoying the warm sun in the cool of the mountain air – and breathing the fragrances of the alpine herbs and flowers. On leaving for an evening elsewhere, he met some fine-looking young ladies who gazed at him admiringly. *"Yesterday"* they said *"you killed and ate sheep – and returned them to life! Because of this we have great devotion. You must have been a very great Lama in your last life – will you tell us about it?"*

"Yah, yah, yah – sure. That is no terrible problem – I have plenty of time. During my many lives, I have taken the form of every creature. I remember it only dimly – but it seems as if it went something like this." Then he sang:

> *"Since I thrive now on chang, I must once have been a bee;*
> *Since I am now so libidinous, I must once have been a cockerel;*
> *Since I am now wrathful, I must once have been a snake;*
> *Since I am now so languid, I must once have been a pig;*
> *Since I am now so parsimonious, I must once have been affluent;*
> *Since I am now so unabashed, I must once have been a maniac;*
> *Since I am now such a prevaricator, I must once have been a thespian;*
> *Since my demeanour is now so uncouth, I must once have been an ape;*
> *Since I am now so ravenous, I must once have been a wolf;*
> *Since I have now such a tight anal sphincter, I must once have been a nun;*

> *Since I am now so punctilious, I must once have been a barren woman;*
> *Since I spend now my wealth on prandial pleasures, I must once have been a monk;*
> *Since I am now so avaricious, I must once have been a custodian;*
> *Since I am now so self-enamoured, I must once have been an officer;*
> *Since I now enjoy cheating, I must once have been a businessman;*
> *Since I now am so loquacious, I must once have been a flirtatious girl.*

"I can't really tell you if any of this is true. You'll need to weigh it up and come to your own decision."

The young ladies conferred – and, smiling, one of them answered *"We think that you were pretending to tell us about your past lives – but we think you were really simply illustrating our imperfections; so, we thank you for this teaching."*

"Yah, yah, yah…" Drukpa Künlegs laughed *"So it may be… but we shall meet again later – and then I shall demonstrate other possibilities."*

Drukpa Künlegs then set out for dPal'khor Chörten College where he found the philosophical intellectuals debating. As he observed them with mild distaste, he noticed a ravishing beauty sitting near the Chörten. But one of the monks disturbed his gaze by calling out indignantly *"Drukpa Künlegs! Your magical powers are astonishing – but you have omitted prostrations to the Chörten. This is incorrect behaviour and a bad example to others."*

"Yah, yah, yah…" Drukpa Künlegs yawned *"I know about prostrations and am not remiss in having performed as many as are required and more. If you need a demonstration however, I will gladly perform prostrations – so you can learn how to perform them correctly."*

Drukpa Künlegs then began prostrating to the beautiful girl by the Chörten – singing:

> *"I bow to this beautiful body*
> *– who is not counted amongst the Eight Chörtens;*
> *I bow to this marvellous Art work*
> *– which has not been fashioned by master craftsmen;*
> *I bow to the cheeks of the girl from Gyan-tsé*
> *– even though she is not recognised as Drölma."*

The scholastic monks were horrified *"Kyé-ma – how vulgar! Drukpa Künlegs – you are a licentious libidinous profligate!"*

"Yah, yah, yah…" yawned Drukpa Künlegs *"and so you say – but since ladies are the way in which everything enters the phenomenal world, they have the nature of Mother Wisdom. When you jokers took monastic ordination at the feet of your Lama—offering him gold without concern for the future—did it not occur to you that he entered the world from the kyil'khor between a lady's thighs? So much is obvious to any of these villagers listening to our discussion. This is why I make no puritanical distinction between this lovely lady and the Chörten as a focus of refuge."*

The villagers laughed—understanding the reality of Drukpa Künlegs' statement—but the monastics glowered at him *"You base and boorish bumpkin! We're trying to maintain the superior rules of moral discipline – and all you can do is attempt to demean us with your ignorant vulgarity."*

Then they made to raise sticks to beat him – but Drukpa Künlegs sang:

> *"The resplendent U-Tsang gelding, peerless in light-footed speed. The Black Golok stallion, who lifts his hooves so high. They race each other across the plains – but any youngster at the stable knows who will be first to pass the string of coloured rLung rTa flags.*
>
> *The Bengali peacock, with its unparalleled display of feathers. The wide-winged Tibetan vulture circling at the height of the sky. The peak of the mountain knows which bird has the panoramic view.*
>
> *The blue cuckoo matchless in song. The red breasted rooster with his deafening ko-ké kok-ko-o. Both are aroused by season and both expand their lungs – but everyone knows which can tell the time.*
>
> *Palden Chörten monastic professors, matchless in learning. Drukpa Künlegs of Ralung, relaxing in the natural stream of circumstances. On examining our individual morality, the nature of reality² will bear witness to who attains nonduality."*

---

2   Nature of reality – dé-kho na-nyid *(de kho na nyid* / དེ་ཁོ་ན་ཉིད *)*.

Finishing his song, his listeners were overcome with faith and devotion, and begged the Lama to protect them in this life and the next.

At Tséchen Gompa the monks were conducting a confession ceremony. Drukpa Künlegs offered a pinch of tea in a tingshar cymbal. *"Tea for everyone!"* he announced with great magnanimity.

"Fool!" they jeered *"That's barely enough for three – let alone* 300 *monks. Take your foolishness elsewhere!"*

Drukpa Künlegs decided to wake them up by playfully scampering around the mountainside, leaping over huge boulders – but carefully avoiding smaller rocks.

"Just look at the 'thom yor!" jeered the monks. *"What sort of idiocy will he show us next!?"*

Drukpa Künlegs laughed *"I thought you'd like to see this – because it's so similar to your practice."*

"Sacrilegious 'thom yor – your antics bear no resemblance to our profound practices!" the monks shouted.

One of the younger monks however had thrown Drukpa Künlegs' tea into the communal kettle—not being inhibited by ideas that the tea would be merely hot water—and commenced to pour tea for the assembly. The monks were dumbfounded. They had nothing further to say – but remained with their bigotry nonetheless.

In Jayül, Drukpa Künlegs stayed in the house of the Governor. He enjoyed his generous hospitality in the company of several monastic scholars who wished to enter into discussion with him.

"So… you don't wear the robes of a Lama, monk, or naljorpa?" the senior scholars commented with derisory incredulity. *"You just wear whatsoever you please and set a poor example. You should dress properly and find yourself a gompa in which to practise, rather than roaming like a mangy cur and giving authentic practitioners a bad name. Why do you behave like this?"*

Drukpa Künlegs shrugged *"If I was a Lama, I'd be the servant of attendants and disciples – and lose freedom of action.*

"If I was a monk, I'd have to maintain the 'dul-trim ³. My discipline, in contradistinction, is natural – and spontaneously manifests in all my actions. If I was a naljorpa I'd have to discover the nature of Mind – as if it wasn't self-evident. Whether or not I'm a poor example depends entirely on the sagacity of whomsoever witnesses my existence. Y'know, if I was destined for hell, then imitating a Buddha wouldn't save me. If I'm destined for Buddhahood, my clothes would be irrelevant. If I'm destined for Buddhahood, my activity, whatever it is, would be spontaneously natural. Settling in a gompa and being preoccupied by acquisitive ambitions, would deflect me from reality. Reality is wherever it is – so I've no need to attempt to find it in the last place I'd expect to find it. In any case monastics are venerated. Their propensity for concretising identity is far greater than for those living elsewhere – such as the average villager, or someone like me. You see, although the motivation for founding a gompa is to establish a place for meditation – these places are more-often-than-not hives of gossip, contention, and rivalry."

The scholars were all equally impressed by this speech, and thanked Drukpa Künlegs for his assiduity.

Drukpa Künlegs took to the road again and found a company of Bhutanese revellers. They were drinking chang and singing whilst nearby a protector ritual was taking place. A worthy local Lama was present and enjoying the lively good-natured atmosphere. Drukpa Künlegs joined them and they offered him chang. After a while the company asked whether he would care to sing them a merry song – so he said he'd be happy to oblige them:

> *"Providentially I'm not a quotidian ritualist accumulating wealth and power through attracting an ever-increasing number of students – and leaving no time to experience the richness of phenomena.*
>
> *Providentially, I'm not a monastic scholar immersed in texts of which I understand little because half my attention is absorbed with the desire for the buttocks of young monks.*
>
> *Providentially I don't stay in a hermitage delighted by the smiles of sycophants who come to make their offerings – leaving me no time to practise.*

---

3   'dul khrims / འདུལ་ཁྲིམས་ / vinaya – the monastic vows of discipline.

> *Providentially I'm not a sorcerer obsessed with manipulation, power, and the capacity for vengeance – or I'd be robbed of any hope of considering kindness.*
>
> *Providentially I am not a shaman or I'd become the slave of spirits and demons – with no time to sever the root of duality.*
>
> *Providentially I'm not a petty prince struggling to obtain taxes from hungry families – and lacking time to roam, as I do, in congenial environs."*

The company enjoyed his song and served more chang. When the evening's merriment was concluded a lady by the name of Yeshé Tsomo[4] offered him a place in her bed. He gave her transmission and stayed some days with Yeshé Tsomo providing her with practice instruction and then left for Lhodrak[5]. There he met with Tak Répa[6] who said *"I'd like to sing a song of appreciation for your qualities – but I lack the skill of composition. Would you be so kind as to sing such a song describing yourself, so that I can sing it and remember you?"*

"I have no qualities of which I could sing" Drukpa Künlegs replied *"however, I'll do what I can."*

> *Dancing with the indestructible stream of magical appearances,*
> *I unify a plethora of discrepancies and incongruities.*
> *Holding the power to spin the 'khorlo of form and emptiness,*
> *I am heroic in the face of dualistic deception.*
> *Being recalcitrant in repugnance with mundane societal obsessions, I*
> *I is simplicity itself to short-change duality.*
> *Travelling light I make any place a lodging.*
> *Perceiving mind as indistinguishable from my Lama,*
> *I am a prosperous vagrant.*
> *Understanding all appearances as nondual play,*
> *I see unity and multiplicity as indivisible.*
> *As I'm familiar with many manifestations of relativity,*
> *I savour the one taste of emptiness and form."*

---

4 *ye shes tsho mo* / ཡེ་ཤེས་ཚོ་མོ་ – Lady of the primordial wisdom lake.
5 *lho brak gru shul* / ལྷོ་བྲག་གྲུ་ཤུལ་
6 *sTag ras pa* / སྟག་རས་པ་

Drukpa Künlegs then visited the place where Marpa lived. He saw the tower which Milarépa built. He crossed the mountains from Karchu to Bumthang in Bhutan, where Guru Rinpoche had left his imprint in a rock upon which he had meditated. In Bhutan he beheld the many attractive Bhutanese ladies – who likewise beheld him and called out rapturously *"Drukpa Künlegs you have arrived! Please let us bring you chang to drink – and then please make love to us all."*

Künzang Dorje Rinpoche laughed at this point *"Now Chögyam, bag quickly packing – and Bhutan going?"*

"I don't think so, Rinpoche" I laughed. *"I'd like to go to Bhutan one day – but, apart from not being Drukpa Künlegs, I don't think I'd have the stamina or inclination to help the ladies of Bhutan in that particular way."*

Künzang Dorje Rinpoche nodded *"O yah. Drukpa Künlegs imitating – only 'thom yors are doing. There are Lamas this idea having, that they like Drukpa Künlegs. They too much deluded. They only 'thom yors. This—you—are never doing. This I am seeing – you are not this idea having. In the future you will Lamas like this seeing – and you must separate keeping. Never time wasting with 'thom yor Lamas, who Drukpa Künlegs imitating."*

He continued to say that Düd'jom Rinpoche had all the capacities and miracle powers of Drukpa Künlegs – but he did not manifest Drukpa Künlegs' style. He told me that Düd'jom Rinpoche had also tied a knot in a sword – but he lived a life which drew no attention other than the highest praise. He said that Drukpa Künlegs manifested as he did because it was necessary at the time. *"This time – myön héruka-manifesting not necessary. Myon héruka activity with many girls in West not possible manifesting."* PAUSE *"Anyway, I am this story more telling"* PAUSE *"So... Drukpa Künlegs too happy becoming."*

Whilst Drukpa Künlegs was singing and drinking with the ladies however, a local prince—enraged by Drukpa Künlegs' bawdy behaviour—shot poisoned arrows at him. None of the arrows were able to strike Drukpa Künlegs and the prince then recognised Drukpa Künlegs as a mahasiddha and became profoundly respectful to him.

So Drukpa Künlegs said, *"Yah, yah, yah – I didn't come here to ravish Bhutanese girls because I'm a frustrated seducer. I came here to display expansive benevolence and offer opportunities for liberation. I didn't come here seeking superlative sustenance, fine apparel, and commodious lodgings. As you see I decline everything."*

Then they all requested *"Please give us a teaching with a profound inner meaning – but in the language of villagers so that we can all understand it."*

Künzang Dorje Rinpoche paused for a moment, saying *"This all Drukpa Künlegs story from memory saying—so maybe all is not complete—but this without text, Künzang Dorje remembering."*

I obviously had a certain look in my eye because Rinpoche said *"Chögyam also much remembering. O yah – no problem."* PAUSE *"What last saying?"*

"Then they all requested 'Please give us a teaching with a profound inner meaning – but in the language of villagers so that we can all understand it.' That's what I recall – but it was simple because it's only 30 seconds in the past."

Rinpoche chuckled and said that for some people 30 seconds was like 30 years – and for others 30 years was like 30 seconds. *"Chögyam good memory for Vajrayana having – and good memory Künzang Dorje words also having."* PAUSE *"Anyway – Drukpa Künlegs next singing:"*

> *"Girls find pleasure in desire.*
> *Lads find it in consummation.*
> *The elderly find it in fertile memory.*
>
> *The bed is the place for consummation – it should be wide and comfortable.*
> *The knee is the envoy of consummation – it should be raised in advance.*
> *The arms are the belt of arousal – they should clasp tightly.*
> *Genitalia are libidinous gluttons – they should be satiated frequently.*
>
> *Making love to married people is proscribed.*
> *Making love to children is proscribed.*
> *Making love to celibates is proscribed.*
>
> *Hunger defines an empty stomach.*
> *Desire for a larger penis defines a 'thom yor.*
> *Fervent appreciation defines the gos dKar lCang lo'i sDe.*
>
> *Impotent men have little imagination.*
> *Philosophers have little awareness.*
> *The wealthy have little generosity.*

Religious dignitaries take joy in bountiful bequests.
Politicians take joy in blandishment.
Perfunctory monks take joy in young boys.

Spiritual poseurs hate anyone who is sincere.
Misers hate anyone who is generous.
The puritanical hate anyone who finds pleasure.

For realisation – realise devotion for the Lama.
For power – visualise the yidam.
For efficacy – invoke the protectors.

Pay no respect to parsimonious Lamas.
Pay no respect to lethargic monastics.
Pay no respect to venal scavengers, servile scroungers, or gluttonous idlers.

Starving beggars are rarely happy.
The profane rarely have dignity.
Indiscriminate laissez-faire itinerants rarely have connections or keep vows.

Those without honesty have bad breath.
Those without religious experience make no offerings.
Those without courage make bad generals.

Aristocrats are defined by tight parsimonious prudence.
The elderly are defined by tight mindedness.
Nuns are defined by tight vaginas.

The loquacious inveigle themselves into the centre of the company.
Monastic wealth inveigles itself into the stomachs of pursers.
The thick penises of sodomitic monks inveigle themselves into novices.

Dissipated onanitic[7] monks have thin skirts.
Abandoned widows have thin stomachs.
Overused fields bear thin crops.

---

7 Onanism – inveterate masturbation. From Onan in the Book of Genesis. Onan was the son of Judah.

Drukpa Künlegs never tires of girls.
Ecclesiastic pontiffs never tire of wealth.
Status-monks never tire of young boys:

Although a lamp burns brightly – it still requires oil.
Although mind may be clear – one still requires a Lama.
Although the nature of Mind is self-evident – it still requires direct recognition."

"*O yah.*" Künzang Dorje Rinpoche paused here in his enumeration. He moved his head slightly from side to side as if he were considering whether or not to ask me what I thought. I had some observations so I thought it best to make them – as I was now more-or-less a person who could say something relatively sensible.

"This list is most intriguing Rinpoche. Drukpa Künlegs seems to interleaf the profound, the profane, and the prosaic. It seems that he uses the profane and prosaic to amuse his audience whilst showing people the pattern of duality – and preparing them for his profound statements. When he describes the three things that are hated which begins 'Spiritual poseurs hate anyone who is sincere;' those three seem to parallel the three in the next line – with the Lama for realisation, the yidam, for power, and the protectors for effectuation."

Rinpoche chuckled *"O yah. Many meanings here. You more like this seeing?"*

"Yes – Drukpa Künlegs never tiring of girls, pontiffs of wealth, and fraudulent monastics of novices. That leads on to the lamp requiring oil; Mind being clear – but requiring a Lama; and the nature of Mind is self-evident requiring direct recognition."

Rinpoche nodded *"Yah—good—and so, this is how Drukpa Künlegs makes people remember. When laughing, then remembering. When sex, they remembering. When everyday life, they remembering. When Chögyam laughing – then remembering. So, when Chögyam teaching – always laughter making. Never Vajrayana without laughter."*

I took that to heart. If ever I was to teach, I would remember Rinpoche's injunction. I would make people laugh. *"Well Rinpoche, I am actually quite good at making people laugh."*

Rinpoche eyed me shrewdly but smiled as he spoke *"Why saying?"*

I took Rinpoche to be asking how I made people laugh *"Well, most simply, I make jokes. I have a good memory for jokes. In fact, I never forget any joke I hear – and I can usually retell jokes in ways which make them funnier."*

"How funnier?"

"Well… I make the jokes longer and I act a little – so a joke becomes like a performance. I use my voice in different ways and use facial expressions."

"More also saying?"

"Yes Rinpoche. It's not only joke telling – but word play. I play with words – with words which sound similar and with irony."

"O yah, kun-né gödpa – this Chögyam well doing."

"Well Rinpoche, I've been a comic most of my life – from when I was young at school. I think it may have been to compensate for my stammer. I had a bad stammer – and no one liked having to listen to me too long. So, I probably used humour as a way to make it worth their while. I also found that I stammered much less when I was performing."

"Yah—good—then all well coming. Students much laughing necessary." PAUSE *"So, Drukpa Künlegs saying… what must not without being – not losing:"*

> *"Lamas without disciples, students without persistence,*
> *Scholars without audience, romantics without lovers,*
> *Lords without servants, aristocrats without food,*
> *Farmers without crops, nomads without yak and dri,*
> *Monastics without discipline, meditators without instruction."*

Rinpoche smiled at this point *"Ngakpa chang mindug?"* he said to me in simplified Tibetan. Then he called and the lady of the house appeared rather swiftly with a tray on which stood a jug full of chang and two glasses. *"Then Drukpa Künlegs what not having, saying:"*

> *"Lamas obsessed with sex, monastics obsessed with sodomy,*
> *Women incapable of orgasms, men unable to have erections,*
> *Fame sought with the anus, wealth sought with the vagina,*
> *How preposterous these people appear – and what scorn they provoke.*

Although the clitoris is triangular,
It will not serve as a basis of a wrathful offering to the Sa bDag [8].
Although sexual moisture never dries up in the sun,
It is unsuited for quenching thirst.
Although a scrotum can hang low,
It's unsuitable as a satchel for carrying food to a retreat cave.
Although a penis has a head which is larger than its shaft,
It cannot be used to hammer a nail.
Alhough a human body may be voluptuous,
It will not provide a mistress for Shin-jé. [9]
Although mind may be worthy and unalloyed,
Teachings are not accomplished by living the average existence.

The teaching of Vajrayana is profound
– but liberation cannot be gained without direct experience.
Drukpa Künlegs may show the method
– but you must practise it yourself."

After Drukpa Künlegs had completed his teaching, the villagers alternately laughed and cried – and still crying and laughing they departed filled with devotion. Through his own exuberance and munificence his reputation spread throughout Bhutan – and thereafter everyone respected him.

"This I am telling – because you one day Bhutan going. Then must be Drukpa Künlegs knowing. In Bhutan both laughter and devotion together when Drukpa Künlegs stories hearing." Rinpoche laughed *"Many shop Drukpa Künlegs wooden dorje* [10] *buying."* He stretched his arms. *"Some very large dorje – bigger than Chögyam dorje!"*

This doubled me up with laughter *"For that I am grateful, Rinpoche. With a dorje that size I'd have to become a monk."*

This in turn made Rinpoche laugh *"O yah – Chögyam much laughter making in western countries."*

8   sa bDag / སབདག – Lord of the Earth. A local protective being.
9   gShin rJe / གཤིནརྗེ – Lord of Death.
10 rDo rJe / རྡོརྗེ – in this sense refers to a penis.

The smell of frying had been intensifying and suddenly the lady of the house entered with an impressive heaped bowl of golden brown mo-mos. I'd somehow become either famous or notorious as a human vacuum cleaner where mo-mos were concerned – and Künzang Dorje Rinpoche seemed to share my delight in them. We both preferred them fried rather than steamed. Rinpoche observed this with undisguised pleasure and laughed a great warm wholehearted laugh of enjoyment.

8

a British army rifle

Künzang Dorje Rinpoche was wearing a sheepskin chuba. I'd never seen him wear such a garment before. It was rather chilly however – so I assumed that he was feeling the cold. I should, of course, have assumed nothing at all.

"Today sheepskin chuba wearing." Rinpoche smiled – but it was a wolfish smile. *"Reason coming?"* He laughed *"Maybe, Künzang Dorje 'coldness suffering' – Chögyam thinking?"*

"That possibility had occurred to me, Rinpoche – but not in any decisive way."

"O yah. This answer, natural."

Rinpoche then asked me the word for the buildings in the West which were used for the performance of stories – in which the characters in the story spoke. The story therefore was told through speaking. I told him that it was called a theatre[1] and that those who spoke were called actors[2]. *"Most people speak of actors and actresses. I call them all actors, as I see no reason to make the distinction. Men and women both act and so they're actors."*

Rinpoche nodded and jostled his shoulders as if to say that he had no disagreement with that idea.

"Yah… so, Künzang Dorje actor – and DoKhyentsé Yeshé Dorje[3] becoming. You maybe disciple Nyoshül[4] becoming. Then room, theatre becoming."

---

1   Theatre – tadmo'i sa (*lTad mo'i sa* / ལྟད་མོའི་ས། / *rangashala*).
2   Actor – trab-tönpa (*'khrab sTon pa* / འཁྲབ་སྟོན་པ*) or khar'drab khan (*khar 'grab mKhan* / ཁར་འགྲབ་མཁན).
3   *mDo mKhyen brTse ye shes rDo rJe* / མདོ་མཁྱེན་བརྩེ་ཡེ་ཤེས་རྡོ་རྗེ / 1799–1866 – was the mind incarnation of Jig'mèd Lingpa. He was also the son of the protector Nyènchen Thanglha (*gNyan chen thang lha* / གཉན་ཆེན་ཐང་ལྷ) of the mountain range of Golok. His main teacher was the First DoDrüpchen, Jig'mèd Thrin-lé 'ö-Zér (*jigs 'med phrin las 'od zer* / འཇིགས་མེད་ཕྲིན་ལས་འོད་ཟེར / 1745–1821). His life featured miraculous events – and in later life he lived as a hunter, like some of the mahasiddhas of ancient India.
4   Nyoshül Lungtog Tenpa'i Nyima (*sNyo shul lung rTogs bsTan pa'i nyi ma* / སྙོ་ཤུལ་ལུང་རྟོགས་བསྟན་པའི་ཉི་མ / 1829–1901).

Rinpoche had told me several stories involving Dza Paltrül[5] and Nyoshül – and it had occurred to me that the manner in which he portrayed Nyoshül in these accounts, bore certain similarities to his Inji disciple, in terms of 'thom yor leanings. I put this proposition to Rinpoche.

He laughed *"O yah, many things possible – but not all."* PAUSE *"Nyoshül great devotion having. Chögyam also great devotion having. Nyoshül many time no seeing – not understanding. Chögyam not like this problem having. When first coming, then other problem having. Chögyam not natural. Not false – but much much formal; much correct; much reserved; too much stiff. Always 'accepted answer' giving like from book reading."*

"And now, Rinpoche?"

"O yah! Now" he laughed heartily. *"Now Chögyam, wild man![6] Chögyam, yanpa tang[7] like ar-jag göd![8] Now all saying like mu-göd[9]!"* Rinpoche was evidently highly amused by describing me as having become feral. He then talked a little with the translator and came up with the word sem tral'mèd pa[10]

"Now, natural. Now, we unceremonious easily talking." PAUSE *"Now, Künzang Dorje something Nyoshül telling."*

Nyoshül Lungtog Tenpa'i Nyima received Dzogchen teachings and transmissions from Dza Paltrül and was his greatest disciple. Nyoshül was regarded as an emanation of Zhi-wa Tso[11] and Chenrézigs[12]. He was born into the Nyoshül family of the Mukpo Dong[13] clan in Der-gé. From an early age he demonstrated signs of accomplishment.

---

5 *rDza dPal sPrul* / རྫ་དཔལ་སྤྲུལ་ / 1808–1887.
6 Wild – shèd ngèn (*shed ngan* / ཤེད་ངན་).
7 *yan pa bTang* / ཡན་པ་བཏང་ – running wild.
8 *ar jag rGod* / ཨར་རྒོད་ – bandit.
9 *dMu rGod* / དམུ་རྒོད་ – unruly, savage, untamed, wild, incorrigible, barbaric.
10 *sems khral 'med pa* / སེམས་ཁྲལ་འམེད་པ་ – unceremonious, at ease.
11 *zhi ba tsho* / ཞི་བ་འཚོ་ / *Shantarakshita* / 725–788 – Ocean of Peace. He was an important philosopher who specialised in Madhyamaka. He had studied at Nalanda University under Yeshé Nyingpo (*ye shes sNying po* / ཡེ་ཤེས་སྙིང་པོ་ / *Jnanagarbha*) and became the founder of Sam-yé (*bSam yas* / བསམ་ཡས་) the first Buddhist institution in Tibet. Zhi-wa Tso propounded a philosophy which combined Madhyamaka and Yogacara.
12 *sPyan ras gZigs* / སྤྱན་རས་གཟིགས་ / *Avalokiteshvara* – All Seeing.
13 *sMug po gDong* / སྨུག་པོ་གདོང་

He studied at Dzogchen Gompa with Gyalsé Shen'phen Tha-yé[14] from whom he received the name Lungtog Tenpa'i Nyima. Dza Paltrül was his Lama for 28 years – during which time Nyoshül acted as his attendant and thus heard every teaching Dza Paltrül gave – receiving some teachings almost a hundred times.

"Why teachings needing so often hearing?" Rinpoche asked.

Fortunately, I had a fairly immediate answer *"Because the teaching is not merely information. If the person teaching has realisation of what is being taught – then what is taught can be received as transmission."*

"So why transmission, more than once needing?"

Here again the answer seemed obvious to me *"Because until one realises the teaching oneself – transmission remains valuable."* Then I took a risk *"I would say, in addition, that even when one has realised the teaching, hearing it again would be a celebration of one's relationship with one's Lama."*

"This you are experiencing?" Rinpoche asked – but not in an obviously doubtful manner.

"I would have to answer both 'yes' and 'no'."

Rinpoche laughed loudly at that *"O yah – now diplomacy coming."*

"No, Rinpoche" I said, shaking my head quite emphatically. Rinpoche smiled and motioned me to continue.

"Well, Kyabjé Düd'jom Rinpoche has given me repeated teachings on the nature of Mind. Each time I feel as if I understand – but each time, the physical sense of understanding drifts away after I leave Düd'jom Rinpoche's presence. My understanding is therefore dependent on Düd'jom Rinpoche's presence. Toward the end of my time with Düd'jom Rinpoche however, the understanding seemed to last longer – and then I reached a point where the understanding—although not as intense— remained. It is not nondual realisation – but… it's like finding Bodhanath. When I am not in Bodhanath—when I'm back in Bristol—I remember how to get to Bodhanath. I don't have to read a Nepalese guidebook to find out how to get back to Bodhanath. I can remember quite clearly what it is like there – and how to get there."

---

14 *rGyal sras gZhan phan mTha' yas* / རྒྱལ་སྲས་གཞན་ཕན་མཐའ་ཡས་ / 1799–1879) – an influential Lama of Dzogchen Gompa who played an important role in revitalising the Nyingma Tradition in Kham (*khams* / ཁམས་).

Rinpoche had been looking at me as I spoke. His expression had betrayed no sense of approval or disapproval. Then suddenly his face shifted quite magically into a smile. *"O yah"* he nodded. *"This you are well saying."*

After serving his teacher and spending many years in retreat, Nyoshül was instructed by Dza Paltrül to return to the Nyoshül Valley and live in retreat. Dza Paltrül predicted that Nyoshül would meet an emanation of Dri'mèd Shé-nyèn[15] – Khenpo Ngawang Palzang[16].

"Nyoshül also with Jamyang Khyentsé Wangpo [17] *studying – and Nyingthig Yabzhi* [18] *receiving."*

Later he spent nine years at the encampment of Nyala Pema Düd'dül[19], teaching the gTértön's foremost disciples, including Nyala Rang-rig Dorje, and almost a thousand others. In his sixtieth year, in accordance with Dza Paltrül's instruction, he returned to his native region and settled in an encampment in the Pema Rito mountains of Trom. He died at the age of 72 on the seventeenth day of the fifth lunar month.

---

15 *dri 'med bShes gNyen* / དྲི་མེད་བཤེས་གཉེན་ / *Vimalamitra*.

16 *mKhan po ngag dBang dPal bZang* / མཁན་པོ་ངག་དབང་དཔལ་བཟང་ / 1879–1941 – an influential Dzogchen teacher of recent history. He predicted that he would reappear once every hundred years.

17 *'jam dByangs mKhyen brTse'i dBang po* / འཇམ་དབྱངས་མཁྱེན་བརྩེའི་དབང་པོ་ / 1820–1892, or Pema 'ö-Sel Do-ngak Lingpa (*pa dMa 'od gSal mDo sNgags gLing pa* / པདྨ་འོད་གསལ་མདོ་སྔགས་གླིང་པ་) – a major treasure revealer and last of the five Sovereign gTértöns. Contemporary of Chokgyur Lingpa (1829–1870) and Jamgön Kongtrül the Great. Combined incarnation of Dri'mèd Shényèn and Chögyal Trisong Detsèn (*khri srong lDe brTsan* / ཁྲི་སྲོང་ལྡེ་བཙན་) or Trisong De'u tsen (*khri srong lDe'u bTsan* / ཁྲི་སྲོང་ལྡེའུ་བཙན་ / 742–797) the 38th king of Tibet, he was a main disciple of Guru Rinpoche and founder of the Ri'mèd (*ris 'med* / རིས་མེད་)—without boundaries—movement.

18 *sNying thig ya bZhi* / སྙིང་ཐིག་ཡ་བཞི་ – the Four Sections of Nying-thig, which consists of: Vima Nyingthig, Lama Yangthig, Khandro Nyingthig, and Khandro Yangthig. The Vima Nyingthig and Khandro Nyingthig are also known as the 'Mother Nying-thig' and the Lama Yangthig and Khandro Yangthig are known as the 'Child Nying-thig'. The two collections are therefore called 'The Four Sections of Mother and Child – Nyingthig ma-bu zhi (*sNying thig ma bu bZhi* / སྙིང་ཐིག་མ་བུ་བཞི་).

19 *nyag bla padma bdud 'dul* / ཉག་བླ་པདྨ་བདུད་འདུལ་ / 1816–1872.

"Amongst his disciples was gTértön Sogyal – Lérab Lingpa [20]. His incarnation now in Tibet and one also in Bhutan." PAUSE *"This one in London"* shaking his head ruefully *"only name 'Sogyal' having."* PAUSE *"Anyway nothing further saying necessary."* PAUSE *"Nyoshül prophesy making – thirteen incarnations, all name Nyima having."*

The one who took up residence at his own former seat was Shédrüp Tenpa'i Nyima[21]. His teachings included a text on Dzogchen which he sent to Rang-rig Dorje Rinpoche with the instruction that it should be burnt immediately after he'd read it. Rang-rig Dorje Rinpoche burnt it as instructed – but the text survived because a copy was made by the man who delivered it and this is how it was saved for posterity.

"Yah – what you saying this 'text copying' bad act, or not bad act?"

This time I had no idea how to answer — but I began anyway. *"Well, Rinpoche, it was a bad act with a good result – or possibly a good result. It would be hard to know whether the result was good or bad without knowing why Shédrüp Tenpa'i Nyima wanted the text burnt. Maybe the burning was only an instruction for Rang-rig Dorje Rinpoche, because he needed to be able to take the teaching to heart – and not merely store it for a future time. Sometimes people want to receive teachings but regard them as possessions rather than methods by which they develop. So... as I can't see why a Dzogchen text would prove dangerous to others – I can see no reason why it should never exist to help others... unless there is something here that I do not understand – in which case I would ask if you would kindly tell me."*

"O yah – good answer coming. Nothing more needing." PAUSE *"So now – Paltrül and Nyoshül, DoKhyentsé are one time meeting. I am this story telling."*

Dza Paltrül was in mountain retreat with his disciples and saw that Nyoshül looked somewhat enervated. Dza Paltrül called out *"Nyoshül – this is no way to be. You should be possessed of a livelier mien."*

Nyoshül was startled on hearing his Lama's words and apologised for his dullness and insipidity. Paltrül replied that apologies were unnecessary – but that a long walk was definitely called for.

---

20 gTértön Sogyal Lérab Lingpa (*gTer sTon bSod rGyal las rab gLing pa* / གཏེར་སྟོན་བསོད་རྒྱལ་ ལས་རབ་གླིང་པ* / 1856–1926).
21 *bShad sGrub bsTan pa'i nyi ma* / བཤད་སྒྲུབ་བསྟན་པའི་ཉི་མ / b. 1920 – an incarnation of Nyoshül Lungtog. Disciple of Khenpo Ngakchung, with whom he studied from the age of eight to 22. He was the main Lama of Nyoshül Khenpo.

At that, Paltrül had leapt to his feet and began packing up an overnight bag. Nyoshül seeing what was afoot assembled his own accoutrements and folded them into his travelling bag. No sooner was his bag packed than he found himself almost running to catch up with Dza Paltrül who was walking at a brisk pace towards the high pastures.

Paltrül looked back at Nyoshül – and, in a loud voice, exclaimed "*Sheep abound in this area.*". This obviously amused Paltrül. Nyoshül however had no idea of what might be amusing and concentrated on scrambling uphill behind his Lama.

After three hours walk without a word exchanged - a loud crack was heard. It echoed in the mountains. *"Yah!"* Paltrül shouted to Nyoshül. *"Did you hear that report?"*

"Yes…" Nyöshul had heard the sound.

"What would you say made such a sound?"

"A rock fall – maybe thunder?"

"Thunder!" yelled Paltrül. *"Yes!"* then whispering in a conspiratorial manner *"But—not—the kind that portends precipitation."* Nyoshül was perplexed – so Paltrül bellowed *"That is the sound of liberation!"*

Nyoshül was confused. Paltrül gave no elucidation and Nyoshül failed to enquire further.

Soon they distantly beheld a great flock of sheep. *"There are sheep in the distance"* observed Nyoshül.

"O yah!" Paltrül laughed. *"Now maybe you begin to understand."* But Nyoshül only understood that there was something mysterious to understand concerning *sheep* which he was unable to fathom. They continued to walk and after an hour they reached the high pastures – and were amongst the sheep, who were unusually lacking in nervousness.

"The sheep seem unusually lacking in nervousness" Nyoshül attempted – knowing that he was supposed to understand something.

"These sheep are DoKhyentsé Yeshé Dorje's flock!" Paltrül yelled with elation – and strode on exuberantly in spite of his advancing years.

Having surmounted the final ridge, they halted momentarily to catch breath. *"O yah. See Nyöshul!"* Paltrül shouted – even though he was standing next to his disciple. *"Look Nyoshül! There is the 'gar of my Tsawa'i Lama, DoKhyentsé Yeshé Dorje Rinpoche!"*

Nyöshul was startled by Dza Paltrül's shout – but composed himself having become a little more accustomed to Dza Paltrül's sudden propensity for thunderous proclamations. In the distance he could see white shapes which resembled tents. They were still some distance away – but it was clear that this was their destination.

Nyoshül had heard astonishing reports concerning DoKhyentsé Yeshé Dorje. He was a Myön Héruka – and held in the highest esteem by many Nyingma Lamas.

"O yah… you are Myön Héruka knowing?"

"I know the term and what it means, Rinpoche – but that is all."

"What meaning then – you are explaining."

"Well Myonpa means 'madman' and Héruka in Tibetan is Traktung[22] which means 'blood drinker' – as in drinking the blood of dualism and transforming it into the five wisdoms."

"Yah. Nyingma Eight Traktung having. You are naming possible?"

"Jampal Shin-jé, Dorje Jig-jèd, or Yamantaka in Sanskrit[23]. Tamdrin, or Hayagriva in Sanskrit[24]. Yangdag Héruka[25]. Chemchog Héruka, or Mahottara in Sanskrit[26].

---

22 *khrag 'thung* / ཁྲག་འཐུང་
23 Jampal Shin-jé (*'jam dPal gShin rJe* / འཇམ་དཔལ་གཤིན་རྗེ་); Dorje Jig-jèd (*rDo rJe 'jigs byed* / རྡོ་རྗེ་འཇིགས་བྱེད་ / *Yamantaka*) – wrathful Jampalyang (*'jam dPal dByangs* / འཇམ་དཔལ་དབྱངས་ / *Manjushri*) yidam of body.
24 Tamdrin (*rTa mGrin* / རྟ་མགྲིན་ / *pad ma gSung* / པད་མ་གསུང་ / *Hayagriva*) – wrathful Chenrézigs, yidam of speech.
25 Yangdag Héruka (*yang dag thugs* / ཡང་དག་ཐུགས་ / *Vishuddha* / *Sri Samyak*) – wrathful Chana Dorje, yidam of mind.
26 Chemchog Héruka (*che mChog* / ཆེ་མཆོག་ / *Mahottara*) – wrathful Küntuzangpo, yidam of nondual qualities.

Dorje Phurba, or Vajrakilaya in Sanskrit [27]. "Mamo Botong, or Matarah in Sanskrit [28]. Jig-ten Chod-töd [29]. And finally Mödpa Dra-ngak. [30] But with the last two I don't know the Sanskrit."

"Yah—good—but Sanskrit not needing, unless scholar becoming. No need scholar – already too many scholar coming." PAUSE "Yah... Dorje Phurba for Chögyam I am thinking. Also, Dorje Tröllö. You are from Kyabjé Düd'jom Rinpoche receiving?"

"Yes, Rinpoche. I received Dorje Tröllö – and also Dorje Phurba, Tröma Nakmo, and Seng-gé Dongma."

"O yah – too good, too good. What Düd'jom Rinpoche saying main practice?"

"First Tröma Nakmo – then Dorje Phurba and Dorje Tröllö."

"Then after – then Aro gTér coming."

I concurred. That is what Kyabjé Düd'jom Rinpoche had advised. We talked for some time about the gTér of Khyungchen Aro Lingma and what might lead to its re-discovery. Revealing gTérma, albeit a twice-revealed gTérma, seemed as likely as levitation – but as Düd'jom Rinpoche had told me it would happen, I had no actual doubt about it. I'd simply be some other kind of person when it occurred – and I obviously had to work toward that point with a great deal of practice. Practice would have to change me from what I felt myself to be.

I had no lack of commitment and perseverance – but I was still not so very different from the nineteen-year-old who set out for the Himalayas in 1971. I knew a great deal more and my practice had developed – but I was rather definitely a fairly ordinary person, albeit an Art student. I'd spent time with astonishing Lamas – but I was not astonishing.

27 Dorje Phurba (rDo rJe phur ba / རྡོ་རྗེ་ཕུར་བ་) / Phurba Thinlé (phur ba 'phrin las / ཕུར་བ་འཕྲིན་ལས་) / Dorje Zhonu (rDo rJe gZhon nu / རྡོ་རྗེ་གཞོན་ནུ་ / Vajrakilaya / Vajrakumara) – wrathful Dorje Sempa (rDo rJe sems dPa' / རྡོ་རྗེ་སེམས་དཔའ་ / Vajrasattva) – yidam of purification.

28 Mamo Botong (ma mo rBod gTong / མ་མོ་རྦོད་གཏོང་ / Matarah) – wrathful Namkha'i Nyingpo (nam mKha'i sNying po / ནམ་མཁའི་སྙིང་པོ་ / Akasagarbha) – yidam of summoning and dispatching.

29 'jig rTen mChod bsTod / འཇིག་རྟེན་མཆོད་བསྟོད་ / Lokastotrapujanatha – wrathful Sa-yi Nyingpo (sa yi sNying po / ས་ཡི་སྙིང་པོ་ / Ksitigarbha) – yidam of secular presentation and admiration.

30 mod pa drag sNgags / མོད་པ་དྲག་སྔགས་ / Vajramantrabhiru – wrathful Jampa (byams pa / བྱམས་པ་ / Maitreya), yidam of wrathful mantras.

Künzang Dorje Rinpoche could tell what I was thinking. He gazed at me for a moment and said *"Future time – all things possible. Not now 'critical' needing. Future time Düd'jom Rinpoche is all clearly seeing."* PAUSE *"Düd'jom Rinpoche and Guru Rinpoche not different. Guru Rinpoche gTérma systems creating. Künzang Dorje Rinpoche no doubt having. Future time – all things possible. But now we must more Myön Héruka speaking."*

Künzang Dorje Rinpoche adjusted his chuba and commenced *"Myön Héruka these features having: homeless wandering or home and family leaving; like king or queen living or like beggar living; all style of dress wearing – men or women dress not mattering; any culture style manifesting; alcohol drinking and meat eating; all kind of song singing; all kinds of dancing; many story telling; many joke making; fearless behaving; sexual activity transmission giving. Then Myön Héruka certain activities avoiding possible: spiritual texts not reading; not reciting; prostration, 'khora, and outer forms not performing. Myön Héruka sometimes like ordinary layperson living and no difference anyone seeing – sometimes madness showing and all normal behaviour backwards or contrary."*

Rinpoche hastened to provide the caveat that none of these criteria were mandatory apart from having to partake of meat and alcohol at tsog'khorlo – but then that applied to every Vajrayana practitioner either gö kar chang lo or monastic. He asked me what I would say about all these factors in one sentence.

"So Myön Héruka homeless wandering or home and family leaving." PAUSE *"Chögyam homeless wandering and home and family leaving."* PAUSE *"What saying?"*

"Well… yes – but there is still a home to which I could return."

"Yah – but not returning. Since Art School never home living."

I couldn't deny that.

"Then Myön Héruka like king or queen living or like beggar living."

I knew a comment was required *"Yes Rinpoche – I've certainly lived like a beggar. I've collected unwanted cauliflower greens from the greengrocer and cow bones from the butcher in order to make soup. As to living like a monarch, I'd have no objection to that – and when I have enough money, I feel quite wealthy."*

"Yah good. Then Myön Héruka all style of dress wearing – men or women dress not mattering; any culture style manifesting."

"Yes to that Rinpoche – without any qualification."

"Then Myön Héruka alcohol drinking and meat eating."

"Once I was vegetarian and abstemious – but not anymore." PAUSE "However I am glad that I went through that period of discipline."

"Then Myön Héruka all kind of song singing; all kinds of dancing; many story telling; many joke making."

"That describes me, Rinpoche."

"Then Myön Héruka fearless behaving."

That made me laugh "I don't think of myself as fearless Rinpoche – but neither do I think of myself as apprehensive, fretful, nervous, anxious, or fearful." PAUSE "I know I can take risks."

"O yah – much fearless behaving. Then Myön Héruka sexual activity transmission giving."

"No, Rinpoche. That's not me."

"But khandros enjoying sex with Chögyam?"

"I have had no complaints" I laughed. "But – that's not transmission."

"Why saying?"

"Well… transmission leads to realisation—I'm not being humble here—but I cannot say that this occurred. There wasn't even the intention for transmission to occur."

"Not possible 'no transmission' saying." PAUSE "Maybe 'no intention' saying possible – but transmission natural and spontaneous possible. This meaning Myön Héruka still possible." PAUSE "Then Myön Héruka certain activities avoiding possible: spiritual texts not reading; not reciting; prostration, 'khora, and outer forms not performing." PAUSE "This no need speaking – because all Chögyam doing. In Bodhanath – much 'khora. Ngöndro – much prostration." Rinpoche sat back and surveyed the room. "Myön Héruka sometimes like ordinary lay-person living and no difference anyone seeing."

"Yes Rinpoche – that holds true perhaps more than any of the others."

"Yah… Myön Héruka sometimes madness showing and all normal behaviour backwards or contrary."

"That's just the average hippie in Britain, Rinpoche – but I suppose that I can say that I often used to live contrary to hippie cultural customs. I wash and iron my Levis. I even starch them when they become old and faded." PAUSE "But… everything that identifies realisation can be adopted to give the illusion of realisation."

"O yah – but realisation seeing without conventional indications" Rinpoche concluded "This is Dzogchen understanding possible." PAUSE "Why?"

"Because conventional indications can be meaningless. They can be learnt, copied, imitated."

Rinpoche sat looking at me for a moment. "*Yagpo dug*" he intoned. 'Good' had no need of translation – and I had no doubt whatsoever about my answer. Rinpoche then asked me if I would elaborate – and so I said that Dzogchen was the natural state and that the natural state would merely be obscured by requiring anything that could be specified. A person who appeared entirely ordinary could be *finding presence of awareness* in their ordinary activities. A person who appeared abnormal could be *finding presence of awareness* in their abnormal activities. A person who appeared wild and incongruous could be *finding presence of awareness* in their wild and incongruous activities. Dzogchen was beyond defined restrictions.

"*Yagpo dug.*" PAUSE "But Chögyam is not wild behaviour manifesting. Chögyam unusual possible – but always gentle manner. Chögyam always courteous and even-temper having. No peoples ever saying Chögyam is Myön Héruka." PAUSE "But Chögyam secret Myön Héruka."

This was both a command and a prediction – and so I told Rinpoche that it would be exactly as he stated. I had no interest in acting in a crazy manner… and moreover, I didn't think it would work well in the West – unless there were special circumstances as there were around Chögyam Trungpa Rinpoche's life.

"O yah – so second Chögyam not same like first Chögyam looking?"

"No Rinpoche" I laughed. "There's a saying in English concerning the inadvisability of aping one's betters."

Künzang Dorje Rinpoche found that expression extremely funny – which was odd because I had no sense of its being funny until he started laughing. Then we both laughed as if it was the funniest statement either of us had heard for months.

Quite unexpectedly Rinpoche asked *"You one story DoKhyentsé Yeshé Dorje knowing?"*

I replied that I did and he gave me a startlingly broad grin *"Then now telling."*

"Dza Paltrül once resided at a small Nyingma gompa."

Dza Paltrül was alone in his room, when DoKhyentsé arrived. He was on horseback and rode into the courtyard of the gompa. He sprang from his horse without waiting for the courtesies of assistance and adopted a menacing stance. *"Paltrül!"* he bellowed *"No use skulking in there. If you're not too timid; present yourself – and I'll grant transmission!"* Paltrül was happy that his Tsawa'i Lama DoKhyentsé Yeshé Dorje had come to see him and delighted that he was being offered transmission. He rushed down straightaway and approached DoKhyentsé Yeshé Dorje. He had just begun to perform prostrations when DoKhyentsé interrupted the procedure by seizing his hair. He then proceeded to drag Dza Paltrül around the courtyard. As this was happening Dza Paltrül caught a hint of alcohol on DoKhyentsé Yeshé Dorje's breath.

Now Dza Paltrül was abstemious – and this predisposed him to an inappropriate thought. '*Kyé ma hu*[31] – *this is the danger of alcohol. Thus, was it proscribed by Shakyamuni Buddha. 'Even a great master such as DoKhyentsé Yeshé Dorje can be thrown by its hazardous nature'* and so his conjecture ran on. As soon as this supposition arose in Dza Paltrül's mind, DoKhyentsé Yeshé Dorje released Dza Paltrül's hair – as if he were touching something repulsive.

"You disgusting old dog!" DoKhyentsé shouted *"How do ideas of this kind enter your mind!?"* He then spat in Dza Paltrül's face and presented him with his crook'd little finger.

Rinpoche was clearly amused by my delivery *"Show me this gesture!"*

That made me somewhat squeamish – but although I was highly reluctant I did as I was asked. The gesture betokened that the person to whom one displayed it had a predilection for buggery. My evident discomfort caused Rinpoche to laugh *"O yah! Too funny. You must now show this sign to every monk you are meeting."* Then immediately he shook his head and told me that he was not serious about the suggestion. *"Story now continuing."*

---

31 *kye ma kyi hud* /ཀྱེ་མ་ཀྱི་ཧུད/ – exclamation of deep distress.

"If I remember correctly..."

Paltrül—having heard DoKhyentsé Yeshé Dorje say *'Zhenpa logpa'i khyi-gan!* [32] *How does a thought like this enter your mind!?'*— realised he'd made a serious error. He froze and remained exactly as he was when DoKhyentsé Yeshé Dorje let go of his hair. In that moment he recognised the nature of Mind.

Künzang Dorje Rinpoche nodded and asked *"This – what term using?"*

"Informal symbolic transmission" I replied.

"Yah. Informal symbolic transmission. Three kinds Dzogchen transmission coming: Direct Transmission; Symbolic Transmission; Oral Transmission."

Direct transmission is 'mind-to-mind' in which no word is spoken. Lama and disciple sometimes sit in silence. This accounted for the silences which at first seemed nerve wracking. Symbolic transmission functions through cryptic statements, delivered with the display of an object which symbolises the nature of Mind. Symbolic transmission occurs in two ways. The first is as previously described and is termed 'formal symbolic transmission'. The second is 'informal symbolic transmission'. This defined the encounter between Dza Paltrül and DoKhyentsé Yeshé Dorje. Informal symbolic transmission can assume any form. The example here is forceful – but that is not necessarily characteristic of informal symbolic transmission. A Lama could simply tell a joke, perform a few dance steps, or give a display of animal impressions. A Lama might organise an incomprehensible event or simply act out of character. A Lama could speak nonsense or recite unrelated poetry. A Lama could sing an obscure song or howl like a wild animal. The possibilities are limitless. Oral transmission is any instruction or explanation which is given in the context of Dzogchen.

"Then, what more coming?" Rinpoche asked in relation to my account of Dza Paltrül and DoKhyentsé Yeshé Dorje.

"Well, after that, whenever Dza Paltrül gave the Dzogchen men-ngag-dé pointing out instructions to his disciples – he would tell them 'When I first realised the nature of Mind – it was from the transmission of DoKhyentsé Yeshé Dorje. The secret name he gave me with that transmission was Zhenpa logpa'i khyi-gan.' That is all I know of the story."

32 *zhen pa log pa'i khyi rGan* / ཞེན་པ་ལོག་པའི་ཁྱི་རྒན་ – disgusting old dog.

"O yah. Good telling." PAUSE *"Now other story finishing. DoKhyentsé Yeshé Dorje —trülku of Jig'mèd Lingpa*[33]*—Dza Paltrül and Nyoshül are visiting. They much long walking and highlands sheep seeing."*

Fragments of a picture began to shape themselves for Nyoshül as they walked – but he couldn't tie them together. Dza Paltrül was acting in an uncharacteristic manner and speaking extremely loudly for no apparent reason. Something unusual was taking place – but what it could be, Nyoshül could not guess.

DoKhyentsé Yeshé Dorje had known about his prospective guests since dawn. He espied the pair from a distance and observed their physical mien. He knew that his disciple Dza Paltrül Rinpoche was coming with a disciple of his own. He also knew that this disciple probably needed to overcome obstacles to understanding. They'd have travelled all day. They'd be tired and hungry. So, naturally, preparations had been made: a tent had been pitched for their privacy; bedding had been assigned; and, cushions had been arranged commodiously. Viands had been prepared. Chang had been allocated and awaited their arrival in fine wooden pitchers.

The disciples of DoKhyentsé Yeshé Dorje came to greet Dza Paltrül and Nyoshül, and shepherded them to a majestic tent. DoKhyentsé Yeshé Dorje welcomed them in imposing style and gestured for them to sit down on deeply-cushioned pads covered by opulent carpets. He was dressed in a luxurious chuba made of lambskins and sat regally on leopard and tiger hides[34].

DoKhyentsé was in the final stages of cleaning, oiling, and re-assembling his rifle[35]. The sight of the rifle was a bit much for Nyoshül – he had certain ideas about that kind of thing.

33 *'jigs 'med gLing pa* / འཇིགས་མེད་གླིང་པ་ / 1729–1799 – an important Lama in Nyingma history. He received the Longchen Nyingthig cycle of teaching and practice in vision from Rabjam Longchenpa. With the patronage of the Der-gé royal family, he printed the Nyingma Gyüdbum – a compilation of Nyingma tantras and accompanying catalogue. Longchenpa (*kLong chen pa* / ཀློང་ཆེན་པ་) or Longchen Rabjam (*kLong chen rab 'byams* / ཀློང་ཆེན་རབ་འབྱམས་) was one of the most brilliant Nyingma Lamas. He systematised the Nyingma teachings in his 'Seven Treasures' and wrote extensive material on Dzogchen.
34 Leopard and tiger skins are the symbolic dress of the khandros and dPa'wos respectively, and gö kar chang lo Lamas often used them on their thrones.
35 DoKhyentsé was rarely seen without a rifle.

Nonetheless, he sat down along with Paltrül, and the three Lamas talked. They talked about the way things had been, the way things were going, and the way things might turn out—a somewhat matter of fact conversation, with no particular spiritual inclination as far as Nyoshül could ascertain—but every time DoKhyentsé addressed him, it was with some extraordinary appellation such as 'dangerous ruffian', 'savage barbarian', 'audacious scallywag', 'incongruous reprobate', 'degenerate miscreant', or 'impetuous rapscallion'.

"Nice rifle, Rinpoche" commented Paltrül.

"Yes indeed! British – not some pitiful Indian smooth-bore [36]. *This is an Enfield— Pattern 1853—with rifling* [37]. *This came from India recently. I have been waiting for it for a long time."* DoKhyentsé Yeshé Dorje smiled broadly, passing the rifle to Dza Paltrül.

"Does it shoot well?" Paltrül enquired, whilst examining it.

"With absolute accuracy" laughed DoKhyentsé. Each enunciation of DoKhyentsé was delivered with high volume – similar to the style Dza Paltrül had adopted during the trek to DoKhyentsé Yeshé Dorje's gar. DoKhyentsé continued to discuss powder, shot, and muzzle velocity for a while – but suddenly caught sight of attendants. *"Ah!"* he exclaimed *"I see the banquet has arrived! You will be glad to know—I'm sure—that the sheep were dispatched with this very rifle in honour of your visit!"*

Nyoshül had received charge of the rifle from Paltrül moments before DoKhyentsé Yeshé Dorje's pronouncement. Nyoshül was shocked by the news of the rifle's recent use. *"Butchered!"* DoKhyentsé Yeshé Dorje yelled *"Just for you! What d'you think about—that—young Nyoshül!?"*

Nyoshül was stunned.

Finding himself observed by both Lamas, he squirmed—gave a simpering smile—and passed the rifle back to its barbarous owner. *"Thank you, Rinpoche."* was all he could manage to say.

---

36 The older smooth-bore musket—prior to 1830—was the Baker.
37 The Enfield Pattern 1853 was a Minié .577 calibre muzzle-loading British Army rifle with rifling (1853–1867). Rifling: the machined helical grooves in the internal bore of a barrel which exerts torque and imparts spin to a projectile around its longitudinal axis. This stabilises bullets longitudinally, conserving angular momentum, and improving ærodynamic stability – and hence, accuracy.

Nyoshül felt extremely awkward – speculating why Dza Paltrül had brought him into the presence of this Lama who manifested as a depraved hedonist. He'd heard that DoKhyentsé was a wrathful Lama – but this surpassed his imagination.

Nyoshül knew Dza Paltrül was vegetarian[38] – and that he would exert himself to save life wherever possible. Dza Paltrül would avoid visiting any nomad camps where he knew that a yak would be killed for the specific purpose of feeding his party. He was not one of those who believed in the concept of innocence through ignorance – so the horror escalated when his Lama began to devour the lamb with blatant zeal.

Observing Nyoshül's expression, DoKhyentsé Yeshé Dorje selected an huge portion of lamb and hefted it toward Nyoshül, yelling *"Ho! Nyoshül! You crazed carnivore – get your murderous mandibles into this!"*

Nyoshül was aghast – but his devotion to Paltrül was such that he thanked his host and proceeded to nibble at the butchered meat as if it had been roasted for his individual torment. It was evident that Nyoshül was not relishing the roast lamb – and Dza Paltrül noticed his reticent hesitant manner and prompted him *"Eat—Nyoshül—eat!"* This was an abhorrent ordeal for Nyoshül. Having concluded their feast—and washed it down with chang—Dza Paltrül requested a concise essential teaching. DoKhyentsé delightedly agreed *"For many years I have intended to give you this teaching"* he winked at Nyoshül as if he were about to tell a ribald joke *"So I am extremely happy to give it to you now."*

DoKhyentsé took a long careful look at the discombobulated Nyoshül. *"And this drooling debauchee—this insatiable inebriate—can also receive this teaching. He's a nervous little chap but he has a good heart and a healthy appetite for lamb!"*

Nyoshül had no idea why he was being described as a debauchee – but felt unusually privileged nonetheless. To receive a transmission was rare, especially from such a legendary Lama.

---

38 Paltrül was inspired by Shabkar to follow a kar-zé (*dKar zas* / དཀར་ཟས་) – vegetarian diet. In the same style as Shabkar, Paltrül combined the yanas of Sutra, Kriyatantra, and Dzogchen. His lack of difficulty with eating meat as the guest of his teacher DoKhyentsé conforms with the fact that his vegetarianism was a practice rather than a philosophical stance.

So, no matter how bewildering the circumstances – he felt grateful. The direct *pointing-out instruction* he received was brilliantly eloquent yet concise. Nyoshül was amazed and utterly absorbed with the words of DoKhyentsé Yeshé Dorje, a realised Lama who rode with a rifle slung at his back. He was a Lama with nondual realisation who slaughtered sheep.

Before Dza Paltrül and Nyoshül took their leave at the conclusion of the teaching, DoKhyentsé touched foreheads with them both. He looked lovingly at Nyoshül for the first time since he arrived and wished him a comfortable night in the most gracious manner. It was quite uncharacteristic for DoKhyentsé to adopt the mode of a venerable ecclesiastic. Nyoshül was shocked a second time but in an entirely different way. He hardly felt the ground beneath his feet as he accompanied Dza Paltrül to the tent which had been set aside for them. Before entering the tent Dza Paltrül stood for a while looking at the stars.

"I've been your Lama for a long time, Nyoshül" Paltrül exclaimed taking in the endless view *"but in all that time I have never bestowed anything as marvellous as that which you've just received."*

Nyoshül was speechless – but there was nothing to say.

"I want you to know—Nyoshül—that even given my experience, if you were to die tonight; I could not guarantee to send you to the copper-coloured mountain. What a pity the two of us couldn't be sheep in this marvellous herd." Dza Paltrül chuckled *"Every sheep will find itself liberated into that dimension in the instant of its death."*

Nyoshül had tears in his eyes *"As this is the case, DoKhyentsé Yeshé Dorje is none other than Guru Rinpoche."*

"Exactly" Paltrül replied quietly and gently. *"Exactly."*

Künzang Dorje Rinpoche was gazing at me, at this point – or gazing beyond me. He seemed to be holding me in his visual field as if I was part of his visual dimension. I felt inseparable from him in that time and space. I waited for a time when it might feel right to speak – and after an intangible period his eyes seemed to focus on me.

"Exactly as it is with Kyabjé Düd'jom Rinpoche Jig'drèl Yeshé Dorje, and exactly as it is with you."

Rinpoche said nothing for some minutes. We simply sat together. It was a comfortable companiable silence and I felt no tension. I had no concept that I was being judged. There had been times when silence was judgement – but this was not such a time. There was simply nothing to say.

Rinpoche poured out two glasses of chang and we sipped in silence. After a while he said *"So, what meaning this story?"*

"Transmission" I replied. *"Transmission which broke through a barrier."*

"O yah. This very necessary." **Rinpoche smiled** *"Necessary, because Nyoshül chö trang'gyür* [39] *becoming. Not hard like a stone – but hard like milk, edge of bowl drying. This 'not milk – not cheese'. This rind of grease becoming. No possibility without strong movement."*

"Am I like that, Rinpoche?"

Rinpoche shook his head from side to side. *"No – not like this"* he laughed *"Chögyam much emotional – so not like this becoming."* PAUSE *"Not emotional like 'thom yor – but strongly feeling. This much awake making. Everything well seeing. Strength having, necessary for strong emotion. This chang chub sem* [40] *meaning. Chögyam must warrior manifesting."*

Rinpoche—still smiling—ran his finger backward and forward along the edge of his çog-tsé. Suddenly he was asking me a question. I hadn't noticed how his question had started. I wasn't daydreaming, so I couldn't work out what was being asked.

"Lug min-dug [41].*"* Rinpoche quipped, noticing my bemusement. He repeated this several times. Then our lunch arrived. Lunch was a pile of rice with a few shreds of dark green vegetable matter and somewhat smaller shreds of meat. *"Lug min-dug."* I commented. Rinpoche burst out laughing, occasionally repeating the phrase. Somehow this became hysterically funny and we both laughed till the tears were flooding down our cheeks.

---

39 *chos mKhrang 'gyur* / ཆོས་མཁྲང་འགྱུར་ – Dharma hardened.
40 *byang chub sems* / བྱང་ཆུབ་སེམས་ / *bodhicitta* – awakened heart-mind of empathetic appreciation, active compassion. Changchub Sempa (*byang chub sems dPa'* / བྱང་ཆུབ་སེམས་དཔའ་ / *bodhisattva*) – awakened heart-mind warrior.
41 *lug min du* / ལུག་མིན་དུ་ – no sheep.

It seemed somehow self-explanatory in terms of my naïve apprehension. It was a joke about the story. Nyoshül had to eat a lot of lamb as part of receiving transmission from DoKhyentsé. We were both getting very little sheep to eat. Maybe transmission was there nonetheless. *"Transmission!"* Rinpoche suddenly exclaimed in English – then Tibetan *"… preparation needing. What Chögyam thinking? How Paltrül, Nyoshül transmission preparing?"*

"Paltrül emulated DoKhyentsé Yeshé Dorje, as he and Nyoshül were walking together. He was reflecting aspects of what Nyoshül was going to witness in the personality-display of DoKhyentsé – but I don't think that this was designed so that Nyoshül would get used to it." PAUSE "It seems to have been set up so that Nyoshül would make a connection and realise that there was more happening than was obvious at face value."

"Yah – possible" Rinpoche responded in a noncommittal manner. He then sat silently waiting for me to add something further.

"Paltrül was giving clues all the time. He started saying 'sheep country' as if Nyoshül should understand what that meant. It seemed as if he was teasing Nyoshül, or trying to cause him to be intrigued in some way."

Rinpoche looked at me carefully *"Every word important. Nothing missing. Every word important – but Nyoshül no strength having. Nyoshül no question asking. Nyoshül passive – no powerful Dharma-curiosity having,"*

"Lug min-dug" I ventured.

"Transmission" Rinpoche laughed and poured two more glasses of chang. He then continued *"Nyoshül with all things staying – all circumstances. No matter what thinking. No matter what feeling – Nyoshül strong devotion having. This, transmission possible making."* Rinpoche suddenly looked me directly in the eyes *"Chögyam more saying?"*

"Nyoshül allowed Paltrül and DoKhyentsé to perpetrate mayhem in terms of his conceptual mind. He allowed the disorder to escalate to the point where transmission was inevitable."

"O yah… nothing from Chögyam hidden" Rinpoche laughed. I wondered for a fraction of a second whether he was being ironic – but immediately decided that was merely my residual perceptual patterning. If there was irony, Rinpoche's mien would make it clear and he would go on to interrogate me.

Goodbye Forever

"It occurs to me then, that there were many points of transmission during the story, and many aspects of preparation. The humorous insults that DoKhyentsé threw at Nyoshül, were all variations of ideas in Nyoshül's mind. They were deluded descriptions of DoKhyentsé Yeshé Dorje – of which he was deeply ashamed. He probably tried to force such thoughts out of his mind – but DoKhyentsé Yeshé Dorje kept reminding him, by providing new and more outrageous declamations."

"And more saying possible?"

"Well, it also seemed as if there were stages of transmission – as there are stages within a wang [42]*: the British Raj rifle empowerment, the 'roast lamb empowerment', the 'insult empowerment', and the 'simulation of venerability empowerment'."*

"O yah! One day coming – Chögyam four empowerments [43] *this way giving."* Rinpoche laughed, then proceeded to tease me further *"Every sound, ngak* [44]*. Every movement, chagya* [45]*. Every action, wang. Every moment, ka'bab* [46]*."* PAUSE *"Rifle empowerment, like bum wang. Rifle, like bumpa* [47]*. Flame and smoke, like peacock feathers. Sheep meat, like sang wang* [48]*. Bad-name calling wang like shérab yeshé kyi wang.* [49] *Kyé-bu dampa* [50] *display wang – this like tsig wang* [51]*."*

Künzang Dorje Rinpoche explained that he had not been joking when he said that I would one day give empowerments in unorthodox style – because this was characteristic in terms of the gö kar chang lo'i dé. With such empowerments or transmissions, there were not necessarily mantras or visualisations to be given – because what was given was congruent with the fabric of everyday life.

---

42 *dBang sKur* / དབང་བསྐུར་ / *abhisheka* – an empowerment.
43 For detailed clarification of the four empowerments, see *Wearing the Body of Visions* —Chapter 7—ARO BOOKS inc—1995.
44 *sNgags* / སྔགས་ / *mantra* – awareness spell.
45 *phyag rGya* / ཕྱག་རྒྱ་ / *mudra* – awareness gesture, symbolic hand-ballet.
46 *bKa' babs* / བཀའ་བབས་ – transmission.
47 *bum pa* / བུམ་པ་ / *khumba* – vase.
48 *gSang dBang* /གསང་དབང་ – secret empowerment. Meat is the transitional sphere between form and emptiness—in terms of embodiment and disembodiment—just as Sambhogakaya is the bridge between trülku (*sPrul sKu* / སྤྲུལ་སྐུ་ / *Nirmanakaya*) and chöku (*chos sKu* / ཆོས་སྐུ་ / *Dharmakaya*).
49 *shes rab ye shes kyi dBang* / ཤེས་རབ་ཡེ་ཤེས་ཀྱི་དབང་ / *prajna jnana abhiseka* – knowledge-wisdom empowerment. The 'insult' being an empty-reflection of Nyoshül's mind.
50 *sKyes bu dam pa* / སྐྱེས་བུ་དམ་པ་ / *satpurusha* – holy being, saint, virtuous, wise-man.
51 *tshig dBang* / ཚིག་དབང་ – word empowerment. The charade being the 'empty expectations' which are miraculously and completely unexpectedly fulfilled in the unification of the previous stages of empowerment.

"You are remembering what I am Myön Héruka saying?"

I understood that Rinpoche wanted me to repeat what we had discussed previously.

"Yes Rinpoche. You said that Myön Hérukas could either be homeless wanderers or householders with families. They could live like monarchs or mendicants – and that they could dress in any way they chose, including clothes of either gender. They could adopt the manners of other cultures and times – and sing any kind of song from anywhere."

"O yah. Chögyam already Blues music singing – and this from America coming; from African peoples there living. Düd'jom Rinpoche much—much—liking. He is letter telling – Chögyam powerful voice Blues music singing." PAUSE *"Other qualities saying?"*

"Yes Rinpoche. You mentioned that they engaged in diverse dancing; telling stories and jokes." PAUSE *"You also mentioned fearless behaviour and giving sexual transmission."*

"O yah – this like Drukpa Künlegs." PAUSE *"Then what dharma avoiding possible?"*

"This was something I'd never heard before, Rinpoche – that they would not necessarily be expected to study or recite texts. Neither would they be expected to perform prostrations, 'khora, or the other outer forms of practice. However, you added that it wasn't an obligation to avoid Dharma practice in this way." PAUSE *"Ah… I left out the fact that Myön Hérukas were sometimes indistinguishable from ordinary lay-people, if one had no acuity of perception. Then, sometimes, they might actually appear to be insane."*

"Alcohol drinking and meat eating you are forgetting." PAUSE *"This important for Vajrayana. Important for all gö kar chang lo'i dé. No one ngakpa or ngakma saying and not alcohol drinking and not meat eating."*

Rinpoche stressed that the central point was that a ngakpa or ngakma had to keep the Vajrayana commitments.

"Now Myön Héruka more saying. In Tibet was Ngak'chang Kong Myön [52]. Then Kham Myön Dharma Seng-gé [53] – the Mad Dharma Lion of Kham. Also Tsé-kya Myonpa Chingkar Dönyö Dorje [54] – the Momentous Maniacal Thunderbolt Clad in White Felt – previous incarnation of Trülshik Rinpoche [55]. Then Myonpa Çe-tsun Seng-ge Wangchuk [56] – Insane Lion of Mastery Never Gossiping; and, Tsang Myön Héruka Ru-gyan Çan [57] – the Madman of Tsang Festooned with Human Bone Cemetery Ornaments. It is good even to know their names."

Künzang Dorje Rinpoche refilled our glasses with chang and we each took a few sips before he continued.

"DoKhyentsé Yeshé Dorje jealous 'thom yors in Gyarong finding – so he is leaving."

He travelled through Kham and Golok manifesting drüpchen activities. The Gyalpo of Der-gé heard of this – and felt great desire to have DoKhyentsé as his personal Lama. The Gyalpo sent grand invitations to DoKhyentsé Yeshé Dorje – but never received replies. The Gyalpo then proceeded to send representatives to invite DoKhyentsé – but he always refused. The Gyalpo then became angry and wrote *'you do not come soon, I shall have to send soldiers to escort you to my dzong.'* This failed to impress DoKhyentsé Yeshé Dorje. The Gyalpo—exasperated—promised vast offerings – but to no avail. Finally—in desperation—the Gyalpo decided to ask for advice from DoDrüpchen *"What can I do? Nothing works to entice DoKhyentsé to Dergé."*

---

52 sNgags 'chang Kong sMyon / སྔགས་འཆང་གོང་སྨྱོན་ – also known as Kong Myon Trati Ngak'chang Rigpa'i Dorje (kong sMyon kra ti sNgags 'chang rig pa'i rDo rJe / གོང་སྨྱོན་ཀྲ་ཏི་སྔགས་འཆང་རིག་པའི་རྡོ་རྗེ) and Kong Myon Bé-pa'i Naljor (kong sMyon sBas pa'i rNal byor / གོང་སྨྱོན་སྦས་པའི་རྣལ་འབྱོར་).

53 khams sMyon dharma seng ge / ཁམས་སྨྱོན་དྷརྨ་སེང་གེ – also known as Ra-gang gÇodpa (rwa sGang gÇod pa / རྭ་སྒང་གཅོད་པ) or Sônam Phüntsog (bSod nams phun tshogs / བསོད་ནམས་ཕུན་ཚོགས / b. 1890).

54 phying dKar don yod rDo rJe / ཕྱིང་དཀར་དོན་ཡོད་རྡོ་རྗེ

55 Trülshik kun zangthong drol ('khrul zhig kun bZang mThong grol / འཁྲུལ་ཞིག་ཀུན་བཟང་མཐོང་གྲོལ་).

56 Çe-tsun Seng-ge Wangchuk (lCe bTsun seng ge dBang phyug / ལྕེ་བཙུན་སེང་གེ་དབང་ཕྱུག / 11th–12th C) – received transmission of the Vima Nying-thig. According to Jamyang Khyentsé Chökyi Lodrö, Çetsün Seng-gé Wangchuk attained rainbow body on the 10th day of the 7th month – and took incarnation in the 19th C as Jamyang Khyentsé Wangpo, who, received the teaching again from the khandros as the Çetsün Nyingthig.

57 Tsang Myön Héruka (gTsang sMyon he ru ka / གཙང་སྨྱོན་ཧེ་རུ་ཀ / 1452–1507).

DoDrüpchen answered *"DoKhyentsé's activity is only for those who are ready to understand it. If you abandon your attempts to entice him by conventional means, he may decide to come. If this turns out to be the case – you must not try to change DoKhyentsé Rinpoche. He is a drüpchen – and you cannot place conditions on him."*

The Gyalpo resolved to desist in writing and sending representatives. Then, unexpectedly, DoKhyentsé Yeshé Dorje arrived—dressed as a Mongolian—and gave the Gyalpo empowerments and teachings without any preparation. The Gyalpo was delighted. He requested DoKhyentsé to be his Lama – but DoKhyentsé refused, saying *"The way I express Dharma is not conventional – and my lifestyle is offensive to conservative society."* The Gyalpo asked what he did which was offensive and he replied *"I don't try to look or act like a monk. I drink alcohol. I slaughter sheep with my rifle and eat the meat. Because of this I cannot be a Gyalpo's Lama."*

The Gyalpo, bewildered, said *"But you have just given empowerments and teachings which were all in perfect accordance with Dharma."*

"That may well be the case" DoKhyentsé Yeshé Dorje replied *"but if I remain in your land for a day or two you will see other aspects of me which will probably disturb you."*

Over the following days, DoKhyentsé Yeshé Dorje wore a hat made of tree branches. He rode his horse bareback with the saddle strapped to his own back. One day he dismounted from his horse—removed his clothes—and strolled languidly outside the gompa howling like a wolf. On the next occasion he appeared wearing leaves; then dressed as a woman; then as a Mongolian warrior; then as a drokpa[58] from Hor. The Gyalpo attempted without success to dissuade DoKhyentsé Yeshé Dorje from manifesting eccentric behaviour – but DoKhyentsé Yeshé Dorje replied *"I told you that I am not the Lama you want. I told you that my expression of Dharma is too unconventional and my lifestyle is offensive to conservative society. I knew that this would be the way it would work out. I'm leaving."*

"I'm sorry – please wear whatever you like – but please do not leave" pleaded the Gyalpo.

---

58 *'brog pa* / འབྲོག་པ་ – nomad herdsman of either sheep or yak. Chang thang gi drokpa (*byang thang gi 'brog pa* / བྱང་ཐང་གི་འབྲོག་པ་) – yak herding nomads of the northern highplains.

"No" replied DoKhyentsé Yeshé Dorje *"I told you it wouldn't work – and it hasn't worked. I told you how it would be – and you've seen for yourself."*

DoKhyentsé mounted his horse and rode away – never to return to that area.

"Yah – no need Chögyam tree-branch hat wearing" Rinpoche laughed. *"Lady-clothes also not necessary – but trab-pa* [59] *or changthang drokpa clothes possible. What saying?"*

"Certainly Rinpoche, I do tend to wear whatever I like. I always have done. I used to wear an embroidered Greek shepherd's waistcoat at Art School and an ankle-length embroidered Afghan sheepskin coat for a while."

"Always shock making?"

"No Rinpoche, not on purpose. I never wear anything deliberately to have an effect on anyone. I just wear what I enjoy. If there's any response to what I wear, it probably comes from my not following fashion – and then it's probably derision or pity rather than shock. When I'm not in robes – I still wear what I wore in the 1960s."

Rinpoche nodded and opined that this was sane. Following fashion was mental deficiency[60]. I pointed out that it was sometimes hard to divide following fashion from wearing what one enjoyed – because what I wore was once a trend. Of course, one could genuinely like something that was currently popular with a group of people. Rinpoche explained that the mien of a Myön Héruka could vary a great deal in different cultures because the mien was communicative. There was a two-way process. It was a matter of how the general population apprehended Myön Hérukas. In the Himalayan countries there was a context for Myön Hérukas – and so their behaviour was understood. It was also understood that some self-styled 'enlightened crazies' might merely be narcissistic social aberrants. Rinpoche told me that—as far as he understood—there was no general societal context for Myön Hérukas in the West. Problems would therefore arise from any Myön Héruka who offended general morality or ethics. A genuine Myön Héruka therefore, would not act criminally or immorally. To act criminally would not be of benefit to anyone – unless the criminal acts occurred in opposition to a criminal regime such as Nazi Germany.

---

59 *bKrabs pa* / བསྐྲབས་པ་ – warrior.
60 Mental deficiency – gôb-gôb yid (*sGob sGob yid* / སྒོབ་སྒོབ་ཡིད་).

Due to the pre-established faith of Himalayans – Myön Hérukas were inspiring simply on the basis of their existence. In the West however – it would be different. Western Myön Hérukas would function within the framework of their societies. I asked Rinpoche whether he could describe how a western Myön Héruka might appear – and he stunned me by saying *"Maybe like Jimi Hendrix looking."* I did not understand at first because what I heard was somewhere between *Chhi'mèd Handley* and *Jig'mèd Henley*. I took a long shot – and asked *"The Black American electric Blues musician?"*

"O yah!" he replied *"I am in Delhi hearing music and Jimi Hendrix photograph seeing. Music also hearing – and—very much—Myön Héruka thinking."* PAUSE *"But very beautiful sounds coming."*

How could it be that I was sitting in Tso Pema with Kyabjé Künzang Dorje Rinpoche the Tibetan rTsa rLung and Dzogchen Master – and hear him mention Jimi Hendrix as a postulate Myön Héruka? Rinpoche could see that I was somewhat astounded – caught between hilarity and delighted appreciation.

"O yah – Jimi Hendrix very special clothing and music. Many strange beautiful colour and sound coming."

We spoke further and Rinpoche said that he knew something of western culture from some French scientists he had met. They had told him about the Moon landings and that the Moon was just over 100,000 gyang-drag[61] from the earth. That astonished me because I had no idea how far the Moon was from the Earth – even though I'd had an interest in astronomy in my pre-teen years.

Rinpoche knew about the Renaissance, and the European Enlightenment, The American War of Independence, the Napoleonic Wars, The American War Between the States, and the two World Wars. He knew about Judæism, Christianity, and Islam. He knew about some of the great musical composers and artists. He knew about post-war hippie culture and many other aspects of life in the West. I sat there whilst he enumerated what he knew in detail and what he only knew peripherally.

---

61 *rGyang grags* / རྒྱང་གྲགས་ – roughly 2 miles. The Moon is 119,427 gyang-drag from the Earth. 500 zhu'dom (*gZhu 'dom* / གཞུ་འདོམ་) is 1 mile, and the Moon is 238,855 miles from the Earth.

It was as if I'd spent time with the Vivaldi of Vajrayana who turned out —also—to be Shakespeare, Vincent van Gogh, and Einstein.

Rinpoche explained that he'd enumerated the facets of western culture with which he was familiar to give me confidence in his assertion that the Myön Héruka mode could be manifested in the west. It could be manifested *"… but manifestation not same like Tibet or Bhutan coming."* PAUSE *"Künzang Dorje cannot western Myon Héruka telling – it must be Chögyam telling."*

I looked at Rinpoche for a moment and asked *"You would like me to tell that now, Rinpoche?"*

Künzang Dorje Rinpoche laughed shaking his head *"No, not now telling. In future times telling. Now too early. First must be carefully looking. First must western lands, living and teaching – and then seeing."* Rinpoche looked thoughtful for a few moments, as if considering his previous assertion *"Yah… but maybe now something possible saying?"*

"All I can imagine Rinpoche, would be that a western Myön Héruka would act in ways which would question cultural fashions."

Rinpoche nodded and assumed a look I'd seen before when he meant me to continue a line of enquiry.

"There are fashions in almost everything. There's always a new idea of how life could be better. There's currently the idea that butter is bad for you and the health conscious now eat margarine instead. Personally, I don't see what's wrong with butter. "Human beings have been eating it for thousands of years. Margarine as far as I can see is the result of a great deal of processing – and seems a long way from what is natural. More to the point, it tastes disgusting – so I remain unconvinced by the idea that it's healthier than butter. So, there are fashions in health and medicine. There are fashions in clothing, life-style, music and all the Arts. Every fashion is made to appear an improvement – but every fashion is merely another version of what went before. Sometimes there is improvement and sometimes degeneration – but one can only know by personal research what is better or worse." PAUSE *"So, as far as I can see, a Myön Héruka would leap free of all that; to show people the nature of their obedience to fashion – and the nature of their limitations."*

Künzang Dorje Rinpoche observed me for a moment. I was not quite sure why – but then it occurred to me that he was watching for signs of my being anxious as to his response.

Then he laughed *"O yah – Chögyam Myön Héruka in western lands becoming!"*

Then I laughed *"That is not likely Rinpoche."* PAUSE *"I may well irritate people with my eccentricity... and I may well have unfashionable points of view – but I think that people have to respect you before they regard you as a Myön Héruka."* PAUSE *"Chögyam Trungpa Rinpoche is respected – but I don't think it is possible that I would ever be seen as being anywhere remotely like him."*

Rinpoche was grinning at this point *"Future times"* he began after scratching the side of his head with his index finger *"we are not knowing. Only present time knowing – and in present time only some things knowing. What later coming, is present moment depending. Myön Héruka style of Drukpa Künlegs and Myön Héruka style of Chögyam Trungpa Rinpoche – these very different. Style of Künzang Dorje and style of Chögyam different. Style always different."* LONG SILENCE *"What same!?"* he almost shouted.

Then I did something I'd never done before – and it was a spontaneous reaction.

"This!" I replied, with some insane notion that I understood what the word implied. Künzang Dorje Rinpoche looked delighted.

"Yah!" he laughed *"And so now you are knowing."*

Yes! In *that moment* I knew – but I had no idea what I knew.

9

brug pa kun legs

Kyabjé Künzang Dorje Rinpoche took a sip of chang. He cast his eyes on the three mo-mos, still on my plate. It was intriguing to be with someone who ate faster than I did. *"Would you like my mo-mos Rinpoche?"*

"O yah! All mo-mo in world eating!" PAUSE *"No"* he laughed *"Chögyam mo-mo eating – much writing - then much power needing. Much much power from mo-mo, coming necessary."*

It did not take me long to devour the remaining mo-mos.

"Now playful example, from Drukpa Künlegs telling."

Drukpa Künlegs had wandered into an arid plain – and there he met an old man called Apa Gé-po Ten'dzin, whose sons had left home. Of his daughters, all but his youngest had married and so only she remained. As she and her mother always had much to discuss, Apa Gé-po Ten'dzin was somewhat lonely and dejected. He had little to do other than pick his nose and recite Mani[1].

As soon as he saw Drukpa Künlegs he exclaimed *"How fortunate that I should meet you Rinpoche! My sons have established their own homes – and my daughters have all married but one. I'm sorry to say – but I'm jaded with life. I am seriously in need of a practice that'll enable me to go in the best way when I die. Would you be so very kind as to give me a simple practice which will help me?"*

"O yah! Certainly. I'll teach you how to establish confidence in actuality – but you will have to recite it whenever you think of me. You must however – never discuss it with anyone. Do you agree?"

"Most certainly Rinpoche." Apa Gé-po Ten'dzin agreed – and so Drukpa Künlegs gave him the transmission of the Establishment of Certainty in Actuality which Liberates from Cyclic Experience.

---

1   Om Mani Peme Hung – the mantra of Chenrézigs.

> *I establish certainty in the actuality of an old man's humbled penis, emaciated at the rhizome, collapsed like a felled tree.*
> *I establish certainty in the actuality of an old woman's flaccid vagina, collapsed, loose, and impenetrable.*
> *I establish certainty in the actuality of the virile young tiger's dorje, rising proudly, nonchalant in the face of mortality.*
> *I establish certainty in the actuality of the khandro's lotus, uninhibited by shame – which generates waves of ecstasy.*

"You must remember—always, in any place anywhere, whatever the company—to recite this whenever you think of me."

Apa Gé-po Ten'dzin thanked Drukpa Künlegs reverently and asked him if he could also have a practice that would reinforce his resolve – and Drukpa Künlegs taught him the following:

> *The branches of the Great Eastern Tree continually develop – but the spread of foliage depends on the extent of the roots.*
> *Drukpa Künlegs' dorje may wedge in a petite vagina – but tightness depends upon the dimension of the dorje.*
> *Apa Gé-po's impulse to attain realisation is strong – but the magnitude of his attainment will be dependent upon the potency of his devotion.*

"Never forget this and you will attain liberation."

Apa Gé-po returned home, entirely happy – and as soon as he arrived his daughter asked *"Apa la, did you actually meet Drukpa Künlegs? Did you receive a teaching?"*

"Yes!" smiled Apa Gé-po *"Yes to both. I did meet Drukpa Künlegs – and, he gave me transmission of the Establishment of Certainty in Actuality which Liberates from Cyclic Experience. I have learned it word for word."*

"How is that?" his daughter chuckled *"when you are neither educated nor particularly intelligent."*

"Well…" her father replied *"It's a concise practice. It wasn't so difficult to learn by heart."*

"Will you please recite it for us, then?"

Apa Gé-po placed his hands in Anjali mudra[2] and recited. His daughter hid her face away in embarrassment.

"Have you lost your reason!" his wife cried out in shock *"The words of a drüpchen such as Drukpa Künlegs are always pure – so you must have misheard or misunderstood."*

"Neither" replied Apa Gé-po.

"Even so" his wife exclaimed *"It's not proper to imitate Drukpa Künlegs. You must never repeat this in front of anyone ever again."*

"That, I cannot promise. Drukpa Künlegs taught me to recite these lines whenever I thought of him – and I vowed to do so."

Later, when the family was gathered for their evening meal, Apa Gé-po again repeated the verses. *"Ah kha ka – Apa has lost his wits"* the mother said to the daughter – and taking their dinner bowls, they left the table. When Apa Gé-po opened his eyes, he was on his own. Eventually his wife returned and said *"You must stay in a room on your own if you cannot desist from this madness."* Apa Gé-po looked sorrowful but answered *"I shall continue even if I have to endure lifelong solitude"* at which his wife escorted him to the hayloft where he was to be confined.

Apa Gé-po was content to reside in the hayloft – and there ensconced, he continued to recite all his waking hours. A month or so later when the moon was full – the mother and daughter started to hear the strumming of a dramnyèn[3] and trilling of a trèd-ling[4] in their house. Apa Gé-po's wife could no longer hear Apa Gé-po's voice – and started feeling apprehensive. She said to her daughter *"Maybe Apa is weeping on his own. Maybe it would be good to take some chang up to Apa."* Her daughter filled a jug with chang and went up to the loft. When she got there with the chang all she found was a heap of blankets with nothing beneath them other than a rainbow sphere of light surrounding a syllable A. *"Ama la! Come here quickly! Apa la has vanished!"* she cried out in shock and bewilderment.

---

2   Anjali mudra – thal mo'i chag gya (*thal mo'i phyag rGya* / ཐལ་མོའི་ཕྱག་རྒྱ་). This salutation or prayer mudra is performed with the hands pressed together with straight fingers pointing upwards and the thumbs facing you.
3   *sGra nyan* / སྒྲ་སྙན་ – Tibetan guitar.
4   *khred gLing* / ཁྲེད་གླིང་ – Tibetan transverse flute.

There was a deal of commotion in the house – so much so that the neighbours gathered to find out what was amiss. The rainbow sphere of light rose and travelled out of the hayloft and into the sky – and as it ascended, they could all hear the voice of Apa Gé-po singing *"Drukpa Künlegs has released me from the drudgery of this place. I no longer have to be the servant of duality and remain in servitude to samsara. I now live on the Copper Coloured Mountain of Guru Rinpoche. Alas for you whom I leave behind to regret your pusillanimous prudery and parsimonious primness. "Give my possessions to Drukpa Künlegs as an offering – and do what you can to let your attention rise above paltry prissiness."*

When Drukpa Künlegs visited that house years later, it had collapsed and he built a chörten at the point at which Apa Gé-po entered the sky dimension.

"Drukpa Künlegs" Rinpoche commented *"is Apa Gé-po's teng-ar, chörten inside placing – and Nga-wang Chögyal Rinpoche gompa around chörten building"* he smiled. *"This gompa now, Chhi'mèd Lhakhang name calling – and you must one day, with sangyum visiting."*

Künzang Dorje Rinpoche gazed out of the window for some moments. On previous occasions that had made me anxious – but now I tended to see it as his mode of considering something.

"What Chögyam saying this Apa Gé-po recitation?"

"I think that it could have been anything Drukpa Künlegs gave Apa Gé-po to recite – any collection of words. What was important was that Apa Gé-po applied himself and carried out the instruction. I think also that the nature of the recitation was designed to get Apa Gé-po into trouble – in order that he would have to persevere against the criticism he'd encounter whenever anyone overheard him reciting those verses." PAUSE *"I think that in accepting these verses without judgement or question – Apa Gé-po was already entering into a frame of reference which was nonconceptual. He would therefore have had a great advantage over anyone who had semantic or contextual problems with Drukpa Künlegs' words."*

"O yah." PAUSE *"So, today this, rare finding."* PAUSE *"What saying western students?"*

"Well... I think that many western students like these stories – but they like them because they like 'the idea of Drukpa Künlegs'. Some, of course, don't like 'the idea of Drukpa Künlegs' – but it seems that liking or not liking are little different in terms of being ensnared by self-indulgent notions and fantasies. I know this way of thinking because I've thought in this way quite often in the past. The important aspect of this story is transmission – and transmission can occur in limitless ways. I don't think that the western people who like these stories would take on such a practice – in the way Apa Gé-po did. They'd probably like to—think—they would – but when it came to it, they'd find they had intellectual obstacles." PAUSE *"So, I think it would remain in the realm of fantasy for those people."*

"Yah – so Chögyam no 'penis and vagina' recitation giving."

I erupted with mirth at that idea *"No Rinpoche – I think that one can only work within the bounds of what is possible in any society. Apa Gé-po was a product of his society – and, although western people can be naïve and gullible, they don't really have such unquestioning capacity for devotion."* PAUSE *"Unless of course they're the kind of people who become ensnared by cults."*

Then we had to discuss what was meant by cults and cult leaders. It took some time to distinguish between a Lama such a Drukpa Künlegs and a cult leader – but Rinpoche understood when it came to the discussion of cult leaders gaining personal advantage and making false promises.

"O yah... like this we are also Lamas having." He named a few – but said that these people were not respected by anyone who had any understanding.

"Yah, but Chögyam authentic devotion having – so why other western peoples not authentic devotion having?" This was not issued as a challenge as it would have been at the outset of our relationship – but a clear and cogent answer was required.

"I think they do have capacity for authentic devotion, Rinpoche – because everyone is beginninglessly realised and therefore everyone must naturally have the capacity for devotion."

"Yah!" Rinpoche almost shouted with a broad smile. *"And so?"*

"And so it depends on a variety of factors. With western people, devotion—authentic devotion—is going to arise in the context of study, practice, and retreat. There's not going to be a western person like Apa Gé-po who is culturally set up as a layman to have that kind of devotion. It could occur perhaps in the Christian Church in rural settings in Italy or Greece.

"I think that Roman Catholicism and the Greek and Russian Orthodox Churches could have people like Apa Gé-po – but, I can't imagine them in Britain or any of the Protestant countries."

We then had to discuss the diverse nature of Christianity and I had to admit that my knowledge was severely limited. I explained that in the Christian Church – they had something like tsog'khorlo[5] which was called 'holy communion' where you received a sip of red wine and a wafer. This had to be explained as chang and paleb[6]. This was the blood and flesh of Christ. In the Roman Catholic Churches this sacrament was seen as actual – and in the Protestant Churches it was seen as symbolic. This was one of those discussions where there were continual problems with translation – and continual apologies on my part for being an utter ignoramus with respect to Christianity. I had no idea why Christians partook of the blood and flesh of Christ either symbolically or non-symbolically[7]. I was sure there was a good reason – but it had never been explained to me as a child. I said that it was possible for someone who took the chang and paleb to be actual – to have the devotion of Apa Gé-po – but for those who saw it as a symbol it was less likely.

Speaking of chang and paleb was somehow a cue for dinner. An unusual dinner for Künzang Dorje Rinpoche – but he recalled that I liked scrambled eggs and toasted paleb for breakfast, when I could get it. He decided that he'd like to try it himself and so that is what we ate for dinner. I said that I was delighted because I could eat such a meal at any time of day. This was one of the evenings that I ate dinner with Rinpoche rather than returning to the Nyingma Gompa. I received an increasing number of invitations to dine with Rinpoche as my time in Tso Pema drew to a close.

"Yah… so…" he began after the dinner plates had been cleared away *"Drukpa Künlegs 'three things list' making:*

---

5 *tshogs kyi 'khor lo* / ཚོགས་ཀྱི་འཁོར་ལོ་ / *ganachakra* / *gha na tsa kra* – vajra banquet cycle. This is a practice of generosity in terms of the sense fields.
6 *bag leb* / བག་ལེབ་ – a Tibetan muffin.
7 The *Holy Communion* or *Eucharist* is a sacrament inaugurated by Christ at *the Last Supper* – when he offered his disciples bread and wine. He enjoined them to partake of bread and wine in memory of him. He referred to the bread as his body and the wine as his blood.

It is inappropriate to engage in sexual intercourse with a married person, child, or monastic. That's the teaching on The Three Improprieties.

Hunger is the mark of an empty stomach. Desire for a large penis is the mark of a 'thom yor. Passionate lust is the mark of a laudable lady. That's the teaching on The Three Marks.

Impotent men have no imagination. Orphans have no wealth. Aristocrats have meagre generosity. That's the teaching on The Three Deficiencies.

Ecclesiastical dignitaries take joy in donations. Politicians take joy in flattery. Ladies take joy in their lovers. That's the teaching on The Three Joys.

Malefactors abhor the sincerely religious. Misers abhor profligates. Spouses abhor their partner's paramours. That's the teaching on The Three Abhorrences.

Impecunious scroungers are deficient in happiness. The profane are deficient in religion. Vagrants are deficient in commitment: That's the teaching of The Three Deficiencies.

Parsimonious ecclesiastics are worthy of no esteem. Dissolute monastics are worthy of no deference. Poxed louse-ridden 'thom yors are worthy of no regard. That's the teaching on The Three Contemptibles.

Arrogant scholastics are bereft of real knowledge. Conceited young men are bereft of honour. Vain young girls are bereft of intelligence. That's the teaching on The Three Bereft Conditions.

Those without honesty have dry mouths. Those who are without genuineness make no offerings. Those without courage don't make good generals. That is the teaching of The Three Absences.

The sign of a plutocrat is contracted fists. The sign of an arrogant monk is a contracted mind. The sign of a perfect nun is a contracted vagina. That's the teaching of The Three Contractions.

The glib talkers insert themselves into the midst of social gatherings. Monastic wealth inserts itself into the accounts of monastic bursars. Drukpa Künlegs inserts his vajra into the lotuses of young ladies. That's the teaching of The Three Insertions

The minds of gomchens are smooth. The talk of self-seekers is smoother. The thighs of young ladies are the smoothest of all. That's the teaching of The Three Grades of Smoothness.

Sodomitic monks have thin shamthabs. Widows and widowers have gaunt faces. Fields without manure bear meagre crops: That's the teaching of The Three Emaciations.

Drukpa Künlegs is never fatigued by copulation. Monastics are never weary of wealth. The pleasantly disposed are never tired of sex. That's the teaching of The Three Indefatigables.

Although discernment is clear, the Lama remains a prerequisite. Although a lamp burns brightly, it still depends on oil. Although the nature of Mind is self-evident, it necessitates recognition. That's the teaching of The Three Requirements.

The Hinayana purpose is to pacify. The Mahayana purpose is freedom from selfishness. The Vajrayana purpose is to attain nonduality. That's the teaching on The Three Vehicles.

For authentication invoke the Lama. For power invoke the yidam. For competence invoke the protectors. That's the teaching on The Three Roots."

"So…" Rinpoche grinned *"which in list, 'worst peoples thinking?"*

I thought for a while. Some were mixed with good or natural qualities so I discounted those – and finally ended up with *"The arrogant scholastics, conceited young men, and vain young girls."*

"Which best?"

"The teaching of The Three Requirements: *Discernment is clear – but the Lama remains a prerequisite; Lamps burn brightly, but they still depend on oil; nature of Mind is self-evident, but it necessitates recognition."*

Künzang Dorje Rinpoche nodded *"Yah good. Künzang Dorje nothing more needing asking."*

That was unprecedented. I'd expected an interrogation – but then he asked *"Now Chögyam 'three list' making."*

It somehow didn't take me longer than a few moments before I was able to offer *"Those without kindness have a sad future. Those without joy have a sad past. Those without a Lama are sad and joyless in the present as well as the past and future. That's the teaching on* The Three Times.*"*

Kyabjé Künzang Dorje Rinpoche looked at me expressionlessly as it was translated. A second passed. He burst out laughing *"Now Drukpa Künlegs song making! This too funny! This also too good."* PAUSE *"More coming?"*

That was unexpected. *More coming…* I felt momentarily inadequate to the task – but after a few moments I recited: *"Bigots soil their own minds; slanderers soil their own mouths; sectarians soil their own underwear. That's the teaching on* The Three Bowel Disorders.*"*

Rinpoche laughed – once 'bowel disorders' found a viable translation. *"More coming?"* I could see the way this was going and knew I'd eventually run out of material – but, as long as I could I'd make the attempt.

"Mechanical translators feast on literalism and pedantry; those greedy for secret drüpthabs feast on piles of printed paper; those who are conceited in respect of their knowledge feast on the sophistry of clandestine definitions. That's the teaching on The Three Feasts.*"*

"Now false refuge list making."

"Fundamentalists take refuge in experientialists being in error. Literalists take refuge in essentialists being in error. Narrow minded, myopic, anxiously conservative purists take refuge in anyone being in error who has a sense of humour or who appears relaxed and cheerful in their practice. That's the teaching of The Three False Refuges.*"*

"O yah – much enjoying. Now false monk list making."

"That is more difficult Rinpoche – could it be false western monks as I cannot really comment on Himalayan monks."

"Yah – western monk possible."

"False western monks think themselves superior to lay people because they have succeeded in developing flatness of affect. False western monks think themselves superior to lay people because they get to sit closer to the Lama. False western monks think themselves superior to lay people because they stockpile the anaesthetic spray they apply to their genitals. That's the teaching on The Three False Monks." It took a while to explain flatness of affect and anaesthetic spray – but the anaesthetic spray made Rinpoche roar with laughter.

"O yah—too good—too good. Now same with bad yogi."

"Fake western yogis are expert in making every sordid proclivity they indulge, a sign of practising the Inner Tantras. Fake western yogis are expert in making laziness and self-indulgence seem like a sign of relaxing in terms of the natural state. Fake western yogis are expert in making money from selling Vajrayana implements for extortionate prices in the West. Fake western yogis are expert in praising their Lamas whilst ignoring their advice. Fake western yogis are expert in smoking and using drugs whilst pretending to honour their Lamas' teachings. Fake western yogis are expert in being promiscuous and breaking all the root vows whilst pretending to be disciplined." I suddenly realised I'd gone beyond three examples – but as Rinpoche was slapping his thighs with laughter, I figured I'd not overstepped propriety.

"At one time, Rinpoche… I might have said that I only had one example of a fake yogi – and that was me. Now however… I see that self-deprecation needs to be personal, private, and pertinent."

"Yah – good you are not 'fake Chögyam' saying. Chögyam maybe not always 'very best possible' – but never 'worst possible' or 'middling'. Chögyam mainly good. Sometimes very good – but always 'good' doing." PAUSE "Sometimes wrong girlfriend choosing" he laughed "but no harm coming. No harm in mind coming." PAUSE "Now Inji hippie list telling."

Inji hippies… Well, I probably had something to say there – but mainly in the context of what I'd seen in the Himalayas and at Buddhist Centres in Britain.

"Hippie tantrists adore secret information they can keep from others whilst broadcasting that they have access to it. Hippie sutrists adore learning the taxonomy of classifications, categories and inventories by rote. Hippie freeloaders love Indian toilets, living on Freak Street [8], and eating curry with their fingers. That's the teaching on The Three Adorations*."* PAUSE *"However Rinpoche, I must say that I'm also a 'hippie of sorts'..."*

"Why 'Chögyam hippie' saying?" Rinpoche asked and then we had to have a long discussion concerning the many different things which were meant by the word 'hippie'. I ended up having to confess that I was better described as an *Art student* than a *hippie* – even though people of my father's generation would have categorised me as a hippie. The word hippie had changed in meaning since 1967 in any case and become almost too vague to use. My long hair was now 'uncut hair' and one of the vows which I had taken. I had never taken drugs of any kind. I'd never invested in hippy patois. I did frequent wholefood shops and avoided processed food – but food had never become a religious issue with me. Künzang Dorje Rinpoche was surprisingly fascinated by the details of what constituted hippie appearance and lifestyle. He then asked me what western toilets were like and I provided a general description. I explained that the best of them were places where you could cheerfully sit and read for an hour. He was amazed and said that the west must be paradisiacal. I agreed but pointed out that it also had aspects which were diabolical.

"Now Injï tourist telling."

Of this subject I knew little – but this was not the time to back out. *"Culture-seeking tourists visit the Taj Mahal, the Harmandir Sahib, the Golden Temple of Amritsar, and the Red Fort in Delhi. Thirsty gourmet tourists visit Kulu for apple juice, Maharashtra for mango juice, and Uttarakhand for rhododendron juice.* "*The Beatles go to Rishikesh to take a holiday, attempt meditation, and unmask Maharishi* [9]. *That's the teaching on* The Three Types of Tourist.*"*

---

8   Freak Street—Basantapur—in Kathmandu was well known during the Hippie Trail years of the 1960s and 1970s. The attraction was the government-run hashish shops.
9   Maharishi Mahesh Yogi (*Mahesh Prasad Varma* / 1918–2008) was known for developing and popularising 'Transcendental Meditation'. During their stay, the Beatles heard that the Maharishi had made sexual advances towards Mia Farrow. The Beatles ended their association with the Maharishi and described it as a 'public mistake'. John Lennon's song 'Sexy Sadie' is a satirical reference to the Maharishi.

I had to explain a great deal concerning the last line – but as before Rinpoche showed great interest. He seemed keen to know as much as possible about western culture – and I felt uneasy about the fact that he was getting my highly personal picture of the West. He laughed when I told him this – and said that it didn't matter that I was presenting a personal view. What else could I present? There would naturally be other people who would provide him with their views – and eventually he would build a picture made from many different accounts. He said he valued my view because he was confident that I wasn't given to exaggeration.

"Now three 'beautiful qualities' list making."

"Fast galloping horses have beautifully flowing manes. High flying eagles have beautifully variegated plumage. Kind people have beautiful faces no matter what their age or physiognomy. That's the teaching on The Three Beauties.*"*

Künzang Dorje Rinpoche gazed through the window for some moments. *"One time"* he began *"Drukpa Künlegs different list 'three things' – many joke making."*

He massaged the palm of his right hand for a moment with the thumb of his left hand before he commenced.

> *It is unsuitable to seduce the elderly, children, or hermits. That's the teaching on* The Three Unsuitabilities.
>
> *Hunger is the sign of an empty stomach. Wishing for a large penis is the sign of an impotent man. Lasciviousness is the mark of a realised nun. That's the teaching on* The Three Signs.
>
> *Old men have little ingenuity. Idlers have no prosperity. Lords have a dearth of largesse. That's the teaching on* The Three Shortages.
>
> *Monastic bursars take delight in offerings. Officials take delight in sycophancy. Dilettantes take delight in daydreams. That's the teaching on* The Three Delights.
>
> *Scoundrels loathe the blameless. Profligates loathe the thrifty. Monks loathe competition for the favours of young robe-wearers. That's the teaching on* The Three Loathings.

Philosophers are short of insight. Ceremonialists are short of devotion: The impatient, irritable, and petulant are short of happiness. That's the teaching of The Three Shortages.

Decadent dignitaries shouldn't gain approbation. Desultory monks shouldn't gain applause. Diseased dogs and dirty dishevelled dullards shouldn't gain admiration. That's the teaching on The Three Disapprobations.

Debaters have a deficit of insight. Self-enamoured soldiers have a deficit of resolve. Tyrants have a deficit of courage. That's the teaching on The Three Deficits.

Künzang Dorje Rinpoche adjusted his chuba and gazed at me in what seemed an expectant manner. I took the cue *"Rinpoche, this seems to be a similar list – but which has come down through a different oral tradition. It's shorter – but it makes points which don't appear in the first set you taught."*

Rinpoche said nothing – and so I continued.

"I have the feeling that you want me to comment further – so, I'd say that this threefold pattern is a cogent pattern to follow when describing the sociology of Vajrayana."

Then I had to unpack the word 'sociology'.

"O yah – this jig-ten-gyi tha-nyèd [10]*. This must analyse – not ma-chèd ma-tagpa'i jig-ten gyi tha-nyèd* [11]*."*

Rinpoche said that the study of sociology in respect of Vajrayana was important to any Lama. One could not teach if one didn't understand the social conventions that existed amongst Lamas and practitioners. There were the monastic social conventions – but they also existed amongst the gö kar chang lo'i dé. They existed amongst the religious laity too – and this was why Drukpa Künlegs was always lampooning stereotypes amongst these groups. Rinpoche said that although I wasn't Drukpa Künlegs—to the extent that I couldn't urinate on a thangka and thereby add gold leaf where it had been absent—I could make comment when it was required.

10 *'jig rTen gyi tha sNyad* / འཇིག་རྟེན་གྱི་བསྙད་ / *lokavyavahara* – social conventions.
11 *ma dPyad ma brTags pa'i 'jig rTen gyi tha sNyad* / མ་དཔྱད་མ་བརྟགས་པའི་འཇིག་རྟེན་གྱི་བསྙད་ – unanalysed social convention.

145

Although I might not address people spontaneously with my observations as Drukpa Künlegs did, I could do so in my poetry. I could publish a book of my poetry[12] in which I could lampoon the distorted attitudes I saw. I'd never thought of publishing my poetry. I didn't even think of myself as 'a poet' – I simply wrote poetry from time to time. It was what hippies—as Art students—did. Everyone wrote poetry at Art School in the late 1960s and early 1970s. It was part of the culture – although that culture had almost vanished.

I told Künzang Dorje Rinpoche that the culture was changing – and that there was less interest in the Arts than there used to be. Art students seemed to be more like other students and other young people – primarily interested in more popular enjoyments. Somehow, they seemed less mature and less intelligent. Having a large vocabulary was no longer valued – and Rock Music was enjoyed to the exclusion of Baroque, Classical, and later forms of Serious Music. There had been a time when listening to Eric Satie and Frank Zappa in sequence was not unusual. One could mention the Bach 'cello pieces and Stravinsky's Fire Bird Suite and one would be understood – the music would be known. One could quote Shakespeare, Milton, and Ted Hughes in everyday conversation – but now such conversations were rare.

Kyabjé Künzang Dorje Rinpoche listened as I spoke and shook his head *"This not good coming."*

"No, Rinpoche – this is definitely not good." PAUSE *"But as long as I live – I will try to remind people of the importance of the Arts."*

"O yah!" Rinpoche exclaimed with a joyful expression *"Then all good coming."*

And on that note, we bade each other good night.

---

12 *Ravings of a Mild-Mannered Maniac*—Volume I of Ngak'chang Rinpoche's collected poetry—ARO BOOKS inc—2021.

10

convivial vicar of Vajrayana

Kyabjé Künzang Dorje Rinpoche was perusing a letter when I arrived – but as soon as he heard my voice he called out *"O yah – Chögyam breakfast needing. Much hungry!"*

I went into Rinpoche's room and sat down. He'd waved away the need for prostrations as he usually did – but I always started towards performing them. I was loath to appear as if I was taking anything for granted. For him, the intention was all that mattered – and for him it was more important that we were sitting ready for the arrival of breakfast. It arrived. Boiled eggs and paleb. Pö-ja[1] for Rinpoche and hot lemon and honey for his outlandish student.

"Always must be poetry writing" Rinpoche stressed. *"When skills having, then always must be maintaining."*

This was what Kyabjé Düd'jom Rinpoche had said about Blues. It seemed that the message was clear: I was to employ the Arts to the best of my ability, in order to communicate with my generation and future generations in the West. He explained that although Himalayan Lamas could teach western people, they lacked the cultural background to communicate with versatility, resourcefulness, originality, and ingenuity. It was different with western people who spent enough time in the Himalayas – because there was then a shared culture. It had been different with Chögyam Trungpa Rinpoche – because he had plunged headlong into western culture and understood its etiquettes, protocols, and conventions. Rinpoche enquired whether this not the case.

"Certainly Rinpoche. Chögyam Trungpa Rinpoche once went to hear the St Matthew Passion[2] at Oxford University and described it as a great discovery."

Here I had to explain that St Matthew was one of four great Christian Saints who had been disciples of Jesus. I explained that I had studied the Gospel of St Matthew at School.

---

1   *bod ja* / བོད་ཇ་ – Tibetan butter tea.
2   St Matthew Passion is a sacred oratorio written by Johann Sebastian Bach in 1727.

He asked me why that had not made me a Christian and I explained that I had regarded the Bible as a work of literature rather than a religious work that might inspire me. There had obviously been instances of wisdom and compassion – but there was no comparison with what I had found in Vajrayana. I did not disparage Christianity however, as I'd met entirely worthy Christians – particularly my mother. I'd rejected the idea of 'God' as the 'uncreated creator' from the age of five. Once this was explained, Rinpoche asked me to continue what I had been saying with respect to Chögyam Trungpa Rinpoche having heard the St Matthew Passion.

"Chögyam Trungpa Rinpoche said that he experienced the tremendous heroism and religious passion in its sacred atmosphere. He felt the occasion was a personal feast – the beauty of which increased his appreciation of western Art and culture." PAUSE *"He also said that the Tibetan who accompanied him said that the music sounded like cats being burnt alive."*

Rinpoche laughed at that for a few moments – and then continued *"O yah ... Trungpa Rinpoche, Mind incarnation of Drukpa Künlegs."* PAUSE *"You also name 'Chögyam' having."* He eyed me with a slightly mischievous expression. *"Düd'jom Rinpoche in letter telling – Aro Yeshé, Speech Incarnation of Drukpa Künlegs."* Then he burst out laughing *"This meaning: 'same style' coming – but Chögyam not 'same style' with many khandros having"* he laughed. *"Düd'jom Rinpoche writing – Chögyam only one khandro having. Only one sangyum having."* PAUSE *"Yah... western countries, this best system – and for Chögyam this natural system. What natural, always best."*

This was a surprise. I had no idea that Aro Yeshé was connected with Drukpa Künlegs in this way. I wondered momentarily why Kyabjé Düd'jom Rinpoche had not told me – but then it became obvious. Kyabjé Düd'jom Rinpoche must have wanted Kyabjé Künzang Dorje Rinpoche to choose his own time for imparting the information.

"Yes, Rinpoche – monogamy has always been my preference. I would want to see my wife as being my best friend – and that would not function at all with promiscuity. I think that if one has a good relationship – one has no need to add anything or anyone."

"You saying Trungpa Rinpoche mistake making?" he asked, but in a tone that bespoke curiosity rather than censure.

"No – not at all, Rinpoche." PAUSE *"I feel that Chögyam Trungpa Rinpoche was relating with the West in terms of how it was – in the period of time which was known as 'the sexual revolution'. At that time promiscuity was seen as healthy in the alternative culture – and it was the alternative culture from which almost all his students came. I imagine that this coloured his experience of the West. That was the late-1960s to the mid-1970s. That period is more-or-less over now. The world has changed. "That ethos may linger in certain places – but it was never part of my life. I no longer really see it happening outside a few bizarre examples."*

I told Rinpoche about the 'psychedelic Latihan' in Liverpool[3]. That took a fair while because everything which happened had to be explained. He laughed a great deal and agreed that if one lived in a 'mad-house society' such as this – then one's actions would be commensurate with it in order to be understood.

"So" I continued *"in terms of Chögyam Trungpa Rinpoche, he was a mahasiddha in any case – and so his way of teaching can't be viewed in the same category as whatever mine might be. I don't think I even have a category or belong in a category. If I did… it would probably be the Vajrayana version of an English vicar with a rather small parish."*

I then had to explain the word 'vicar' and 'parish' – and how 'vicars' were viewed. They were seen as good sincere people – but not particularly exalted. I said that I could relate to being described as a *convivial vicar of Vajrayana*. We then had to root around for words which might translate 'convivial' in Tibetan: *kunga'wa* [4]; *kyirog chèdpa* [5]; *'grig po* [6]; *cham-po* [7], *thun'gyur dzèd-pa* [8] and, *nyèn-du* [9]. We settled on *cham-po* as coming closest to *convivial*. Künzang Dorje Rinpoche thought about cham-po for a moment and decided that it described me well enough – even though it lacked a certain degree of chom-pa[10]. I was amused by the idea of being a *cham-po chom-pa* – and that seemed to amuse Rinpoche as well.

3   See *Goodbye Forever—Volume II—chapter 12—Fear and Loathing in Liverpool—*Aro Books WORLDWIDE—2022.
4   *kun dGa' ba* / ཀུན་དགའ་བ་ – kind and friendly.
5   *sKyid grogs byed pa* / སྐྱིད་གྲོགས་བྱེད་པ་ – friendly and rejoicing with friends.
6   *'grig po* / འགྲིག་པོ་ – harmonious.
7   *'cham po* / འཆམ་པོ་ – convivial agreeable, amiable, congenial, amicable, cordial, genial, affable.
8   *mThun 'gyur mDzad pa* / མཐུན་འགྱུར་མཛད་པ་ – concordant and well-wishing.
9   *gNyen du* / གཉེན་དུ་ – benevolent and helpful.
10 *sPyom pa* / སྤྱོམ་པ་ – chutzpah, splendour, lavishness, ebullience, or even ostentation.

I said that there'd been a guitar-playing vicar and a motorcycle-riding vicar[11] – so maybe there was a niche for me, being as I had both of these covered. Rinpoche surprised me then by saying that this was a good idea. Vajrayana was not disconnected from life. The Mahasiddhas had shown this.

"Vinapa, guitar playing like Chögyam – but different style coming. Vinapa not Blues playing." PAUSE *"Then, Camaripa, shoe and boot making."* At that point Rinpoche asked to see my boots. He examined them and nodded approval. *"Chögyam not making – but good boot wearing."* PAUSE *"You also town shoe wearing?"*

"Yes Rinpoche – I have a variety of boots and shoes at home." Rinpoche asked so I told him that I had some Grenson Oxford[12] shoes – and few pairs of western boots from America.

"O yah – good shoe and boot wearing necessary. Then when old coming – feet are also good. Anyway, Dhahulipa, rope making. Khadgapa, much stealing. Tantépa, much gambling." PAUSE *"I am thinking, Chögyam never gambling?"*

"No Rinpoche – but not on moral grounds. Some students played cards and gambled – but I always found money too hard to earn to risk losing it."

Rinpoche nodded, as if this was sensible. He commented that he'd never gambled. *"Then… Tantipa, weaving. Savaripa, hunting. Sarvabhaksa is too much always eating. Samudra, is diving and pearl finding. Pacharipa, is pastries making. Minapa, fishing."* PAUSE *"O yah. Then Manibhadra coming; she perfect joyous housewife – and this one incarnation Tibet coming. She after gZa' Druk-tsal Sheldrakma and before Rangbar Tromtsal Düd'dül Dorje. Rangbar Tromtsal Düd'dül Dorje is captain under General Shengpa in Ling Gésar army."* PAUSE *"Then, Kumbharipa, pot making. Kantalipa, tailor – but clothes from rag making."* Rinpoche laughed at this point and asked if I had ever made clothes from rags.

---

11 Reverend Bill Shergold—the 'ton-up vicar'—discovering that young motorcyclists were banned from most cafés, founded the legendary 59 Club which he set up as a church-run youth club based at Hackney Wick. 'Ton-up' refers to reaching 100 mph.
12 Grenson – shoemaker in Northamptonshire founded in 1866 by William Green. William Green died in 1901, and left the business to his son. In 1931 it was renamed as 'Grenson'. Oxford shoes have 'closed lacing' shoelace eyelet tabs that are attached under the vamp. Oxfords are plain, formal shoes, normally brown or black.

"Not exactly, Rinpoche – but I have always patched my trousers, and used fabric from older pairs. I also save all my old trousers – because one day I hope to make other clothes from them." This caused Rinpoche great amusement – and I had to explain the social custom of faded and patched jeans not being seen as a sign of poverty. There was a special kind – a make called Levi 501s which had a certain cachet to which I was not immune. That made Rinpoche laugh *"Yah – all good coming."* PAUSE *"So... Kamparipa, Blacksmith."* PAUSE *"Blacksmith in Chögyam family coming?"*

"Yes, Rinpoche. My grandfather on my father's side was a blacksmith – when he lived in Lancashire, in the North of England. His father had also been a blacksmith. When he moved south to Kent he worked in the dockyards."

"O yah – good that blacksmith in family. Tibetan 'low class' saying – but this foolish. Damçan[13] *Garwa Nagpo*[14]*, blacksmith – so much honour coming. Dorje Legpa*[15] *also – he is thousand phurba for Guru Rinpoche making."* PAUSE *"Then Goraksha, cowboy—like western film—but not boot like Chögyam wearing."* PAUSE *"I am one time in Delhi cowboy film seeing. Zangpo, Dugpo, dang Dog-nyépo."*

It took a while to work out what this film may have been – but after a little discussion it turned out to be *The Good, the Bad and the Ugly* [16]. Rinpoche had stunned me in various ways over the weeks we spent together – but this was unexpectedly unexpected. I was sitting in an ancient house in Tso Pema with almost no connection with the 20th Century, and suddenly Kyabjé Künzang Dorje Rinpoche tells me that he has seen *The Good, the Bad and the Ugly* in Delhi – albeit with someone giving him a running translation. Somehow the incongruity of this was similar to his shouting the mantric syllable *Phat* as a means of transmission. After some discussion of the film—and Rinpoche commenting that I looked like Clint Eastwood—he returned to his listing of Mahasiddhas.

---

13 *dam can* / དམ་ཅན་ – *protector.*
14 *mGar ba nag po* / མགར་བ་ནག་པོ་ – a Nyingma protector.
15 *rDo rJe legs pa* / རྡོ་རྗེ་ལེགས་པ་ / *vajra sadhu* – one of three main Nyingma protectors, who rides a goat or snow lion.
16 The Good, the Bad and the Ugly, is a 1966 Italian film (*Il buono, il brutto, il cattivo*) directed by Sergio Leone and starring Clint Eastwood as 'the Good', Lee Van Cleef as 'the Bad', and Eli Wallach as 'the Ugly'. Zangpo (*bZang po* / བཟང་པོ་) – good; dugpo (*sDug po* / སྡུག་པོ་) – bad; dog-nyépo (*mDog nyes* / མདོག་ཉེས་པོ་) – ugly.

"Then Godhuripa, birds catching. Dombi Héruka is with musician gipsy-girl, tiger riding. Dhobipa, is laundry – clothes washing. Kilakilapa, too loudly talking and always too much talking. Thaganapa, is many lies always telling and swindling. Also, many others coming – all in the world. All many things making and doing." PAUSE *"So – modern time others coming. Kyabjé Düd'jom Rinpoche many—many—books writing. Dung-sé Thrin-lé Norbu Rinpoche is unique language powerfully teaching. Trungpa Rinpoche also own style language, horse-riding, and military wearing. Then…"* he chuckled *"Mahasiddha Chögyam – he Blues singing, poetry writing, Arts painting."* Then he laughed *"and many khandro happy making."*

I decided not to dissemble. Rinpoche strongly disapproved of 'statutory humility'. It was artificial and unnecessary. It was an affectation. He said that no one needed to tell anyone that they were just a humble monk or just a humble anything. Humility was simply lack of arrogance – and that as I was not arrogant, I was obviously humble – or obviously without grandiosity. Statements of humility were an irritation as they interrupted the flow of otherwise congenial conversation – besides which, disavowing potential as a Mahasiddha was simply silly, when it was perfectly obvious that I'd only just been reprieved from being designated *a terminal 'thom yor.* Instead I made a joke about being a 'mahasiddha' deliberately bilingually misinterpreted as 'big tree' – 'maha cedar'. Fortunately, there wasn't too much to explain. Rinpoche responded *"Ya – Chögyam not so tall for 'De-wa da-ru* [17] *chen' calling – so must drüpchen becoming!"* Rinpoche went on to say that there had been many Mahasiddhas in Tibet – but that they were not viewed in the same way as the Indian Mahasiddhas. This was because Tibet deferred to India as the sacred land from which Buddhism had originated. It was his feeling however that someone, somewhere, at some time – should make a collection of hagiographies of 84 Tibetan Mahasiddhas.

"Wouldn't the gTértöns fit into that category, Rinpoche?"

"O yah. You are naming?"

Rinpoche went through a long list of gTértöns[18] – after which my hand ached from note taking, and sadly there was insufficient time to obtain all the spellings in Tibetan U-chen script.

---

17 *rDe ba da ru* / རེ་བ་དར་ – cedar.
18 *See:* appendix I – gTérma and gTértöns.

I had my Sony Walkman Professional tape recorder, so I had backup on my notes – and maybe I could play the tapes to someone who could write the names for me in U-chen. It was hard work – but I enjoyed every moment with Künzang Dorje Rinpoche. After this inundation of names of gTértöns and their texts – we stopped for refreshments. It was chang rather than Eagle Beer[19]. I far preferred chang – even though I defined it in Britain as having a flavour not entirely unlike a subtle blend of kerosene and low fat yoghurt.

Rinpoche then wanted to know whether gTérma existed in the West

"That is not easy to answer, Rinpoche. There is certainly nothing that I would describe as having come from Guru Rinpoche or Yeshé Tsogyel—or anyone with nondual realisation—but then I cannot say that I have studied any of the revelations that might resemble gTérma in terms of their discovery." PAUSE *"The only thing I can name is The Book of Mormon."*

"O yah – this name I am hearing once. Please you are telling."

"Well… I do not know much – but the Book of Mormon is a text which contains writings of ancient prophets who lived on the American continent, about the time of Shakyamuni Buddha. It was published by Joseph Smith in the early 1800s *as an account written by 'Mormon'. According to Joseph Smith the Book of Mormon was originally written in unknown characters engraved on golden plates. He said that Mormon, the last prophet to contribute to the book, buried it in Cumorah, a hill in New York State, before his death. He then appeared in a vision in* 1827 *as an angel, revealing the location of the plates and instructing Joseph Smith to translate the plates into English."*

"And what western peoples saying this book?"

---

19 Eagle beer – in the 1850s Solan-based Dyer Meakin Breweries Ltd launched India's first beer brand Golden Eagle.

"People say all kinds of things — but the least negative view is that Joseph Smith authored it, drawing, whether consciously or subconsciously, on material and ideas from his contemporary environment, rather than translating an ancient text [20]*."*

"Yah — so Chögyam thinking?"

"I hope you won't mind me saying this — but I prefer not to think anything about it. It's not my religion — so I feel I have no cause to have any opinion. I have not studied it or practised it — and I know almost nothing about it. I only know what I know because some Mormons knocked on my door one day and wanted to tell me all about it. They seemed nice people and gave me a Book of Mormon. They didn't have a good attitude toward Buddhism however — and so I had to tell them they'd be better off looking for other people to convert. I told them I'd been a Buddhist almost all my life and was not likely to change by virtue of anyone's arguments."

Rinpoche was silent and expressionless as this was being translated — but after a few moments consideration he burst out laughing and said *"Yah… kind and friendly always good — but firm remaining also good."*

He went on to say that although there was no purpose in looking at every religion — it could be valuable to know something about the ways in which other people thought. He told me that it was not good to argue against those of other religions — but because I would teach in the West, I would need to know something about Christian thought. He explained that it would often influence the way in which people interpreted what I taught. People tended to understand through comparison, and that if *this* looked like *that* — it was surely the same. In this way, he explained, many people confused Buddhism and Hinduism. Kyabjé Düd'jom Rinpoche had told him this.

---

20 The Book of Mormon presents subjects such as the fall of Adam and Eve, the nature of the atonement, eschatology, priesthood authority, redemption from physical and spiritual death, the nature of baptism and communion, personal revelation, economic justice, the nature of God and the angels. The pivotal event of the book is the appearance of Jesus in America closely after his resurrection. The Book of Mormon is said to fulfil numerous biblical prophecies by ending apostasy and signalling a restoration of Christianity. It provides a critique of western society, which condemns immorality, individualism, social inequality, ethnic injustice, and nationalism. The English text emulates the King James Version of the Bible — and its grammar and word choice reflect Early Modern English.

There were apparently quite a few western people who had the Hindu view of karma. They thought they were Buddhists – but believed in karma as merely a form of predestination. They failed to see that dissolution of the cause removed the effect. There was only cause and effect as long as the cause was not experienced as empty.

"If effect always coming then realisation not possible. If realisation possible from this view then realisation for cause coming. If realisation from cause coming, then realisation duality remaining."

This was why I loved Vajrayana. It was so entirely comprehensible. If effect inevitably and unavoidably followed cause – it created a closed loop. The effect would simply create another cause which would give rise to another effect. There would be no way out of the closed loop. The way out, of course, was that the patterning of karma was merely an overlay which obscured the beginningless nondual state. If one realised the nondual state, then the patterning of karma vanished in the same instant.

11

many corpses

Künzang Dorje Rinpoche spoke at length about the right frame of mind for hearing the stories of Drukpa Künlegs. *"Must both laughter and devotion same time coming – or no understanding."*

He said that there were western people in particular who were unable to experience laughter and devotion at the same time. There were some puritanical students who found the stories upsetting – and some 'nonsense students' who found them exciting because they merely enjoyed breaking rules or being iconoclastic. *"Both type – only 'thom yor."*

That there had to be *both laughter and devotion or there'd be no real understanding* was an entirely astonishing statement – or rather, it was astonishing to me. It hit me as transmission – because the words ignited a state of awareness. I sat there speechless for some moments – and in those moments I understood the nature of transmission and the nature of everything which Künzang Dorje Rinpoche had ever communicated. It was not simply the words – but the words had been a vehicle through which volumes of teaching coalesced as a seamless expanse of understanding. Rinpoche smiled at me – and filled my glass with chang.

Rinpoche then began another account *"Drukpa Künlegs, is one monastic academy visiting. Every monk, chang having…"*

So, as he had no desire to become a drunken sot, he decided to move on and remain alone. He hadn't walked for more than a day before he found another such academy – where he found the monks quibbling about minute doctrinal differences. Rather than clutter his mind with useless pedantry he took to the road again. At least on the open road no one would ask him whether he believed the road was there or not. Proceeding further, he came to a large town and in that town there was a most prestigious academy. Every other monk however, was pining for a boyfriend – so being unwilling to risk his buttocks, he took to the road again. Drukpa Künlegs decided he'd had enough of monastic academies and thought it preferable to visit hermits – but in every hermitage he visited, the gomchen was keen to find a wife.

So, as he had no desire to become a householder husband with a herd of howling children, he decided that hermitages were no place for someone of his temperament. Next on the list was a place where gar'cham was the order of the day – and the monks were all keen to outperform each other with regard to who was the best 'cham dancer. He watched them twirl and gyrate. He watched them in their efforts to leap and remain on one leg for long periods of time – and thought *'This is all well and good – but walking in the mountains is all the exercise I need.'*

So, he walked into the mountains for some days and eventually came to a charnel ground in a remote and deserted place. He encountered several sorcerers, evidently keen to become powerful by invoking demons – but having no desire to make pacts with duplicitous denizens of the indeterminate dimensions, he passed them by.

"Some western peoples this desire having." Rinpoche snorted. *"They ugly-mind 'thom yors. Also, some too ugly faces also having. Maybe no girlfriend finding and this why they mThu-gyé jèd* [1] *making. You are western peoples like this knowing?"*

"Yes, Rinpoche. I've met a few."

"É hong! [2] *Not near these people staying."*

"Rinpoche" I began tentatively *"How do you know they're ugly? Have you met such people?"*

"O yah – but not speaking to these peoples. One is Ngakpa Yeshé Dorje visiting. Other is Kathmandu sometimes staying. Big beard having. Not like Chögyam beard. Deceitful eyes having – middle part too small. Eyes not direct looking. Eyes narrow. Possible drug using." PAUSE *"This one Ngakpa Yeshé Dorje visiting – you are knowing?"*

"Yes, Rinpoche – I think so, although he might not be the same person."

"What name?"

"… Gilbert Harris…" I replied, feeling a little uneasy about naming names.

---

1   *mThu rGyas byed* / མཐུ་རྒྱས་བྱེད་ – performing black magic.
2   *e hong* / ཨེ་ཧོང་ – an expression of disgust.

"Yah—yah—yah… this name – this name, I am hearing one time. I am also Gilbert Harris photograph with Ngakpa Yeshé Dorje seeing. Gilbert Harris much broken vows. Much lying. Much bad action. Much ugly face from arrogance coming."

This was somewhat shocking. Rinpoche noticed my expression and said *"Yah… ugly-mind, ugly speech, ugly face 'thom yor – but Künzang Dorje, can nothing doing. Chögyam, can nothing doing. "Not helping possible – only in practice remembering. Künzang Dorje many 'thom yor in practice remembering. Many 'thom yor – too many 'thom yor."*

He went on to say that this song of Drukpa Künlegs—and he couldn't remember it all—enumerated all the places of practice and styles of practitioner which one could find in Tibet and Bhutan. Drukpa Künlegs found fault with them all – but that was not to say that there were not good places and good practitioners. These songs were for Himalayan audiences – and it was important for them to know that outer display didn't always betoken anything of value beneath the surface. Himalayan people were too easily taken in by appearances. He asked whether western people were generally more suspicious.

"Yes, Rinpoche. Many western people are more suspicious, or perhaps cynical – but they're not mainly the ones who study with Lamas."

"Yah—yah—yah…" Rinpoche laughed *"This song of Drukpa Künlegs, they must reading!"*

> *If you have no authentic relationship with a Lama*
> *– what's the use of your massive intellect?*
> *If you fail to realise reality within the nature of Mind*
> *– what other reality do you expect to find?*
> *If you fail to see the essence*
> *– what's the use of adhering to religious laws?*
>
> *If you can't intuitively comprehend nonduality*
> *– what's there to be gained from doctrinal research?*
> *If you're unable to love others as your children*
> *– what's the use of prayers and rituals?*
> *If you're ignorant of the central point of your vows*
> *– what's lost by breaking each in turn?*

> *If you're estranged from awareness*
> *— what's there to be gained from subduing thought?*
> *If you can't regulate your life in terms of the seasons and times of the day*
> *— what are you but a 'thom yor?*
> *If you waste your life, living on borrowed money, time, and energy*
> *— who'll repay your debts?*
>
> *If you opt for asceticism and inadequate clothing*
> *— what's to be gained but imitating the cold hells?*
> *Striving without instruction, is like an insect climbing a sand hill,*
> *accomplishing nothing.*
> *Gathering instructions but ignoring the nature of mind*
> *— means you'll starve, next to the food cupboard.*
>
> *Lamas who refuse to teach or write*
> *— are as useless as the jewel in the head of a snake;*
> *Ignorant 'thom yors prattle constantly*
> *— proclaim their ignorance to anyone who will listen.*
> *Those who understand the essence of the teaching*
> *— they are the ones who actually practise it.*

Rinpoche concluded and looked at me in the way I recognised. He wanted me to ask something or say something.

"So, Rinpoche" I asked *"the first line makes me wonder about the nature of 'authentic relationship' with the Lama. In terms of western people being drawn to thu-tèd* [3] *— it seems that unless they had thu-wo* [4] *as their Lamas; they would lack authentic relationship."*

"O yah—good—now principle and function seeing." PAUSE *"... but, Thu-tèd anyway too stupid."* PAUSE *"So, other lines something saying?"*

"Yes, Rinpoche — adhering to laws when failing to see the essence. The laws would just be laws rather than guidance. They would be form disconnected from emptiness."

Rinpoche gestured for me to continue.

---

3   *mThu gTad* / མཐུ་གཏད་ – power, strength, force. black magic, casting spells.
4   *mThu bo* / མཐུ་བོ་ – wizard, witch, magician, sorcerer, necromancer.

"Then there are prayers and rituals being useless if one is unable to love others as one's children." PAUSE "That one is difficult for me because I don't actually like everyone. I'd like to like everyone—and I try to like everyone—but the 'trying' doesn't remove the sensation of dislike. It's not a strong dislike and I don't invest in it – but the trace of dislike remains. I try to keep in mind that these people are beginglessly realised. I try to keep in mind that I can't be likeable to everyone either. I try to keep in mind that the unlikeable characteristics of others are based on their circumstances and previous painful experience – but… loving them as if they were my children is beyond my capacity."

Rinpoche had sat listening to this banal confession in silence. His face was expressionless. It was impossible to tell whether his expressionlessness betokened disapprobation or simply concentration. Suddenly he burst out laughing *"O yah. When children bad behaving – then must be punishing! Punishing – but still loving. 'Punishing' not meaning 'not loving'. When punishing needing – then must be punishing. When Chögyam first arriving – he like 'thom yor speaking. Then Künzang Dorje must be shouting. Künzang Dorje shouting – not meaning 'Künzang Dorje, Chögyam not loving'. Künzang Dorje too much, Chögyam loving."* PAUSE *"So, same with Thu-wo 'thom yors."*

Künzang Dorje Rinpoche's realised-pragmatism always hit me sideways. He explained that as I had no investment in my dislike – it was not lack of love. It was merely seeing people as they were. Naturally I would help such people if I could *"Yes."* Naturally I would be of benefit to such people if I could *"Yes."* Naturally I would speak in a kindly way to such people *"Yes."*

"Then!" Rinpoche laughed *"No problem coming – Chögyam much loving."* PAUSE *"Yah – anyway… Lama Tsé-wang* [5] *, Drukpa Künlegs asking – and so new house consecrating."*

He wanted whatever 'auspicious invocation' would cause good fortune – so Drukpa Künlegs began:

"As the door's as solid as a mountain – your house will be bestowed with endurance. As bows and arrows are hanging on the pillar – your house will be bestowed with wealth. As the ceiling beams are straight – your house will be bestowed with righteous accommodation. As its roof is slated – your house will be bestowed with benevolent security. May your house endure to entertain many inhabitants and many corpses."

---

5   bLa ma tshe dbang / བླ་མ་ཚེ་དབང་.

"A kha kha!" Lama Tsé-wang exclaimed in lamentation *"Please don't make this last wish!"*

Drukpa Künlegs shrugged *"Fine by me"* he replied. He then changed the final line of his benediction.

"May your house endure – but may it never entertain a corpse."

This amendment suited Lama Tsé-wang perfectly, but his family line was broken and today the house stands empty and ruined – a khang ral-zhig[6].

Künzang Dorje Rinpoche smiled. He took a sip of beer and said *"One day when you tsam khang having – I many corpses wishing. Many, many—many—corpses."* By this he meant that he hoped that many people would come to study and practice when I established a retreat centre[7]. Many people eventually become many corpses.

Drukpa Künlegs, decided to confront the Rong-thong kLu,[8] subdue her – and bind her, to be a Guardian of Vajrayana. As he descended to the river—on the Punakha trail—the kLu saw him coming, and assumed her most terrible appearance – hovering in a dazzling mist of spray from the torrent.

She sang him this song: *"Come here and listen to me! This celebrated Ti-sé white peak*[9] *and Chang Thang realm of wind. What are they but inhospitable snowbound escarpments of rock? Is that so damn marvellous? This celebrated white snow lion with white fur and turquoise mane, who roars ineffectually in the valleys. Is that so damn marvellous? This celebrated Drukpa Künlegs – impoverished mendicant who talks nonsense and tells obscene jokes. Is he so damn marvellous? Don't expect homage from me! If you have realisation – answer me, or go away!"*

"Listen here you lamentable kLu" Drukpa Künlegs replied *"don't imagine that attempting to scorn me is interesting to anyone, anytime, anywhere. I come here today, in answer to a request – so keep your thoughts to yourself and pay attention."*

---

6   *khang ral zhig* / ཁང་རལ་ཞིག / – ruined house.
7   A Nyingma gö kar chang lo Retreat Centre was finally established in 2019 – *Drala Jong*, Aro gTér Nyingma Vajrayana Retreat Centre, Pant-y-Porthman, Banc-y-Ffordd, Llandysul, Carmarthenshire, Wales.
8   *kLu* / ཀླུ / *naga* – extra-dimensional serpent entity. Rong-thong (rong thongs / རོང་ཐོངས་) – 'abandoned gorge', a place in Bhutan.
9   Gang-kar ti-sé (*gangs dKar ti se* / གངས་དཀར་ཏི་སེ་) – White Glacier, Mount Kailash.

Drukpa Künlegs fixed her eyes and continued *"On the celebrated white peak of Ti-sé, 500 siddhas reside serenely. Khandros ride upon great white snow lions. As the universe naturally respects this innately famous Drukpa Künlegs—although he be an indigent, impecunious, penurious, itinerant peripatetic—he has no complaints. He's turned his back on avarice, aggression, obsession, paranoia, and oblivious torpor – so he's free to say whatever enters his mind. He never has to work – because he's content to hang loose, so whatever occurs becomes the means of liberation. So, Rong-thong kLu – be content with being a protectress! You spawn of the eight classes – why not choose to be a consort who's worthy, charming, and attractive. Follow me and hold to the path of blissful freedom. Why, you could attain liberation in one life. Now, answer me genuinely."*

On hearing this the kLu immediately assumed the form of a beautiful lady – and brought Drukpa Künlegs chang in a vast crystal receptacle; singing this song: *"Hear me, Duty-Free* [10] *Drukpa Künlegs—dignified in descent —empowered in actuality—with a heart of a hero! You carry the bow and arrow of experience and insight. You bear the shield and armour of patience and tolerance. You lead the dog which destroys sorcery. You who have the power of a universal emperor, so I request you to lead me to blissful freedom. I shall be a spatial jewel. Above my waist I am entrancing – and below my waist is the dKyil'khor of ecstasy. My muscles are strong and I am possessed of sexual expertise that would delight Drukpa Künlegs. "I am a kLu with fervent lust – so our meeting augers joy. Please stay here with me tonight and I'll offer the requisite devotion."*

She took Drukpa Künlegs to her dwelling—provided him with chang— and promised to serve Vajrayana and never harm anyone again. On receiving this promise Drukpa Künlegs entered into ka-jor with the kLu and through this means she attained liberation.

Künzang Dorje Rinpoche explained that this account—and many of the others—described the dimension of vision. The narratives wove in and out of vision, and it was not always possible to define which was which. He said that Drukpa Künlegs had existed in the world – but that aspects of his life existed in the visionary realm. The main point was to hear the stories without engaging in speculation, conjecture, or supposition. There was no need to divide what happened in the ordinary world from what happened in terms of visionary experience.

---

10 Chatral (*bya bral* / བྱ་བྲལ་) – free of duties or occupations; effortlessness – free of any deliberate actions; free of anything that has to be done.

He said that when I got home to England and told stories of my time in the Himalayas – they would be suffused with the colours of my experience – and therefore they would have a certain visionary aspect for others. There may not be accounts of sexual exploits with kLu – but there would be material that would be equally otherworldly for many people. History was composed of what happened and what was sensed – what was ordinary and what was extraordinary. The important factor to bear in mind about history—in the Vajrayana sense—was its subtle function in terms of perception. Drukpa Künlegs was thus a catalyst. He was a figure who became an active ingredient in the lives of those who imbibed his lore.

"Rinpoche" I began somewhat tentatively *"the Rong-thong kLu story seems to be quite simple – in terms of being an exchange of statements. The Rong-thong kLu makes her disparaging statement and Drukpa Künlegs answers her – and that ends the confrontation."*

Rinpoche grinned and explained that some situations were obvious. People—or entities—who considered themselves powerful were almost invariably inclined to test their power against others. This was because they fundamentally lacked confidence in their own power. If one actually had power, one would not need to test it. If one's power was only there for the benefit of others – then the fact that others had greater power would have no relevance. Drukpa Künlegs had nothing to prove and so his answers were playful. The Rong-thong kLu knew from Drukpa Künleg's style of answer that she was entirely unequipped in the presence of Drukpa Künlegs. The power differential was overwhelmingly apparent.

"O yah – now lunch must be eating. Today many mo-mos."

Künzang Dorje Rinpoche gazed out of the window for some moments.

"Yah so… Early in morning, Drukpa Künlegs across the valley from Künzang Ling to Khyung Sé-kha, gazing. There he Gyal'dzom seeing."

Gyal'dzom was dancing merrily under a tree, and he sang a song for her.

> "*Looking out from Shar Künzang Ling I see Khandro Khyung Sé-kha swinging and swaying like the lha* [11]. *She must be the lady Gyal'dzom for whom I have sought! Today when the sun reaches its zenith I will visit you – so fill a yak horn with chang, and we'll tell stories and make love.*"

Drukpa Künlegs crossed the valley and arrived at Gyal'dzom's door. She was just setting out to draw water – so she invited him to take his ease and await her return. "*You have no need of drawing water Gyal'dzom la*" Drukpa Künlegs exclaimed with a beaming smile. "*We shall cause it to rise from your own spring!*" Gyal'dzom took his meaning immediately and they made love on the doorstep.

She served him ara[12] and chang – and then sang to him as follows:

> "*Drukpa Künlegs of Tibet! Not only are you handsome and regal – but you spread astonishing benefit. In the rising spring breeze, which is so delightfully cooling, there is no substance to be found. In the plummeting Tsangpo there is no obstruction.*"

> "*Gyal'dzom gZa' of Khyung Sé-kha. Not only are you voluptuous and charming – but you also have a magnificent pelvic thrust. So, let me ask you this – if there is no substance in the ascending spring breeze, on what do vultures glide? If there is no obstruction to the cascading Tsangpo, what of the boulders of the mountains? Then you may well wonder—if the mind of Drukpa Künlegs contains no fantasy—what is Gyal'dzom gZa'?*"

He then made as if to leave – but Gyal'dzom gZa' detained him, saying "*But you must surely take some nourishment before you leave here. I have cooked no meat this evening – but I have eggs I can cook for you.*"

"*Yah-yah-yah…*" Drukpa Künlegs yawned "*I would rather eat chicken than their eggs.*"

Suddenly a chicken appeared at the window—squawked loudly—and fell dead on the floor. Gyal'dzom gZa' immediately prepared and cooked the bird – serving it with fresh vegetables from her garden.

---

11 *lha* / ཬ — extra-dimensional beings.
12 *a rag* / ཨ་རག — spirit liquor made from barley or other grains.

When Drukpa Künlegs had finished eating he clicked his fingers over the chicken bones and commanded that they animate themselves. *"Arise glorious fowl!"* The chicken instantly reassembled itself as a living creature and flew back through the window from which it had previously emerged. *"Now that's the right way to eat a chicken!"* he laughed.

She then besought him to stay with her forever and Drukpa Künlegs replied *"Since your secret lotus is comfortably tight, I'll return for a further nine days. Because you're a postural artist, I'll return for another nine days. Because you're good-hearted and kind, I'll return for yet another nine days."* Having made this promise, he departed.

He returned for nine days three times and on each occasion, he gave Gyal'dzom gZa' religious instruction. After each visit Drukpa Künlegs made to her home, she went into retreat for 21 days – but after the third he instructed her to find a retreat cave and remain in practice until she had gained realisation. She did as she had been instructed and within three months, she had attained full realisation.

"So, miracle chicken – what saying?"

"Well, the miracle of the chicken is something on which I cannot comment – other than saying that it seems to be symbolic of Drukpa Künlegs' natural conjuring with the situation."

"What story in Bristol coming with lady and Drukpa Chögyam?"

"I suppose that if this were to happen in Bristol, the lady might say 'I've not been to the shops for groceries – so I can only make you a snack.' Then I'd reply 'That's easily remedied – I'll just telephone the local Tibetan restaurant, order a Chicken Tsecho and two large servings of fried beef mo-mos, and pay by credit card.'…"

Kyabjé Künzang Dorje Rinpoche smiled very slightly *"And then saying"* by which I understood that he wanted me to comment on the difference.

"Well, if that story was told in Drukpa Künlegs' time – it would be equally as miraculous as resurrecting a chicken that had just been eaten."

Kyabjé Künzang Dorje Rinpoche was silent for some moments *"Good answer – but better answer coming."* Another few silent moments. *"Now"* he began – but without the sense of threat that used to accompany such questioning *"Carefully looking."* PAUSE *"Until perfect answer finding – silent remaining."*

many corpses

I sat and looked at the question. What was the difference. The difference in one sense was obvious – one was a supernormal miracle and the other was a seeming miracle of the modern western world. The perfect answer —I knew—would involve principle and function. The point of everything lay in the result. I had the answer before I had the answer – because I didn't see the answer as an answer when it appeared. The answer was that the end result of both scenarios was the same: a meal was provided.

"From the perspective of result, there is no difference between the stories – because the outcome is the same: a meal is provided."

"O yah!" Rinpoche roared – but with pleasure. *"Chögyam perfect answer finding – not always perfect answer finding. Always principle and function remembering. Always fruition thinking. Always base, path, and fruit thinking. Then answer always perfect."*

Künzang Dorje Rinpoche smiled after a pause in which we sipped chang *"Yah. so… afterwards she him chang serving."* Drukpa Kunlegs and Gyal'dzom gZa' laughed and discoursed until it was time for him to take his leave. *"Why not stay here?"* she enquired with enthusiasm *"You would be more than welcome."*

Drukpa Künlegs sighed *"Kyé ma… I cannot stay. I must be going."*

Gyal'dzom heard these words – but clearly had other ideas. She promptly filled a jug of chang and pursued him along the track. At the crest of the first hill Drukpa Künlegs sat down and asked Gyal'dzom the name of the surrounding countryside. *"This place is called Pang-yul*[13] *and the hills are called Log-thang Kya-mo."*

"Well, this Pang[14] *is profound and auspicious – and as this arid land needs feeding you'd better pour out the chang."* They sat together—partook of the chang— and as they were thus engaged Drukpa Künlegs said *"You Eastern ladies are famous singers, are you not?"* to which Gyal'dzom replied that she could not deny it. *"Then sing me a song, if you please."* So Gyal'dzom sang.

---

13 *pang yul* / པང་ཡུལ་.
14 *pang* / པང་ – bosom.

> "O Wandering Drukpa Künlegs, Listen to the song of Gyal'dzom.
> The meadows in the mountains become white in Winter – but Drukpa Künlegs is whiter in his happiness. Alpine meadows change from white to green and back again – but Drukpa Künlegs remains always white with joy. Sharp-eyed vultures soaring high have no dominion over tempests of karmic winds – so they must obey the storm. This Gyal'dzom of Khyung Sé-kha, is incapable of governing future events – and must thus await your return alone. Gyal'dzom eventually found her sangyab [15] – but now he has to leave and this evanescent encounter leaves me lonely."

Drukpa Künlegs then sang in the way of a reply.

> "O beauteous radiant perspicacious Gyal'dzom. The grass in the valleys is lush – but not as lush as the many qualities of Gyal'dzom. The valley grass changes with the seasons – but Gyal'dzom remains rutilant with expectation of my return. Vultures glide high above mundane concerns – as does Drukpa Künlegs. This wandering Drukpa Künlegs must go where he goes. He must go irrespective of the mountain ranges over which he glides – to return to Gyal'dzom at the perfect juncture."

Having sung their songs, they parted – Gyal'dzom entered retreat and within three months, gained realisation.

Künzang Dorje Rinpoche had an expression that betokened curiosity *"What Chögyam, Drukpa Künlegs language style thinking?"*

"It's not how we speak in the West Rinpoche – but that's only in the present time. When I read books which were written a hundred years ago—or much older books—people had something far closer to this way of speaking."

Rinpoche nodded and motioned for me to continue.

"People used to compose their speech as they spoke – and prided themselves on their fluency and ability to use simile, metaphor, and quotations from poetry and other great works of literature." PAUSE *"This has even changed since I was at school. We were expected to know a great deal of poetry by heart – so that we could quote in examinations.*

---

15 gSang yab / གསང་ཡབ་ – literally 'secret father' – but meaning *consort, religious husband.*

many corpses

"This seemed to act as an encouragement to do the same with Rock Music lyrics – and almost everyone would use such quotations in their everyday speech. Now it seems to have died out and the standard of literacy has dropped to a noticeable degree."

"Then Drukpa Künlegs not easy understanding."

"No Rinpoche – I think that most people would find it difficult to understand his allusions."

"Yah…" Rinpoche sighed *"Maybe Chögyam 'simple writing' possible?"*

"I can certainly try Rinpoche. I can shorten the sentences, which would make it easier for people."

"Yah, good." PAUSE *"More saying?"*

"Well yes – I would say that Drukpa Künlegs' puns would be understood and appreciated."

"Chögyam pun[16] making?"

"Certainly Rinpoche." I felt like saying *'Pun is my middle name'* but it would have been funny and it would have taken far too long to explain what was even slightly amusing about it. *"I make puns quite often."*

"All peoples enjoying?"

"Not everyone, Rinpoche. Some people say they don't enjoy them."

"Why this saying?"

"I really don't know Rinpoche… It always seems better to me to have more causes for laughter rather than fewer causes – and I feel that if a pun is clever and arises spontaneously in conversation, it really should cause laughter to anyone with a sense of humour."

"O yah – some people no sense of humour having. These people realisation too difficult. These people never realisation accomplishing. Humour very—very—important. Laughing must possible. Always laughing must possible." PAUSE *"Laughing not possible then Drukpa Künlegs never understanding."* PAUSE *"Anyway, songs singing and then parting. Then Gyal'dzom retreat going and liberation attaining."*

---

16 *Pun* – *tsig gyag* (*tshig rGyag* / ཚིག་རྒྱག་).

12

chaotic humour

The light streamed through the windows of the wonderful room at the Nyingma gompa. The light rays animated the colours of the room – and they radiated as intensely as unprecedentedly heavy silk-velvet. The greens and reds were impossibly deep yet light and spacious. What more could one want than colour when one arose from sleep. I sang the 'A' and the note continued for a surprising length of time. I wondered when my breath would finally fail – but it seemed all the air on the planet was in my lungs. And then it ended. It ended naturally without making effort to protract the note further. I arose, washed and dressed, and went straight to see Künzang Dorje Rinpoche as arranged. It was nearing the end of my time in Tso Pema and he wanted me to come and eat breakfast with him every morning.

I arrived and the smell of freshly baked paleb was evident even before the door opened. Rinpoche welcomed me with a great beaming smile and not long after I had taken my seat, breakfast arrived. Somehow Rinpoche had obtained coffee. He knew I liked coffee and had obviously procured some – probably from Mandi, through the auspices of one of the Nyingma monks who went there occasionally. I expressed great appreciation – but Rinpoche gave me a certain grin. He knew that the coffee was terrible – but instead of reprimanding me for being a mealymouthed fawner, he simply said *"Yah… not like Chögyam best 'tshig ja*[1]*."*

"No, Rinpoche, it's not – but I haven't had good coffee ground from real beans for so long that this is really quite enjoyable especially on a cold morning."

Then Rinpoche laughed *"O yah 'tshig ja 'burnt tea' meaning."*

"That's quite a good definition for this Rinpoche – but my appreciation is more for your kindness in obtaining it for me."

Then we both laughed for a while about 'burnt tea' – and progressed onto Drukpa Künlegs and his proclivity for word play.

---

1   *'tshig ja* / འཚིག་ཇ་

Goodbye Forever

"Drukpa Künlegs head of Jela'i La pass reaching…"

Whilst he was wondering whether he should descend through Mang Dewa to Khyen Yül, he encountered an aged man with a heavy load. *"What've you got in that large bag?"* he enquired.

"Barley is what I carry in my bag, venerable sir" the old man replied – and Drukpa Künlegs thought *'Mmmm… there's no prophecy concerning my coming to this place'* and so he asked *"what villages would I find if I were to wander down into that valley?"*

The old man rubbed his nose in thought and replied *"Well, first there's Ru-khu'ching, then Jang dang'ching and also Tang-sé'ching."*

"É hong." Drukpa Künlegs wrinkled his nose *"I shan't go down into the valley of triple urination. Thank you for the warning, old fellow."*

Künzang Dorje Rinpoche grinned and asked *"Why you thinking Drukpa Künlegs joke making – and decision, this way making?"*

That was an imponderable question *"There is obviously some joke here – but I do not understand it."*

"O yah – there is joke in speech contained. Each village 'ching ending – and 'ching like gCin sounding. 'ching is 'bound' or 'contained' meaning – and gCin is urine meaning."

"Ah…" I replied as if I'd understood something. Then I pondered. Künzang Dorje Rinpoche gazed at me – but without impatience. An idea emerged. *"It occurs to me Rinpoche – that, first, Drukpa Künlegs recalls that there's no prophecy concerning his coming to this place. So … this means he needs some reason either to go down into the valley, or avoid it. He maybe needs a reason because there are more than a thousand such valleys – and he cannot visit them all."*

Künzang Dorje Rinpoche nodded *"More coming?"*

"Yes… then, it strikes me that humour is—or can be—symbolic. It can be based on coincidence or accident—or the confluence of improbable phenomena—such as you hearing the music of Jimi Hendrix in Delhi. That made me laugh – but not because it was 'funny'… it was because it was delightfully unlikely. Thinking of you and Jimi Hendrix in the same context was outside my conceptual structures."

"O yah. So…" Rinpoche prompted.

"So – Drukpa Künlegs chooses not to go into the valley as a whimsy. The choice had to be based on something; so he chose humour as his reasoning – because humour is a chaotic element, like the play of emptiness and form which reflects nonduality."

Rinpoche gazed at me. First, he was expressionless – then, slowly, a smile emerged. *"Chögyam subtle analysis making."* Then he laughed and slapped his thighs repeatedly *"Yag po dug—yag po dug—yag po dug!"* Rinpoche spoke then of humour and the importance of humour in teaching. Humour was often linked with sudden understanding. He said that every good Lama made jokes and found humour in situations. The fact that we were both beginninglessly realised and fettered by duality – was funny. The more one realised the patterns of duality the funnier the situation became in terms of one's experience. There was also sadness when observing those who created their own suffering without any understanding of what they were doing. He said that it could be like watching someone hitting their toes with a hammer whilst screaming *"Will this pain never end?"*

Rinpoche returned to his account of Drukpa Künlegs.

Drukpa Künlegs journeyed on to Gyeng Ling Nyi-shar in Wangdü. There he drank chang with the local ladies – and sang them songs of realisation. One of the ladies—Sharmo Künzang—served him her best chang and sang for him:

> *"Kyé ma – please listen to my song of woe. Drukpa Künlegs, I have come to resemble a wooden doorstep fixed in place by stout door-posts. I am trampled alike by dogs and pigs. Drukpa Künlegs, please do not leave me here in this horrid hovel – but rather, please take me to the Lhakhang in Ra-lung, Upper Tsang in order that I may attain liberation.*
>
> *"Drukpa Künlegs – I have come to resemble hammered iron on the anvil of a blacksmith. I am gripped by tongs and pincers and unable to escape the hammer. Drukpa Künlegs, please don't leave me here – but rather take me to the Lhakhang in Ra-lung, Upper Tsang so I may attain liberation.*
>
> *"Drukpa Künlegs, I am miserable because I love my parents – and so, I feel obliged to stay here where my imbecilic, ineffectual, impotent husband makes life utterly frustrating, exasperating, and wearisome.*

"Drukpa Künlegs, please don't leave me here – but rather take me to the Lhakhang in Ra-lung, Upper Tsang so I may attain liberation."

"Traversing the sky from east to west, the sun illuminates the four continents" Drukpa Künlegs replied "so why should this wandering yogi need companions on his travels?"

Sharmo Künzang had no answer – so Drukpa Künlegs continued "Then consider this. The most fortunate tree is able to grow tall in the inaccessible southern jungles, where callous woodmen cannot hack it with their axes. Isn't it better to be a spreading tree than a temple door-post? Isn't it better to be a rock on the mountain than a cellar door-step made of stone?"

Sharmo Künzang had no answer – so Drukpa Künlegs continued "Yah-yah-yah – so consider this." Drukpa Künlegs laughed "The most fortunate iron finds the anvil of the blacksmith – but is it not better to be a staff or a begging bowl than a temple door. You need not sweat on the blacksmith's anvil when wood and stone can replace the blacksmith's iron. You are fortunate. You need not bear the weight of that lumbering ox of a husband – and rather, become my lover, find a meditation cave. Let your sister-in-law replace you as your parents' servant."

Inspired by Drukpa Künlegs' words, she committed to doing as he had advised. She entered into ka-jor and received instruction in meditation. She then made the ascent to Paro Chum-phuk and stayed there for three years – after which she attained 'ja'lü.

At sunset in Jé-nang Wa-ché, Drukpa Künlegs was looking for a place to spend the night, when he met the Go-kyé dPal-mo at a spring and asked "Would you be so kind as to give me lodging for the night?"

But Go-kyé dPal-mo was offended "Drukpa Künlegs you lecherous dog! You won't find anyone who'll give you accommodation. You demand hospitality, employ obscene language, and make libidinous advances on the womenfolk – I therefore have no accommodation for you."

"What about chang then?"

"There is no chang."

"Never mind the lack of chang – what say you to conjoining with me?"

"I can give you tea if you like – but then you'll have to take your leave."

They went inside. Go-kyé dPal-mo served him tea and Drukpa Künlegs proffered these verses of benediction. *"Listen"* he began *"From the fontanel of a frog, the red syllable Om emerges and vanishes into the western sky. Many people have observed this miracle – and that frog can still be seen preserved in the wall of the temple that was built there."*

"What does this mean?" Go-kyé dPal-mo asked. *"I do not understand this."*

"Yah-yah-yah" replied Drukpa Künlegs *"I see the way of it. Maybe listen to this instead. People say Drukpa Künlegs is insane – but with insanity all sensory forms become the way of realisation. People say that Drukpa Künlegs has a prodigious dorje – but his long schlong brings joy to the hearts of young ladies. People say that Drukpa Künlegs is an avid fornicator – but copulation occasions a host of fine children. People say that Drukpa Künlegs has an amazingly tight anal sphincter – but a resolute rectum precludes being buggered by duality. People say that Drukpa Künlegs has bright red veins – but red veins gather a cloud of khandros. People say that Drukpa Künlegs does little other than blather – but this raconteur has abandoned the customary places of peregrination. People say that Drukpa Künlegs is surpassingly handsome – but his attractiveness endears him to the hearts of the ladies from Mön. People say that Drukpa Künlegs is fully realised – well yes, of course, because awareness grows through subjection of inimical indifference to phenomena."*

"O yah!" Künzang Dorje Rinpoche smiled *"Then Go-kyé dPal-mo filled with joy and certainty becoming. Then Drukpa Künlegs singing:"*

> *"Some prefer the blissful space of the Dewachen – some men prefer the wealth of the nether regions. Good luck to lha and kLu!*
> *Some enjoy the pleasure of virtue – some enjoy the wealth of royalty. Good luck to cheerful drüpthobs and despondent aristocrats!*
> *Go-kyé dPal-mo likes her house – Drukpa Künlegs likes vaginas. Good luck to lover of houses and the lover of vaginas.*
> *Go-kyé dPal-mo likes tea – Drukpa Künlegs likes chang. Good luck to the drinker of tea and the imbiber of chang.*
> *Go-kyé dPal-mo's husband enjoys playing dice and losing – Drukpa Künlegs enjoys singing songs. Good luck to gambling loser and successful singer.*
> *Sodomitic monks are happy inside young boys – Drukpa Künlegs is happy inside his hostess. Good luck to young boys who can avoid being buggered and to Drukpa Künlegs who has no desire for it.*

> *Young men of heroic strength drink good chang and wear fine clothes. Good luck to youthful exuberance.*
>
> *Girls of great beauty and wisdom dress in silks and enjoy sex. Good luck to the exuberance of women.*
>
> *The meaning of the Lama's teaching, is in the student's ears – and in the path that is practised. Good luck to Lamas and students."*

Kyabjé Künzang Dorje Rinpoche looked at me in the way I recognised as 'expectation'. He wanted me to comment *"There are some interesting references here. The way Drukpa Künlegs says 'Some men prefer the blissful space of the Dewachen – other men prefer the wealth of the nether regions.' But he doesn't continue as he does later by wishing good luck to the pious and the debauched. He says 'Good luck to lha and kLu!' – and this seems to elevate the proclivities and make them equal."*

"O yah – and more coming?"

"Only that he echoes this first wishing of good luck to the young heroes in fine clothes who drink good chang – and the girls of great beauty and wisdom who dress in silk and enjoy sex." PAUSE *"I think that some people would think this was sung to be shocking. What I see however, is an expression of Vajrayana in terms of our fundamental nondual realisation – and how it can be seen in the vividness of everyday life. It seems to be a reflection of generosity, munificence, liberality, bounteousness, and benevolence."* It took a while to translate all these words and distinguish them from each other. It tuned out that there were fewer different words in Tibetan[2].

Künzang Dorje Rinpoche, thinking of generosity, then told a final story of Drukpa Künlegs. *"O yah – generosity important. In Drakwok Nang—in regions of Pungthang—Drukpa Künlegs with Apa Tashi and Ama Nanga Lhamo staying."*

Tashi and Ama Nanga Lhamo were very happy indeed to have Drukpa Künlegs in their home.

---

2   Chog-jin (*mChog sByin* / མཆོག་སྦྱིན་ / *varada*) – perfect generosity. Tong-phöd (*gTong phod* / གཏོང་ཕོད་) – magnanimity. Du-ngö zhi (*bsDu dNgos bZhi* / བསྡུ་དངོས་བཞི་) – the four modes of magnetising in the four attractive aspects of a changchub sem-dPa': jinpa (*sByin pa* / སྦྱིན་པ་) – liberality; nyènpa mrawa (*sNyan par sMra ba* / སྙན་པར་སྨྲ་བ་) – affectionate speech; dön chodpa (*don sPyod pa* / དོན་སྤྱོད་པ་) – resolute endeavour; and, dön thünpa (*don mThun pa* / དོན་མཐུན་པ་) – concord in resolution.

"We are most honoured to have you in our house today" they exclaimed. *"Please stay and be our daughter's husband."*

Drukpa Künlegs smiled *"If I am going to marry your daughter, I need chang"* so they brought him a large pitcher of chang. After quaffing a quantity, he opined *"The chang is excellent – I really must reimburse you."* At this he transformed the boiled chang grain into gold. Later Apa Tashi was about to go out to cut a tree to replace a pillar in the house when Drukpa Künlegs immediately offered *"I'll do it for you. I'm used to erecting pillars!"* Then he spontaneously manifested a pillar and put it in place. *"I am utterly astonished!"* Apa Tashi exclaimed in great exuberance *"Two men could hardly have carried such a great pillar!"* Drukpa Künlegs laughed *"That's the least of it. We now require good clear water, to make further chang!"* and at that he performed a water divination – and with a little digging water burst forth from under the rocks. The spring which Drukpa Künlegs discovered near Apa Tashi and Ama Nanga Lhamo's house is there even today.

I was expecting that Künzang Dorje Rinpoche would ask me to comment – but he did not. He simply poured out two glasses of chang and smiled very broadly.

13

perchance to dream

Künzang Dorje Rinpoche had told me, the previous day, that he was going to give detailed information concerning the gos dKar lCang lo'i sDe. I was eager to hear everything he could tell me on this subject – as I had made a promise to Kyabjé Düd'jom Rinpoche that I would attempt to establish what he had called the 'tradition of ngakpas'[1] in the West. That would require me becoming an authority on the tradition as well as living the tradition – or as much of an authority as it was possible for me to be.

"O yah – good!" Rinpoche exclaimed in mixed Tibetan and English, as I entered *"Now much all day gö kar chang lo teaching and writing."*

Then he took a long look at me and nodded. He told me that he was concerned for me – in how my life would go with keeping my promise. He said that he had no doubt that I would keep my damtsig[2]. He knew this because the very first time that I'd stood up for myself in relation to him—and not backed down—was when he'd assailed me as to keeping my word. It was when he called my honour into question.

"Then like great tiger becoming – and Künzang Dorje fearful becoming" he made a pantomime of shielding himself from me and looking frightened. Rinpoche trying to look frightened was the only thing I ever saw him do that was unconvincing. That made me laugh. The idea of his being afraid of me was too absurd. He was joking—of course—but it was a meaningful jest, as he followed it by telling me that this was something he'd noticed about me on several occasions. I came across *"… like flower – then great stone suddenly becoming."* He said that he was rarely surprised by people – but this way I had of flipping into megalithic mode was something he'd not encountered before.

---

1 Although there are ngakpas (*sNgags pa* / སྔགས་པ / *mantrin*) and ngakmas (*sNgags ma* / སྔགས་མ / *mantrini*) – the word 'ngakpa' can be used to mean both male and female mantrikas / tantrikas.
2 *dam tshig* / དམ་ཚིག / *samaya*.

We talked for a while about the quality of being *gentle yet firm* and I told him that there was a saying or expression in English that concerned the proper way to manifest authority. *"It's described as having an iron hand in a velvet glove."*

He liked that expression. He said that he had come to see that I had this *iron hand* – but he also knew that it was extremely rare that I ever manifested it. He said that it was good that strength was kept in reserve – and only used when it was required.

"Anyway… not too much 'this and that' saying" he chuckled *"today, gö kar chang lo telling – because everything clearly detail must be knowing. Too many people in this time are ignorant and foolishly about gö kar chang lo'i dé speaking. Much nonsense talking – and worse, some deliberate bad lies telling. This must not allowed – must not continuing. When home travelling and teaching – then people questions asking. Then clear explanation must be giving. When 'thom yor scholars criticising – then Chögyam must strongly answering. Then must iron fist showing and 'thom yor nonsense contradicting. You always must be correctly telling – gö kar chang lo'i dé from Guru Rinpoche and Yeshé Tsogyel coming."*

He then began to itemise every aspect of gos dKar lCang lo appearance.

Gö means clothing – which is mainly represented by the religious lower garment or skirt. *Kar* means white or undyed. So, 'gö kar' mainly refers to the white shamthab – but it also refers to white clothing in general. Künzang Dorje Rinpoche often dressed completely in white. This gö kar must be cotton if you follow the Milarépa tradition of the Kagyüd because répa or réma means 'cotton wearer'[3]. Nyingmas wear any white fabric – but it is undyed rather than necessarily pure white. The idea of wearing white cotton for répa and réma, is based on its lack of warmth. These practitioners specialise in gTummo[4]—the yoga of spatial heat—and wear cotton in the coldest weather as a mark of accomplishment.

---

3   Milarépa (*mi la ras pa* / མི་ལ་རས་པ་ / 1040–1123) – Mila the cotton-clad. Those who follow in his tradition are called répa (*ras pa* / རས་པ་ – male) and réma (*ras ma* / རས་མ་ – female).
4   gTum mo / གཏུམ་མོ་ / chandali – the practice of spatial heat, one of the Six Yogas of Naropa or Six Yogas of Niguma. The Naro or Nigu Chödrug (*na ro* / *ni gu chos drug*) are: gTummo – spatial heat; gyu-lü (*sGyu lus* / སྒྱུ་ལུས་) – illusory body; mi-lam (*rMi lam* / རྨི་ལམ་) – dream yoga; 'ö-Sel (*'od gSal* / འོད་གསལ་) – clear light; 'pho-wa (*'pho ba* / འཕོ་བ་) – transference of consciousness; bardo (*bar do* / བར་དོ་) – intermediate state.

Ngakpas and ngakmas wear the white shamthab. Monks and nuns wear the maroon or red shamthab. Both are of the same design – because both are religious costume. Idiots speak of 'lay tantrikas' but there is no word in Tibetan that means 'lay tantrika'. The Tibetan word for 'lay' is kya[5] which means 'grey' – and that refers to the natural colour of undyed wool. *Kya* does not mean 'non-celibate'[6] – it simply means secular and tantrikas cannot be described as secular.

"Kyabjé Düd'jom Rinpoche cannot kya-wo being! This is lying 'thom yor slander!" Künzang Dorje Rinpoche exclaimed, banging his fist on the table so hard that his bell rose momentarily from the table with a ringing sound. *"How Guru Rinpoche, kya-wo calling? How great gTértön, kya-wo calling? How can Mind-incarnation of Düd'jom Lingpa, kya-wo calling? How Dung-sé Thrin-lé Norbu? How Shen'phen Dawa? How Minling Trichen? How Dilgo Khyentsé? How 'Khordong Chhi'mèd Rig'dzin? How so many—many—great gos dKar lCang lo Lamas? How 'kya-wo' saying? This much—much—lies telling. This 'kya-wo' word impossible for such Lamas using!"* Then he laughed *"Impossible also for Chögyam using. Chögyam 'Inji' saying – but kya-wo, not possible saying."*

"Anyway, Kyabjé Düd'jom Rinpoche – first the Buddha Rig'dzin Nuden Dorje. In the future Buddha Möpa Tha-yé. In India Shakyamuni's disciple Shariputra. Then Mahasiddha Saraha. Then in Tibet Khye'u chung mKha'lDing[7] *– 25 disciples of Guru Rinpoche inside appearing."*

---

5 *sKya* / སྐྱ – means grey, pale grey, light, colourless; yellowish-white, light-blue, light green, or light yellow. Kya-wo (*sKya bo* / སྐྱ་བོ) – means layman; a person clothed in the coarse grey serge.
6 The word 'lay' does not mean 'non-celibate' in English either. It means 'unprofessional / not of the clergy'. It has the same meaning in every Scandinavian, European, and Eastern European language. It cannot be used to mean non-celibate because there are non-celibate religions such as Judæism and the Protestant Churches.
7 Khye'u chung mKha' lDing was more commonly known as Khye'u chung Lotsa. Drüpchen Drog-mi Khye'u chung Lotsa (*grub chen 'brog mi Khye'u chung lo tsa* / གྲུབ་ཆེན་འབྲོག་མི་ཁྱེའུ་ཆུང་ལོ་ཙ) was born into the Drog (*brog* / འབྲོག) clan. Khye'u chung Lotsa was accomplished with mantra and mudra. He was able to attract birds in order to teach them.

He sat—spatially glowering—for a brief moment, then grinned entirely warmly – and gave me the entire list of Kyabjé Düd'jom Rinpoche's previous incarnations[8]. He concluded, saying *"Anyway – with ngakpa and ngakma, shamthab folding is different coming."*

With the ngakpas and ngakmas there are various styles according to tradition. Our tradition of folding is the large pleat at the front and back. This represents the indivisibility of emptiness and form. The six panels of the shamthab are the six classes of Tantra[9]. The doubled bands at the top and bottom are the same taste of samsara and nirvana[10]. The white cotton shamthab is uncontaminated by the stain of duality – as the lotus is uncontaminated by the effluvium of the swamp in which it grows. White is the colour of undyed cotton and represents kadag – primal purity.

The word *chang* comes from gya-chang[11]. Gya-chang were the weeping willows planted by princess Gya-za Kong-jo[12] when she came from China to marry King Song-tsen Gampo.

8   Kyabjé Düd'jom Rinpoche Jig'drèl Yeshé Dorje (1904–1987) had seventeen incarnations: **1.** Nuden Dorje Buddha prior to Shakyamuni Buddha; **2.** Shariputra: chief disciple of Shakyamuni Buddha known for his detailed precision in wisdom; **3.** Mahasiddha Saraha: poet and master of yogas; **4.** Mahasiddha Krishnadhara: chief minister of Indrabhuti of Ögyen; **5.** Hungkara: one of the eight Rig'dzins; holder of Yangdag thugs received form the Khandros; **6.** Khye'u Chung Lotsa: translator and one of Guru Rinpoche's 25 Tibetan disciples; **7.** Smritijnana: one of the Indian Panditas in Tibet; **8.** Rongzom Pandita: scholar and redactor of the Nyingma Kama; **9.** Dampa Desheg: founder of Kathog Gompa in Kham; **10.** Ling Jé Repa: founder of the Drukpa Kagyu School; **11.** Chögyel Phagpa: nephew of Sakya Pandita, ruler of Tibet, Lama to Kubla'i Khan; **12.** Drumkhar Nagpopa: Khampa yogi who resided in dark retreat for 18 years; **13.** Héwa Chö-jung: Khampa siddha and subjugator of violently bellicose heretics; **14.** Traktung Düd'dül Dorje: the gTértön who revived Kathog; **15.** Gyalsré Sônam Détsen: head of Kathog Gompa; **16.** Düd'dül Rolpa'i Tsal: Ngak'chang Lama of Jig'mèd Lingpa; **17.** gTértön Düd'jom Lingpa (1835–1904) – born in Chak-kyong in Kham in Gili gö kar chang lo family; known for magical powers and wrathful appearance.

9   Six classes of tantra – gyüd-dé drug (*rGyud sDe drug* / རྒྱུད་སྡེ་དྲུག). In the Nyingma Tradition the tantras are divided into six classes: the three outer tantras (*common to Sarma and Nyingma):* are Kriya tantra; charya or upa tantra; and yoga tantra. The three inner tantras (*specific to Nyingma):* are Mahayoga, Anuyoga, and Atiyoga or Dzogchen.

10 'Khor'dé (*'khor 'das* / འཁོར་འདས) – cyclic experience and its transcendence.

11 *rGya lCang* / རྒྱ་ལྕང.

12 Jétsun Drölma'i Trülpa Gya-za Konjo (*rJe bTsun sGrol ma'i sprul pa rGya za kong jo* / རྗེ་བཙུན་སྒྲོལ་མའི་སྤྲུལ་པ་རྒྱ་ཟ་ཀོང་ཇོ) – a manifestation of Drölma (*sGrol ma* / སྒྲོལ་མ / *Tara*).

So *chang-lo* therefore means *long hair like a weeping willow*. Gö kar chang lo'i dé therefore means the assembly of those who wear white raiment and have uncut hair.

"*O yah*" Rinpoche announced with some satisfaction. "*I think you are hair-vows keeping since young age.*" PAUSE "*This true?*"

"*Yes… I stopped cutting my hair when I was fourteen years old, Rinpoche*" I replied with surprise that he should know this "*… but there was no 'vow'. I made no promise. It was just something I wanted to do. At that time I didn't know about the vows – and only learnt that when I came to Nepal in 1971. It was the hippie period and many people stopped cutting their hair. It was the fashion of the time – but now people are cutting their hair again. The fashion has changed*"

"*Fashion changing – but Chögyam not changing?*"

"*No, Rinpoche, I don't follow fashion – I never have done. I don't go against fashion deliberately – if there is something I appreciate, then I accept it whether it is fashionable or not. When what I wear goes out of fashion I don't stop liking it.*"

"*Then 'thom yors laughing – but Chögyam not caring?*"

"*Exactly Rinpoche. I stopped being the slave of other people's opinion when I was eleven-years-old. That was when the first change in fashion came to my attention.*"

I then gave Künzang Dorje Rinpoche an account of the first time I was laughed at for wearing clothes that had gone out of fashion. My German grandmother had bought me a pair of elastic sided Chelsea boots[13] when no one I knew wore them. Other boys laughed at them. Then the Beatles started wearing them and they became fashionable. Then I was admired for wearing them, apart from the fact that they were brown rather than black. Then in the 1970s they fell out of fashion – but I got a new pair. They were always available for the horse-riding market. I said it was the same as when the hippie period was dwindling. One was no longer supposed to wear 'period clothing', cavalry frock coats, or Chelsea boots.

13 Chelsea boots are close-fitting ankle-boots with elasticated side panels which utilised *Charles Goodyear's vulcanised rubber*. Designed in 1840 by Queen Victoria's shoemaker J Sparks-Hall – they became popular with walkers and equestrians. In the 1960s they became fashionable as *Chelsea Boots* after Chelsea, London – where Jimi Hendrix and the Rolling Stones shopped. Anello & Davide created a variant in 1961. John Lennon and Paul McCartney saw them in their window display and commissioned them with Cuban heels. These became known as *Beatle Boots*. John Lennon had his several inches above the ankle which necessitated zips on one side.

"O yah" he smiled at the conclusion of my lengthy explanation. "Fashion always 'law' for 'thom yors. Anyway, all good coming. 'Vow' or 'not vow' with hair – no difference coming. Hair not cutting. This is most important. I see you, this knowledge inside having."

"So… hair topknot having" Rinpoche began his discourse. "Topknot – this, Buddha and Buddha-consort of space element [14]. Ornaments – this Buddha and Buddha-consort of fire element [15]. We are Buddha and Buddha-consort of water element [16] becoming – through mélong wearing. We are Buddha families becoming through dressing and through life circumstances practising. Sashes – and gold or copper amulets: this, Buddha and Buddha-consort of earth element [17]. Phurbas in waistband – this Buddha and Buddha-consort of air element [18]."

Rinpoche smiled at me effusively. "Then…" he announced with glee "gDang, rolpa, and rTsal [19]. This, Dzogchen meaning. gDang – meaning 'shining emptiness'. Rolpa – meaning 'clear unimpeded play of energy'. rTsal meaning – radiance of energy. This is pervasively compassionate – purity of phenomenal world."

Unadorned hair symbolises gDang – the Lama manifesting as vast space. Adorned hair symbolises rolpa—the Lama manifesting as rolpa—realised display. Matted locks symbolise rTsal – the Lama manifesting within the sphere of realised manifestation.

Conch earrings are the outer symbol of hearing extraordinary instructions; the inner symbol of hearing all sound as mantra; the secret symbol of realising the nature of sound as unborn; the most secret symbol is the realisation of all sound as self-liberated potency.

---

14 Space element: Nampar Nangdzé (*nam par sNang mDzad* / ནམ་པར་སྣང་མཛད་ / *Vairochana*) and Ying-chugma (*dByings phyug ma* / དབྱིངས་ཕྱུག་མ་ / *Dharmadhatvishvari*).
15 Fire element: 'od Pa'mèd (*'od pags 'med* / འོད་པགས་མེད་ / *Amitabha*) and Gö-kar mo (*gos dKar mo* / གོས་དཀར་མོ་ / *Pandara*).
16 Water element: Mikyöpa (*mi bsKyod pa* / མི་བསྐྱོད་པ་ / *Akshobhya*) and Sanggye Chanma (*sangs rGyas sPyan ma* / སངས་རྒྱས་སྤྱན་མ་ / *Locana*).
17 Earth element: Rinchen Jungné (*rin chen 'byung gNas* / རིན་ཆེན་འབྱུང་གནས་ / *Ratnasambhava*) and Dorje Mamaki (*rDo rJe ma ma ki* / རྡོ་རྗེ་མ་མ་ཀི་ / *Vajra Mamaki*).
18 Air element: Dön-yö Drüp-pa (*don yod grub pa* / དོན་ཡོད་གྲུབ་པ་ / *Amoghasiddhi*) and Damtsig Drölma (*dam tshig sGrol ma* / དམ་ཚིག་སྒྲོལ་མ་ / *Visvapani* / *Green Tara*).
19 gDang (*gDang* / གདང་), rol pa (*rol pa* / རོལ་པ་), rTsal (*rTsal* / རྩལ་) – three aspects of energy: inner-outer undivided, internally manifesting, and externally manifesting.

"Ngakpas and ngakmas on left-hand ring-fingers, drilbu-emblazoned wisdom ring wearing. Ngakpas and ngakmas on right-hand ring-fingers, dorje-emblazoned method ring wearing. This must gold making – because rTsa protection on these fingers needing." Künzang Dorje Rinpoche then indicated the line of the rTsa that runs down the ring fingers[20] and up the arms connecting with the heart. He explained that those who had little awareness and no power did not draw attention to themselves with respect to beings in other dimensions. If, however, one became aware of other dimensions – there would be reciprocal attention. Just as there are malignant human beings, there are malignant entities in other dimensions – just as there are malignant animals. *"If Bengal never going – then Bengal tiger never meeting. If Bengal jungle going – then must be rifle having. In Tso Pema and Bodhanath – no tiger coming, so no rifle needing. This why ngakpas and ngakmas gold rings wearing necessary."* Rinpoche took a sip of his Eagle beer. *"So, Gos dKar lCang lo'i sDe with Vajrayana vows beginning. Ngakpas and Ngakmas, they all these vows are holding."*

Historically the gö kar chang lo'i dé began in India with the 84 Mahasiddhas. There were two traditions at that time: those with partners – and those without. Normally Vajrayana is practised with a partner – but it is also allowed without. In ancient India both systems were found. It was at this time that the gö kar chang lo'i dé started wearing long hair on the top of their heads and the white shamthabs were worn. Guru Rinpoche founded the gö kar chang lo'i dé in Tibet – although it actually had a small beginning with Srong-tsan Gampo. At that time, 21 texts of Chenrézigs were translated and introduced. Dharma was not spread in a complete way at that stage – but there were ngakpas and ngakmas at that time, even so. Then at the time of Trisong Détsen, Dharma was spread in a vast way by Guru Rinpoche and Yeshé Tsogyel.

Trisong Détsen established the religious code laid down by Guru Rinpoche. This was the code concerning the appearance and comportment of the monastics and the gö kar chang lo'i dé.

---

20 Thun-srin (*mThun srin* / མཐུན་སྲིན་) – ring finger. *mThun* means corresponding, conducive, favourable, harmonious. *Srin* means barbarous or savage. The *Lha* channel runs from the heart to the ring finger along the ulnar artery. If the *Lha* channel is damaged the person begins to suffer, feel lonely, weak, or mentally disturbed. The symptoms of damage or loss of the *Lha* can be: insecurity, unhappiness, depression, fear, nihilism, difficulty in concentrating, anxiety, panic attacks, and recurrent nightmares.

"Concerning clothing..." Rinpoche said shaking his head *"... only monastics yellow wearing... but now some ngakpas and ngakmas also yellow wearing."* PAUSE *"This... not so good – but this Tibetan culture."*

Yellow is the colour of the vinaya – the colour of monastic discipline. Of course, this special bright yellow became popular in Tibet because this was the colour of the Chinese Imperial court. Only the emperor and the highest in the court are allowed to wear this yellow – so Tibetan nobles started imitating that. Then of course religious dignitaries started wearing it rather than wearing the common *sulphur yellow* of Buddha Shakyamuni's monks.

Ngakpas and ngakmas—unlike monks and nuns—may wear all colours. They may even wear yellow in the gar'cham – or if they are Lamas, giving an empowerment of Dzambhala—or any other yellow yidam—but otherwise yellow is reserved for monastics. *"If leather wearing and natural leather yellow-looking then no problem. Monk and nun anyway, not leather wearing allowed."*

The gö kar chang lo'i dé—according to Guru Rinpoche's advice to Trisong Détsen—should wear white, red, and blue. They can also wear black and the five colours depending on their activity. The black robe is for the phurba master and is usually worn with a green shirt.

Concerning food, monastics were only allowed to eat vegetables with the three whites and the three sweets.[21] They should not drink wine or eat meat. The gö kar chang lo'i dé on the other hand were advised to drink wine and eat meat in order that their lives would be no different from the tsog'khorlo. It was advised thus because in Vajrayana practice one has to visualise oneself as the yidam – and within that experience one cannot entertain dualistic thoughts concerning alcohol or meat. The gos dKar lCang lo'i sDe could enjoy things considered as 'impure' within Sutrayana, because the inner tantras transcend the pure-impure dichotomy. So, the gö kar chang lo'i dé must relish the five objects of sensual pleasure and make that the path of bliss which brings them to yeshé.[22]

---

21 Kar-sum (*dKar gSum* / དཀར་གསུམ་) – the three whites: milk, butter, and yoghurt. Ngar-sum (*mNgar gSum* / མངར་གསུམ་) – the three sweets: sugar, honey and molasses.
22 *ye shes* / ཡེ་ཤེས་ / jnana – primordial wisdom.

"Guru Rinpoche said '... the gö kar chang lo'i dé should practise on Yeshé basing. They must all existence as practice employing. Senses and fields of senses all methods of nondual realisation becoming.' If we alcohol taking – then alcohol with awareness drinking. Then access to Yeshé increasing. At the time of Guru Rinpoche in Tibet, many practitioners the same realisation as 84 Mahasiddhas of India obtaining."

There were excellent practitioners at that time: King Trisong Détsen[23]; the 25 siddhas of Chimphu; 25 female disciples; the 111 Siddhas of Chu-wo ri; the 80 ngakpas of Yérwa; the 55 Togdens of Yang-dzong; the 30 Ngakpas of Sheldrak; and, the 25 Ngakmas of Khar-chu. *"So, 'thom yor scholars 'no ngakma' saying are not 25 Ngakmas of Khar-chu knowing. This ignorance and arrogance. First Spread in Tibet many—many—ngakmas coming. Soon in West many ngakmas coming when Chögyam and sangyum are gos dKar lCang lo'i sDe establishing."*

Künzang Dorje Rinpoche raised his eyebrows at that point. *"This Düd'jom Rinpoche clearly saying. What Chögyam saying?"*

This was one of those times when knee-jerk humility would have cut in – but I noted the impulse and let it evaporate. *"I shall make it happen – or die in the endeavour. As Kyabjé Düd'jom Rinpoche wants it to happen, it will happen. I have confidence that Düd'jom Rinpoche put his trust in me for a reason – and that you have done the same. Anyway – it's not just me. I have centuries of history to validate the endeavour. The power of that history is colossal and if I remain honest in being a conduit for it – the endeavour cannot fail."*

Rinpoche laughed with pleasure and slapped his thighs rather violently *"O yah! Now my—SON—speaking!"* PAUSE *"So… hundreds of gTértöns in Tibet and Bhutan coming. All are gö kar chang lo. Maybe some small number are gé-long vows holding – but then secret consort having. When Guru Rinpoche Tibet leaving, Yeshé Tsogyel gos dKar lCang lo'i sDe longer establishing. Thousands of female practitioners then coming – thousands of ngakmas.* "Guru Rinpoche and Yeshé Tsogyel established gos dKar lCang lo'i sDe – and female practitioners and male practitioners together practising. That is why 'ngakma name' coming – not only ngakpa.

"Present time, in Golok and Amdo still word 'ngakma' using. Some 'thom yor scholars say 'no word like ngakma'. Only reason coming – they never hearing or reading. This like 'æroplane not existing' saying – because æroplane never seeing.

---

23 Trisong Détsen (*khri srong de'u bTsan* / ཁྲི་སྲོང་དེའུ་བཙན་ / 790–844 AD).

"This like 'hundred floors house not existing' because New York never going." PAUSE
"Then… other 'thom yors say ngakmas existing – but must be 'ngakmo' calling. This 'thom yor stupidity – because thousands of ngakmas in time of Yeshé Tsogyel living. Yeshé Tsogyel over three thousand ngakma disciples having."

Yeshé Tsogyel practised in the area of Sang-chö La, and also in Amdo, where thousands of ngakpas and ngakmas gathered. These days there are fewer practitioners than before – but still the tradition was handed down to the present day. The two divisions of the ordained sangha renowned in Tibet during the time of the Khen-lob-chö-sum[24] were the monastics with shaven-heads and saffron robes;[25] and the sangha of white shamthabs and long plaited hair – the gö kar chang lo'i dé. Both sanghas had equal sovereignty. This was clearly specified during the reign of Trisong Détsen.

King Tri Ralpaçan[26]—who came after Guru Rinpoche left Tibet—was a great king who respected both sanghas. To show this—and to show that both were more important than himself—he laid out his long hair across the place where the monastics and gö kar chang lo'i dé sat. He then tied silk ribbons to the end of his hair in order to extend his hair along the entire seating area of all the ordained practitioners. He placed the monastics on his right side and the gö kar chang lo'i dé sat on his left. This is clearly stated in reliable histories of the Tibetan monarchies – so it is widely known and indisputable. Let no one say there is no gö kar chang lo'i dé as an authentic ordained sangha. One day I will write this in Tibetan so that Tibetans cannot be ignorant of their own history.[27]

---

24 *mKhen sLob chos gSum* / མཁེན་སློབ་ཆོས་གསུམ་. 'Khen' refers to Khenpo Shantarakshita, 'Lob' to the Tantric Buddha Lopön Padmasambhava, and 'Chö' to the Dharma King, Trisong Détsen.
25 Monastics with shaven-heads and saffron robes – Rabjung ngur-mig gi dé (*rab byung ngur sMrig gi sDe* / རབ་བྱུང་ངུར་སྨྲིག་གི་སྡེ་).
26 *khri ral pa can* / ཁྲི་རལ་པ་ཅན་ – ruled central Tibet in the years of 866–896.
27 Künzang Dorje Rinpoche wrote this—as intended—in 1999. It was published later as a booklet called '*A Descriptive History of the Rig'dzinpas and Rig'dzinmas of the Great Secret Mantra Vehicle – they who are dignified in White Skirts and resplendent with Long Hair*'. This text varies in various respects from the oral instruction given in 1975. Although there are both omissions and additions which make them dissimilar – they carry the same import. The printed booklet also contains details of Mahayoga symbolism—which Künzang Dorje Rinpoche did not mention in 1975—which would prove of great interest to anyone studying Vajrayana in a gö kar chang lo lineage. See: Appendix III.

perchance to dream

Guru Rinpoche established these sanghas himself in Tibet, Bhutan, and many areas over the Himalayas – so there is no reason to lack confidence that the gö kar chang lo'i dé are Guru Rinpoche's ordained Vajrayana sangha.

In Tibet—in the upper and lower regions of Kham—those ngakpas are known as A-mé. In Ngari[28], the far-western region of Tibet, they are known as Jopa[29], and in the Ü-tsang[30] region, they are called Ngak'chang.[31] In Sikkim and other bordering kingdoms, these practitioners are known as Ser-khyimpa.[32] In Bhutan they are called gomchen.

In the Tibetan histories, four Jopas are described who, in service to Dharma kings of Töd Gugé[33] and Gungthang,[34] reversed harmful forces causing illness. Similarly, for the Dharma Kings of Nangchen[35] and Dé-ge,[36] there were three groups consisting of four A-més in the low part of the valley, four great Lamas at the centre, four ministers in between. The four A-més were renowned for dispelling illness.

Künzang Dorje Rinpoche seemed to be gazing through me – but then focused sharply on my eyes *"O yah! In three valleys of Nangchen and Dé-ge, are ngakpas and ngakmas 'Triangle of Earth and Sky' practising. Triangle lines of earth, sky, valleys, and rivers: syllable 'Ham' inside triangle placing. This too dangerous for all but ngakpas and ngakmas – but great benefit coming.*

"If people fearful mental experiences having, then presence of ngakpas and ngakmas who sharp, swift, powerful energies of wrathful activity having – then extreme benefit. Ngakpas and ngakmas always great value to people bringing."

28 *mNga' ris* / མངའ་རིས་
29 *jo pa* / ཇོ་པ་
30 *dBus gTsang* / དབུས་གཙང་
31 *sNgags 'chang* / སྔགས་འཆང་
32 *ser khyim pa* / སེར་ཁྱིམ་པ་ – 'Ser' refers to the yellow monastic colour and 'khyimpa' means householder.
33 *sTod gu ge* / སྟོད་གུ་གེ་
34 *gung thang* / གུང་ཐང་
35 *nang chen* / ནང་ཆེན་
36 *sDe dGe* / སྡེ་དགེ་

In Central Tibet, at the time of Drogön Chögyal Phakpa,[37] there were four great ngakpas in the four directions of Drogön Tsang.[38]

"Generally speaking, two kinds of ngakpa and ngakma existing: those of family lineage and those without family lineage. Ngakpas of family lineage are connected father to son lineages. These through generations passing. At this time the main family lineages are these: Nyingma Tradition there is Kyabjé Minling Trichen Rinpoche;[39] *Sakya School there is Sakya Tri'dzin Rinpoche.*[40] *They are 'Family Lineage Ngakpas who Hold Succession', title calling. Many others also who family lineage holding—especially with the Nyingma—but Minling Trichen Rinpoche and Sakya Trichen Rinpoche, most important.*

'Ngakpas and ngakmas without family lineage in both the Nyingma and Sarma traditions finding. Ngakpa family lineage not necessary having. Chögyam not necessary having. Anyone gö kar chang lo vows receiving, kyil'khor entering – whatever yidam through the Wang, rLung, and Tri from their Tsawa'i Lama receiving. Only necessary accomplishment of practise[41] *demonstrating. This way Chögyam gos dKar lCang lo vows in western countries giving.*

"*So, Gos dKar lCang lo'i sDe three categories showing: White Ngak'phang, Multi-coloured Ngak'phang and Black Ngak'phang. These all western ngakpas and ngakmas may be practising – according to the wish of Kyabjé Düd'jom Rinpoche.*"

The White Ngak'phang primarily practise Dzogchen. They also practise Anuyoga – but from the perspective of Dzogchen. Their retreat however, is that they live in the midst of the secular world – or wherever they find themselves. This does not mean that they cannot enter into long retreat or live in mountain hermitages – but it is not a requirement. The main feature of the White Ngak'phang is that every aspect of life is integrated with practice. There is no reliance on rituals. White Ngak'phang practise is mainly formless – and entering into the nature of the elements through the sense fields.

---

37 '*gro mGon chos rGyal 'phags pa* / འགྲོ་མགོན་ཆོས་རྒྱལ་འཕགས་པ / 1235–1280
38 '*gro mGon tshang* / འགྲོ་མགོན་ཚང
39 Lachen Minling Trichen Rinpoche (*bla chen sMin gLing khri chen rin po che* / བླ་ཆེན་སྨིན་གླིང་ཁྲི་ཆེན་རིན་པོ་ཆེ).
40 Drölma Potrang-gyi Trichen Rinpoche (*sGrol ma pho brang gi khri chen rin po che* / སྒྲོལ་མ་པོ་བྲང་གི་ཁྲི་ཆེན་རིན་པོ་ཆེ).
41 Mantra accumulations of the three activities of drüpthab: approach, accomplishment, and activity.

Some practise the essential forms of the Six Yogas of Naropa or Niguma – particularly 'pho-wa[42].

"White Ngak'phang – entire lives indistinguishable from practice. Whatever doing – this practice becoming. We are this category – and we are all white clothes wearing: white shamthab, white to-nga, white ku-tö [43]*. Ku-zèn*[44] *– white with red and blue like sKu gSum and rTsa gSum."*

The Multi-coloured Ngak'phang primarily practise Anuyoga – and Mahayoga from the perspective of Anuyoga. They are masters of rTsa rLung. They are those who accomplished practice in long retreats and then devote their lives to retreats and the performance of drüpthab. They are experts in ritual – but they have complete knowledge of the inner meaning of the rituals they perform. They may also practise Dzogchen – but their approach is from the view of the Mahayoga and Anuyoga. The Multi-coloured Ngak'phang wear white shamthabs and red or maroon waistcoats. They should wear a five-coloured shamthab sash – but it can be red or white.

The Black Ngak'phang primarily practise the Outer Tantras – and Mahayoga from the perspective of the Outer Tantras. They are primarily ritualists who specialise in manipulating outer circumstances for the benefit of the people. They practise the srog-tad sum[45], make amulets[46], perform exorcism, make predictions[47], scry mirrors in divination[48], and prevent hailstorms for the benefit of farmers. The Black Ngak'phang should wear a black chuba with a green or five-coloured sash. They should wear a ngakru suspended from their chuba sash – as well as any other implements that they use in their central practices.

---

42 Kyabjé Künzang Dorje Rinpoche was a master of all the rTsa rLung practices – and was asked by Kyabjé Düd'jom Rinpoche Jig'drèl Yeshé Dorje to write a text on rTsa rLung practice. This text was then incorporated into the Düd'jom gTér.
43 sKu sTod / སྐུ་སྟོད་ – upper garment.
44 sKu gZan / སྐུ་གཟན་ – shawl.
45 Srog-ser tad sum (*srog ser gTad gSum* / སྲོག་སེར་གཏད་གསུམ་) – the three aspects of protective tantric ritual: life-wheel, hail, and spells.
46 Amulet – Tag-chog (*bTags chog* / བཏགས་ཆོག་).
47 Prediction – ma'ong lung tèn (*ma 'ongs lung bsTan* / མ་འོངས་ལུང་བསྟན་), lung tén (*lung bsTan* / ལུང་བསྟན་), or lung tön (*lung sTon* / ལུང་སྟོན་).
48 Divination – tra-se-na (*pra se na* / པྲ་སེ་ན་).

"Black Ngak'phang sometimes 'village ngakpa' calling – but just because ngakpa is poor and village-living not 'village ngakpa' making." Rinpoche shook his head and asked me whether a ngakpa who lived in a city should be called a 'city ngakpa' – and whether a ngakpa who lived in a town should be called a 'town ngakpa'. Or what is a ngakpa living on a ship – should he be a 'ship ngakpa'? This caused him great amusement – and this emphasised the fact that the term 'village' ngakpa was a meaningless slur.

"Some monks are accountant, bursar, and trader working. Some dob-dob [49]*"* Künzang Dorje Rinpoche gave an expression of distaste when he mentioned the dob-dobs. *"Dob-dob over young monk fighting – for best sex having"* shaking his head in displeasure. *"Some cooking. Some cleaning. Some sweeping. Some butter-lamp cleaning and filling. Some 'this' doing. Some 'that' doing. But—all—monk robe wearing! But many not more practise than lay people. Some lay people more devout than people monastic robe wearing! Therefore, no reason coming, 'village ngakpas' bad words speaking! Plenty in monastery not as good. Some bad. Some worse. Sometimes much worse in many monastery finding!"*

In Tibet, three ngakpa dratsangs were highly exalted. They were situated in Amdo[50], Chakri Phurdrak[51], and Shangzab Phulung.[52] In Amdo there was Repkong[53] – and there, the gos dKar lCang lo'i sDe either left their hair long-flowing or allowed it to become matted. They wore multi-coloured shawls. At Chakri Phurdrak where there is a self-arising letter 'A' on a rock cliff, the clothing of the gos dKar lCang lo'i sDe was the same. In Shangzab Phulung – on the border of Ü[54] and Tsang[55] are zabphu[56] gos dKar lCang lo'i sDe. They have long, free-flowing hair, the multi-coloured zen[57] and the nambu karpo.[58]

---

49 *lDob lDob* / ལྡོབ་ལྡོབ་ – police monks who existed in large Gelug gompas such as Sera, Ganden, and Drepung. These monks were often keen on sport, fighting, and other secular pursuits.
50 *A mDo* / ཨ་མདོ
51 *chags ri'i phur brag* / ཆགས་རིའི་ཕུར་བྲག
52 *shangs zab phu lung* / ཤངས་ཟབ་ཕུ་ལུང
53 *reb kong* / རེབ་གོང
54 *dBus* / དབུས
55 *gTsang* / གཙང
56 *zab phu* / ཟབ་ཕུ
57 Zen-tra (*gZan phra* / གཟན་ཕྲ) – multi-coloured shawl.
58 *gNam bu dKar po* / གནམ་བུ་དཀར་པོ – white woollen shamthab.

"In Tibet – so many small ngak'phang dratsangs. So many I cannot all in list making. No purpose coming long list making and no time for making. This just for you to know—and tell western people—that the gö kar chang lo'i dé widespread in Tibet – and rich and powerful history having. Finally saying." PAUSE *"Perfect and proper – father or mother with children becoming. Perfect and proper – home having for gö kar chang lo'i dé. But hair cutting in fear of what people saying – this vow breakage. You should never ashamed or fearful becoming, robe wearing. You are vows for robes holding. Kyabjé Düd'jom Rinpoche is robes vows giving. Künzang Dorje is also robes vows giving. So, no question. So, no one arguing. Maybe some with bad-mind 'this' and 'that' saying. Bigoted 'thom yor all kinds of nonsense saying – but Chögyam must always ignoring."*

Rinpoche went on to tell me that one of the many difficulties that beset the gos dKar lCang lo'i sDe was the lack of commonality in their dress. To some extent the gos dKar lCang lo'i sDe are characteristically heterodox – but one of the reasons for their current lack of uniformity was due to past persecution. He explained that when the gos dKar lCang lo'i sDe became scattered all over Tibet – they became isolated from each other. There were no large encampments or dratsangs – and so differences emerged over time. Some differences were due to evolution through the influence of particular Lamas – but often it was a matter of poverty. Where there was insufficient money to have the proper robes made, the gos dKar lCang lo'i sDe would wear the nearest equivalent – and this then led to the style being adopted as conventional. This was why many of the gos dKar lCang lo'i sDe now wore monastic shamthabs. Monastic shamthabs were easily available. This was now also the case with the Bön monastics who should wear blue shamthabs – but now many wore the Buddhist maroon, the only difference being that the panels in their waistcoats were blue rather than yellow. Künzang Dorje Rinpoche's final comment was that the correct dress was exactly what I had been given by Kyabjé Düd'jom Rinpoche. If anyone wanted to know what the gos dKar lCang lo'i sDe should wear – then this was the example that should be followed.

"Yah – now we must be eating, then later back to gompa sleeping necessary." Rinpoche chuckled *"Chögyam much tiredness from writing."*

"I am a little tired, Rinpoche – but this has all been so valuable to me. If you were to talk far into the night I'd be happy to keep writing."

"O yah – but teeth must also working, not only hand."

The fragrance of mo-mos had been detectable for ten minutes and soon they appeared – with Golok sauce and Eagle beer. We sang the Seven Line Song of Guru Rinpoche and ate with gusto. Or rather, I ate with gusto and Rinpoche ate with perfect measured zest. After a while Rinpoche asked me about the West and why people were leaving Christianity and Judæism – and adopting Buddhism.

"I can't answer that from my own experience, Rinpoche – because I was never a Christian. I have heard it explained that they found Christianity too dogmatic and concerned with rules that are not explained."

"Tibetan Dharma also dogmatic. Many rules, and no meaning giving." PAUSE "Other reasons coming?"

"They say there is too much hypocrisy – pretences, insincerity, duplicity…"

"O yah!" he laughed *"we also much hypocrisy having. Powerful monk, sex having in secret – but not karmamudra practising."* PAUSE *"Yah . . . Other reasons coming?"*

"Yes… there's the question of faith – they don't like having to have faith. They see Dharma as logical and Christianity as illogical."

"Yah – we also faith having. Dharma logical – but when people not logic understanding then no logic. Vajrayana saying all primordial realisation having – but Tibetan culture, women inferior making. Vajrayana saying 'women all khandro' – but then Tibetan culture badly treating. All logic losing when bad mind having." PAUSE *"Other reasons coming?"*

"There is the question of God – but that was always my problem. I have never believed in a God who created everything."

Rinpoche had his questioning expression, so I continued. *"Even as an eight-year-old, it was evident to me that if everything was the creation of God then that also applied to the Devil. The Devil was initially the angel Lucifer – but he rebelled against God saying 'I will not serve'."*

"What then happening?"

"Well—and you must keep in mind that I never studied Christian theology—God cast him out of heaven."

"And there many bad actions making."

"Yes."

"And God not stopping possible?"

"It would seem not – but I do not know how a Christian theologian would address that."

The translator had asked about the word theologian and so I replied *"Like a lopön* [59], *khenpo* [60], *or geshé* [61].*"*

"O yah – not 'God' believing. This one good reason coming. Dharma no 'God' having."

On that Rinpoche bade me good night – and I strolled back to the Nyingma Gompa feeling as if I could spend the rest of my life in this way. I took care not to be a 'thom yor when I was with Künzang Dorje Rinpoche – but I had to be careful not to lapse into infantilism as soon as I was out of his sight. I had a task to fulfil. It was good to feel so happy about being exactly where I was. The night sky was clear. The stars sparkled in the endless black of space. A faint breeze ruffled the surface of the lake and I realised I had time to make a circumambulation of the lake in almost utter silence. My feet seemed a greater distance from my ears than seemed normal and the slight crunch beneath my feet seemed unusually distant.

It was then that I woke up in the dream. I understood that I had gone straight back to the Gompa and from taking my leave of Künzang Dorje Rinpoche – and gone to sleep. So as I seemed to be circumambulating, I simply continued. I realised that walking could be effortless and soundless and that all I wished to hear was the wind on the lake. That then, that was all I heard. Eventually I heard nothing. Then I saw nothing. Then I woke up in the bed in Kyabjé Düd'jom Rinpoche's room in the Nyingma Gompa. I was still not used to making use of dreams. Sometimes there were astonishing revelations. Sometimes I could travel to other places entirely – and other times. This time however, I failed even to wonder whether Aro Yeshé had ever been to Tso Pema.

---

59 *sLob dPon* / སློབ་དཔོན་ / *acarya* – preceptor.
60 *mKhan po* / མཁན་པོ་ / *upadhyaya* – one who has completed the major course of studies in philosophy, logic, and vinaya.
61 *dGe bShes* / དགེ་བཤེས་ – Gélug academic title; holder of a high academic degree in Buddhist philosophy.

Goodbye Forever

I rose and ate a pleasant breakfast and it was early enough to circumambulate the lake. I was surprised that no one was to be seen. Usually there would have been Tibetans circumambulating the lake. Still, it was wonderfully serene. Yes, *serene* was the word. I considered the word *serene* that had come to mind – because it was not a word I used in particular. I stood for a while by the edge of the lake. It was entirely calm and mirror-like. I had never seen it quite as placid and reflective. I was gazing toward the other side of the lake and decided to move closer. I suddenly realised I was walking on the water. There seemed to be a trick to it. If I didn't allow my feet to dip below the ankle, all was well. Then the fact that I was dreaming dawned again. The breakfast had been a dream. I could not recall who brought it and where I had eaten it. I'd been in some sort of refectory that was quite unlike anywhere in the gompa. As I settled into the nature of the dream it occurred to me that I should wish to see Guru Rinpoche and Mandarava[62] on the lake. As soon as I had the idea they appeared – but they were only a painted scene as one might see in a thangka. This was disappointing – and I renewed my effort. I tried to see through the thangka-like image but nothing happened. The image just became increasingly vague. I began to sing Guru Rinpoche's mantra – and awoke in the room in the gompa. Finally, I was actually awake – but it took a while to convince myself of the fact. I rose and ate a real breakfast. It was equally as pleasant as the one I had dreamed.

62 *man da ra wa* / མན་ད་ར་ཝ

14

mantra hurling assembly

"O yah – Chögyam last night—much—dreaming. Lake 'khora making and clarity finding." This was not the first time that Kyabjé Künzang Dorje Rinpoche had known what I had dreamt. I was therefore not surprised. *"Yah – Düd'jom Rinpoche's room sleeping – then dream of clarity arising. Maybe now in home land, same clarity finding."*

Künzang Dorje Rinpoche then continued speaking on the subject of the gos dKar lCang lo'i sDe, where he had left off on the previous day.

"Many thousands ngak'phang tradition in Tibet before…" there followed a discussion with regard to Tibetan and western chronology and it was decided it was the 11th Century. *"… after this, then, diminishing – and female practitioner in particular into background being forced. This time large gompas arising, and the gos dKar lCang lo'i sDe out of central Tibet being forced. Then many Kham, Amdo, and Golok going. Many to Tibet border lands going – like Bön practitioners before going. Then in remote villages living – so in peace practice continuing. They anywhere living far from large monastic places."*

"So, this disparaging 'village ngakpa' term, Rinpoche, this comes from this period?"

"O yah, this term of disrespect then coming and respect for gö kar chang lo diminishing – but not places where large monasteries less influence having. So, then, Nyingma Tradition decision for survival making. Nyingma stronger monastic form adopting. Second spread coming and Nyingma must be surviving. Then original non-monastic style gradually losing. Then great Nyingma Lamas in history as monks showing. This false representing. Longchenpa not celibate monk – and many other great Lamas not celibate monk. As yesterday saying, our costume Guru Rinpoche giving. Guru Rinpoche telling, monastics yellow and red wearing. They must be ngar-sum kar-sum eating." Rinpoche smiled *"Also vegetable and tsampa[1] eating. Not meat eating. Pö-ja drinking not chang drinking."* Rinpoche laughed *"Pö-ja, Chögyam much—much—hating, so monk never becoming."*

---

1   *tsam pa* / ཙམ་པ་ – barley that is roasted, crushed, and roasted again.

Künzang Dorje Rinpoche roared with laughter at this point. Somehow the idea that I was disqualified from becoming a monk on the basis that I didn't like Tibetan tea, was something that was more hilarious than anything he'd considered before. He stopped laughing for a while and then erupted into mirth again. This recurred three times. This then set me off and we both laughed until the tears were streaming.

Kyabjé Künzang Dorje Rinpoche then decided it was time for chang – so he called to the lady of the house to bring glasses.

"Yah, yah, yah…" shaking his head *"then time passing and different coming. From second spread gradually monks and nuns meat eating. Now no restriction coming for monks and nuns meat eating. Guru Rinpoche telling ngakpas and ngakmas must be meat eating—must be chang and Ara drinking—and all sense fields, practice becoming. They must artificially pure and impure not discriminating. Gos dKar /Cang lo base is yeshé – primordial wisdom. Everything pure from beginninglessness. Gö kar chang lo all based on yeshé. We are never into 'pure / impure difference' view falling."* Rinpoche took a sip of chang. *"Because emphasis on yeshé establishing – second spread monastics are gö kar chang lo'i dé dismissing. They wrong thinking gö kar chang lo'i dé. They monk superior thinking. Gompa building superior saying. Monks not gö kar chang lo'i dé understanding and false judgement making. Monk 'thom yor much jealousy, much power seeking. Then monk, tantras controlling. They Sutrayana must power over Vajrayana. They bad view of women having."*

This was a somewhat grim picture – and I realised where I stood in a long chain of events that stretched back as far as the Battle of Hastings. Thinking of what was happening in Britain at the time was useful in getting a sense of the time scale involved – but when it hit home, I felt somewhat weighed down.

"And I have to change all that, Rinpoche. That is a great deal of history. I will do as I have promised – but it is difficult at this moment to see to what degree I may succeed."

Rinpoche observed me for a moment – but not in a stern way *"You maybe Kyabjé Düd'jom Rinpoche idea, not possible thinking?"*

Of course. A smile gradually appeared on my face. It wasn't an enormous smile – but it was a smile.

"Of course. Düd'jom Rinpoche has asked me to do this and so it—must—be possible – and, if Kyabjé Düd'jom Rinpoche asked me; it—must—be possible for me." PAUSE *"And of course – you also feel it is possible that I can accomplish this."* PAUSE *"I should have no doubt – but I don't want to be the kind of 'thom yor who believes himself capable of anything and everything."*

It was not possible to explain to Künzang Dorje Rinpoche that I felt like Frodo at the Council of Elrond agreeing to taking the 'one ring' to Mordor and cast it into the fire in Mount Orodruin[2]. It was perhaps just as well – because it was a somewhat ludicrous analogy. Then it occurred to me that Frodo succeeded in the end. The analogy was not entirely valueless – just not something I could explain to Künzang Dorje Rinpoche, without spending several hours explaining the plot of *'The Lord of the Rings'*.

Rinpoche noticed that thoughts had crossed my mind – because he said *"Demon empty. Many demon coming – but all empty. Düd'jom, 'demon destroying' meaning – so you also dud'jom becoming. Empty demon with empty dagger destroying."*

He'd pictorially fathomed my thoughts. It struck me then—as it did so many times—that Vajrayana was Art. Künzang Dorje Rinpoche had just brought out logic through poetry – the poetry of Düd'jom Rinpoche's name. He was Jig'drèl Yeshé Dorje too – the Fearless Primordial Thunderbolt of Wisdom.

Künzang Dorje Rinpoche pointed out that although I was indeed supposed to change the world – I did not have to accomplish that task in a few years, a few decades, or even a few lives. The only necessity was to begin – and then everything would take care of itself. People would help me. My sangyum would help. Other Lamas would eventually help. People who had never heard of me would help. *"Like landslide coming"* he laughed. *"Like avalanche and this you are well knowing."*

---

2 See: *Lord of the Rings* – an epic of fiction by JRR Tolkien. The title refers to the Dark Lord Sauron, who had in an earlier age created the One Ring to rule the other Rings of Power as the ultimate weapon in his campaign to conquer Middle-earth. From sedate pastoral life in the Shire, a place similar to Dorsetshire, the story follows the course of the War of the Rings through the eyes of its characters, most notably the Hobbit Frodo – and his friends Sam, Merry, and Pippin.

"Yes, Rinpoche – or rather, I know it – just not that well. I have dreams—and I see many scenes in my dreams—but nothing that lasts very long and the scenes are disconnected." PAUSE *"On rare occasions I remember having felt as if I was Aro Yeshé – but that sense never comes through into my waking life."* PAUSE *"Do you think it will ever come through and that there will one day be no division between what I once was and what I am now?"*

Künzang Dorje Rinpoche said nothing. He simply sat and observed me. So, I continued *"It's not that this is something that I actively want. I don't see that anything absolutely depends upon it – it's just that I have the idea that I could be a better example of the teaching I've received if I was more like Aro Yeshé than Ngakpa Chögyam."*

Künzang Dorje Rinpoche shook his head *"Why Chögyam bad thinking? Why Aro Yeshé better thinking?"* PAUSE *"Aro Yeshé dead. Chögyam alive. Dead no use. Alive much benefit."*

I couldn't argue with that.

"Anyway Chögyam all good doing. Nepal going – and Kyabjé Düd'jom Rinpoche meeting. Then Kyabjé Düd'jom Rinpoche saying Chögyam must be Künzang Dorje, in Tso Pema going. Then" he laughed *"Künzang Dorje much shouting and Chögyam remain. Other Inji away running – but Chögyam staying. Every day shouting and bad word 'thom yor using – but Chögyam always staying. This great strength. This good strong mind. No need Aro Yeshé becoming. Only sangyum needing – then all things good coming."* PAUSE *"Aro Yeshé never Tso Pema pilgrimage making. Bhutan going one time—short time—with older and younger sangyum. Maybe one time you also Bhutan going."*

"I would certainly like to go just once – because I would wish to make a pilgrimage to Taktsang. Every time I see photographs of Taktsang I feel drawn to it."

"Then must be Taktsang going – but only when sangyum finding."

"Can you tell me anything about Taktsang, Rinpoche?"

"O yah. Takstang is building around Taktsang Seng-gé Samdrüp [3] cave, where Guru Rinpoche meditating. He is from Tibet flying on sky tigress. Yeshé Tsogyel manifests as flying tigress at cliff edge landing."

---

3   sTag tshang seng ge bSam grub / སྟག་ཚང་སེང་གི་བསམ་གྲུབ

He then established Vajrayana in Bhutan. Later, Guru Rinpoche visited Bumthang to subdue demons. Guru Rinpoche's body impression is imprinted on the wall of a cave near Kur-jé Lhakhang. Langchen Palgyi Seng-gé came to the cave to meditate[4] and so it is named Palphug – Palgyi's Cave. After he died later in Nepal, his body was miraculously returned to the gompa by Dorje Legpa – and is now sealed in a chörten in a room to the left at the top of the gompa entrance stairway.

Many drüpthobs went to Taktsang to meditate, including Milarépa PaDampa Sang-gyé, Ma-gÇig Labdrön[5] and Thangtong Gyalpo[6]. Later[7] the Lapa School was established in Paro. Then later[8] many Lamas came from Tibet and established gompas in Bhutan. The first was built[9] when Sônam Gyaltsen—a Nyingma Lama from Kathog—came from Tibet. He had paintings made which can still be faintly discerned on a rock above the principal building that dates back to the 1400s. Taktsang was under the governance of Kathog in the middle of the 17th century. The Taktsang Ögyen Tsémo Lhakhang was rebuilt after a fire in 1958. In the 17th century gTértön Pema Lingpa of Bumthang founded many gompas in Bhutan. He originated many religious and secular dance forms connected with Zangdog Palri – the Copper Coloured Mountain of Guru Rinpoche.

"This same as Taktsang. His dances in Paro Tshé festival performed."

It was during this time that the Drukpa Lama, Ngawang Namgyal, fled from Tibet to escape persecution by the Gelugpas. He established Bhutan with a system of rulership known as Shabdrung. It was during a Tibetan invasion of Bhutan in the mid 1600s that the Shabdrung—and the Nyingma Lama, gTértön Rig'dzin Nyingpo—invoked Guru Rinpoche and the protectors at Taktsang to give success over the invaders. He performed the Kagyèd Gong'dü[10] and Bhutan won the war against Tibet – but the Shabdrung was not able to build a lhakhang at Takstsang to celebrate the event.

4   In 853.
5   *ma gCig lab sGron* / མ་གཅིག་ལབ་སྒྲོན་ / 1054–1146).
6   *thang sTong rGyal po* / ཐང་སྟོང་རྒྱལ་པོ་ / 1384–1505).
7   The later 12th century.
8   Between 12th–17th centuries.
9   14th century.
10 *bKa brGyad dgongs 'dus* / བཀའ་བརྒྱད་དགོངས་འདུས་

"It's sad…" I commented *"that people can't leave each other alone. It's been the same in Europe with different Christian schools battling against each other. It seems to be that those who want to dominate others have no understanding of the religions they're supposed to be following."*

"Yah…" Rinpoche sighed *"when religion understanding – then no aggression arising. When aggression arising then religion not different from other 'thom yor kingdom."* PAUSE *"Buddhist 'thom yor, Bönpo 'thom yor, Christian 'thom yor, Muslim 'thom yor, Hindu 'thom yor – all same. All 'thom yor. Real practising each religion then difference but compassion no difference. Difference in view and method coming – but freedom for other peoples – all same view."* PAUSE *"What Chögyam saying?"*

"I would say the same – but maybe I would qualify the statement in case anyone thought that this was agreeing with the Hindu idea that 'all religions are one'. This idea has proved popular in the West because it sounds all-embracing and all-accepting – but if you believe that 'all religions are one', you become a Hindu. This is not what you said, Rinpoche – but I know how people think and I have found that it is important to make this distinction. "I would say that it is impossible to say that all religions are one if you have not studied and practised all religions. More than this – you would have had to have taken all religions to the point of accomplishment. I think all religions have a similarity in terms of ethics, morality, and kindness – but in terms of ultimate view, they can be quite different. Buddhism is an atheist religion – and there is no way that 'God' can be said to be the same as nonduality. I think that 'God' is a valuable method for those who are enthused by the idea of a creator – but, the idea has its problems. I don't need to go into what those problems are – but they affect the view at the relative level, sometimes quite considerably. Having said that – there are good Christians and bad Buddhists. Anyone in any religion can distort the religion to their own purposes."

I suddenly became aware that I'd delivered some sort of sermon and wondered what Künzang Dorje Rinpoche would make of it. It took a while to translate everything I had said – but when the translation came to an end, Rinpoche stroked his beard and grinned at me.

"O yah. Yah—yah—yah. Now all things teaching." Then he laughed *"You telling 'I not teaching methods knowing.' But you teaching method very well knowing. You Künzang Dorje carefully teachings hearing and 'principle and function' applying. Now Vajrayana in West no problem teaching."*

The wish of the Shabdrung to build a lhakhang was fulfilled during the reign of the 4th Druk Desi Ten'dzin Rab-gyé[11], the 1st, and only successor of Shabdrung Ngawang Namgyal[12]. During his visit to the sacred cave of Taktsang Palphug during the Tséchu he laid the foundation for building the lhakhang dedicated to Guru Rinpoche called the Guru Tsengyèd Lhakhang[13] At this time, he was leading the Tséchu festival dances – and at that time the only lhakhangs at the highest elevations, were the Zangdog Palri[14] and Ögyen Tsémo [15].

The Taktsang gompa consists of four main lhakhangs and residences designed to adapt to the rock ledges and caves. Out of the eight caves, four are easy to access. The cave where Guru Rinpoche first entered, riding the Tiger, is known as Tholu Phug and the original cave where he resided and meditated is known as Palphug. He directed disciples to build the gompa here. The gompa is precariously perched and clings to the side of the mountain like a gecko. The main cave is entered through a narrow passage. The cave houses many images of yidams. In an adjoining room, the texts are placed. All the buildings are interconnected through steps and stairways made in the rock. There are a few wooden bridges along the paths and stairways that cross over. Each building has a balcony, which provides views of the Paro Valley.

"Yah... so, when Taktsang going – then you will something knowing." PAUSE *"But, knowing or not knowing – not so important as devotion arising"* Rinpoche stressed. *"But... this I am not worrying."* PAUSE *"One day Chögyam Taktsang going. This I am knowing – and when Taktsang seeing, then Guru Rinpoche in person seeing. This possible. If Künzang Dorje still living – then you are telling."* PAUSE *"Maybe much visions coming.* PAUSE *If Kyabjé Künzang Dorje Rinpoche not then living – then must be Sam'phel Déchen telling."*

---

11 (1635–1697).
12 *zhabs drung ngag dBang rNam rGyal* / ཞབས་དྲུང་ངག་དབང་རྣམ་རྒྱལ — a cousin from the line descending from Drukpa Künlegs.
13 *gu ru mTshan brGyad lha khang* / གུ་རུ་མཚན་བརྒྱད་ལྷ་ཁང — Lhakhang of the Guru with Eight Names.
14 *zangs mDog dPal ri* / ཟངས་མདོག་དཔལ་རི
15 *o rgGyan rTse mo* / ཨོ་རྒྱན་རྩེ་མོ

15

miraculous mistresses

It had turned cold – cold as only Tso Pema seemed to turn cold. It wasn't the temperature in particular – it was the bone-chilling damp. A faint drizzle was descending. I could just make it out through the window of Künzang Dorje Rinpoche's room. He took a sip of hot chang with honey. He had just poured out two glasses. We both sipped in silence for some moments.

"*You maybe khandros thinking?*" Rinpoche observed.

"*Occasionally Rinpoche – but mainly those in the past rather than the future.*"

"*O yah… many famous khandros in Guru Rinpoche time coming. Many all are knowing and Mandarava – but many—many—other khandros. Yeshé Tsogyel is heart disciple who is all transmission from Guru Rinpoche receiving. All mastering—all perfectly accomplishing—Buddha becoming.*"

Yeshé Tsogyel became the living embodiment of Guru Rinpoche's lineage in Tibet. Through her siddhis she could bring the dead to life. Her memory was unfailing. She transcribed every word of teaching Guru Rinpoche uttered – and codified them into khandro-cypher[1] to be discovered as gTérmas in future generations. After Guru Rinpoche's departure from Tibet, she encoded further gTérmas, both as texts and as Mind-transmissions[2]. Together with Nubchen Sang-gyé Yeshé she transcribed many more volumes of Guru Rinpoche's teaching. She spent the rest of her life wandering throughout Tibet teaching many thousands of gö kar chang lo disciples. Yeshé Tsogyel has taken many incarnations in Tibet – within the Nyingma lineages and within the lineages of the Kagyüd and Sakya.

---

1 Khandro Da'yig (*mKha' 'gro'i brDa' yig* / མཁའ་འགྲོའི་བརྡ་ཡིག) – khandro cypher / dakini script. Also thiglé'i yi-ge (*thig le'i yi ge* / ཐིག་ལེའི་ཡི་གེ) – essence cypher; pung-yig (*sPung yig* / སྤུང་ཡིག) – amassed cypher; bé-yig (*sBas yig* / སྦས་ཡིག) – hidden cypher; shur-yig (*bShur yig* / བཤུར་ཡིག) – burning cypher.
2 Mind-transmission – Gong gTer (*dGongs gTer* / དགོངས་གཏེར).

Yeshé Tsogyel was the living embodiment of every manifestation of Yangchen-ma³.

Rinpoche took a sip of chang and smiled *"Then Mandarava. Mandarava born in Zahor, and through the cremation fire with Guru Rinpoche passing. She the siddhi of longevity gaining and throughout Himalaya region wandering transmission and instruction in the practice of Vajrayana giving. She 'secret activity' manifesting and so her accomplishments less known. Her effectiveness in world less known – but most powerful becoming. Great realisation. She also Buddha becoming."* PAUSE *"Then, Tashi Khyi'drèn*⁴*. Tashi Khyi'drèn born in region of Mön. The place is Mön Tsa'og calling. She is in Bhutan much fame."*

Tashi Khyi'drèn had spontaneous visions and complete memories of previous lives. She was first given empowerment and transmission by Yeshé Tsogyel, who then brought her to Guru Rinpoche. He took her as one of his major consorts in the practice of the Buddha-karma of destruction.

"When Guru Rinpoche, Dorje Tröllö manifesting – Tashi Chhi'drèn as Tiger manifesting. Some saying Yeshé Tsogyel as tiger of Dorje Tröllö manifesting. This also true. Many khandros tiger manifesting with Dorje Tröllö."

Rinpoche sat gazing into space for some moments. *"Kala Drüpchen*⁵*. Parents of Kala Drüpchen are weavers – and Kala Drüpchen learning Vajrayana from early age through the method of weaving."* PAUSE *"This meaning 'tantra knowing'…?"* Rinpoche asked.

"Yes Rinpoche. As far as I know, Tantra is connected with the idea of weaving and with the loom of lucency."

---

3   dByangs chen ma / དབྱངས་ཆེན་མ་ / Sarasvati – the Buddha of Knowledge and Eloquence. Yangchen-ma's manifestations are as follows: Rinchen Yangchen ma (*rin chen dByangs chan ma* / རིན་ཆེན་དབྱངས་ཆེན་མ་) – Melodious Ratna Buddha; Dorje Yangchen-ma (*rDo rJe dByangs chan ma* / རྡོ་རྗེ་དབྱངས་ཆེན་མ་) – Melodious Vajra Buddha; Padma'i Yangchen ma (*pad ma'i dByangs chan ma* / པདྨའི་དབྱངས་ཆེན་མ་) – Melodious Padma Buddha; Thrinlé-kyi Yangchen-ma (*'phrin las kyi dByangs chan ma* / འཕྲིན་ལས་ཀྱི་དབྱངས་ཆེན་མ་) – Melodious Karma Buddha; Sang-gyé Kün-ngö Yangchen-ma (*sang rGyas kun dNgos dByangs chan ma* / སངས་རྒྱས་ཀུན་དངོས་དབྱངས་ཆེན་མ་) – Melodious Embodiment of all Buddhas; and Ngawang Yangchen-ma (*ngag dBang dByangs chan ma* / ངག་དབང་དབྱངས་ཆེན་མ་) – Melodious Buddha of Powerful Speech.

4   bKra shis khye'u 'dren / བཀྲ་ཤིས་ཁྱེའུ་འདྲེན་ – one of the five major consort disciples of Guru Rinpoche and Yeshé Tsogyel.

5   ka la grub chen ma / ཀ་ལ་གྲུབ་ཆེན་མ་ / Kalasiddhi.

'Loom of lucency' proved untranslatable and so I had to unpack the term. *"It means that emptiness and form are the warp and weft of reality. For there to be a warp and weft there has to be a loom — so the loom is a symbol of nonduality. That is how it was explained to me by Kyabjé Dilgo Khyentsé Rinpoche. So, the image concerns the warp of form and the weft of emptiness."*

"O yah! This good coming, good saying." PAUSE *"Maybe nangsèl'i thag-tri* [6]*"* PAUSE *"Anyway… when both parents dying, Kala Drüpchen bodies to charnel ground taking and leaving. Kala Drüpchen then found by Mandarava who as tiger manifesting. Mandarava like Yeshé Tsogyel and Tashi Khyi'dren — all one time tiger manifesting. Tiger caring for Kala Drüpchen. Tiger instruction giving — then to Guru Rinpoche bringing. Then Guru Rinpoche transmission giving. Kala Drüpchen then Yeshé Tsogyel — concealment of gTérmas assisting. Then end of life Kala Drüpchen is rainbow body attaining."*

We sat in silence for some minutes. This happened periodically and it was an unspoken aspect of our time together. Meditation permeated these times. *"You wish all khandros hearing?"* Rinpoche asked.

"Yes, Rinpoche. I would value that. I find this account of the khandros extremely important because there is so little information about women in Vajrayana and women will be happy to know this information."

"O yah… then you telling and western khandros much smiling — too much smiling. Then sangyum quickly arriving." Rinpoche laughed *"O yah… 'Khordu khandro mangpö 'khor* [7]*. Then next Shakya Lhamo* [8] *coming. Shakya Lhamo daughter of the Queen of Nepal. Then Queen in childbirth dying and Shakya Lhamo mother's body to charnel ground taking. There wild animals feeding and care giving before Guru Rinpoche discovering. Guru Rinpoche then Shakya Lhamo as major consort taking and all necessary teachings and transmissions giving. At end of life Shakya Lhamo rainbow-body manifesting."*

---

6 *nang gSal'i thags khri* / ནང་གསལ་འི་ཐགས་ཁྲི་
7 *'khor du mKha' 'gro mang po 'khor* / འཁོར་དུ་མཁའ་འགྲོ་མང་པོ་འཁོར་ — surrounded by hosts of sky dancers or dakinis.
8 *sha kya lha mo* / ཤཱཀྱ་ལྷ་མོ་ / *Shakyadevi*.

"O yah! Then... most important khandro now coming! Mélong gZa' Rinchen Tso.⁹" Rinpoche fixed me with a knowing expression and his eyes seemed to grow larger and wider. *"When Chögyam incarnation of Mélong gZa' Rinchen Tso finding – then very long living and too happy. She was Mistress of the Jewel-Mirror Lake. White robes on the rays of the sun hanging – and naked in the mountains dancing. Never clothes again wearing – only rainbow light."*

"Rinpoche... you said 'If I meet her'...?" PAUSE *"How would I meet her? How would that be possible?"*

Rinpoche laughed *"Same way Düd'jom Rinpoche meeting. Same way Künzang Dorje meeting."* PAUSE *"Meeting always possible. Many tulkus of these khandros possible finding. Chögyam practising well. This I am seeing. Good practice coming, then meeting possible. For you this good – and much help."* PAUSE *"Anyway past—present—future – all potential present every moment. Just continuing. Simply practising. Practising as we together practising... and Chögyam same good natural mind keeping. With 'thom yor not involved – then good circumstances coming and khandro finding. Maybe Mélong gZa' Rinchen Tso finding. This I am thinking. Yes. Chögyam incarnation of Mélong gZa' Rinchen Tso finding."*

There was not much I could say about that. I wanted to ask '*how, when, why, where...?*' but I realised Rinpoche wasn't going to be specific. This was obviously something he simply knew. It was something which he knew – but not in the way that things are normally known. Something had just appeared in his mind and he'd spoken of it directly. Kyabjé Düd'jom Rinpoche also did that. He'd simply say something about the future because it arose. It made me wonder about what was possible for me. Would I ever simply receive trans-temporal impressions? Did they already occur? Maybe they occurred and were subject to conditioned filtration.

If I pushed for anything specific, it would ruin the atmosphere which had evolved. I always had to be sensitive to that. There's always the tendency to make everything concrete and if a person's too persistent – then they cease to hear such statements.

9   *me long gZa' rin chen mTsho* / མེ་ལོང་གཟའ་རིན་ཆེན་མཚོ་ – . according to Künzang Dorje Rinpoche she was the originator of the incarnation line that preceded A-yé Khandro (*A ye mKha' 'gro* / ཨ་ཡེ་མཁའ་འགྲོ་), who was one of the two sangyums of Aro Yeshé (*A ro ye shes* / ཨ་རོ་ཡེ་ཤེས་) and the previous incarnation of Khandro Déchen Tsédrüp Rolpa'i Yeshé (*mKha' 'gro bDe chen Tshe grub rol pa'i ye shes* / མཁའ་འགྲོ་བདེ་ཆེན་ཚེ་གྲུབ་རོལ་པའི་ཡེ་ཤེས་).

Of course, this sometimes leads to enduring mystery – but I always relied on Rinpoche to give me information when he assessed the time as being conducive.

Rinpoche poured a tot of whiskey for both of us *"Yah… then Tshan-ma Za Dorje Tso* [10] *– Mistress of the Hot Vajra Lake realised the siddhi of gTummo and could cause the lake in which she bathed to give rise to steam as if it were a thermal spring."* Rinpoche looked at me and chuckled at this point *"Maybe you can do this without gTummo."* Rinpoche was accustomed to the fact that I couldn't tolerate heat very well and seemed to suffer no ill effects from drinking cold water. He often teased me about having some form of naturally arisen gTummo because I was too hot most of the time. *"Maybe you will have to sit in the lake and make steam!"* he laughed.

"Now that would be entertaining for the local people – but I don't think my heat would last that long at this time of year."

Rinpoche chuckled and shook his head. *"Yah… possible, not possible – no meaning. Anyhow Mélong Za Rinchen Tso… at the end of life rainbow body attaining."* PAUSE *"You gTummo practising?"*

"I began Rinpoche… but I don't have the legs for it. My legs are too short for lotus posture. I tried quite hard to perform the exercises – but only succeeded in hurting my ankles." PAUSE *"Kyabjé Düd'jom Rinpoche said I should practise 'phowa instead."*

Rinpoche nodded *"Yah… I can see this."* PAUSE *"This will be good for Dzogchen men-ngag-dé – you will need Phat shouting!"* Rinpoche shouted a sudden 'Phat!'

I felt myself *splatter* across the room.

I didn't jump as I had done on many previous occasions. I probably flinched slightly as my autonomic nervous system reacted involuntarily – but the effect was still *violent*. I sat there as my 'self' or my reality reassembled. It was as if disassembled particles of 'me' slowly came back into focus—as something self-recognisable—something like 'a person sitting in front of his Lama'. It was for a moment as if I was viewing the movie of what had just happened – and the movie was dissolving into what was actually taking place.

---

10 *Tshan ma gZa' rDo rJe mTsho* / ཚན་མ་གཟའ་རྡོ་རྗེ་མཚོ

Rinpoche grinned at me and continued his account as if nothing had happened *"Then… Tshom-bu Za Pema Tso*[11] *– Mistress of the dKyil'khor-clustered Lotus Lake, such mastery of her rTsa rLung accomplishing that body of yidam materially manifesting. And then… Tshé-nam Za Sang-gyé Tso* [12] *– Life-sky Mistress of the Indestructible Lake, rainbow body attaining."*

As Rinpoche explained – it was said of her, that after abandoning both physical clothing and the clothing of delusion she entered into the naked expanse of being in which, whether she swam like a fish in water or flew like a bird in the sky was incidental – both elements were her natural home.

Rinpoche peered out of the window into the night. *"Darkness now coming."* PAUSE *"Another day going… but still… we have days together remaining."* PAUSE *"Many great Lamas, appearance of yidam manifesting – but mainly this during empowerments happening. Düd'jom Lingpa always this manifesting. Kyabjé Düd'jom Rinpoche and his son Dung-sé Thrin-lé Norbu Rinpoche always this manifesting. This I have seen."*

Rinpoche adjusted his chuba sash and gazed into space for a moment. *"Yah… and so… then Shel-kar gZa' Dorje Tso* [13] *… She on water walking – as if solid ground."* PAUSE *"This siddhi I am in Tibet seeing. There was one khandro—A'dzin Namkha—in Golok this siddhi manifesting. I saw her once – but she was far away and she had reached the shore before I am close coming – but others peoples closer and they are seeing her on water walking."* PAUSE *"I am never again seeing. This because she is not pleased too many people meeting. She was a great master and mainly Dzogchen long-dé practising."* PAUSE *"Anyway… Shel-kar gZa' Dorje Tso much devotion to Guru Rinpoche – like river plant by water currents moving, according to suggestion of Guru Rinpoche. Through devotion she all siddhis realising and rainbow body attaining.*

"Then Rü thog gZa' Thönrüpma [14] *– Mistress of the Thunderbolt Clan. She subdued the protectors by her mere gaze.*

---

11 *tshom bu gZa' padma mTsho* / ཚོམ་བུ་གཟའ་པདྨ་མཚོ
12 *tshe gNam gZa' sangs gyas mTsho* / ཚེ་གནམ་གཟའ་སངས་རྒྱས་མཚོ
13 *shel dKar gZa' rDor rJe mTsho* / ཤེལ་དཀར་གཟའ་རྡོར་རྗེ་མཚོ
14 *rus thog gZa' don grub ma* / རུས་ཐོག་གཟའ་དོན་གྲུབ་མ

"And Shubu gZa' Sherpa-ma [15] *had perfect insight into every text and commentary without the need of study. She gave transmission of everything within the nine yanas."*

"Yah..." Rinpoche smiled after lunch had been cleared away *"Next 'ö-ché gZa' Kar-Gyalmo* [16] *– Mistress of Primordial Starlight."*

"That's a remarkable name, Rinpoche" I exclaimed.

"O yah! Remarkable! All questions concerning the teachings, yidam asking and answers to everything without other teachings receiving."

"Which yidam did she practise?"

"It is not recorded. With most of these khandro disciples little is known."

This was because there was a great deal of persecution of the gö kar chang lo'i dé in the second spread of Buddhism in Tibet. The new monastic powers at the beginning were antagonistic to the Nyingma lineages which had continued from the time of Guru Rinpoche. They outlawed the Inner Tantras and any of the outer tantras which did not sit comfortably with Sutrayana. They made it punishable by death to translate such Tantras from Sanskrit. Because of this a great deal was lost – especially concerning the female siddhas. Anything which promoted the idea of women attaining realisation was suppressed – and women were relegated to a lower status. Now, since the Chinese invasion—Rinpoche explained—many Tibetan texts were no longer available. He thought that some could possibly be found in Kham and Golok – but now it would be difficult to find them.

"Maybe later in my life... I can try to find some of these texts, Rinpoche – if the situation in Tibet ever changes."

"Yah... good... maybe—maybe not—but anyway, if possible – then please try." PAUSE *"But Tibet... maybe be difficult for you."* PAUSE *"Chögyam Tibet going possible?"* Rinpoche shook his head. *"Maybe. Maybe not. I 'maybe not' thinking. I thinking Bhutan going. Bhutan going, then all good things coming."*

---

15 *shu bu gZa' shar pa ma* / ཤུ་བུ་གཟའ་ཤར་པ་མ—Lady from the East—was the sister of Shubu Pagyi Seng-gé (*shu bu dPal gyi seng ge* / ཤུ་བུ་དཔལ་གྱི་སེང་གེ), one of the 25 disciples of Padmasambhava.

16 *'o ches gZa' sKar rGyal mo* / འོ་ཆེས་གཟའ་སྐར་རྒྱལ་མོ

Künzang Dorje Rinpoche told me about Bhutan and what a marvellous country it was. It was a real Vajrayana Kingdom – the last such country in the world. Guru Rinpoche had been there as had Yeshé Tsogyel and Tashi Khyi'dren. Thangtong Gyalpo had been there and built suspension bridges. Drukpa Künlegs had spent a long time in Bhutan. Bhutan had not suffered the misfortune of theocracy – which meant it was still a free country. Bhutan had joined the United Nations whereas Tibet had preferred to trust the Chinese before their invasion of Tibet in the 1950s. *"Bhutanese Kings much intelligence having. Tibetan government too stupid and western peoples fearing. Modern idea fearing. Democracy fearing. Too much fearing – and too much China trusting. Now all slaves becoming."*

Rinpoche talked at length concerning Tibetan history and what had led to the Chinese takeover of Tibet. He spoke extremely frankly about the corruption of power in Tibet and about the sectarian rivalry which had led to the imposition of Chinese suzerainty over Tibet. He explained how the powerful political Lamas had basically sold Tibet for their own ends. It was not the fault of the ordinary Tibetans—or the authentic practitioners of all schools and traditions—it was the power-hungry political ecclesiastics who had been to blame. He said that these powerful ecclesiastics were still playing the same invidious games – but that it could not go on forever. They would all eventually be exposed by the modern world and lose their power. Their power was based on an ignorance which could not withstand world-wide communication. There were books now—on Tibetan history—and western people were studying historical texts. He said that it had once been too easy to falsify the past – but this was now becoming increasingly difficult.

"Yah—and so—Yamdrok gZa' Chökyi Drölma[17]. She is Liberated Mistress of Turquoise Lake – and teachings to all beings giving. Whenever speaking – her words hearing and great joy in people arising. Every aspect of existence there is joy coming."

---

17 *yar 'brog gZa' chos kyi grol ma* / ཡར་འབྲོག་གཟའ་ཆོས་ཀྱི་སྒྲོལ་མ་ — Yamdrok is one of the Dragpa'i Tso-chen Gyèd (*grags pa'i mTsho chen brGyad* / གྲགས་པའི་མཚོ་ཆེན་བརྒྱད་) – the Four Renowned Lakes: **1.** Yamdrok Yu-tso (*yar 'brog gYu mTsho* / ཡར་འབྲོག་གཡུ་མཚོ་) – the Turquoise Lake; **2.** Tri shöd Gyalmo (*khri shod rGyal mo* / ཁྲི་ཤོད་རྒྱལ་མོ་) – the Blue Lake in Do-mé; also known as Ko-ko nor, Ling Tso Ngön-mo (*ling mTsho sNgon mo* / གླིང་མཚོ་སྔོན་མོ་); **3.** Tso Mapham (*mTsho ma pham* / མཚོ་མ་ཕམ་ / (Manasarowar) – the Invincible Lake; **4.** Chang-gi Nam Tso (*byang gi gNam mTsho* / བྱང་གི་གནམ་མཚོ་) – the Celestial Northern Lake.

Rinpoche explained that a mark of authentic teaching—stemming from authentic realisation—gave rise to joy. If what was taught was merely intellectually profound – there would be no natural joy. People might listen with great interest. They might be highly impressed – but their lives would be unlikely to be changed by it. Teaching which was merely intellectually perfect had a short life. People might hear such teaching as a huge revelation – but days, hours, or sometimes minutes later the impact would dissipate. This was because joy was lacking – and there could only be joy when the teaching arose from authentic realisation. Rinpoche compared it to winning a great prize and being given a cheque for a huge sum of money. The joy of receiving this sum would only last if one gave the cheque to one's bank and the bank accepted it. Then later one would have to see the sum of money reflected in one's bank account. One would then have to withdraw actual money and spend it. Only then would the joy be real.

"O yah" Rinpoche pinned me eye to eye with a penetrating gaze almost as if he were furious. Then he smiled extremely broadly and exclaimed *"Much joy must be bringing. Chögyam must be much joy bringing!"*

Every time Rinpoche said something like this, I had to remind myself not to play the 'humile' card to him – or secretly to myself. How did I know what was possible? To deny the possibility was not to trust Künzang Dorje Rinpoche – and as I trusted him implicitly in every other respect, it was somehow asinine to distrust him just because he made a positive statement about me. I knew that he was not given to giving 'pep talks' like some sort of sports coach – but I felt so limited. If he was telling me about the teacher I would be in my next life, it would have sounded reasonable – but how would a person who'd led such a bizarre life ever cause joy through teaching? I was too whimsical. I was too fascinated by too many things.

"Then… 'dzem-ma gZa' Lhamo [18] *– The Divine Blushing Mistress."*

"Blushing, Rinpoche?"

"O yah – blushing. Like Chögyam" he chuckled *"when western khandros much pleasure giving."*

---

18 *'dzem ma gZa' lha mo* / འཛེམ་མ་གཟའ་ལྷ་མོ

Rinpoche had read my mind again. This had now become a relief—every time it happened—because I knew that I was an open book. It was exactly what I wanted to be in respect of Künzang Dorje Rinpoche – and, of course, the relief was in knowing that there was nothing in me to cause him to shout at me ever again.

"Blushing, red and white thig-lés mixing this meaning – but this you are already knowing."

"Oh yes – the pink complexion which is the sign of integrating the male and female aspects of being."

Rinpoche nodded and proceeded *"O yah… She sustenance from food and wine directly from the nature of the sky taking."*

"Is that like çud-len, [19] *Rinpoche?"*

Rinpoche shook his head *"No, this fruitional. This result. This not practice. With çud-len still water drinking necessary."*

"Is this something that I should practise, Rinpoche?"

"Maybe. Maybe not. Maybe not so necessary for you." PAUSE *"Künzang Dorje çud-len practising – because it is valuable for retreat when no provision coming. Chögyam always provision having – I am thinking…"* PAUSE *"Maybe you once the long-ku çud-len practising. For vision this valuable. I rilbu giving for this – and then… maybe in some years… you are trying. You are time and place knowing."*

There are three forms of çud-len. The first is trülku çud-len, in which one only eats rice. One eats less-and-less rice every day until only one grain per meal is ingested. The second is the long-ku çud-len. With this one ingests three rilbus per day.

---

[19] *bCud len* / བཅུད་ལེན་ – çud-len pa is the Tibetan equivalent to *rasayana* in Sanskrit, and means 'extracting the essences' and subsisting on the essences. Çud-len means vital essence, distilled essence, quintessence, taste, elixir, potency, nutritional substance, extraction, essential aspect. It also means the preparation of elixirs for the elderly to prolong life. Çud-len involves the extraction of essences from stones and mineral deposits (*rDo'i bCud len* / རྡོའི་བཅུད་ལེན་), earth (*sa'i bCud len* / སའི་བཅུད་ལེན་), roots (*rTsa ba'i bCud len* / རྩ་བའི་བཅུད་ལེན་), flower petals (*me tog gi bCud len* / མེ་ཏོག་གི་བཅུད་ལེན་), and breath (*rLung gi bCud len* / རླུང་གི་བཅུད་ལེན་). There is also nondual presence (*rig pa'i bCud len* / རིག་པའི་བཅུད་ལེན་), which requires nondual absorption. The practice is eating incrementally less until one can survive by sucking a special kind of stone.

The third is chö-ku çud-len – in which one eats nothing at all – but simply sucks a special kind of stone. In this, one can only drink water – and the time of the retreat is three weeks. *"Yah... if çud-len practising, I am thinking... maybe only once necessary – and only long-ku çud-len practising.* [20]*"*

Rinpoche and I sat in silence for some time after he concluded his instruction of çud-len. This often occurred after he imparted some specific instruction. He never told me why we sat in silence and I never asked – but it made sense to me in terms of transmission. I'd been given an important teaching and I needed to sit with what I'd been given.

"Then..." Rinpoche resumed *"... 'bar Za Lha-yang* [21] *Mistress of Blazing Melody. She pacified the perceptions of disciples without need of activity. Merely to see her was to have one's confusion resolved and one's relationships with others harmonised."* PAUSE *"This siddhi is wonderful. Such a khandro – great benefit for many 'thom yor in this world."* PAUSE *"When there are too many 'thom yor – too much suffering in this world. Suffering anyway as long as 'khorwa peoples experiencing, but 'thom yor suffering worse making – then too difficult for people good circumstances for practise finding."*

Cha-rog gZa' Changchubma[22]—Compassionate Mistress of Ravens—through the Dzogchen men-ngak-dé practice of integrating with moving elements – gained the siddhi of transforming her physical body into the moving elements: wind, fire, or water in order to benefit her disciples.

"Ha ha!" Rinpoche exclaimed rather loudly. I'd not heard him raise his voice for quite a while and so the hair on the nape of my neck prickled with it. *'Aro gZa' Druk-tsal Shèldrakma* [23]. *This... means she is one taste knowing. Primordial 'A' taste knowing – and radiance like Dragon having. Mistress of Crystal Crags.* "*Siddhi of thunder in sky commanding. Mind identical with the sky experiencing. What arising in mind – in sky manifesting as cloud and all are seeing."*

Rinpoche sat in silence for some minutes at this point. It was one of those times when—although looking straight at me—his vision seemed to be taking in some vast horizon.

20 I practised this—according to Rinpoche's instruction—in July 1983 at Lam Rim Chöling in Raglan, Wales.
21 *'bar gZa' lha dByangs* / འབར་གཟའ་ལྷ་དབྱངས
22 *bya rog gZa' byang chub ma* / བྱ་རོག་གཟའ་བྱང་ཆུབ་མ
23 *A ro gZa' 'brug rTsal shel brag ma* / ཨ་རོ་གཟའ་འབྲུག་རྩལ་ཤེལ་བྲག་མ

It could easily have felt as if I was not there and that Rinpoche was sitting in an empty room – but I did not feel excluded from his gaze. Then, quite slowly, he said *"Kyabjé Düd'jom Rinpoche is telling. Chögyam incarnation—in time of Guru Rinpoche and Yeshé Tsogyel—Aro gZa' Druk-tsal Shèldrakma."*

At first, this information seemed to disappear into itself – like an idea which arises in a daydream, which is immediately forgotten. Rinpoche continued to sit absolutely still – but it was not one of those occasions in which I knew he wanted me to speak. After a few moments I remembered what he had said and the words hung in space like gossamer on the wind – something barely visible. Then incrementally the words formed a pattern – but the pattern made less sense than the fleeting gossamer of his words. I became aware that concept consciousness had intervened and I was merely wallowing in a stew of ideas. Sometimes 'linear understanding' converted experiential knowledge into incomprehension.

"Thinking – no value coming" were the next words I heard — but it was as if I was remembering them rather than hearing them in the present.

"I understand that, Rinpoche." Then, after a moment, I took a risk with the question which arose *"Rinpoche—I apologise if this is discourteous—but is there a reason why you just told me this?"*

"No discourteous coming" Künzang Dorje Rinpoche chuckled *"Chögyam—never—discourteous – always too polite. No reason. Just what Düd'jom Rinpoche is telling – and we are together khandros talking. All are past life having. All long story having. Every Lama long story having."*

Then he explained that I might have memories of this time – or I might never remember anything. Apparently, many Lamas remembered nothing of their incarnation lines. He said that Düd'jom Rinpoche was different. His memory was continuous and stretched back to the time of Shakyamuni Buddha. What was important for me was that I practised – and that I continued to practise. I should not fixate on the past – but nor should I ignore it. It was important because Düd'jom Rinpoche had mentioned it – but beyond this, there was nothing to do with what he had told me. He asked me what I knew of my grandparents. I told him a little. I told him what my brother Græham had discovered – that my grandfather on my father's side had left school at the age of twelve to support the family after the death of his father.

His reading ability was poor but he taught himself—with limited help—to read to a good standard. He then taught himself history by reading an encyclopaedia. My grandmother was a farm worker in a milking parlour. In the army—during the Boer War—my grandfather was a soldier in an insignificant company which tended to the Cavalry horses. He contracted yellow fever and was then discharged and returned home.

"*O yah.*" Rinpoche nodded. "*Father also army?*"

"Yes, *my father left school at fourteen years of age. He became a dock worker. After a few months of this work he decided it was not what he wanted to do with his life. He therefore falsified his age in order to join the army. He then worked his way up the ranks, through taking engineering qualifications. He was finally promoted to the rank of major.*"

"*And mother family knowing?*"

"Yes. *My grandmother—on my mother's side—was related to the Classical composer Franz Schubert. My grandfather was the headmaster of a large prestigious school. They were seriously reduced in circumstances during the Second World War because of their opposition to Hitler. My grandfather refused to have Nazi propaganda material taught in his school – because he believed that education concerned imparting factual information. It destroyed my grandfather's health and he died earlier than he might have done. My grandmother survived him but had to escape to Denmark because of the help she had given to Jewish families.*"

"*Yah… father like zo-zhing* [24]*– and mother like ku-drag* [25]*.*" Rinpoche nodded whilst he contemplated this. "*This Chögyam, this understanding making. So, how Chögyam Zo-zhing or ku-drag understanding? Why zo-zhing for father thinking? He major becoming – so why ku-drag not thinking?*"

My answer was a lengthy discourse in my mind before I even began – so I asked whether Rinpoche wanted to hear a long explanation. He agreed and so I presented him with my reasons for thinking of myself as working class.

"*I see my father as zo-zhing – because his parents were zo-zhing. Even though he studied in the army and became a major – he was only a 'wartime major' and that is not regarded in the same light as being a major during a period of peace.*"

---

24 *bZo zhing* / བཟོ་ཞིང་ – working class, peasantry.
25 *sKu drag* / སྐུ་དྲག་ – noble, aristocrat, gentry, high official.

Rinpoche nodded his acceptance of my explanation.

"So… it's a given understanding, in Britain at least, that social class comes from one's father rather than one's mother. That's the first point. The second is that whatever one's social status was – one drops in social status in another country unless one is royalty or from an extremely wealthy and influential family. My mother's family became quite poor as a result of the Nazi regime. They fell from having servants to having very little. My mother therefore entered my father's social situation rather than he entering hers – and my experience of life was conditioned by education in a school with largely working-class children."

This was translated to Kunzang Dorje Rinpoche with a few clarifications required – and all the while he nodded. Then he asked *"Your own idea – what coming?"*

"My own idea, Rinpoche, is probably the main thing rather than who my parents are – or who my grandparents were. I suppose I could see myself as middle-class – but I see myself as working class."

Here we had to have a discussion to find out what would equate to 'middle-class'. There were a few suggestions: *tshong pa* 'merchant' and *tshong dPon* 'trade agent' and I said that this was more-or-less the origin of the middle classes in Europe – but that they were now higher level office workers, school teachers, professionals such as doctors and architects and governmental bureaucrats. This made sense and so we moved on.

"So, although I have an Art School degree—and I enjoy tshong dPon interests such as literature, poetry, music, and theatre—I don't see myself as a tshong dPon. I don't see myself that way – because I don't have a tshong dPon mind. I say this because there's an aspect of tshong dPon attitude which I don't appreciate. Typically, tshong dPons are concerned with status. They're competitive with each other. They look down on those they see as lower in society – and try to ingratiate themselves with those they see as higher. That doesn't suit me. I don't want to look down on anyone or ingratiate myself with anyone. I feel there is more integrity in being a zo-zhing. There were tshong dPons at Art School – although some were kindly open-minded people, they were mainly status conscious. The three ladies with whom I shared a house were ku-drag with wealthy parents – and they were far less interested in status. They were good friends and didn't treat me as an inferior merely because I had little money. So… this is why I am happy to be a zo-zhing."

Künzang Dorje Rinpoche nodded *"O yah. This good. This natural. This Dharma view. All equal treating. All kindness showing. Arrogance and haughty not feeling – then all happiness naturally coming."*

He told me that my family information was 'a facet of the multifaceted crystal of my empty continuum' – and that Aro gZa' Druk-tsal Shèldrakma was simply another aspect of that. There was no more to think about it.

This whole discussion suddenly became quite astonishing to me. I understood in the moment, that he summed it all up by asking me about my family in order to make me relax. The information which he had given me concerning Aro gZa' Druk-tsal Shèldrakma, had somehow thrown me into a rather strange state emotionally. I could not describe what the emotion was because it was nothing like anything which I understood. It was perhaps a little bit like the reverberation of something which was being flustered in the wind – or like the weird whirring of the world just prior to fainting. I'd only fainted once in my life. It had been at the home of my Aunt Rikchen and Uncle Arnold in Ahlten[26] near Hannover in Germany. The memory came back to me at that moment and I wondered if I was about to faint again. I didn't. By the time I'd talked about my family history I felt fairly normal again and the information concerning Aro gZa' Druk-tsal Shèldrakma was simply there – as the room was there and as the glass of Eagle beer was there. Rinpoche indicated my glass of beer and I took a drink. I'd become quite thirsty and had not realised it. Perhaps it had made me feel a little faint. I had no way of knowing.

"O yah… Drom gZa' Pema-sèl[27], *Lotus Light Mistress from Drom Clan coming"* Rinpoche recommened. *"Siddhi of flight having. She, daughter from prince of the Drom clan – but dying when age sixteen. Parents much grief and Guru Rinpoche asking for life bringing. Guru Rinpoche then Chimphu taking and life bringing. Guru Rinpoche red vermilion Hri on each breast writing. Then transmission of Men-ngak Khandro Nying-thig*[28] *giving and authenticating as gTértön in future time."*

---

26 Ahlten is a village three miles to the East district of Lehrte. Ahlten is seven miles east of Hannover, the capital town Niedersachsen.
27 *'brom gZa' padma gSal* / འབྲོམ་གཟའ་པདམ་གསལ
28 *man ngag mKha' 'gro sNying thig* / མན་ངག་མཁའ་འགྲོ་སྙིང་ཐིག

Guru Rinpoche concealed the treasure within her Mind-stream and she later revealed this gTérma in her incarnation as Pema Le'drèl-tsal[29] in the eighth century. Pema Le'drèl-tsal withdrew the gTérma of Khandro Nying-thig from the rock at Daklha Tramo Drak in the province of Dakpo in the year of the Female Water Ox[30]. He only partially decoded it during his life. He transmitted the gTérma to his main disciple Gyal-sé Legden[31]. Pema Le'drèl-tsal was incarnated as Rabjam Longchenpa, who received the entire cycle of Khandro Nying-thig from Gyal-sé Legden, and thus ensured the lineage was maintained.

Rong gZa' Siddhi[32], Mistress of Siddhis – could live on stones as nourishment.

Trum gZa' Shèl ma[33], Mistress of Crystal – manifested floral apparitions in the sky and inspired visions to arise within other practitioners.

Khu gZa' Pal-tsün[34], Mistress of Glorious Wrath – could make her phurba vibrate merely by resting her attention on its outer form.

"O yah… now…" Rinpoche yawned *"tired becoming…"* shaking his head with a grin. *"Too many khandros—too many khandros"* he laughed. *"You still young – so problem for you not coming. Maybe you now dreaming many khandros. Now maybe sleeping necessary – but before . . . I am something telling and you must be writing in good English so I can again hearing."*

This was something which Düd'jom Rinpoche had asked from time to time: that I should write down what he had taught and then edit it into English as I would speak it. Then the translator would deliver what I had written to Kyabjé Düd'jom Rinpoche in Tibetan – so that he could hear what I had understood.

> *Confidence arises from understanding the state of intrinsic awareness immediacy.*
>
> *Intrinsic awareness immediacy is uncreated.*

---

29 *pad ma las 'brel rTsal* / པད་མ་ལས་འབྲེལ་རྩལ་ / 1231–1307
30 Crossing the years 1253 and 1254.
31 He also transmitted this gTérma to the 3rd Gyalwa Karmapa, Rangjung Dorje, and to Rinchen Lingpa.
32 *rong gZa' siddhi* / རོང་གཟའ་སིདྡྷི་
33 *khrum gZa' shel ma* / ཁྲུམ་གཟའ་ཤེལ་མ་
34 *'khu gZa' dPal tsun* / འཁུ་གཟའ་དཔལ་བཙུན་

It is self-existent—and its essence is Zhi [35]*—the primordial ground.*
Everywhere the manner in which it arises—as diverse appearances—is uninterrupted and free of obstruction.
Everything which appears arises spontaneously as the self-perfected display of chö-ku – the Space of Being.
That which arises is liberated directly due to intrinsic awareness immediacy.
This is none other than rig-pa – nondual instant presence.
Nondual knowingness is present in the hearts of all Buddhas.
Rigpa is encompassed within the intrinsic awareness immediacy of every being.

Künzang Dorje Rinpoche nodded. He smiled when these words were translated back to him. *"Now sleeping necessary – and khandros dreaming."*

---

35 *gZhi* / གཞི་ / *alaya*.

16

Charong Drüpchen

Künzang Dorje Rinpoche adjusted his chuba. It had once been black Tibetan serge. Now the fabric was many shades of the deepest grey – rippled with a black that was almost vivid. It had been sumptuously refined by the weather: sun, wind, and rain. It was an old garment but clean and perfectly pleated. The piping and edgings had been replaced. He was always utterly refined in his appearance. Always dignified – but never triflingly fastidious. He simply arranged his apparel so that it sat or lay as it should.

"So… today history coming [1]*."* PAUSE *"This because Chögyam asking"* Rinpoche announced with a smile. *"Not too much saying – but something."* He gazed at me benevolently – but it was as if I was part of a landscape that I could not see. Or maybe it was a time which I did not currently inhabit. I have seen people daydreaming or seeing images in the mind's eye – but this has never included me as part of the vision. It was as if I'd been placed within his vision of another time and another place.

---

1 In 1975 Kyabjé Künzang Dorje Rinpoche wrote a brief life history at my request. This can be found in *wisdom eccentrics* published by ARO BOOKS inc in 2011. Kyabjé Künzang Dorje Rinpoche wrote as a colophon: *Knowing of my life, my Dharma friends requested the history of my life and liberation. Furthermore, my English friend Chögyam—the Aro Tulku—(Ngak 'chang Chos dByings rGya mTsho) sincerely requested an account of my life and the Lamas with whom I have taken refuge. He asked me to describe the places I lived and practices in which I engaged. At his request I composed this brief history in the* 17th *rabjung, the fire rat year in Nepal whilst living at Tsogyel Gé'phel Jong near Yang-lé-shöd.* de lTar rang gi chos grogs 'ga' nas khyed kyi chos phyogs / kyi rnam thar zhig dgos zhes bsKul ma byung ba dang / lhag par dByin yul gyi grogs po **A ro sPrul sKu chos rGyam** / nas kyang rNam thar zhig dgos zhes nan bsKul / la brTen nas rang gis bLa ma bsTen tshul / gNas dang sGrub brGyab pa'i lo rGyus mDor 'dus 'di bZhin / bod rab byung me byi lor bal yul gNas chen yang le shod kyi / nye 'dabs mTsho rGyal dGe 'phel lJongs su sDod sKabs bris pa dGe'o / bal yul sGo mang gLog rtsis (kam pu'i tar) dPe sKrun khang nas 'phrul par du bTab pa'o. དེ་ལྟར་རང་གི་ཆོས་གྲོགས་འགའ་ནས་ཁྱེད་ཀྱི་ཆོས་ ཕྱོགས། ཀྱི་རྣམ་ཐར་ཞིག་དགོས་ཞེས་བསྐུལ་མ་བྱུང་བ་དང་། ལྷག་པར་དབྱིན་ཡུལ་གྱི་གྲོགས་པོ་ཨ་རོ་སྤྲུལ་སྐུ་ཆོས་རྒྱམ། ནས་ཀྱང་རྣམ་ ཐར་ཞིག་དགོས་ཞེས་ནན་བསྐུལ། ལ་བརྟེན་ནས་རང་གིས་བླ་མ་བསྟེན་ཚུལ། གནས་དང་སྒྲུབ་བརྒྱབ་པའི་ལོ་རྒྱུས་མདོར་འདུས་འདི་ བཞིན། བོད་རབ་བྱུང་མེ་བྱི་ལོར་བལ་ཡུལ་གནས་ཆེན་ཡང་ལེ་ཤོད་ཀྱི། ཉེ་འདབས་མཚོ་རྒྱལ་དགེ་འཕེལ་ལྗོངས་སུ་སྡོད་སྐབས་བྲིས་པ་ དགེའོ། བལ་ཡུལ་སྒོ་མང་གློག་རྩིས་ (ཀམ་པུའི་ཏར) དཔེ་སྐྲུན་ཁང་ནས་འཕྲུལ་པར་དུ་བཏབ་པའོ།།

"Father" he commenced *"ancestral lineage from Horsog Déma coming. Family clan Jya-rig Tse'phel Chawo."* PAUSE *"This 'Bird Tribe' meaning. Bird Tribe from Cha-rig A-sé'i lineage descending – in Sang-zhung Ma-gyo Ga-den of Nagchu Dzong.*

"Iron horse year—16th rab jung ^{2}—before dawn. 25th day of 5th month – being born. Mother is Dung'dok and father A-Dok. One month after birth, Dzigar Potrül Rinpoche arriving and parents asking, he name giving. Dzigar Potrül Rinpoche happy with request – and 'This one, trülku of Charong Drüpchen. He is then 'Künzang Dorje' name giving. Then he is saying 'Thirteen children 'Dorje' now I am naming – and Künzang Dorje foremost coming."

He said all this in a matter-of-fact manner. And I was intrigued by his lack of involvement with either pride of humility. It was simply reportage. This is what Dzigar Potrül Rinpoche had said – and he was merely repeating it. I realised that I would have dissembled and said something about my not really being the foremost in anything. I recognised instantly how stupid it would have been for me to have made such a disclaimer. After all, I had a first-class honours degree – and I had no hauteur about it. I don't even think I was lucky. I simply worked hard. I'd deserved it – as anyone would have done who had worked as hard as I had worked. It was all quite simple and uncomplicated.

"Magyo Gaden where Mi-nak Tobchen living. Tobchen 'Great Strength' meaning – like Chögyam many bricks, ladder all-day climbing." Künzang Dorje Rinpoche beamed. He was referring to the fact that I'd worked all Summer hodding bricks^3 on a building site. He'd asked me to explain in detail and to be honest about the nature of the work – so I'd explained that there were not many who would endure the work for long. Tibetans, generally, seem to admire physical prowess almost as much as meditative capacity.

"Mi-nak Tobchen lord of Lhothri Dé-gu – Tak-zig Gyalpo: King of Tigers and Leopards." Kyabjé Künzang Dorje Rinpoche explained that being the King of Tigers and Leopards had a great breadth of meaning.

---

2 1929
3 A hod is a three-sided brick carrier – with a long handle for carrying over the shoulder. Arranging bricks herringbone fashion, 12 bricks can be carried – if the hoddie is strong. Hoddies serve bricklaying teams of two or three and deliver 1,000 to 2,000 bricks a day.

The tiger and leopards symbolised Form and Emptiness; Method and Wisdom; and, dPa'wos and Khandros. The robes of gTértöns were often edged with the fur of tigers and leopards.

"When Mon and Ling warring, Mi-nak Tobchen manifested as dPa'wo Kulha-thok so his peoples helping." Kyabjé Künzang Dorje Rinpoche explained that war was a great horror in the world – but that it occurred. Because it occurred – one had to be able to act for the benefit of the defenceless. It was thus not wrong to be a soldier, a great general, or a Warrior King like Ling Gésar. He spoke of the World Wars and the fact that Hitler had to be opposed. It was not wrong to oppose Hitler or other dictators of this kind – because they caused the most severe suffering. War which is based on greed and expansion was always wrong – and to oppose such warmongers through force of arms was necessary for Vajrayana practitioners.

"After battle victory, Lhothri Dé-gu—the enemy of Mi-nak Tobchen's tribe—comes forward. 'I am the Protector Dorje Bérnakchen of Druga province!' Lhothri Dé-gu is loudly boasting. Mi-nak Tobchen is hearing boasting of Lhothri Dé-gu – and then, with name 'Kulhathok', he riding and vanquishing Lhothri Dé-gu."

"But how vanquishing?" Künzang Dorje Rinpoche asked rhetorically. Then he shook his head in negation *"Not by ordinary warfare vanquishing."* At this point he indicated the phurba he wore in his chuba sash. *"Mi-nak Tobchen only on yidam and Lama's prophecy depending. No weapon carrying. No protection. No sword. No armour. No helmet. Mi-nak Tobchen—with name dPa'wo Kulhathok—transforming by power of protector Nyènchen Thanglha [4] into Dorje Bérnakchen! Then arising with black hat, triangular-sleeved gown, and meteorite iron phurba in belt sash."* As Kyabjé Künzang Dorje Rinpoche explained this – it all seemed to be happening in front of my eyes.

---

4 Nyènchen Thanglha is the Protector of Künzang Dorje Rinpoche's homeland. Regarding Nyènchen Thanglha, Drigung Rig'dzin Chödrak wrote his invocation of the Protectors: 'In the centre of the fragrant celestial realm of the northern direction – external phenomena spontaneously formed a four-peak snowy mountain, and inner phenomena manifested a treasure trove of precious jewels – there lives the oathbound wealth-lord Nyènchen Thanglha. Great protector, Jowo Shakyamuni, and female celestial beings of fragrance, purify the warriors of Mon.' Also Trülshik Pema Düd'dül wrote: *'The heart son of the great celestial being Tshangpa; holder of the treasure of the trans-dimensional water being's crown. Great liberator Nyènchen Thanglha – purify the vast assembly of Mon.'*

That is not to say that I saw anything changing. Künzang Dorje Rinpoche did not manifest visually as Dorje Bérnakchen. It was as if he had but I could not comprehend what I was seeing. Then suddenly the invisible vision passed and the previous reality resumed.

Künzang Dorje Rinpoche then explained that there had been four powerful athletic dPa'wos: the Black Chinese Ha Yang Tobchen; the Yellow Mongolian Takmar Tobchen; the Northern Tak-zig Mi-nak Tobchen and Northern Mi-chen Tobchen – and; also, Nyènchen Thanglha from Dru-dag province. *"Künzang Dorje, from lineage of Mi-nak Tobchen coming. This one is dPa'wo Kulhathok manifesting – and his people helping."*

This was like something from the history of Genghis Khan[5]. I'd seen the film and felt some strange affinity with Mongolia. As the thought of the film flickered in my mind, Künzang Dorje Rinpoche made a movement of his head and eyes which betokened that he'd seen something move behind me. Maybe the lady of the house bringing chang? This happened from time to time. Kyabjé Künzang Dorje Rinpoche laughed *"Chang not yet coming"* then seriously *"You also Mongolia thinking. You must be explaining."*

"I had a flash back—a vivid memory—of a film I once saw of Genghis Khan." PAUSE *"I was unusually impressed by the film – but also by the landscape and culture of Mongolia."*

After some discussion with the translator about who Genghis Khan might be, Künzang Dorje Rinpoche nodded *"O yah… This one Tibet in Fire Hare year[6] coming. This one maybe like Ling Gésar. What are you saying? This one, 'warrior realisation' having like Ling Gésar – or ordinary warrior?"*

"There are conflicting accounts, Rinpoche. He is a hero in Mongolia – so I feel that I would rather see him as the Mongolians see him."

Künzang Dorje Rinpoche looked at me shrewdly – but with a hint of gleeful mischief in his eyes *"Why this saying?"*

---

5 Genghis Khan (1155–1227) was the first Great Khan of the Mongol Empire, which became the largest contiguous empire in history. He came to power by uniting many of the nomadic Mongol clans.
6 1206.

"Because history is written by historians, and historians are mainly academics who believe that the present and the past are disconnected." Künzang Dorje Rinpoche had a slight smile at this point. *"So, historians aren't interested in what people think in the present. In the West—for example—the historians no longer accept that King Arthur existed – or many other heroes such as Beowulf – or Robin Hood in England or William Tell in Switzerland. They also want to portray the ignoble aspect of people who were once thought to be entirely worthy and noble. It seems to me that the reality of these people lies in the value they provide in helping people become kindly, honourable, and heroic. The academics also doubt the existence of Guru Rinpoche – so I have no trust in academics."*

"Why no trust having… ?"

"Because academics take refuge in pieces of paper and script which could have been written by anyone with any motive. I could write an account of Tso Pema explaining that there was no lake here – and in a thousand years an academic would quote my account as if it was true, merely because my account was a thousand years old. There are stones lying around here which are far older – and they are completely true. These stones aren't pretending to be mangos."

Künzang Dorje Rinpoche doubled up laughing at this. *"O yah! You are too well saying!"* PAUSE *"So, now you Genghis Khan something telling."*

"Genghis Khan" I began *"was born near Onon River in Mongolia in the 12th Century. He is named Témujin, which means blacksmith or made of iron."*

"O yah! Good name."

"He didn't receive the name Genghis until he was proclaimed leader of the Mongol people and father of the Mongol clans. Genghis means 'oceanic' and 'Khan' meaning 'ruler' – so the whole name means something like 'universal ruler'. From an early age, he was confronted by the brutality of life on the Mongolian Steppe. Rival clan leaders poisoned his father when he was nine years old – and his tribe expelled his family, leaving his mother to raise her children alone. He grew up having to hunt so that his family could survive."

During his teenage years, rival clans abducted and enslaved him and his wife Bör-té – but he made a daring escape in which he suffered many hardships. By his early 20s however, he'd established himself as a fearless warrior and leader, who was so well loved and honoured that he gathered warriors to him and united all the Mongol clans under his leadership.

He had an astute perception of people's qualities and promoted them on their skill and intelligence rather than class or wealth. One famous example was during a battle with the Taijut clan, when he was nearly killed after his horse was shot from under him. After the battle he addressed the Taijut prisoners and asked who was responsible for causing him to fall from his horse. The warrior who had shot the arrow stood forward as the archer – and Genghis Khan made him a warrior of rank in his host.

Unlike other warrior kings, Genghis Khan passed laws of religious freedom for all and granted tax exemptions to religious institutions. Although he followed a shamanic way which revered the spirits of the mountains, winds, and sky – he also had a personal interest in Buddhism.

Genghis Khan understood the evil of slavery as he'd been a slave in his teens – so when he unified the Mongol clans, he outlawed slavery. He instituted a system of law which prohibited theft, adultery, blood feuds, and fraudulent testimony. He also outlawed the pollution of rivers or streams and demanded that warriors left no litter. In the enforcement of his law, he instigated the creation of a writing system – which, although not the first writing system in Asia, was the first to be widely adopted and taught. Genghis Khan was one of the richest people in history – but only in terms of land. Rather than hoard wealth he gave it to his warriors, who were prohibited from looting.

Genghis Khan is a national hero and the founding father of Mongolia – but during the era of Soviet rule in the 20th century, even mentioning his name was banned. The Soviet government tried to remove all traces of Genghis Khan by removing his story from school textbooks and forbidding people from making pilgrimages to his birthplace. Genghis Khan was eventually restored to Mongolian history after independence in the early 1990s. *"He now appears on Mongolian currency."*

"O yah! Good! Good history telling. How Genghis Khan informations knowing?"

"I was told by a Mongolian man called Bor-ji-gin[7] I met in McLeod Ganj. He'd come to see the Dalai Lama. He said that 'Genghis' had the same meaning as 'Dalai' which meant 'oceanic'.

---

7   Bor-ji-gin—Blue-grey Wolf—an ancestor of Genghis Khan.

"He said there were many distorted accounts of *Genghis Khan* – and that it was a shame people believed what was written in western books. He said what was written was biased according to Russian and Chinese accounts. These, he said, were no better than reading a Nazi description of *Winston Churchill*."

"Yah – so what Chögyam believing?"

"Well – I think what people believe is a matter of choice. There are those who believe what the academics tell us about Genghis Khan. I prefer to accept the way he is seen by modern-day Mongolians – because that is the living aspect of history. Genghis Khan is extremely important to the Mongolian people today – and this seems to be what matters most. I would always far rather believe what was meaningful, than an academic text. Today the style in the West is to want to discover what may have been bad or corrupt about a person in the past – but I would rather have heroes and heroines than people with mixed motivation, or people who were no better or worse than I am. I would rather have people to admire. I would rather have figures to emulate. I'd rather be in the position of wanting to be as great as they were – and struggling to achieve it."

"*O yah!*" Rinpoche affirmed – almost with a roar "*Genghis Khan manifestation of Ling Gésar!*" PAUSE "*Yah – now like warriors we are walking.*" Suddenly Künzang Dorje Rinpoche was on his feet and seconds later I was on mine. We hurried out of the door and walked at a rather brisk pace up to the caves above Tso Pema. The pace was such that Pema Dorje the translator found it difficult to translate and breathe at the same time – so Künzang Dorje Rinpoche occasionally stopped to let him catch his breath. Fortunately, although I've never had 'running legs'—and couldn't run to save my life—I've always had 'up-hill walking legs'. I was therefore able to keep up with Künzang Dorje Rinpoche without undue exertion. I was however amazed at his pace – because, at his height, his legs must have been somewhat shorter than mine.

"*When five-year-old – blue goat, size of mountain seeing.*" PAUSE "*Chögyam also one time seeing.*"

It wasn't a question – but I answered because I was stunned by what Rinpoche had said. "*Yes, Rinpoche. It happened one evening when I was sitting on the steps of the Art School looking out at the evening sky.*"

"More saying, possible?"

"Yes Rinpoche. The colour of the sky was every shade of pink, orange, and red imaginable – together with purple, violet, and indigo. There were also streaks of blue and hints of green. Then, suddenly I saw something I'd often seen as a child. I'd often seen 'entities' in the clouds as a child. I thought they were real when I was very young – but I was told as I grew older that they were just my imagination. On this evening though, there was a goat and rider who were quite well defined – but only for a second or two. The wind was gusting through what I saw. The clouds continually made the image and interfered with the image. I tried to get what I saw into focus – and this is probably what dispelled the apparition."

"O yah. This is good." **Rinpoche nodded** *"Future time – Chögyam more seeing."* PAUSE *"Düd'jom Rinpoche telling?"*

"No, Rinpoche – but not for any reason. It simply didn't occur to me."

"Yah – next time Kyabjé Düd'jom Rinpoche seeing, you must be telling." PAUSE *"When seeing – no fear coming?"*

"No, Rinpoche – no fear… just… I don't know how to describe what it felt like. It was like knowing something without knowing what it was I was knowing. That was a feeling I remember having many times when I was young."

"O yah – too funny" he laughed *"Chögyam mighty dPa'wo! Like Genghis Khan! No fear having! This too happy making."* PAUSE *"Anyway, Künzang Dorje terror feeling—when vision of goat seeing—and so, mother calling. When mother arriving, nothing there finding. Later, Lamas are mother telling 'This goat, is goat Damçan Dorje Legpa is riding'."*

Rinpoche said that when he was seven years of age, he saw a beautiful girl wearing a dress completely ornamented with turquoise and coral. In her right hand she brandished a gri-gug. In her left hand she held a skull bowl. She also carried a lasso. He had told his mother and father of this and they told a Lama – who said *"This was Palden Lhamo."* [8]

When he was nine years old, he saw a red man the size of a mountain. He was stepping from one mountain peak to another. He told his mother and relatives. When asked, the Lama told them: *"That is the Protector Zangs Ri-tèn Dam Rolpa Kyadun."*

---

8   dPal lDan lha mo / དཔལ་ལྡན་ལྷ་མོ་ / *Sri Devi* – the female consort of Nakpo Chenpo (Mahakala).

We walked in silence for a while and then Kyabjé Künzang Dorje Rinpoche said *"Today we Wangdor Rinpoche* [9] *visiting. Today visiting because no other visitor."* PAUSE *"There is one American woman who is nun pretending – but she sex with many Indian men having. Her name Khé-drub – one time she maybe Gélug nun. Maybe true maybe not true – but not mattering. Now too much arrogance."*

Rinpoche then regaled me with an account of how this woman had made a nuisance of herself by repeatedly propositioning him in respect of practising karmamudra[10] with her. I was astonished she'd had the temerity to ask more than once. *"Knowing your wrathful demeanour, Rinpoche – I could not imagine asking anything more than once, if I met with your refusal."*

"O yah! This too funny." Rinpoche laughed *"Chögyam never such—very— complete 'thom yor. This Khé-drub, one complete myönpa – but not like sickness myönpa suffering. She kun-né mong-pa* [11] *and lang chen myön pa* [12]*! Too much arrogance. 'Tibetan speaking' is much much haughtiness making."*

It turned out that Khé-drub had to be driven away by the house owners because she sat outside every day and wouldn't go away. It seemed as if Khé-drub was under the illusion that she was either Yeshé Tsogyel or like Yeshé Tsogyel. It was vital to her that she had to have sexual relations with Künzang Dorje Rinpoche. He had told her that she wasn't qualified for such a practice – to which she spouted gibberish about Mahamudra as if she had the realisation with all the signs. *"I am Khé-drub telling 'sometime sign seeing* breakfast *saying – but no breakfast possible eating because: no bread; no butter; no egg; and, no kerosene for cooking.' Then I am telling 'You must breakfast somewhere else eating – because when no food then light-headed becoming.' But . . . she is not understanding."*

9 Lama Wangdor. Drüpwang Wangchuk Dorje Rinpoche (*sGrub dBang dBang phyug rDo rJe* / ༒ / 1923–2019) lived in the Tso Pema, Retreat Caves. He was a Nyingma-Kagyüd exponent who trained first in Dzigar in Kham where he became a main student of Thug-sé Rinpoche. He fled from Tibet, carrying Thug-sé Rinpoche upon his back. He spent over 60 years in cave retreat, under the direction of Kyabjé Düd'jom Rinpoche Jig'drèl Yeshé Dorje and Khunu Ten'dzin Gyaltsen Rinpoche. He is thus is a lineage successor of both.
10 Karmamudra – lé-kyi chagya (*las kyi phyag rGya* / ༒): tantric sexual yoga.
11 *kun nas rMongs pa* / ༒ – deeply ingrained delusion.
12 *gLang chen sMyon pa* / ༒ – crazed elephant.

Künzang Dorje Rinpoche had apparently not shouted at her. This amazed me. I asked him how it was that he had not shouted at her – and he replied that it was because she was not worth shouting at. That was astounding. I'd foolishly imagined that he would have shouted at her and shown signs of fury – but no. Rinpoche chuckled at the idea. He explained that shouting had to have a purpose – and that he would not honour a 'thom yor, such as Khé-drub, by raising his voice. He'd simply explained, in simple terms, that she was confused – that she had misinterpreted her experiences as meaning something profound. He told her that many people had such experiences – but that they were merely nyams. Rinpoche told her that merely because she could speak a basic Tibetan was no reason to believe she had meditative insight. He warned her about having sex with Indian men. He told her she was in danger – because far from seeing her as a yogini, they'd see her as a prostitute who wasn't attractive enough to charge for her services. Rinpoche tried to explain to her that she couldn't behave as if she were in the West – because the consequences might lead to her being harmed. She had not listened however – and was eventually serially raped. She'd then claimed the experience as evidence of her exalted spiritual status.

Kyabjé Künzang Dorje Rinpoche asked me what I thought about that story.

"Well Rinpoche… I'm very sorry indeed that she was raped…" I sighed *"She certainly has temerity, audacity, and strength of endurance."* I wanted to say chutzpah – but knew it would not be understood by the translator.

"O yah… much impudence—much insolence—much presumption." PAUSE *"but… maybe this rape-story mind-created. She many stories making."* PAUSE *"Maybe she now telling many stories Künzang Dorje sex having."* He laughed *"Are many western women like this behaving?"*

"Not many, Rinpoche – some perhaps. The closest are probably the groupies who seek out Rock Stars – but I've never heard of them having pretentions to grandeur. There are also plenty of men who are worse in terms of pretentiousness. I've met some western men in India and Nepal who have been self-delusional and self-obsessed. It's sad."

"Yah, sad – maybe next life, better soon coming."

Hearing this story made me realise that there was good reason why Künzang Dorje Rinpoche didn't wish to teach an Inji. As our conversation reached this point, we arrived at the retreat cave of Ani Bumchung. She welcomed us and made tea for Künzang Dorje Rinpoche. I received a glass of water as Rinpoche had explained that I never drank tea – only cold water. *"Chu dangmo"* he advised. Ani Bumchung looked amazed *"A tsi!* [13] *"* she exclaimed. I knew this reaction – and it had been explained to me. There was a Tibetan saying which ran *'Only saints and madmen drink cold water.'* Rinpoche was obviously amused by the reaction. They conversed for a while and it was evident that Rinpoche was explaining who I was – because Ani Bumchung kept glancing at me and smiling. She was sitting on the doorstep as there was no room in her cave for three people. I did offer to sit outside but Ani Bumchung would not hear of it.

There were as many as 50 retreat caves on the stony mountainside. They are called caves – but most of them are shallow indents in the rock which have been excavated. These are then sealed off from the elements by a wood wall with a door. Some caves have wooden floors. They are mainly only large enough to contain a bed. Ani Bumchung's cave had a fissure in the 'ceiling' which led to some point higher up – and this served as a smoke hole when she was cooking over her kerosene burner. I looked back on this first meeting with Ani Bumchung years later when she loaned me her cave for retreat. She went on pilgrimage to Nepal and I stayed there for three months. Rinpoche explained that Ani Bumchung was an accomplished practitioner of Düd'jom gTér Tröma Nakmo – and she was delighted that I engaged in the same practice.

Our visit to Ani Bumchung was made while en route to Lama Wangdor Rinpoche and the retreatants – for whom Künzang Dorje Rinpoche was to give empowerment. Pema Dorje was apparently unqualified to attend the dBang – which led to my suggesting I sat outside with him. Rinpoche wagged a finger at me and indicated that I should remain.

The empowerment of Dorje Tröllö was not lengthy as it was given in the unelaborate style from the inner tantras. It concluded with Rinpoche holding up a crystal. As he held it up, it sparkled in the single shaft of light which entered the cave through a crevice.

---

13 *A rTsis* / ཨ་རྩིས་ – a sound betokening astonishment.

He first shouted "*Hri!*" – and after a few moments "*Phat!*" I say 'shouted' but his voice was not loud. It was not a shout – it simply felt like a shout. It pierced the environment.

After the empowerment we all partook of a feast. Momos had been prepared. Kyabjé Künzang Dorje Rinpoche laughed when he saw the mo-mos – and I was not sure why. I discovered why almost immediately – as he had requested them especially for me. He had laughed at my expression of pleasure in seeing them. Pema Dorje had returned by this time and had explained to me *"Künzang Dorje Rinpoche – surprise making. He is many mo-mo requesting."*

I thanked Rinpoche and Lama Wangdor. They both laughed and said that they too enjoyed mo-mos. There was much conversation between Lama Wangdor and Künzang Dorje Rinpoche – and sometimes Rinpoche would give me an inkling of what they were discussing. Khé-drub had apparently gone to McLeod Ganj – which was why Rinpoche had chosen this day to give the empowerment. He did not wish there to be any Vajrayana connection between them. Lama Wangdor understood this and had therefore let Rinpoche know of her absence. Lama Wangdor said that he was pleased to have met me – and Rinpoche and I set off back down the mountainside.

Rinpoche had to make use of my guidance as the daylight diminished. He was surprised that I could see so well in the dark. *"It's the other side of having light-sensitive eyes, I think. I have to wear sunglasses outside for the greater part of the year – but in the twilight I seem to be able to see as well as in broad daylight."*

"Yah – but now not twilight. Ya-tsan! And now is darkness – and you still seeing!"

"Yes Rinpoche – but maybe not seeing so clearly. I can see enough to guide us all down this track—because there is starlight and moonlight—even though it is only a crescent moon."

In time we got back to Rinpoche's lodging and sat comfortably sipping hot chang and savouring some rather excellent khap-sé[14] which the lady of the house had made fresh for our return.

---

14 *kha zas* / ཁ་ཟས་ – strips of plaited dough which are fried.

17

ma-dzé da-gyüd

I could imagine many another western person finding it easy to be natural and free with their opinions. I put this to Kyabjé Künzang Dorje Rinpoche near the end of our time. *"I think it would have been much easier for you, Rinpoche – if I'd been relaxed, confident, and forthright."*

This made him laugh *"No"* he replied in English. *"No good. No good."* Also in English. *"No good result then coming"* he laughed. *"Not good functioning. When too relaxed – then importance, too little seeing. Too little 'intelligence-respect' having. Too much 'thom-yor arrogance. Too much rigid opinion coming. Too much 'thom yor pride. Too much 'thom yor trust in fixed western culture view. Too much 'thom yor trust in fixed Tibetan culture view. Then no 'intelligence-devotion' possible."* PAUSE *"What best coming – is what Chögyam is first showing. What best coming is —now—is what—now—Chögyam showing. Each moment coming, best moment coming. Then Dzogchen men-ngag-dé is possible."* PAUSE *"Otherwise not possible."*

This was altogether unexpected. I must have worn an expression of utter surprise – because Rinpoche asked *"Now you question asking."*

"I am not sure how to ask this question Rinpoche… but – if how I was at the beginning and at every point was how it was best for me to have been." Then I had to say it again so that the translator could follow what I was saying *"… then… it seems as if you orchestrated, or created, everything as it happened."* PAUSE *"It's more as if everything was ma-dzé da-gyüd* [1] *– like DoKhyentsé Yeshé Dorje throwing Dza Paltrül to the ground and dragging him around by his hair."*

Künzang Dorje Rinpoche nodded *"O yah."* He widened his eyes slightly and tilted his head fractionally, as if to say *'That—is—the obvious conclusion.'*

I continued *"… but, you made it look as if there was a process and you were gradually coming to trust me."*

"O yah!" Künzang Dorje Rinpoche exclaimed and laughed for some length of time.

---

1 *ma mDzes brDa brGyud* / མ་མཛེས་བརྡ་བརྒྱུད་ – informal symbolic transmission or unconventional symbolic transmission.

"Düd'jom Rinpoche in his letter – 'Aro tulku' telling. This I am also seeing when dream having. White-hair man seeing – but young man, not old man. Young white-hair man – and eyes are coral colour. I know this man. I am thinking this is Chögyam. But now brown hair having and—too—large beard having like mahasiddha – but anyway, same. No difference." PAUSE – and then with a grin *"Now what asking?"*

"So… all the time you knew that Düd'jom Rinpoche had told me about being the incarnation of Aro Yeshé."

Rinpoche nodded. He began to smile. His smile broadened until he burst out laughing.

"Did he also tell you" I ventured *"that I was supposed to make a second revelation of Khyungchen Aro Lingma's gTérma cycle in the future?"*

"O yah. This also telling." PAUSE *"So, you not asking—why—Künzang Dorje too much shouting?"* he laughed.

"No, Rinpoche" I laughed. *"It had not occurred to me to ask that. It became obvious to me why you had to shout at me."*

Rinpoche made his usual gesture of hand when he wished me to continue.

"Well… apart from informal symbolic transmission – there was also the question of breaking through my unconscious affectations and habits of 'spiritualised perception'. I had studied a great deal before I came to the Himalayas and inadvertently taught myself to be stilted, mechanistic, and narrow… That was one aspect."

Rinpoche nodded as if to say that I'd made a reasonable assessment.

"Then there was my sense of fear. I think it was valuable in terms of making me far more present than I could otherwise have been. It seemed to—retard—the progress of time. It seemed to make the situation like . . . looking—or feeling—through an emotional magnifying glass." I had to repeat that a few times before the translator could grasp what I was saying. *"It enabled me to see myself moment-by-moment – and, to observe my thought processes. Through this I was able to see how mechanical I was – how much I thought with habit patterns. I discovered that what I did most of the time was to call dogs 'small hornless cows' merely because they had four legs."*

"O yah – this too well saying" Rinpoche nodded. *"Later years you must be other peoples teaching"* he laughed *"but Künzang Dorje 'shouting system' not necessary, for Chögyam using."* He sat back and smiled. We sat in comfortable silence for a few minutes. *"Something now important concerning tobacco from Kyabjé Düd'jom Rinpoche telling. His teaching 'Guide that Leads the Blind on a False Path which Ends in a Precipice'. What is written, in brief telling so you will be knowing and advising people in west countries when you teachings giving."* PAUSE *"You once smoking?"*

"I never tried it because my lady friend didn't like the smell. She said that it was an expensive habit which was more-or-less like burning foul-smelling money."

"O yah!" he laughed *"Good! Khandro wisdoms giving. Tobacco is poison. It kills body and mind. Kyabjé Düd'jom Rinpoche, cannabis and opium – same saying. He is writing: opium and other related intoxicants, taken by mouth or nose, thirst not quenching or hunger satisfy. Not delicious taste possessing."*

He continued to explain that these substances were bereft of anything which promoted health or strengthened the life force. These substances merely served to increase nervousness and blood pressure. They caused cancer and pulmonary disease.

"At this time, many people, in all levels of society have attraction for these substances. They consume without intelligence. In the West you are seeing?"

"Yes, Rinpoche, smoking is fairly common and smoking cannabis was common at Art School. I think that no one really understands the problems – but I've seen the way in which cannabis makes people vague and detached from reality."

Rinpoche then spoke of the gTérmas from which Düd'jom Rinpoche had quoted: Chögyal Ratna Lingpa[2]; Sang-gyé Lingpa; gTértön Rig'dzin Gö'dem; gTértön Düd'dül Dorje; gTértön Longsel; gTértön Thugchog Dorje; gTértön Dro'dül Lingpa; and Ma-gÇig Labdrön.

"There are innumerable predictions concerning tobacco – and the use of tobacco has been particularly forbidden by accomplished masters of both Sarma and Nyingma traditions. But still 'thom yors are smoking – and 'thom yor Lamas are disciples smoking allowing. The vajra words of Guru Rinpoche are not deceiving. Sincere practitioners must not doubts having.

2   Ratna Lingpa (*rat na gLing pa* / རཏྣ་གླིང་པ / 1403–1478)

"Some 'thom yors 'How problems from smoking natural plant arising?' saying. Aconite also natural plant – but small quantity eating and death coming. Many natural plant – death coming. 'If this is true with plant—at physical level—why will not also rTsa rLung death causing? You must strongly speaking when teachings giving. Then those who are not 'thom-yor will this poison of tobacco and narcotics avoiding."

"It's good to know about this text from Kyabjé Düd'jom Rinpoche. I will try to find the text and have it translated into English – and maybe also into German.[3]"

"This is good. Important for people knowing. If anyone respect for Kyabjé Düd'jom Rinpoche having – they must his advice seriously taking – and never smoke tobacco, cannabis, or opium." Then he laughed "People not liking when this telling! Much arguing and bad words! But already people not Chögyam liking." He laughed uproariously about that. Rinpoche thought it was particularly amusing that some people didn't like me. He shook his head as he laughed "O yah! And future times even more people not liking! Many bad word saying – this really too funny."

"I'm looking forward to that" I chuckled. Rinpoche understood my irony quite clearly. He had got used to such comments and found them amusing.

"O yah – some people much hating and many bad words saying."

"I eagerly anticipate it, Rinpoche." I smiled – because it was both funny and vaguely harrowing. I knew that Rinpoche was joking – but he was also telling me something serious at the same time. It was a tremendous breakthrough for me when Rinpoche realised that I had a sense of humour. At first, he'd thought I was almost irredeemably lacking in wit. Tibetans understand irony quite well – but something is often lost in translation if the translator doesn't feel one's irony to be respectful. Once Pema Dorje understood that Rinpoche enjoyed my ironic comments our interactions became far livelier.

"É hong!" Rinpoche snorted "Kyé-ma… some people Künzang Dorje not liking…" with a theatrically sad face.

---

3 The text of the Smoking Booklet – Tobacco: 'the Guide that leads the Blind on a False Path which ends in a Precipice' has been translated into six languages, including Enlgish and German. These are published as booklets by Aro Books WORLDWIDE.

Then he laughed *"But always 'thom yor idea having. For 'thom yor, all authentic Vajrayana practice despising. Religious 'thom yor only wealth and status caring. Most Dharma 'thom yor only for the opinions of famous Lamas caring. Many Tibetan 'thom yor only the Dharma of superstition understanding. Vajrayana and Tibetan culture not intelligent dividing. Women not respecting – even when 'khandro' calling! This in lives of many Tibetan yoginis seeing. Lives of Ma-gÇig Labdrön and Jomo Menmo*[4]. *They much persecution suffering. This Vajrayana? No!"* Rinpoche thumped the table. *"This Tibetan cultural stupidity! They are nun, looking down – but nun like Ani Bumchung – they real practitioners! Why does Künzang Dorje say this? Because no 'status' in nun, becoming. Any woman nun becoming – is only for Dharma, not status."*

It was unusual to see Rinpoche displaying wrath. It had been some time since that wrath was levelled at me – but even though I was not the subject of his wrath; it had a similar effect. Rinpoche smiled and shook his head *"Yah… no need thinking this angry Künzang Dorje again as before coming"* he laughed.

"No Rinpoche, I don't think that – but, I must say, you still have a strong effect on me when you are displeased with anyone or anything anywhere."

"O yah!" Rinpoche laughed uproariously *"This is not problem – this devotion. You must remember this when own students having. They also like this. They Chögyam seeing – just as you are Künzang Dorje seeing."*

Now it was my turn to laugh *"Rinpoche – for anyone to see me—as I see you— would mean that I would have to be a thousand miles from where I am now."*

Rinpoche shook his head laughing *"O yah – thousand miles west, your land finding – so no problem."*

I realised that Rinpoche had not misunderstood me – he'd simply made a joke through deliberate literalism. I decided that I wasn't going to be the 'thom yor whom Rinpoche had found tedious by virtue of my sanctimonious humility – and so I just laughed at Rinpoche's humour.

"What you say about Tibetan culture, Rinpoche…" I began, changing tack from what Rinpoche had previously stated *"… is something that I can see as an issue in the future. I have found that many western students mistake culture for Vajrayana – but they do so in a way which is quite determined.*

---

4 *jo mo sMan mo* / ཇོ་མོ་སྨན་མོ་ / 1248–1283.

"I've found that there are many of them with whom I simply cannot hold any kind of conversation. Not that I make Vajrayana a subject of conversation—I don't like to do that—but they tend to engage me in such conversations and then become irritated by what I say. This is not a question exactly – because I know what to do… it's just that I wonder what it would be like to teach western people when so many of them seem to have such extremely fixed ideas. Might it not be better if I didn't teach?"

Rinpoche shook his head *"No. Teaching important – otherwise gö kar chang lo'i dé forgotten. How vows keeping to Kyabjé Düd'jom Rinpoche if not teaching?"*

"I could just give lectures on the gö kar chang lo'i dé."

"No." Rinpoche shook his head again *"Not possible. From obstacles you must be learning. You must these people with fixed ideas answering – then same time learning."* I was to give teachings and learn how to teach through the experience of teaching. He said that not every Lama taught as he had taught me. This was not common, he laughed *"Chögyam, not this bad Künzang Dorje teaching needing."* He gave me to understand that he could have approached teaching me in another way altogether. He could have simply given me Dzogchen men-ngag-dé teaching—which would have lasted a day, at most—and then wished me farewell. He considered however, that we should spend time together. He felt that it was possible to get to know me personally – and the only way to do that was to be explosive. He had to find out who I really was – and the only way to proceed with that, was to find out what I was like under stress and provocation. He didn't want me as a person who came to him every once in a while, for blessings and a never-ending series of requests for additional information. Vajrayana had a great deal of information – but the information was not *the essence of Vajrayana;* neither was it the essence of relationship between Lama and disciple. This was a revelation. Kyabjé Künzang Dorje Rinpoche hadn't actually immediately disliked me. He hadn't even thought I was a 'thom yor – even though I occasionally spoke like a 'thom yor. He had seen a future in which he could play a part. This was the way I would work with people. Not through wrath – but through seeing people's characters and modes of being. I was to perceive how people thought and respond accordingly.

"You 'thinking', clearly seeing. Then you—know—what saying. Then students 'essential nature of Vajrayana' understanding. This naturally coming – just as we together speaking. Problems coming – but always for every Lama problems coming. Mi-kha [5] also coming – but past times also mi-kha coming. Tibet—so much—mi-kha."

I was to remember the stories he had told – such as the story of DoKhyentsé Yeshé Dorje and how he was treated by the Gyalpo when the Lamas of Dzogchen Gompa tried to make him behave conservatively.

"Yes indeed *Rinpoche*, that was when he wore a hat made from tree branches, and rode his horse bareback with the saddle strapped to his back."

"O yah! Then dismounting—clothes removing—and back and forth walking in front of Lang-da gompa howling like wolf. More remembering?"

"Yes, Rinpoche. The next time he appeared wearing leaves; then dressed as a woman; then as a Mongolian warrior; then as a drokpa from Hor. The Gyalpo saw these displays and attempted to dissuade DoKhyentsé Yeshé Dorje from manifesting wisdom-eccentricity. Then DoKhyentsé Yeshé Dorje said 'As I told you – I am not a Lama you would want. My understanding of Dharma is too unconventional. My way of living is too offensive to conservative society.' That is all I remember without looking at my notes."

"Then… that is good. Many people in Tibet with bad minds and bad attitudes toward Lamas having. Too many! No one believed Düd'jom Lingpa, until old – and now very famous coming and gTérma practised even in America. Why should easier for Chögyam than Düd'jom Lingpa?" He laughed "You are argument having?"

That made me smile *"Rinpoche – you must know that I can have no argument with anything you say. There is nothing I can say now. I'll just go ahead and deal with whatever happens."*

"Yah good!" he replied in English.

---

5   *mi kha* / སྨྲ་ཁ་ — slander, libel, defamation, vilification calumny, scandalising, gossip, character assassination criticism of the ignorant; literally 'bad mouth'.

"This will sound ridiculous, Rinpoche" I smiled *"but it has the feeling of the eve of a great battle – not that I know what that would be like apart from how it is described in books and films."*

"O yah! Great battle! Like Ling Gésar." PAUSE *"Maybe one day Rangbar Düd'dül Dorje* [6] *remembering. Künzang Dorje too well remembering. Much brave—much courageous—much fearless hero. Ling Gesar many great heroes having and many enemies defeating."*

Künzang Dorje Rinpoche said he'd heard that western people didn't like Ling Gésar – because they were opposed to warfare of any kind. What did I think of this?

"Well Rinpoche… I think that they have forgotten World War II. I think that when you're faced with Nazis – war becomes necessary. I think some western people see Buddhism as being aligned with pacifism – which seems a misunderstanding. One's motivation must be peaceful – but one's actions may sometimes need to be wrathful. I think that sometimes there is no choice – in terms of having to contend with a great and dangerous evil. If you just allow an evil force to have its way – then the results are far worse than the armed conflict which could have been set against it. As it was… over six million Jews were killed by the Nazis. It is hard to imagine how it could have been worse – but unless Hitler had been stopped, the death toll could have tripled." PAUSE *"It is at these times that Ling Gésar is needed. Pacifism in terms of not opposing Hitler is a tragically naïve philosophical theory."* Rinpoche nodded in grave agreement – so I continued *"It worked for Gandhi against the British – but Gandhi would not have succeeded with Nazis."*

When the figure 'six million' was translated, Rinpoche shook his head. He looked sad beyond anything I had ever seen. He sat silently staring into space. After a weighty moment he said *"Sa-ya drug* [7]*."*

"Yes…" I sighed *"Sa-ya drug… that's the population of Tibet"* and that was the one time I ever saw Kyabjé Künzang Dorje Rinpoche look shocked. *"Ya…"* he sighed *"these times, Ling Gésar much needed."*

---

6   *rang 'bar khrom rTsal bDud 'dul rDo rJe* / རང་འབར་ཁྲོ་རྩལ་བདུད་འདུལ་རྡོ་རྗེ – a lieutenant under General Shengpa in the host of Ling Gésar. He was the incarnation of Mahasiddha Manibhadra (Drüpchen Norzang / *grub chen nor bZang* / གྲུབ་ཆེན་ནོར་བཟང་) – the perfect housewife). Manibhadra was the incarnation of Aro gZa' Druk-tsal Sheldrakma, one of the disciples of Guru Rinpoche and Yeshé Tsogyel.

7   *sa ya drug* / ས་ཡ་དྲུག – six million.

Künzang Dorje Rinpoche then spoke of how he had been General Shengpa at that time – and I had been Captain Rangbar Düd'dül Dorje. Once we had been warriors, and we were warriors still – because Changchub Sempa meant realised mind warrior. The syllable dPa' in Changchub Sempa (*byang chub sems dPa'*) meant warrior – and one needed the mind of a warrior to deal with a world which had been ruined by 'thom yors.

"Some must sword and gun fighting—but we—we, must corrupt view fighting. We must with fearless power of practice fighting. We must politics disregarding."

Rinpoche explained that there were always people in powerful positions who would try to dominate others – but we should resist their domination. Such people had tried to imprison Düd'jom Rinpoche – but they had failed. They had used political strategy – but its corrupt nature had been exposed. Düd'jom Rinpoche had not fought – but not because he was not a great hero. He had not fought because he knew that he had no need to fight. Hundreds of Tibetans and Bhutanese had lain on the railway lines to prevent the trains taking Düd'jom Rinpoche to the Indian prison[8]. The Royal families of Bhutan, Sikkim, and Nepal had petitioned Prime Minister Nehru, and Kyabjé Düd'jom Rinpoche had been released. The allegations that Düd'jom Rinpoche was a paid Chinese collaborator were seen to be entirely bogus.

---

8   See: *Goodbye Forever*—VOLUME I—chapter 21 *Born in a Dragon Year*. After leaving Tibet, Kyabjé Düd'jom Rinpoche Jig'drèl Yeshé Dorje settled in Kalimpong, India. He gave extensive teachings there and in Darjeeling. His teachings were extremely popular and he became famous throughout the Tibetan community. Once it became evident that Düd'jom Rinpoche was becoming a focus of great devotion amongst the exiled Tibetans he was arrested and jailed in Siliguri on the basis of fabricated testimonies that he was a Chinese spy. India was highly sensitive to the Chinese presence so close to their northern borders. The accusation emanated from a person or persons in the Tibetan Government in Exile. Düd'jom Rinpoche had not concurred with their idea that there should be a union of all Tibetan lineages under the Dalai Lama. The idea was that it was necessary to unite all the lineages in order to create unity in the Tibetan community. Düd'jom Rinpoche's response to this was *"Any person well-grounded in their practice should continue in that practice and with the lineage of that practice. It should be our purpose to preserve all lineages as methods for attaining realisation. As practitioners we should sustain our own traditions while respecting and rejoicing in the qualities of other traditions."*

Kyabjé Düd'jom Rinpoche had given me this account himself – but I listened to Kyabjé Künzang Dorje Rinpoche with rapt attention nonetheless. It was part of his explanation of why it was necessary to be a hero—a dPa'wo—and why I would need to be a dPa'wo.

"Yah... and so... our time is over. Tomorrow you last time coming – and then... I must Tso Pema leaving and Sikkim going." PAUSE *"So—now—you are my son."* He looked at me with a kindly grin and took both my hands in his. *"You are my son... but our time together here in Tso Pema is over."*

And so it was that I received the Dzogchen men-ngag-dé teachings and transmissions. It came at a point where I'd given up all hope of ever receiving it. More than this however – I would have felt entirely satisfied in not receiving it at all. I'd not merely given up hope – but I'd forgotten all about hope. I think I'd forgotten fear as well.

My time in Tso Pema had turned into the most stupendous discovery. I learnt that I could—to some linear extent—be my own teacher. I could not be my own Lama – but I did not have to ask questions about technicalities. I could understand the parameters of Vajrayana by simply identifying the principle and function of the subject in question. Rinpoche had taught me how to see the principle and function of the teachings – and in so doing unlocked the enormous wealth of Vajrayana.

Vajrayana was no longer something to be learnt word-by-word—fact-by-fact—category-by-category. It was a living coherent organism which was entirely open to understanding – as long as one was possessed of the experience of silent sitting. There were the building blocks—of course—such as: emptiness and form; duality and nonduality; the five elements; and, the principles of khandro and dPa'wo. Beyond that however, there was not so very much to know beyond the functioning of the individual practices. I knew a variety of taxonomical structures such as the nine yanas and the three series of Dzogchen – so, with those tools, there was nothing which could not be understood unless one was a recalcitrant recidivistic 'thom yor.

Künzang Dorje Rinpoche—fortunately for me—had seen that I was a 'thom yor who was capable of redemption. I imagine it was touch and go at times – but in the end his patience bore fruit to the extent that he was sure I was no longer a 'thom yor. That didn't mean I had any degree of realisation – but, for me, to have ceased to be a 'thom yor was most of what I wanted from life.

Beyond that, there was simply practice – and, by the time I was on the verge of leaving Tso Pema, Künzang Dorje Rinpoche seemed to feel I was capable.

I made my last farewell to Künzang Dorje Rinpoche in early March. He made a final joke about my dark maroon to-nga – the woollen waistcoat I'd had made in Bristol. I'd had no idea that dark maroon was the colour favoured by the monastic elite. It had made me look like some kind of aristocratic trülku and Künzang Dorje Rinpoche had repeatedly ridiculed it. He asked *"What does Kyabjé Düd'jom Rinpoche think of this magnificent to-nga?"*

"Düd'jom Rinpoche has never seen it. I left it in McLeod Ganj."

"O yah!" he laughed. *"This is best. I am happy Düd'jom Rinpoche, never this— very—shameful thing seeing."*

The serious ridicule had abated vis-à-vis the to-nga – but I was still teased about that wretched garment from time to time. I promised I'd have a new to-nga made as soon as I could. A red cotton one suited to my station in life. Rinpoche laughed *"O yah – red! Then cheeks matching."* He always seemed amused by my red cheeks. At first, he thought it was some kind of make-up like lipstick – and was relieved to know that my idiocy didn't extend to painting my face.

Rinpoche gave me a gö kar chang lo shawl before I departed – and I was both amazed and inordinately grateful. Düd'jom Rinpoche had told me that I should try to find one – but I never expected Künzang Dorje Rinpoche to give me such a shawl as a present. It was as hard as cardboard—being new—but Rinpoche assured me that it would become as soft as silk in a year.

Rinpoche wanted to see me on the morning of my departure – and said that he would come to the Nyingma gompa where I had been residing. He wanted to see Düd'jom Rinpoche's room. I was surprised that he had never seen it before. When he arrived however – he told me that he simply wished to say goodbye at the actual time of my departure from Tso Pema. This was deeply moving. That Kyabjé Künzang Dorje Rinpoche should come to wave goodbye was something I would never have imagined.

From being an unwelcome 'thom yor to being treated as his son – was a huge shift. It was easier to understand myself as a 'thom yor. Not that being told I was his son was not utterly valuable – but it said far more about Rinpoche than it said about me. How he saw me was based on his nondual realisation. From that perspective, I could only be what he saw. The difficulty was that I couldn't see it. This was not a statement of humility – it was simply a statement of reality as I understood it. Maybe one day Rinpoche's reality and my reality would merge. That after all was the purpose of practising Lama'i Naljor – Unification with the Mind of the Lama.

A knock on the door. The taxi had arrived. I swung my rucksack onto my back. Kyabjé Künzang Dorje Rinpoche and I left Kyabjé Düd'jom Rinpoche's room – and went to the gompa entrance. Rinpoche prevented me from offering prostrations. I took his guidance and climbed into the taxi. Rinpoche stood waving until I was out of sight. I looked back until he was out of sight.

I almost burst into tears – but it occurred to me that Künzang Dorje Rinpoche would not have been too impressed by this. I stared out of the taxi window at the shapes and colours of the world. In a few moments concept was absent – and colour was present.

part three

nothing to know other than knowingness

Retracing my steps. From Tso Pema to McLeod Ganj to Bodhanath – and surprisingly back to McLeod Ganj, before setting out overland for Britain. It was a well-known route – and time spent travelling was part of the experience of being in the Himalayas of India and Nepal. There could have been little said about this final period – but I somehow failed to expect the unexpected.

I had no idea that Kyabjé Düd'jom Rinpoche would have more time for me than a brief interview. I had no idea that an aerogramme would arrive and change my travel plans. I had no idea that I'd observe someone being strafed by bat guano – or that I'd meet a high-rolling free-wheeling diamond-ringed dégagé dentist. I had no idea that I'd run into my old Swiss friend Johannes Frischknecht, or that he'd translate the Tibetan equivalent of Edgar Allan Poe.

I felt the fact I would be continually walking into an unpredictable future, should have been obvious to me. I knew the future was mysterious – but it was often far more mysterious than I imagined. A slight twist of the existential kaleidoscope would change the picture of reality.

When I was eight or nine years old, I used to ponder the future. There were two routes I could take from West Street Junior School to the bus stop in Farnham. It often occurred to me that the choice could change my life. It wasn't that it would change my life—I was not superstitious—but the possibility was there. I'd stand at the point at which the choice had to be made – and go whichever way I felt drawn. If I wasn't drawn, I'd simply toss a coin in order to decide. This coin tossing mode was not something I used often – but when there was no obvious preference, it seemed practical. On most occasions I preferred to use linear reasoning – but sometimes this form of cogitation availed no clear result. Sometimes there was nothing to give weight to different options.

It occurred to me, as a boy, that there must be many junctures in life – where life-changing decisions are made without realising the portentous nature of the choice. To walk or catch a bus. To run for a bus or accept that one had missed it.

To stroll through Farnham Park rather than follow a shorter route along the main road. To visit the library to see whether a requested book had arrived – or get home half an hour earlier. To go to Aldershot outdoor Swimming Pool or cycle into the countryside to sit amongst the trees in the Devil's Punch Bowl[1].

There seemed to be so many alternatives which could be pivotal – but the fact that these pivotal points occurred, still caused me wonderment.

---

1   *The Devil's Punchbowl* is a 700-acre natural amphitheatre to the east of Hindhead, Surrey. The highest point of the rim is Gibbet Hill – 900 ft above sea level. The skyline of London can be detected on a clear day – roughly 40 miles to the east.

18

dön'dré

It was hard to leave Tso Pema – and my departure was made with mixed feelings. I was sad to be leaving Künzang Dorje Rinpoche—who was now utterly my Tsawa'i Lama—but I was glad I'd come through. I'd accomplished what I'd set out to accomplish. Now I could return to see Kyabjé Düd'jom Rinpoche before returning to England. First however, I would need to go back to McLeod Ganj. I had a return ticket – and had things to pick up in McLeod Ganj: things I'd left rather than schlepp them to Tso Pema.

At the end of the day—having arrived in Mandi—I caught the bus to Upper Dharamsala, and the continuation bus to McLeod Ganj. I unpacked in the hut I still rented and fell asleep shortly after crawling into my sleeping bag.

When I awoke, the friendly rat was looking at me. It had almost become a pet; I gave it food every day and it seemed to sense some kind of kinship with me. It was sitting quite near my face on the pillow. "*Good morrow, righteous rodent*" I smiled. It stopped cleaning its whiskers for a moment—and gazed at me—almost as if it had understood what I'd said. I recited Guru Rinpoche mantra for the rat until it went to sleep next to me. That was my cue to rise and launch into the day. I washed and dressed and took the track up to see Ngakpa Yeshé Dorje and Khandro Ten'dzin Drölkar. I'd be in McLeod Ganj for a few days before heading out for Nepal.

Ngakpa Yeshé Dorje and Khandro Ten'dzin Drölkar already knew that I was back in McLeod Ganj and so they were expecting me. They were there to greet me at the entrance to their expansive shack. Once I'd taken my seat and was provided with a glass of hot chang and honey – it was explained in a mixture of English, Tibetan, and sign language that Sônam was coming to translate and that he'd be arriving shortly. No sooner was it explained than Sônam arrived. Khandro Ten'dzin Drölkar was keen to know whether I had been able to meet Karma Gyalpo Rinpoche.

I replied that I had. I was now somewhat at a loss for how to continue because Düd'jom Rinpoche had instructed me not to mention Künzang Dorje Rinpoche to anyone – not even Ngakpa Yeshé Dorje. I felt intuitively that it was not a breach of promise to answer direct questions from Khandro Ten'dzin Drölkar – although I suddenly realised that I was a 'thom yor. Why had I not asked Künzang Dorje Rinpoche what to do? He had told me that Khandro Ten'dzin Drölkar was his disciple – and I could easily have discussed the promise I'd made to Kyabjé Düd'jom Rinpoche with regard to secrecy.

"You are teachings receiving?" smiled Khandro Ten'dzin Drölkar.

"Yes – I was extremely fortunate."

Fortunately, also, nothing else was asked – and so I volunteered nothing further. That was both viable and dubious. It was viable because I was keeping my word to Düd'jom Rinpoche – but dubious because I felt I was not being open and candid with Khandro Ten'dzin Drölkar. Maybe at some point in the future I'd be free to tell her what had occurred. I'd ask Düd'jom Rinpoche when I next saw him – and that would be within a week. That was also questionable because after my time with Künzang Dorje Rinpoche, I felt I ought to be able to reach such a decision without having to pester Düd'jom Rinpoche on the subject. Künzang Dorje Rinpoche had expended considerable effort in trying to make an adult of me—in Vajrayana terms—and yet here I was, unable to resolve this dilemma. Was it even a dilemma?

Ngakpa Yeshé Dorje on hearing I'd met Künzang Dorje Rinpoche—or rather Karma Gyalpo Rinpoche—said *"Best, always Kyabjé Düd'jom Rinpoche relying"* and I replied that I would always rely on Kyabjé Düd'jom Rinpoche. I detected something in the atmosphere around the mention of Karma Gyalpo Rinpoche – and it became obvious that there was something I did not know. This I *would* need to mention to Düd'jom Rinpoche. He might elucidate – but maybe I didn't need any details. I was aware that it was only sensible to seek information if it could serve some purpose. Curiosity for its own sake was the mark of a 'thom yor as far as Künzang Dorje Rinpoche was concerned. Why ask the cost of an apple if you do not propose to buy it? I steered the subject away from Karma Gyalpo Rinpoche.

"I'm going to see Kyabjé Düd'jom Rinpoche in a few days. I promised to see him once more before going home to England."

"O yah! Very good – very good!" Ngakpa Yeshé Dorje said in mixed Tibetan and English.

"It is good you are today coming – because tomorrow I must 'dré [1] dispelling." PAUSE "You know 'dré meaning?"

"Yes Rinpoche, ghost."

"O yah – you are 'dré in England knowing?"

The idea of answering 'not personally' flitted through my mind – but, I ignored it and said "We know of 'dré in England."

"And peoples 'dré believing or not believing?"

"Well… some people believe in 'dré, some not. Most are not sure – or never consider them."

"You are believing?"

"Yes… although I have never encountered one. You have mentioned their existence. I have no doubt about anything you have told me – but in the West most people need to have personal experience before they will believe anything; unless they're the kind of people who like to believe in…" here we had to hunt around for words for 'supernatural'. "Of course being able to study Tröma Nakmo with you enables me to accept much that people would not accept in the West."

"Yah…" Ngakpa Yeshé Dorje pondered "peoples must be believing – or much danger possible from 'dre. Sometimes 'dré much—much—trouble making." PAUSE "Now, I must something important explaining, and you must all peoples telling – all people who 'ghost' not believing. Peoples much foolish when not 'dré believing. I must often 'dré dispelling. Many places India I am travelling and 'dré dispelling." PAUSE "So, you must 'dré dispelling learning – and all things. Chir-dog, already something learning, but you must complete study making – also char gÇod. Then all things ngakpa practising."

I indicated that I would be grateful to hear anything he had to tell – but felt slightly guarded in respect of being expected to learn how to be a Mahayoga ngakpa in the style he was describing. Kyabjé Düd'jom Rinpoche had said nothing of this. Neither had Künzang Dorje Rinpoche – in fact Künzang Dorje Rinpoche had grimaced slightly when I'd told him about assisting Ngakpa Yeshé Dorje with exorcism.

1   'dre / འདྲེ – ghost; dön 'dré (gDon 'dre / གདོན་འདྲེ) – demonic ghost

I'd asked him whether he would recommend my studying exorcism further – because I felt it might be a side-track in terms of Dzogchen. He'd nodded and said *"No harm – no benefit. Best you are sem'dzin* [2] *practising."* He'd said that practising Tröma Nakmo as a yidam was good – but that I should avoid the lower paths [3]. *"Lower activity – enemies and obstructers liberating* [4]. *This 'og rim* [5] *– like mouth opening and 'og lung* [6] *coming."* He had laughed *"When lha min mèd-ri* [7] *power giving – then you, lha min mèd-ri prisoner becoming. Düd'jom Rinpoche also same saying."*

So here I was with Ngakpa Yeshé Dorje—for the first time—in a state of lack of enthusiasm. More than that – I was conflicted. On the one side there was my deep affection for Ngakpa Yeshé Dorje – and on the other was unquestionable devotion and respect for Düd'jom Rinpoche and Künzang Dorje Rinpoche. There was no choice as to my direction – but I felt sad nonetheless. I felt as if I was betraying his kindness. I felt false. Ngakpa Yeshé Dorje had been extremely kind to me. He had allowed me into areas of practice which were not readily open—especially to western people—and here I was inwardly refusing what he was offering – yet being courteous in listening.

Having signified that I would be appreciative of hearing anything he had to tell me, Ngakpa Yeshé Dorje began. *"Golok, many nomad living – and there one ngakpa family. They ngakpa family lineage having. Two brothers – both young maybe 23 and 25 years old. Ngakpa Tséring Wangpo and Ngakpa Namgyal Dorje. One younger sister also – she is Ngakma Sônam Dé-kyi. All are gÇod empowerment and teachings from Shérab Dorje Rinpoche receiving. Shérab Dorje Rinpoche is one very great ngakpa. Not many people knowing – but very powerful."*

Having received the empowerment, the siblings committed to visit 108 mountain sites, 108 places haunted by 'dré, and 108 charnel-grounds. They had to practise gÇod at each of these sites as part of their commitment.

---

2 *sems 'dzin* / སེམས་འཛིན་

3 The lower paths – man-lam (*dMan lam* / དམན་ལམ་) or nyan rang-gi lam (*nyan rang gi lam* / ཉན་རང་གི་ལམ་).

4 The lower activity of liberating enemies and obstructers – tö-lé (*sTod las* / སྟོད་ལས་) and also mè-lé dradeg dralwa (*sMad las dGra bGegs bsGral ba* / སྨད་ལས་དགྲ་བགེགས་བསྒྲལ་བ་).

5 'Og-rim (*'og rim* / འོག་རིམ་) – lower level, subordinate, inferior.

6 *'og rLung* / འོག་རླུང་ – lower wind; flatus, flatulence.

7 *lha min sMad ris* / ལྷ་མིན་སྨད་རིས་ – lower class of animalistic entities (dud-dro / *dud 'gro* / དུད་འགྲོ་).

When practising gÇod, it is important to practise in places which are home to harm-bringing bDüd[8], nyèn[9], tsèn[10], nöd-zhin[11], and 'dön-dré and therefore there is great danger. One could easily die in such places. The siblings recognised that it would be unwise to put themselves at risk as a group – because, were they all to die, their family lineage would terminate. They decided they would take it in turns to complete the gÇod pilgrimage – each one engaging with the practice only after another had accomplished the practice. The other two would take care of the food requirements of the one practising.

The younger brother Tséring Wangpo went first to take his brother Namgyal Dorje supplies. After some weeks he returned to check how Namgyal Dorje was faring. When he arrived, he felt extremely fearful as he approached the tent as he could hear nothing. There was no sound of bell and gÇod damaru, there was no chanting. He called *"Namgyal, I've arrived bringing food supplies"* but there was no answer. He called three times – but the silence remained. Finally, he decided to open the front flap of the tent to see whether Namgyal Dorje was inside. Maybe he had decided to practise on a nearby ledge of rock. There were many such places to sit. When he opened the flap he beheld his brother's corpse. Namgyal Dorje's body was white and had dried blood all over his chest – that had evidently issued from his nostrils.

He could not ascertain the cause of his brother's death and there was no doctor with whom he could enquire. He knew what to do however – and fed Namgyal Dorje to the vultures after having performed bardo rites. He decided it was best to begin practice in his brother's tent. His sister Sônam Dé-kyi would obviously bring food after a while – as she was an intelligent young woman and would assume that he had stayed close to his elder brother for some reason.

After a few weeks, Sônam Dé-kyi arrived with provisions. As she approached the tent a sense of dread arose in her. There was no sound. No bell, gÇod damaru, or kangling. No sound of chanting. She called *"Tséring, dear brother, I'm here with food supplies."* There was no answer. She called three times – but was answered only by silence.

---

8 *bDud* / བདུད – mara, demon, negative influence.
9 *gNyan* / གཉན – malevolent mountain entity.
10 *bTsan* / བཙན – demon.
11 *gNod sByin* / གནོད་སྦྱིན / *yaksha* – storm-bringer.

Not knowing what else to do, she opened the front flap of the tent and was confronted by the sight of Tséring Wangpo's dead body. It was white and splattered with dried blood which had issued from his nostrils.

Where was Namgyal Dorje? She had no idea. She wanted to discover the cause of Tséring Wangpo's death but without recourse to a doctor she could make nothing of it. She knew how to proceed – and fed his body to the vultures after performing the bardo rites. She decided it was best to begin practice in her brothers' tent. It was late and so after arranging everything she prepared her sleeping blankets and went to sleep. Whilst sleeping, she dreamed of her brothers. Each appeared in turn saying *"It is the milk."* Each in turn vanished with no further explanation. This same dream occurred on two nights. She could find no sense in the dream and decided to ignore it. There was no purpose in thinking about dreams when she should be practising gÇod.

On the third night Sônam Dé-kyi's brothers appeared again – making the same statement *"It is the milk."* Shortly before dawn she was awoken by the sound of a female voice in song. The words were of some other dialect – or perhaps some other language. Sônam Dé-kyi listened for a while as the sound came closer. The melody sounded like gÇod – so maybe she was a gÇodma. Maybe this was good. Maybe she could travel together with her. She was deeply saddened by the loss of her brother Tsering and had no idea where her older brother was. Sônam Dé-kyi had a bad feeling about her older brother Namgyal Dorje – as it seemed that he might also be dead.

She opened the tent flap to see who was singing – and was slightly startled to see a woman almost immediately at the entrance to her tent. The woman was dressed in outlandish clothing which was hard to define. *"Reverend Ngakma – I have come to bring you milk to drink. I have just milked my dri and there is more milk than I require. It seemed as if a gÇodma sister might be happy to receive some fresh milk."*

It was a kind offer – but there was something unnatural in the woman's voice. Sônam Dé-kyi could not identify what it was – but it was as if she was speaking words which she had memorised. The words sounded rehearsed, as if she had used them often before. Still there was nothing wrong with fresh milk. The woman passed her the bowl of milk – but Sônam Dé-kyi was faintly uncomfortable about the expression on the woman's face.

She looked pleased – but her pleasure had some aspect that seemed unwholesome. She was just about to take a sip when her brothers' words occurred to her *"It is the milk."* An idea immediately occurred to her *'Yes —it **is** the milk—it is the **milk** which caused my brothers to die. This woman is not normal. She could be anything. She could be from somewhere other than the human realm.'*

Sônam Dé-kyi had slid her phurba from her waist-sash as she was thinking – and surreptitiously held it below the bowl as she pretended to drink. Then suddenly shouting an activity mantra of Dorje Phurba she threw the milk into the woman's face with great force. The milk passed through the woman's face and turned into air. Hideous sounds emitted from where the woman had stood and her form disappeared in smoke; blown away by the wind. The woman had been a dön-dré. Sônam Dé-kyi then understood how her brothers had died.

"Yah…" Ngakpa Yeshé Dorje commenced once he had finished relating the story. *"This in father's lifetime happening. He is grandson of Ngakma Sônam Dé-kyi meeting and this he is telling – so you can all peoples telling."*

I replied that I would convey the story just as he had told it – but failed to add that few people would believe it. I was not sure what I made of it – as the story had been handed down through a few too many people. Speaking from direct personal experience was one thing – but this was possibly another.

It also struck me that I lived in a world where there was so much bogus verbiage that people weren't inclined to believe anything. I'd believed a few urban legends as a teenager – and had been surprised to find a book about urban legends. In reading the book I found the stories I'd been told – defined as typical urban legends.

People were now more cynical than they had been when I was young. In a way this was good – but it made me feel sad that Ngakpa Yeshé Dorje had told this story in order to be helpful to people… but they'd mainly regard it as mythology. I didn't believe everything I heard – but I didn't actively disbelieve accounts merely because they were outside my experience. There was a point between the two stances of belief and disbelief – the point where one simply does not know. Why either believe or disbelieve something of which one has no experience? I didn't understand how a jet aircraft functioned—or how it rose from the ground—but I still took flights to India every year.

Then Ngakpa Yeshé Dorje had another account to give me. "*One time there is one young gé-nyèn* [12] *Thrin-lé Dorje and he is with one very fat Geshé Tsültrim Tsöndrü*[13] *living. They small gompa in Kham living. This story also my father telling.*"

Geshé Tsültrim told Thrin-lé to go and buy some yak meat from a particular zhan-ma[14] who lived in a tent near the drokpa encampment. '*Buy plenty for tonight's dinner – but accept only what the butcher woman provides for the money. Don't ask her for more.*'

Thrin-lé had never heard that there were women engaged in this kind of work – but he set out and found the zhan-ma where his Lama said she would be. He made his request and paid the price – but he noticed a discrepancy. It seemed that there wasn't the amount of yak meat he'd expected. So, Thrin-lé told the zhan-ma that there wasn't enough yak meat for the money he'd paid. This displeased the zhan-ma who scowled at him silently – but nonetheless added a little more yak meat.

Thrin-lé still felt the amount of yak meat didn't represent the price he'd paid and asked for more. The zhan-ma then appeared irritated – but added a little more yak meat; again, without saying a word. Thrin-lé still felt cheated and being a brave lad – ventured to ask again for more. Again, a fraction more was added in silence – but with an expression of rage. This was disconcerting to Thrin-lé but he was at least satisfied that he had enough yak meat for the Geshé's dinner. He knew the Geshé to have a large appetite and he would be grumpy if his dinner appeared skimpy.

Thrin-lé took the yak meat back to the gompa, and told Geshé Tsültrim what had occurred – expecting to be praised for his persistence. Instead, however, Geshé Tsültrim was horrified and looked anxious. "*Ah kha kha! Bad—bad—bad! You didn't follow my instruction. I told you not to ask for more than she gave you. There may be extremely serious consequences. Let me see your arms.*"

---

12 *dGe bsNyen* / དགེ་བསྙེན་ / *sravaka* – a monk with eight vows to observe. Celibacy is not enjoined upon gé-nyèns or gé-nyènmas, Buddhist lay adherents who maintain the five precepts.
13 *dGe bShes tshul khrims brTson 'grus* / དགེ་བཤེས་ཚུལ་ཁྲིམས་བརྩོན་འགྲུས་. Tsültrim means discipline (*Sila*) and tsöndrü means diligence (*virya*).
14 *bZhan ma* / བཞན་མ་ – butcher (female).

Thrin-lé proffered his arms – and Geshé Tsültrim examined them. There were curious marks upon them. *"Ah kha kha! Terrible—terrible—terrible!"* he exclaimed in fear. *"I told you explicitly to take whatever the zhan-ma gave you and not to ask for more. You have made a terrible error! The marks on your hands signify that you will be her food tonight!"*

"How can that be!?" asked Thrin-lé in great trepidation.

"She is a dön'dré! She will eat you alive!" Geshé Tsültrim gasped – having come out in a cold sweat.

"Please save me Geshé la!" Thrin-lé pleaded in terror – but the Geshé replied *"I cannot save you – I don't have the knowledge, capacity, or power."*

"What can I do? Where can I hide!?"

"There is nowhere you can hide! The only thing you can do is find my brother and plead with him to help you. He is a ngakpa. He has not studied the Sutras and is ignorant of the noble doctrine. He is ignorant and has no training in debate – but he has training for this kind of work. His name is Gyür'mèd Rinchen and he lives amongst the nomads. They like him because he is a shaman who casts spells and makes protective amulets. He will be able to help you. Tell him that I sent you and be extremely polite – because he is extremely proud and haughty."

So that's what he did. He found Gyür'mèd Rinchen quite easily and explained his predicament in as polite and reverential a manner as he could. He mentioned that it was his brother's request and hoped fervently and solicitously that the Lama would be so very generous as to grant his venerable brother's request.

"Ah…" responded the Lama *"so that's the way of it. I'm happy to help you – but not for the sake of my fat gluttonous brother. We have the same father, yes – but not the same mother. And this shows too well in his life. He is addicted to status and makes a great deal of his academic erudition. If he were not so acquisitive, impractical, and incompetent he wouldn't have ventured to have dealings with that pernicious maleficent dön'dré."*

"Then you will help me, Rinpoche?" Thrin-lé asked in some degree of excitement. *"Certainly, I will help you – but you must do exactly what I tell you to do. My greedy brother did warn you not to ask for more – and you didn't heed his instruction. That was not entirely stupid – because he didn't warn you that she was a dön'dré. Had he told you – you might have remembered his admonition.*

"As it was, he didn't want you to be too afraid to buy meat from her. That was an act which he will come to regret."

"You will punish him?" Thrin-lé asked nervously.

"No… Tsültrim will punish himself. I need have no hand in it. Our actions are their own punishment. I may not have studied the Sutras or learned how to debate – but I am not so ignorant that I do not understand lé. [15]*"*

"I will do whatever you say to save my life" Thrin-lé promised.

"Well… you must learn something from this which will help you in life. I could simply deal with her myself – but you must do it in order to find out what your priorities are in life."

And so, Lama Gyür'mèd Rinchen gave Thrin-lé his instructions. He was to go far beyond the drokpa encampment in the direction of the mountains. There he would find a large black tent which was the home of another *dön'dré*. He was to ask her for her help, in respect of accommodation for the night. Thrinlé was to be highly solicitous and make her an offering of tsampa and butter. She would prove unwilling – but then he was to offer cheese. She would still prove unwilling – and then he was to offer her chang. Then she would help – and the sign of her being willing to help was that she would slap his face with some force. Lama Gyür'mèd Rinchen would provide him with the offerings – but he would have a long way to carry them. Thrin-lé followed Lama Gyür'mèd Rinchen's instructions and left immediately for the hills. It was a long walk and the weight of the tsampa, butter, cheese, and chang proved more of a burden than he would have imagined. He eventually saw the black tent in the distance and made his way towards it. There were ravens flying over the tent and a black dre'u[16] which started braying horribly as soon as it saw him approach.

A woman suddenly appeared from the tent brandishing a whip. She cracked the whip in the air and a gust of wind was aroused. It blew against Thrin-lé and made it difficult to walk uphill to the tent. He persevered however and eventually stood before the dön'dré. He somehow didn't feel as terrified as he had expected.

---

15 *las* / ལས་ / *karma* – perception and response, more commonly known as cause and effect.

16 *dre'u* / དྲེའུ་ – mule.

He had demanded better service from the previous dön'dré he'd met and so he thought that if anything he was safer than on the previous occasion. He had come, after all, on Lama Gyür'mèd Rinchen's instructions – and he was a ngakpa. He understood such situations whereas Geshé Tsültrim Tsöndrü did not.

Thrin-lé without a word offered the tsampa and butter and the dön'dré took it from him – but just made howling noises at him and shook her head violently. Thrin-lé then offered the cheese. The dön'dré took it from him – and made howling noises as before but without the violent head shaking. Thrin-lé then offered the chang. The dön'dré took it from him with something approaching pleasure. She then slapped him sharply around the face. She howled – but now he could understand the howling. There were words in the howling which became clearer as the howling seemed to subside. *"What do you want! Tell me now – or go away!"* she barked.

Thrin-lé explained the situation and requested her, extremely politely, to let him stay the night in her tent. *"Usually I would not do this – but I see that a ngakpa has sent you here. I also see that you are not avaricious, injudicious, and impudent like that Geshé. I will help you – but you must do exactly as I tell you."*

To save his life, he was to hide silently inside a large iron vessel as soon as dusk fell. The dön'dré would seal it closed – all but for a small hole which would allow him to breathe. She would then tie down the cover with a length of magical rope in which she'd tied nine knots.

Dusk fell quite soon as Thrin-lé had arrived toward the end of the day. *"You arrived only just in time"* the dön'dré announced *"because very soon that vile dön'dré sister will arrive with other dön'dré who come to feast with me. She has always been avaricious, voracious, and stupid. I have no reason to side with her."*

Once Thrin-lé was secured inside the iron vessel, the dön'dré sat on it as a chair. Thrin-lé was not happy to be incarcerated in the iron pot – but it was better than being eaten alive. After a short time, several other dön'dré arrived and proceeded to howl at each other. It took some time to adjust to the awful sound – but eventually he could understand some of what they were saying.

"Yah, yah, yah – and so" announced the dön'dré in whose tent Thrin-lé had sought protection *"who is the shar-jin [17] tonight? Bring the meat now!"*

---

17 *sha sByin* / ཤ་སྦྱིན་ – meat bringer.

On hearing this the dön'dré who had sold Thrin-lé the yak meat said *"I am she. Tonight, I have a special treat for you all – a fresh young monk! I shall go and fetch him."* At this she left the tent – but within a few minutes she reappeared. She looked haggard from what Thrin-lé could see through the airhole beneath the lid of the iron vessel. *"The meat I obtained for this night – it has gone!"*

"Is that so!" screeched the dön'dré who owned the black tent. *"Then you know what must happen!"* The meat-selling dön'dré cowered by the entrance to the tent – but not for long. She was torn apart by the other dön'dré and devoured. Thrin-lé could not bear to look and fainted with fear.

When he awoke, he was lying on the ground wrapped in black blankets. There was no dön'dré and no tent – only ravens cawing and the dre'u braying. Thrin-lé folded the blankets neatly and left them where he had slept. He was intelligent enough not to take what had not actually been given to him. He returned to Lama Gyür'mèd Rinchen and explained everything which had occurred. Thrin-lé never returned to the gompa to study with Geshé Tsültrim Tsöndrü, but became a disciple of Lama Gyür'mèd Rinchen and lived amongst the nomads – where meat was not as perilous to obtain.

By the time these stories were concluded it was time for me to leave and return to my hut.

"Not frightened in dark walking?" Ngakpa Yeshé Dorje asked with a chuckle.

"Well, I've taken the walk many times before in the dark and tonight isn't different from those other nights – unless you feel that there are dön'dré out there tonight."

"Always dön'dré possible" Ngakpa Yeshé Dorje laughed *"but you Tröma practising so no fear having."*

Khandro Ten'dzin Drölkar also laughed, but she looked at me 'knowingly' – or so I thought. I wondered what that *look* had betokened – but unless she ever referred to it, there was no way I would know. It would be impolite to ask such a question. I noticed that Sônam was really quite uneasy and so I said I'd accompany him back to the Tibetan Astro-Medical Centre where he lived. Sônam seemed grateful.

We walked back and Sônam chattered nervously as if he wanted to keep all thoughts of dön'dré out of his mind. I obliged by chattering with him in order to calm him.

I reminded him that it was my custom to sit in the graveyard of *St John's in the Wilderness*[18] – the deserted little English church between McLeod Ganj and Forsyth Bazar. At first Tibetans thought I was crazy to sit there because of the 'dré – but when I failed to die or fall sick, they started looking at me as if I was an accomplished ngakpa. I wished it had been possible to have told them that I was just an English art student. This was my main qualification. It wasn't that I was fearless or so accomplished that I terrified the 'dré. It was merely because I'd never been frightened of ghosts – or the rumour of ghosts. I'd never encountered a ghost – and had never thought of Khyungchen Aro Lingma as a ghost. She'd simply been the beneficent White Lady who appeared in my room at night.

Be that as it may, I told Sônam *"I have no fear of dön'dré so you need have no fear as long as you're with me."* This cheered him up noticeably and gradually the lights of McLeod Ganj took away the last shreds of Sônam's anxiety.

My reassurance of Sônam was entirely bravado – but it came from a kindly intention and so I didn't reprimand myself. It was true however, that I wasn't unduly worried by the supernatural. I never had been. It wasn't because I was cynical on the subject – but because I'd never witnessed anything of that nature. It was always possible – but until it was, I didn't feel it worthwhile to feel anxious. Ngakpa Yeshé Dorje's stories had been strange to hear – because they had a culturally based pattern. It was a pattern which was different in some ways to the pattern of western ghost stories – but similar in others. The fact that I saw a pattern was what made the stories difficult to wholeheartedly believe.

I did not feel comfortable about this point of view however. I would rather there'd been no idea of that kind in my mind – but there was. I couldn't quite imagine non-human entities having conversations and emotions which were so similar to human modes. I decided that there was little purpose in speculating. If one doesn't know – then belief and disbelief are of little value. Not being able to believe did not automatically mean that one disbelieved. That was the usual western assumption – but for me, *not knowing* was always preferable to belief or disbelief. Maybe—one day—I'd know.

---

18 St John's in the Wilderness – a Neo-Gothic Anglican Church dedicated to John the Baptist, built in 1852, set in a deodar forest. It is known for the Belgian stained-glass windows donated by Lady Elgin.

The next day I went to see Khandro Ten'dzin Drölkar. Sônam was unavailable and so Pema Wang-gyal came with me. He was another student at the Tibetan Astro-Medical Centre.

We arrived at the shambling hut and Khandro Ten'dzin Drölkar made tea for herself and Pema Wang-gyal – and a glass of hot lemon and honey for the tea-abstemious Inji. She then said *"I am one story telling."* It was a long story and she asked if I had time to listen. Naturally I had all the time in the world to listen to anything she had to tell me.

"One time mother and daughter alone living. Mother name Yang-çan [19] *and daughter is Samdrüp* [20]. *They barley growing and chang making."*

Each day—when Samdrüp went out to guard the crops—she had to drive the birds away throughout the day. When she came home in the evening, she saw her mother Yang-çan climbing a ladder to the roof, and asked what she was doing. *"I'm climbing so that I can see further into the distance – but tell me, did birds eat our barley?"*

"No. I drove them all away" Samdrüp replied.

"Then you are a good daughter. You have done well."

The next day she noticed Yang-çan on the rooftop.

"Ama la" she asked *"what are you doing? One day you're on the ladder attic – and now you're on the roof."*

"I'm looking for someone" Yang-çan replied.

"Who are you looking for Ama la?"

"I am looking for someone who may be coming to visit us soon – but I cannot not tell you who it is."

The next morning, Samdrüp again went to the field to drive the birds away as usual. When she returned home that evening, she found her mother in the sky above their house. The daughter was alarmed *"Ama la – how can you be in the sky?"*

---

19 dByangs can / དབྱངས་ཅན་ / Sarasvati – powerful speech.
20 bSam 'grub / བསམ་འགྲུབ་ – fulfilled wishes.

"Never mind about how I am where I am — I'm going away for some days. Anyway, you just stay here and I will make sure you are safe. There is food to eat for many days — so you will not go hungry."

Now, Yang-çan was a natural jig'tèn khandro[21] who had the power of flight — but this power had not passed to her daughter. Samdrüp didn't know what to do, but Yang-çan had thrown her a magical woollen rope before she disappeared into the sky — and so she went out and started to play with the rope. As she was occupied whirling the rope in the air and watching scenes unfold at the end of the rope, the daughter of a srinmo[22] arrived disguised as a pretty young girl, and asked Samdrüp *"What are you doing?"*

"I'm playing with a rope that my mother gave me" she replied.

"Why? What fun is there in a piece of rope?" the srinmo asked.

"It helps me see my mother" Samdrüp answered. *"My mother gave it to me before she flew into the sky and when I whirl the rope I see her in the sky."*

The srinmo, being curious, asked *"Can I whirl that rope and see what I can see?"* The girl agreed and the srinmo began to whirl the rope in the air looking to see if she could see the girl's mother at the rope's end. The srinmo seeing nothing at the rope's end said *"I see nothing with this rope. Maybe I will try again tomorrow to see your mother. Will you still be here tomorrow?"*

"This is my home" the girl replied. *"Where else would I go?"*

Having heard this reply the srinmo left — and Samdrüp was left alone wondering who the strange girl might have been. She coiled up her mother's rope and hid it in her dress. The next morning as Samdrüp sat at the window of the house eating an apricot — the srinmo arrived, carrying a black sack and asked Samdrüp *"What are you doing?"*

"I'm eating an apricot from my mother's food store" the girl replied.

"May I have one of your mother's apricots?" asked the srinmo.

"I'll throw you one."

---

21 *'jig rTen mKha' 'gro ma* / མཁའ་འགྲོམ / Lokadakini.
22 *srin mo* / སྲིན་མོ / *rakshasi* — often translated as demoness, ogress or vampire, but there is no useful translation.

"Don't throw!" said the srinmo. *"I cannot catch anything which is thrown!"*

"Right then – just hold your sack open and I'll throw one into it."

"The neck of my sack is too small" the srinmo replied. *"Will you be so kind as to pass it to me?"*

Samdrüp stretched her hand down from the window holding out an apricot. The srinmo caught hold of her wrist and swiftly pulled her into the sack. Once the srinmo had secured Samdrüp in the sack, she bounded away and kept bounding until she had crossed several valleys. Samdrüp heard Yang-çan's voice from somewhere outside the sack saying *"Tell the srinmo she needs to rest."*

So Samdrüp shouted from the sack *"Hey! You've travelled too far! You must be tired – why not rest for a while?"*

The srinmo agreed *"Yes—now you mention it—I am indeed tired. I think I will take a rest."*

As they were resting, the srinmo found that her head was itching unpleasantly and said *"You could make yourself useful now – will you be so good as to de-louse my hair?"* Samdrüp agreed because it would give her time to think about how to escape. As she was looking for lice, she heard Yang-çan's voice coming from the sky *"Look for stones to fill the sack."* So Samdrüp searched the srinmo's hair for lice with one hand, whilst feeling the ground for stones with the other hand. Every stone she found she surreptitiously slipped into the sack. After a while the srinmo fell asleep – because the de-lousing had been so soothing. As soon as the srinmo was asleep, Samdrüp ran home.

Eventually the srinmo awoke – but mysteriously forgot what had happened before she went to sleep. She assumed Samdrüp was still in the sack – because it felt as heavy as it should feel with a little girl inside it. She continued on her way and eventually reached her home.

"As I promised Ama la, I have brought meat today" announced the srinmo as she emptied her sack onto the floor next to the boiling pot which her mother was preparing.

The srinmo was shocked as she watched the pebbles fall onto the floor. Her mother and relatives rebuked her angrily for her foolishness.

Her mother told her that she'd have to seek the human girl as soon as she awoke the next day. The next day the srinmo dutifully returned to the human girl's home. She caught her outside her house – this time by creeping up behind her and slipping the black sack over her head. *"This time"* she snarled *"we're not stopping to rest on the way! Tonight, you will be dinner for my hungry family!"*

On the srinmo's arriving home, Samdrüp heard her mother's voice *"Say you're too little to be worth eating."* The srinmo was about to drop Samdrüp from her sack when Samdrüp shouted *"Not so fast! I'm just a little girl. I'm too small to be worth eating. My body would never feed your family. Best to let me first grow bigger if you want a decent meal."*

The mother srinmo agreed *"Yes, that's reasonable. She's right – she is too small. Maybe she'll be bigger tomorrow."* The family all agreed and they decided to leave cooking Samdrüp for another day. The next day the family members went hunting while the srinmo daughter remained to guard Samdrüp. Samdrüp was clever however – and decided that her mother had thrown her a rope from the sky for a good reason. She took the rope out from her dress and started to climb it. As she climbed the rope she yelled in glee *"I can see my mother from here!"*

The srinmo was immediately interested. She told Samdrüp to get down from the rope so that she could also see her mother. Samdrüp descended and the srinmo ascended. Samdrüp then heard her mother's voice *"Srinmos cannot see unless they wear human clothes."*

Sure enough the srinmo saw nothing and snarled with annoyance.

"But you can't see my mother in your clothes" Samdrüp stated as if it was a commonly understood fact. *"You will only be able to see her if you wear human clothes."*

The srinmo believed the girl and exchanged her clothes for Samdrüp's dress. As the srinmo climbed the rope the girl threw a cooking knife that cut the rope, precipitating the srinmo into the boiling water – where, after some horrible screams, she began to cook.

Not long after, the family returned – and the mother srinmo laughed *"Ah good! I see you have boiled the human girl."*

"Yes, indeed I have!" replied Samdrüp *"with plenty of salt and butter."* Samdrüp was dressed as a srinmo and so the family mistook her for one of them.

Goodbye Forever

The family found the meal delicious. Whilst they were enjoying the meal Samdrüp heard her mother say *"Time to leave and find a tall tree to climb."* So, she quietly left whilst the family were busy eating – saying *"I'm not hungry because I'm too hot after all that cooking – so I'm going to stand outside to cool down."* When the family were coming to the end of their meal, they wondered where their daughter had gone. *"She's surely cooled down by this time."* When they found no one outside, they began to suspect that they had eaten a family member rather than the human girl. Maybe the girl had somehow dressed in srinmo clothing.

They sought for Samdrüp – but she was nowhere in sight. They followed her footprints and found her perched in the higher branches of a tree. A srinpo brother began to climb after her – so she called out *"Ama la make the tree grow taller."* Immediately the top of the tree started to grow towards the moon. The srinpo however, continued to climb – and the distance was narrowing between him and Samdrüp. So Samdrüp called to her mother *"Throw an iron chain from the moon so that I can escape."* Her mother replied *"so far you have used ropes to achieve everything."*

"But this time" Samdrüp insisted *"a woollen rope will not be strong enough."*

As Samdrüp gained the highest branches—and the srinpo was almost upon her—Yang-çan threw down an iron chain. Samdrüp caught the iron chain and climbed to the moon. When Samdrüp was safe, she said *"Ama la – throw down the woollen rope for the srinpo."* Yang-çan—smiling—threw down the woollen rope.

"Then srinpo woollen rope grasping and too far climbing – but before moon arriving, woollen rope breaking. Then srinpo from too great height falling. Srinpo falling on family – and so fast falling that all family dying. Then Samdrüp and Yang-çan home going and chang making."

On concluding the story, Khandro Ten'dzin Drölkar asked *"Srinmo story believing – or not believing?"*

This was a change in my experience of Khandro Ten'dzin Drölkar. I had never known her to put me on the spot before.

"Well… I hope this does not sound rude… but it sounds like a folk story – a story for children."

"Why children story thinking?" Khandro Ten'dzin Drölkar asked with a smile.

"Well..." I replied *"because it has many similar features to western children's stories – and I have heard stories which are like this from many different European and Scandinavian countries. I've also heard Chinese and Japanese stories which have similar features. When I was at Art School, we had a project on illustrating children's stories and I read quite a few before choosing one to illustrate. One thing they all seemed to have in common was that the characters acted in ways which were not believable."*

"O yah!" Khandro Ten'dzin Drölkar laughed a warm and merry laugh. *"Children's story. Story is emptiness. All reflections, emptiness. All manifesting in Mind mirror, empty. Srinmo empty. Dön'dré empty. Believing, empty. Not believing, empty."*

Then Khandro Ten'dzin Drölkar and Pema Wang-gyal had to discuss a word. It came out as culture[23] – after which Khandro Ten'dzin Drölkar said *"Tibetan culture, empty"* and laughed. *"Western culture, empty. But culture both also form. When form different coming – one must be empty becoming. When Tibetan culture, form – then western culture emptiness becoming. When western culture, form – then Tibetan culture emptiness becoming. Chögyam must in both worlds living. So, 'form culture' is emptiness becoming – and 'emptiness culture' is form becoming. This knowledge applying – then, no problem having."*

That was a perfect analysis of the subject – based on principle and function. Khandro Ten'dzin Drölkar was so obviously a disciple of Künzang Dorje Rinpoche. To address the *emptiness* and *form* of different *cultures* – seemed exactly what Künzang Dorje Rinpoche would have done. There was a beauty to the simplicity of it. When one believes explanations which come from Tibetan culture – then the beliefs of western culture become emptiness. When one believes explanations which come from western culture – then the Tibetan cultural beliefs become emptiness. And it's not that you have to choose one or the other. Both can function alternately depending where one finds oneself – and beyond that, both are relative. The only reality is the nondual state.

We sipped our respective beverages before Khandro Ten'dzin Drölkar recommenced. *"Dzogchen practice you having – so srinmo and dön'dré empty remaining. No fear. No action needing – only awareness. This, Kyabjé Künzang Dorje Rinpoche teaching"* she laughed. *"This too funny. I am Karma Gyalpo Rinpoche calling – and Chögyam not knowing, this—same—Lama."*

---

23 Culture – rig-né (*rig gNas* / རིག་གནས་).

Khandro Ten'dzin Drölkar told me that she was very happy that I had studied with Künzang Dorje Rinpoche – because now we were vajra brother and sister. This was a bond which would last throughout our lives and future lives. We would always be connected.

This was a wonderful statement. We sat together in an atmosphere permeated by her warmth and kindness. An idea arose but I decided immediately not to act on it. It was not that I couldn't ask Khandro Ten'dzin Drölkar – but I could not ask her through a third party. It was too personal a question. I wanted to know why Ngakpa Yeshé Dorje had seemed to cast doubt on Künzang Dorje Rinpoche. He said *"Better to rely on Kyabjé Düd'jom Rinpoche."* Then it occurred to me that even if I could speak Tibetan sufficiently to ask the question – it might not be a question which Khandro Ten'dzin Drölkar wanted to answer. It might be an invasive question. No, it *would* be an invasive question. I'd been saved from it, only by my ignorance of Tibetan language.

On my way back to my hut I pondered what Khandro Ten'dzin Drölkar had intended by telling me this Tibetan children's tale – and asking me whether I believed it represented reality. I pondered mere seconds before it was obvious that she was making a comment on the dön'dré accounts which Ngakpa Yeshé Dorje had given. Perhaps the fact that Pema Wang-gyal had translated rather than Sônam, had given her the chance to comment without seeming to criticise her husband. Pema Wang-gyal had not heard the stories on the previous evening – so he would not have linked the events.

That then, was my conclusion. Khandro Ten'dzin Drölkar was excusing me from having to believe the dön'dré stories. Was there any other conclusion? I could see no other conclusion – but was I to trust my conclusion? If I trusted my conclusion, it would affect my view of Ngakpa Yeshé Dorje – and that was a difficult position. I was probably going to have to put the question to Kyabjé Düd'jom Rinpoche. The thought of laying the matter before him rather than trusting my own judgement didn't feel a desirable option – but as it concerned *pure vision* in respect of the Lama, I felt I had no choice. Life had been simple up to that point – and I wondered how the cards would fall. One thing was certain – I was not going to train as an exorcist. At some point I was going to have to own up to my reluctance – but maybe Düd'jom Rinpoche would provide me with the necessary exemption. I was sure this was possible.

19

perfect, just as it is

I said farewell to Ngakpa Yeshé Dorje and Khandro Ten'dzin Drölkar. They were both happy that I was going to see Kyabjé Düd'jom Rinpoche again. I reminded Ngakpa Yeshé Dorje that I'd not forgotten my promise to seek out conch shell earrings for him. *"Also, Chögyam necessary finding"* he'd replied – and with that I wandered down to wait outside Narowjee's for the bus. *'Also, Khandro Ten'dzin Drölkar necessary finding.'* I thought as I stood there. If Ngakpa Yeshé Dorje should have them—and I should have them—then certainly Khandro Ten'dzin Drölkar should have them. She should have them before me, certainly.

What followed my catching the bus, was merely an itinerary subsequent to arriving in Bodhanath. I was used to the journey. It hadn't become a great deal easier – but it wasn't the ordeal it once was. Long journeys provide plentiful time for conjecture, speculation, and surmise – if required. Even if not required – conjecture can begin to require itself. I did ponder a few matters. I pondered the stories told by Ngakpa Yeshé Dorje – or, not so much the stories, as his having taken them as real accounts when I took them as folk tales. Khandro Ten'dzin Drölkar also took them as folk tales – or, such was her intimation. There was nothing I could do with that conjecture. There was no obvious resolution – other than discomfort. I decided the subject was best left alone until I could discuss it with Düd'jom Rinpoche. Another field of conjecture was where I'd settle in Britain in terms of finding work. Farnham and Aldershot were not the best places to find manual labouring jobs. There were once roadworks on the M3 motorway – but the roadworks had moved on. They were now out of range of my parental home. Bristol would be far easier in terms of finding accommodation – but the cost of rented accommodation had risen quite ridiculously. Maybe there were other towns or cities I could explore. Purposeless to dwell on it. *Age Quod Agis* [1] – I'd do what I did: as and when it proved expedient.

---

1 Age Quod Agis is attributed to Ignatius Loyola the founder of the Jesuit Order. It means *'Do what you do'* and is basically an encouragement to focus on the task at hand.

The journey was behind me—yet again—and I was glad to be back in Bodhanath; apart from not knowing whether Kyabjé Düd'jom Rinpoche would be there or not. If he was not there then I would see whether Dilgo Khyentsé Rinpoche was there and able to see me. If this also was not possible then I would be happy to live in Bodhanath for three weeks and circumambulate the chörten 21 times, three times a day. Actually, I'd ceased to count. I knew by the sensation in my legs approximately how many 'khora I had performed. I wasn't performing 'khora for merit[2] in any case – as I considered *everything I did* to be a giveaway for everyone and everything everywhere. If I drank a bottle of *Sprite*, it was for everyone and everything everywhere. If I saw something beautiful it was for everyone and everything everywhere. I did not always remember – but I tried to remember as often as possible.

Düd'jom Rinpoche smiled a huge smile at me as I entered the room and, after I'd performed my prostrations, he laughed *"O yah – Künzang Dorje not eating! You liking and much learning!"* PAUSE *"He transmission Dzogchen men-ngag-dé giving?"*

"Yes Rinpoche – to all three" I smiled. *"I was intimidated by him at first – but, in the end, he told me that I was his son."* Then I did something that I do from time to time. My eyes brimmed. Düd'jom Rinpoche observed me in a kindly way and waited 'til I gained control of myself. *"Yah – it is as I am wishing. You are all things well doing – and now time is coming your own country returning."*

"Yes, Rinpoche, I am sorry to say that it is. Do you have any advice for me before I go home… in terms of the future?"

"O yah – but today not only 'time with me' talking."

Düd'jom Rinpoche had a short period of completely free time – and he wanted to see me every day until I had to leave Nepal.

"After some time Bodhanath coming, again – Tso Pema again, Künzang Dorje seeing. But one day you must return – and your own country living. All life you cannot India and Nepal staying. Bad for health.

---

2   Merit (*bSod nams* / བསོད་ནམས་ / *punya*). It is translated as 'merit' but actually has a meaning closer to 'skill' or 'capacity'.

"Then when you old – you must have support for life and somewhere staying." PAUSE *"First practices and retreats completing – then returning, own land."* PAUSE *"Future times peoples teaching requests making – then must be teaching. Before—as much as possible—you must time with Künzang Dorje staying close."*

"Künzang Dorje Rinpoche told me that in the future there would be a time when I would not see him for 13 years."

"O yah…" PAUSE *"This one full cycle of the Tibetan calendar – and one year more coming. This means that you must something without him completing. Künzang Dorje indications for what is necessary giving?"*

"Yes. He gave me practices – and said that I needed to fulfil them in the interim. He said that by the time we met again, I would have my own students and that he wanted me to establish this and be self-reliant. He said that in the West I would learn a great deal in terms of self-reliance and that this was a vital part of learning how people perceived and what motivated them. He said that I would not learn these things if I was seen as someone who was not an authority in his own right. He said that I would have to see how people responded and what their real intentions were."

"Yah… good." Düd'jom Rinpoche gazed both at me—and through me—into space for almost a minute. *"This you can doing. This you can accomplishing. Difficulties coming – but not too much difficulties. You all difficulties overcoming."*

'Difficulties' had been an occasional theme with both Düd'jom Rinpoche and Künzang Dorje Rinpoche. Both Lamas had said that I would have *difficulties*. That was not the most cheerful news – but they had both said I'd *overcome the difficulties*; so… I assumed that whatever didn't kill me would make me more resilient.

"So… do—you—have advice for me Rinpoche, on Lamas with whom I should study in that time? Künzang Dorje Rinpoche said that I should continue my studies and practise with other Lamas in the 13 year interval."

"Künzang Dorje names giving?"

"He suggested Chatral Rinpoche, Dung-sé Thrin-lé Norbu Rinpoche , Chag'düd Tulku Rinpoche, and 'Khordong gTérchen Tulku Chhi'mèd Rig'dzin Rinpoche."

Düd'jom Rinpoche pondered for a moment *"My son Thrin-lé Norbu—and also Chag'düd—America now living. This too far travelling. Maybe America later travelling."* PAUSE *"Chatral… yah… maybe."*

Rinpoche made movement with his fingers as if counting. *"No."* Pause with further finger movements. *"O yah! Chhi'mèd Rig'dzin for you, much best."* PAUSE *"Yah – Chhi'mèd Rig'dzin—good Lama—fierce like Künzang Dorje."* PAUSE *"Chang gTér³—Mahayoga—practising but Dzogchen also perfectly knowing. Teachings from Künzang Dorje learning, he is all understanding."*

"And Ngakpa Yeshé Dorje…" I asked *"Would you recommend that I continue to study Tröma Nakmo with him?"*

Düd'jom Rinpoche looked at me knowingly for a moment *"Yah… possible – but maybe no Chir-dog learning. For Yeshé Dorje Chir-dog good – but for Chögyam…* he shook his head *"No benefit coming."*

"I am relieved to hear you say that Rinpoche – because I have been worrying about it. It seems that Ngakpa Yeshé Dorje wants me to train in all those areas of his expertise – and… it's not really…" PAUSE *"I'm appreciative of his openness to teaching me – but, I have no enthusiasm for it."*

Düd'jom Rinpoche smiled *"O yah. Chögyam always natural remaining."* Then he laughed *"Mind like sky – not like tree root. Much complicated no good. No purpose in western countries. When Dzogchen accomplishing, all demon naturally banishing—naturally subduing—no effort making."* PAUSE *"I am thinking time with Yeshé Dorje, end coming. Chögyam not always, time for McLeod Ganj travelling. Not always possible. Ten'dzin Drölkar always future meeting. Maybe Nepal one day staying – not always McLeod Ganj. Then Chögyam often seeing. For Khandro Ten'dzin Drölkar, Künzang Dorje is Tsawa'i Lama – and also my son, Thrin-lé Norbu. She is very well Dzogchen knowing. Also rTsa rLung. Much retreat. Khandro Ten'dzin Drölkar is profound practitioner."*

Khandro Ten'dzin Drölkar's words returned to me at that point. She'd thought *'it would be good to be together in view of the fact that my time was running out in McLeod Ganj – and we never knew when we might see each other again. There could be obstacles to us meeting – and so we should make sure that we made full use of the time we had.'*

Düd'jom Rinpoche smiled at that point – having obviously read my mind *"No problem coming – always Chögyam is Ten'dzin Drölkar meeting. Many—many —time meeting."* PAUSE *"Then—after 13 years—again Künzang Dorje meeting. Then too much happiness – and all difficulties in space dissolving."*

---

3   *byang gTer* / བྱང་གཏེར་ – Northern gTérmas, revealed by gTértön Rig'dzin Gödem (*gTer sTon rig 'dzin rGod kyi lDem 'phru can* / གཏེར་སྟོན་རིག་འཛིན་རྒོད་ཀྱི་ལྡེམ་འཕྲུ་ཅན་ / 1337–1408).

"And… will I also be able to meet with you again, Rinpoche?"

"Yah… you also again meeting – but not easy as before, or like now. I must travel. I must teach many places. Maybe in your own land meeting. Maybe in London teaching. There is one Düd'jom gTér place there now – and they are inviting me. 'Ögyen Chöling' name I am giving – and there is one Sönam Gyaltsen there. He is young – maybe same age as you – maybe few years older. Maybe you see him there. He gives some help with Dharma there I think."

"Should I study with him when I am in England Rinpoche?"

"No" he laughed "he is no retreat or study having – but help giving with Tibetan language. Help with circumstances when you teachings giving." The idea was that I could help him with English and he would help me with Tibetan – and with introductions to people which would lead to my giving public teachings.

"Rinpoche, you have mentioned that I will have difficulties, several times now. Is it possible to say what these difficulties will be?"

"Difficulties from people coming. This in Tibet also coming. Where people 'powerful' wanting, 'status' wanting, money wanting – then always difficulties coming." He said that it was not that I wanted these things – but that the desire of others would cause conflict because of jealousy and rivalry. He told me that jealousy and rivalry had been behind his being sent to an Indian prison at one time. He asked me whether I remembered the story – and I answered that I remembered it all too clearly. Then he laughed "Dzogchen practising, difficulties coming – not bad seeing. Chögyam all circumstances with the same taste experiencing – but help still needing. Nyingmas are brothers – and brothers must be friends. Important you Nyingma Lama friends finding. Then not alone. Alone then too much difficult. If gö kar chang lo Lamas in West travelling, then I am telling – you must Chögyam friend becoming."

I thanked Kyabjé Düd'jom Rinpoche for his help and advice – and said that I would write it all down. I would never forget what he had said.

"Yah… not everyone trusting. Not everyone trusting who tells 'I am Vajrayana practising'. Many bad people in the world living – and some 'big monks', gö kar chang lo'i dé not liking." PAUSE "When you are father to your students—like Künzang Dorje is father to you—then you, strength like Künzang Dorje needing. This not meaning 'wrathful' becoming. Just be natural—as you are—but you must strong staying." PAUSE "Always strong staying."

"Künzang Dorje Rinpoche also warned me of difficulties if I tried to establish the gö kar chang lo'i dé in the West. He was extremely happy that you asked me to do this – but he said that it would not be easy for me."

"You still wishing?"

"Yes, Rinpoche – certainly. I will do this whatever happens. There is nothing in life more important to me than following your suggestion."

"Then you must Tibetan history studying. If Tibetan history studying you will know more what you must expecting."

He went on to say that there had been terrible Dharma politics in Tibet and still now there are terrible actions which were the reverse of Dharma. There were powerful people who did not want to see the gö kar chang lo'i dé known in the West. They thought the gö kar chang lo'i dé would take money away from the monasteries. They thought that if people in the West saw the gö kar chang lo'i dé they would lose interest in the monasteries and the monastic lineages. This was false and reverse thinking – but still, they had these ideas. Then Düd'jom Rinpoche laughed with considerable mirth and repeated what he'd said previously *"These people once had me thrown in prison as a Chinese spy!"*

Düd'jom Rinpoche saw the regret in my eyes and continued *"Yah… this is why I say you must always strong. You must always careful…"* But the West was different from India and Nepal. The powerful politicians who had him put in prison had no power in my land – but they would try to do what they could to make life difficult for me if I ever became well known. It was when I began to teach that it might become difficult. If people liked me—and I wore gö kar chang lo—it would make them angry because they did not wish gö kar chang lo'i dé to be seen in the West. *"Chögyam always in mind keeping. No separation. Maybe … all is well for you."* PAUSE *"Maybe when you are father to your own gö kar chang lo children you will be clearly what is necessary seeing."*

Düd'jom Rinpoche was unique in having received the transmission of all extant lineages of the Nyingma Tradition. He was renowned as a great gTértön – and his gTérmas are widely taught and practised throughout the world. He was one of the last remaining masters who was thoroughly conversant with all three series of Dzogchen – and, above all else, he was regarded as the living embodiment of Guru Rinpoche.

As Guru Rinpoche's representative in the world, he was often referred to as 'The Lama of Lamas'. He was acknowledged by the leading Tibetan teachers of his time as possessing the greatest power and facility in giving transmission of *the nature of Mind* – and it was to him that the great masters sent their students when they were ready for mind-to-mind transmission. Düd'jom Rinpoche is the Tsawa'i Lama of many of today's most prominent Lamas.

We ate lunch together in the company of several other Lamas. They had become accustomed to the presence of the Inji who spoke no Tibetan – or precious little. They spoke with Düd'jom Rinpoche – and I was content to listen to their voices. Sometimes I recognised words and phrases.

Once the meal was concluded the Lamas left. They bade me goodbye and I reciprocated. I knew how to bid Lamas an honorific goodbye. A few letters had arrived with the Lamas and so Düd'jom Rinpoche spent some time reading them before he turned his attention to me. Not that his attention hadn't included me – he smiled at me between letters, to let me know that my presence was welcome. Having spent ten minutes or so in writing, Kyabjé Düd'jom Rinpoche called for Tséwang—the monk who often translated—and we awaited his arrival. He appeared fairly quickly and when he was seated Düd'jom Rinpoche said *"Mind of every living being – fundamental nondual nature having."*

Although we all have this fundamental nature, it is not recognised. It seems unknown. This fundamental nature however—this spontaneous awareness—has been there from beginninglessness. It is mirror-like.

"When Chögyam in front of mirror laughing – he is laughing face reflection seeing." Then he laughed *"When girlfriend not there, Chögyam sad face seeing."*

Düd'jom Rinpoche and Künzang Dorje Rinpoche occasionally teased me about girlfriends – because young ladies seemed to loom large in my accounts of my life in the West. I had once enquired as to whether my partiality for young ladies was an obstacle but both had said that it was quite the reverse – particularly because I was primarily intent on having a long-term relationship, and eventually marriage. It was necessary that I should have a sangyum – and so naturally I had to see what was possible in the liaisons which presented themselves.

Düd'jom Rinpoche had once asked me about my girlfriends and asked me to enumerate and describe them. It may seem an unusual request – but to me, at the time, anything which Düd'jom Rinpoche asked me was part of something fundamentally meaningful. Whatever he asked was congruent with Vajrayana – and so it was only later when writing about it that it occurred to me that it was unusual. I began with Alice Rosalind Trevelyan at the age of five[4] in 1957. I described each young lady and he asked me questions concerning their appearance and interests. He mainly asked questions about Alice and Lindie Dale. He told me that these were the two most important young ladies and that either could have become a sangyum. He thought that although Anelie Mandelbaum had been a valuable ladyfriend she would not have been suitable as a sangyum.

Then he asked me which of the two—Alice Trevelyan or Lindie Dale—I would choose as the ideal sangyum. *"That's a difficult question to answer"* I explained *"because I knew Alice when I was 5 and 6 – and Lindie when I was 16 to 18. So, the experiences are quite dissimilar."* PAUSE *"However… if I look at potentialities… although at first I would have chosen Lindie – I would choose Alice."*

"Ya, 'A-li'[5] *is 'little girl' meaning – or 'a li khug ta'*[6]*…"* Here Düd'jom Rinpoche and the translator had to discuss different birds. *"Maybe 'swallow' meaning – this auspicious name. So, why Chögyam Ah-lees choosing?"*

"Because Alice was a stronger person. Lindie ended our relationship at her parent's insistence. They saw me as being a degenerate." The word degenerate had to be explained – and I had to provide a picture of 1960s upper middle-class values and mores. I explained that long-haired hippies were seen as little short of criminals. They were seen as drug users and people who were worthless to society. Düd'jom Rinpoche took in this information. He found it surprising but had no comment to make. He asked me to continue – so I did. *"I don't think Alice would have discontinued our relationship at her parents' insistence. In any case Alice's parents liked me."* PAUSE *"Then also, Lindie said that her parents had been right about my future. They'd pointed out that my being a Blues musician, if I became successful, would have meant constant travelling around the world. She would not have wished either to accompany me or to remain at home alone."* PAUSE *"So, she was a little fearful of the unknown.*

---

4   See *Goodbye Forever*—Volume I—chapter 2; and *an odd boy*— Volume I—chapter 1.
5   *a li* / ཨ་ལི — an infant.
6   *a li khug ta* / ཨ་ལི་ཁུག་ཏ — swallow.

"She wanted an understandable future and a relatively normal life. I don't think Alice would have had such fears about the life of a professional musician – or a wandering ngakpa. I think Alice would have wanted to join me in whatever adventure it was."

"O yah! Good answer coming. Sangyum must powerful. Must strong – same like Chögyam. When not powerful and strong, then no inspiration coming. When no powerful and strong, then no continuing good practice."

That was most interesting. Düd'jom Rinpoche often asked about aspects of my life – and there was never an occasion when his questions were simply curiosity. His questions always led somewhere which proved valuable. When I'd described Alice – it was as if he was seeing a photograph. It was not that my description was so vivid – but that he saw beyond the words into the image of Alice which I held in my mind. My speech was simply the mirror of this period of my life.

"This mirror – primordial ground. Reflection of Chögyam with laughing face into perfect mirror of primordial ground looking."

This, he said was Küntuzangpo[7] – and in this I would discover the ultimate nature of awakening. Küntuzangpo was the empire of the primordial ground. Finding myself to be there was the ultimate nature of awakening. Then the beginningless natural freedoms would manifest as my individual nature.

Ordinary beings fail to recognise this nature – this mirror-like primordial ground. A subtle identity-fixating consciousness emerges from it – and the sense of 'identity' and adhering to fixed 'identity' appears. From this, arises the need to project conceptual references onto phenomena – and relate to those projections, rather than to what is actually there.

'Identity apprehension' functions through the six sense perceptions – which could be said to be like the windows of a house. Some colour is seen. Some sound is heard. Then a second thought arises which interprets what is seen or heard in terms of what is already thought to be known concerning the world. At first there is simply colour or sound – but then there is the projected identification as this or that, or any one of a great number of possible categories.

---

7   *kun tu bZang po* / ཀུན་ཏུ་བཟང་པོ་

This apprehension of colour characteristics is seized upon as objectified reality. Similarly, we project onto sound – and then hear sounds according to categories. Next, more heavily concretised concepts develop and pursue the colours and sounds – identifying them as pleasant, unpleasant, or indeterminate. Then there is the perception which projects onto fragrances and odours. These are apprehended as fixed realities which are either pleasant, unpleasant, or un-noticed. The conceptualisation occurs in respect of taste—and that which can be tasted—and is apprehended as delicious, disgusting, or bland.

Finally, there is tactile perception, which apprehends physical contact as: pleasurable, uncomfortable, or nondescript. It is therefore evident that *whatever state of mind* it is which apprehends – thinks of itself as valid, according to the nature of what is experienced. There are six consciousnesses: the five sense perceptions and ideational perceptivity, and when they take what is subjective to be objective – duality becomes exponentially complex.

The root of delusion is duality – and occurs simply because we do not recognise the essential nature of being. Due to this, the idea of self and other as entirely separate arises – along with all other 'subject / object' dichotomies. Due to maintaining the sense of fixed identity – the vectors of dualistic derangement (*territorialism, aggression, obsession, paranoia, and denial*) develop to protect this identity.

"For us however, as practitioners of Vajrayana, only one instruction necessary: everything liberating. This is essential nature of phenomena experiencing."

I'd written it all down – and Kyabjé Düd'jom Rinpoche asked me to re-draft it in my own English in order that it could be translated back to him. This happened fairly frequently. I had been given to understand that it was a crucial part of my training – and that it would be valuable in later years that I had these texts which had been checked in this way.

"Some western students meeting" Düd'jom Rinpoche continued. *"They saying 'Profound teachings from our Lamas understanding.' but signs of progress not coming – only ideas and words. You people like this meeting when teaching beginning – so there are things you must be understanding."*

There can be a gulf between what is intellectually known and how people live. One can read many books. One can remember many words and phrases which can be quoted. One can seem to understand emptiness – but if meditation is sporadic there will be no result.

Profound methods are worthless if one merely toys with them as a child plays with novelties. If one merely lives according to indoctrinated habit there is only eating and defæcating fantasy; sleeping and waking fantasy; working and idling fantasy; desiring and reviling fantasy; thinking and obliviating fantasy. In these ways of passing time one can merely live life following habituated routines. As soon as one arises in the morning one begins to make plans. One is concerned about what might happen next. One is proud of apparent success. One is dejected by apparent failure. This can go on until death – and nothing will have changed in a way which means anything.

The reason why people toy with methods like children is because they have no real devotion – they only have fascination. Fascination will prompt practice – but it is fickle and easily worn out. Unless one has the devotion to be loyal to Lama and lineage, profound methods will achieve nothing – because one will not apply them with any diligence. One has to be diligent in the face of not experiencing a result. One must be content to practise even though there seems to be no success. One has to practise because one is a practitioner – and one is a practitioner because one has a Lama. One may think there is no success, but one will be changing – and one day the change will seem obvious and startling. This happens for an authentic practitioner – but not for one who is merely obsessed with gaining special experiences.

"Gap between view, meditation, and action is like between day and night, between the sky and abyss – unless radical leap of devotion taking. Then no intentional effort needing – simply with complete spontaneity living."

No intention is no plan, no effort, and no purpose. One has to have the courage and confidence to let anything happen. Then one's actions are always spontaneous and playful. This is because there is no connection with dualistic derangement. The world is already perfect, just as it is.

20

awareness

"Rinpoche…" I began *"I have some rather strange questions to ask — and I do not feel at ease about asking them."*

Düd'jom Rinpoche laughed *"Asking always possible."*

"Well… Künzang Dorje Rinpoche instructed me extremely well in terms of recognising principle and function. He told me stories and then questioned me about the motivation and intentions of the people in the stories. I had to concentrate. I had to examine the stories in every detail — and I had to be precise in my answers."

Düd'jom Rinpoche nodded with a smile to indicate that this was good.

"So… he thought after many sessions… that I had an understanding of principle and function."

Again, Düd'jom Rinpoche nodded with a smile to indicate that this was good.

"So, now it comes to life and how it is outside 'stories of Lamas' — and I am wondering how to approach real life situations." PAUSE *"So, what I would like to ask concerns Ngakpa Yeshé Dorje and something he said that made me feel… ill at ease for the first time in all the time I have known him."*

Düd'jom Rinpoche nodded but there was no smile.

"You instructed me not to mention Kyabjé Künzang Dorje Rinpoche to anyone — even Ngakpa Yeshé Dorje."

Düd'jom Rinpoche nodded agreement.

"So, of course, I did not. But Khandro Ten'dzin Drölkar mentioned that I should meet Karma Gyalpo Rinpoche when I went to Tso Pema."

At this Düd'jom Rinpoche smiled *"O yah — she is disciple."*

"Yes… and during my time with Künzang Dorje Rinpoche, Khandro Ten'dzin Drölkar came up in conversation and he said that she was his student. He said she knew him as Karma Gyalpo Rinpoche."

"O yah — so you are secret name discovering."

"Yes, Rinpoche. Well, that was fine – but when I got back to McLeod Ganj, Khandro Ten'dzin Drölkar asked me if I'd met Karma Gyalpo Rinpoche and whether I'd received teachings from him." PAUSE *"Then, I had to say something."*

"What saying?"

"I said that I had met him and had been fortunate enough to receive teachings – but said no more. Fortunately, she asked no more on the subject." PAUSE *"But then, Ngakpa Yeshé Dorje said it was better to rely on you – and I replied that I would always rely on you. That seemed to end the subject – but I did not feel the discussion had a good atmosphere and I wanted to ask you about it in order that if there was anything to understand… I would understand it."*

Düd'jom Rinpoche observed me for a moment *"Yah… some difference coming. This why I am saying not Yeshé Dorje telling that you are with Künzang Dorje Rinpoche studying. Khandro Ten'dzin Drölkar high practitioner – she is Dzogchen profoundly practising and much retreat. She is much from Kyabjé Künzang Dorje Rinpoche learning. Ngakpa Yeshé Dorje is good ngakpa – but not experience like Khandro Ten'dzin Drölkar. This some difficulty making."* PAUSE *"This difficult for you – but you are good conduct and behaviour. Chögyam no error making. Also, good explaining so I am knowing."*

That was both a surprise and a relief. The surprise was not pleasant and the relief was not exactly gratifying. Düd'jom Rinpoche gazed at me for a few moments and asked *"Chögyam more saying?"*

"Yes Rinpoche" I replied. *"The other part of my concern is about the stories that Ngakpa Yeshé Dorje told me. They concerned dön'dré and my problem was that I found them unbelievable. Then the next day Khandro Ten'dzin Drölkar gave me an account about demons which was obviously a children's story. She then asked if I believed or disbelieved the story. I said that it sounded like a children's story – and she replied that it was. It was a folk tale. She seemed to have a purpose in telling me this story and asking me this question – and I guessed that she was telling me in an extremely careful manner that Ngakpa Yeshé Dorje's accounts of dön'dré were of the same category."*

Düd'jom Rinpoche asked me to recount the stories. I did so. On my conclusion of the stories—which I tried to keep quite brief—he said *"Yah… all stories. These stories I am also knowing. Many Tibetans these stories telling. This srinmo story from Bhutan coming. These stories children and simple people are enjoying. You well principle and function from Künzang Dorje learning."*

He said that Khandro Ten'dzin Drölkar had been both diplomatic and clever in how she dealt with the situation. She had wanted to help me – but without seeming to call her husband into question. I had come to the right conclusion. Where did this leave me however, in relation to Ngakpa Yeshé Dorje? Düd'jom Rinpoche smiled and said that Ngakpa Yeshé Dorje was a good Tröma practitioner and had much to teach on Tröma – but for Dzogchen I should rely on Künzang Dorje Rinpoche, and on Khandro Ten'dzin Drölkar, whenever I happened to see her on her own.

On that note I went for lunch in order not to take up too much of Düd'jom Rinpoche's time. He often invited me to stay for lunch – but on this occasion I felt I needed to ponder. I went to perform 'khora. I recited mantra and avoided thinking – but over lunch ideas erupted. It seemed to me that I'd hit some sort of point in life. It seemed like a loss of innocence or the collapse of naïveté. Life was more complex than I had imagined in the world of Vajrayana – and I was not entirely happy with how that felt. I had no doubt in Düd'jom Rinpoche or Künzang Dorje Rinpoche. I wanted to have no doubt about Ngakpa Yeshé Dorje – but it was evident from recent events that although Ngakpa Yeshé Dorje was a great practitioner and accomplished weather-maker – he was not always able to distinguish 'fact' and 'fiction' in certain areas. He was still affected by emotions which were common to others.

I know that some great practitioners still had bag chags[1]—I had a copious bag of them—so there was no need to wallow in infantile disappointment. I couldn't expect every Lama to be like Düd'jom Rinpoche or Künzang Dorje Rinpoche. After all, I was a tulku – yet I was a bumbling buffoon at times. I had the usual range of emotions – and, although 'anger' was almost absent, I could still afflict myself with sadness. And now—right in this moment—I was experiencing some degree of enervation. This was pitiful. It was time I grew up and faced reality as an adult ngakpa rather than a cloistered child. I would look to Ngakpa Yeshé Dorje in terms of the wonderful teachings he had to offer rather than looking at him as if he was a realised being. By the time I'd finished lunch – I felt entirely different. The world had changed and my perspective had shifted. I had a greater sense of self-reliance. I had made the right deductions.

---

1 *bag chags* / བག་ཆགས་ / *vasana* – karmic traces, dormant thought-habits.

I returned to Kyabjé Düd'jom Rinpoche's house in a lighter and more spacious frame of mind. Once he had enquired whether I'd enjoyed my mo-mos – he said *"O yah! Now Chögyam happiness mind returning. This Chögyam natural mind. Always natural remaining. Always Tsawa'i Lama relying. Always happiness mind having."* PAUSE *"So – practitioner, always principle and function knowing. Always incisive knowledge needing. Always phenomenal existence as infinite purity seeing."* PAUSE *"From infinite purity of phenomenal existence – dKyil'khor of yidam is magical wisdoms-gestures displaying."* PAUSE *"Too often I am opposite seeing. Some western students are good mind having. Some just vanity from information collecting. Some just stupid from intellect* [2] *becoming."*

Düd'jom Rinpoche said that it was important for me to know what the common errors were—especially in western people—according to his experience of meeting them. They were the ones I would be teaching – and so I had to know what their particular obstacles were. He said that Himalayan people also had obstacles. It wasn't that western people were lesser mortals. There was no better or worse with east or west. The obstacles were the five dualistic derangements – but the patterns were externally different. Intellectualism was less of a problem with Tibetans – but they were not as good with questioning and critical thinking. Tibetans were also far keener to receive blessings than to receive teachings. Westerners were not satisfied by blessings but would rather have teachings. Some western people were obsessed with advanced teachings – even though they had no actual use for them. *"I am helicopter much liking – but not possible flying"* he laughed.

"That describes me, Rinpoche. I am keen to receive Dzogchen teaching – but I am not such a good practitioner."

Düd'jom Rinpoche smiled at that, negating it with a side-to-side movement of his head. He told me that my predilection for Dzogchen was different inasmuch as it was not motivated by wanting something advanced. It was simply my practice style.

---

2 Kun-tag dag'dzin (*kun brTags bDag 'dzin* / ཀུན་བརྟགས་བདག་འཛིན་) – conceptualised self-referencing; theoretical self-referencing habituation.

It was what had drawn me first to Theravada³, then to Chögyam Trungpa Rinpoche and Shunryu Suzuki⁴. We'd had discussions of these influences in 1971 – and Düd'jom Rinpoche had given commentary on quotations from Shunryu Suzuki's book. I had looked for *formless methods* rather than *highly advanced methods*. I had looked for teachings which dealt with integration into everyday life. My case was clearly different.

"I cannot say though, Rinpoche, that I experience no excitement concerning Dzogchen."

He laughed – and told me that if I had no excitement about Dzogchen then I'd have no understanding of it either. It was natural to have such excitement – and my excitement was reasonable. It was not mere curiosity and the desire to possess something secret.

I could not question Düd'jom Rinpoche's good opinion of me without questioning his understanding – so I had to accept that I wasn't a cretin. The problem was that I had to **be** *who he saw me as being* – and never deviate from that. He saw what I was thinking however – and told me to relax. *"You good emptiness experience having. This necessary foundation – and you are having."*

It was true that I had engaged in a fair deal of silent sitting since the age of 14 – and that practice had increased year by year. Even in my final two years at school, I'd sat for at least an hour a day.

"Without realisation of emptiness – view of duality and nonduality as 'none other than own perception' meaning rudrahood, not dödma'i sang-gyé ⁵*."*

Rinpoche said that grasping at the form of yidams as if as if they were solid 'possessions', leads to the same result. If one engages in protector practice without nondual experience – the protectors become demons. If one interferes with electrical wiring without experience – one stands the risk of electrocution.

---

3   Rear Admiral EH Shattock. *An Experiment in Mindfulness: an English Admiral's Experiences in a Buddhist Monastery*, published in 1958. A highly literate account which deals with the problems of daily living – which conveys a serious and moving religious experience.
4   *Zen Mind, Beginner's Mind* by Shunryu Suzuki (published in 1970) became a spiritual classic, which serves to steer meditators away from the trap of intellectualism. This book was strongly advocated by Chögyam Trungpa Rinpoche.
5   *gDod ma'i sangs rGyas* / གདོད་མའི་སངས་རྒྱས་ – primordial Buddhahood.

Without the capacity to transform mentally created offerings into magical emanations of the sky treasury – one's meagre array of material offerings will delight no one. Without the vital instructions to transform and transfer impure appearances of duality into the display of the pure nature of phenomena, the mere recitation of words and repetition of mantras will not accomplish anything.

"Wouldn't one have to be a mahasiddha to achieve this?" I asked.

Düd'jom Rinpoche smiled *"You are result of Four Naljors experiencing?"*

"Yes Rinpoche…" PAUSE *"but that is not what I experience all the time."*

He laughed when I said that *"But not each moment offerings creating and magical emanations of the sky treasury transforming."*

"So, one can be a momentary mahasiddha?"

"Also, momentary demon coming. But Chögyam, no demon idea or behaviour having – only sometime, khandros too much liking."

The wisdom of seeing the infinite purity of the phenomenal world, is impossible without the vital instructions for experiencing authentic yidam appearances.

Accomplishing the Buddhakarmas is impossible without the vital kyé-rim and dzog-rim instructions for mantra recitation and the visualisation of light rays shining out and returning.

Without understanding the meaning of practice – an aeon of adhering to meditative technique without devotion to Lama and lineage, will not lead to realisation.

Without the vital instructions of one's Tsawa'i Lama, the attempt to abandon hope and fear – can only be a pretence in which the fourteen root vows of Vajrayana will wither.

Phenomenal existence—experienced either as duality or nonduality—is simply display. One must realise their inseparability as the natural state. The natural state is all-encompassing, all-pervasive space. It is inexpressible spacious clarity. This is the inconceivable view of Dzogchen – so do not ruin presence of natural mind with obsessive techniques and mental constructs.

Relax and remain in the natural stream which is without meditation. This is the natural mind of liberation without obsession[6]. Relax in the natural arising of whatever arises and behaviour will naturally be congruent with Vajrayana. Relax in the gestalt in which everything occurs of itself. This is the unsurpassed activity. Just cultivate this without searching for results – and in this way the primordial nondual awareness is actualised.

At that point Düd'jom Rinpoche concluded and suggested that I might like to take a walk before dinner. He had to see 'too many people' and he did not want me to have to sit there too long with discussions which I would not be able to follow. I was always happy in such circumstances – but took the cue to leave. I said that I'd have my dinner in Bodhanath – as I did not wish to intrude too much. Düd'jom Rinpoche said that he liked having me there – but it might be good on this occasion to walk a little. He did not know quite how long his discussions would take. They might extend over the dinner period. With that, I set out and performed 'khora for an hour before settling on where I'd eat.

After my final 'khora I decided to peruse the Tibetan stalls – some of which were simply blankets on the ground, covered with assorted items neatly arranged. I made a point of looking for examples of plain simple old pieces which could serve as models for reproduction – for the time when this proved possible. There would be a shrineroom in the future. It would mark the beginning of a tradition in the West – and so I wanted to give attention to æsthetics. It would be congruent with Vajrayana tradition—naturally—but the parameters of what was traditional were quite wide.

Düd'jom Rinpoche had told me that I would have to make a variety of choices in terms of the outer form – but that this would not be difficult for me, as I was an artist. My first choice, then, was to opt for simplicity. I had noticed a trend in Tibetan refugee culture for elaboration. The butter lamps made post-exodus in India and Nepal were all far more decorative – so I gravitated to what was older and simpler. I'd seen photographs of shrinerooms in small off-the beaten-track gompas in Tibet and Bhutan – and had seen unpainted wood. I appreciated the unpainted wood and the preponderance of copper rather than silver and gold. It was all merely a matter of taste – so I gave my personal predilections no superiority.

---

6   Natural mind – rang bab kyi dranpa (*rang babs kyi dran pa* / རང་བབས་ཀྱི་དྲན་པ).

It was more a question of the atmosphere I wished to inculcate. I had an appreciation of natural materials – and purity of line. It was the same with British architecture. I preferred Georgian to Victorian particularly in ceiling mouldings. The Victorian penchant for clusters of plaster grapes seemed to make a room less spacious. It occurred to me that the Aro gTér which I would inherit was a Dzogchen lineage – and this would be better represented by a certain minimalism. Of course, *minimalism* in Vajrayana would still seem fairly Rococo to a Zen practitioner – or to a Lutheran like my mother.

I found a small damaged silver butter lamp and purchased it, as it was surprisingly cheap. Phüntsog the silversmith in McLeod Ganj would repair it for me – along with the other damaged items I'd found. I'd been told in the past that I'd ruined the antique value of these items – and replied that as I had no intention of selling them, the value was simply what it was to me. Someone, from another perspective, told me I'd destroyed the 'vibrations' of the old items I'd repaired. There are a wealth of attitudes in the world – and a host of people who seem happy to voice them, uninvited. Fortunately, the ethos seemed to have shifted since I'd first travelled East – and I met fewer people who objected to my existence. It could have been because I was more self-contained. It could have been because I was generally silent. I sought no conversation – and it no longer seemed to seek me. I'd spoken with Düd'jom Rinpoche about western people and their tendency to act as thought-police. He had said *"Whatever good or bad words people using – no meaning having."*

In speaking of me – I should not be affected by them. I should have no doubt or fear. Acceptance and rejection were irrelevant. I should let people say what they liked. No one but my Lama was qualified to speak of me. I was to retain full control over my life. Why place a rope through my nose so 'thom yors could pull me from one place to another?

"You are good-nature having. You know how harmonious with others being – without nose pulling."

If anyone tried to hinder me in my life's work, I should be immovable " … *like iron ball size of yak with silk scarf pulling."* It didn't matter whether such hindering people were superior or inferior. I should not let my intention bend according to the prevalent wind, like grass in a mountain pass. I should know what I must do – and where I must go.

I should be happy in fulfilling the predictions Düd'jom Rinpoche had made for my life – and follow my own intelligence.

With that in mind I went in search of the fried buffalo-beef mo-mos which I'd been told were bad for me. I ended up in a small restaurant run by Tséring Drölma – a Tibetan lady who spoke very little English. The place was empty and she was glad to have a customer. She also seemed glad that the customer was a ngakpa. She pointed at me and then pointed back at the chörten – and said *"Kyabjé Düd'jom Rinpoche?"* I nodded and answered *"La so* [7]*"* in the affirmative.

"Yagpo dug" she replied. *"Ngakpa, yagpo dug"* she continued in simplified Tibetan. I thanked her for her kind comment and ordered the mo-mos.

The fact that I was recognised as a ngakpa seemed wonderfully wholesomely supportive. There was no sense of veneration – simply joyful acceptance. I was an understandable object in her world – and I was glad to be in her restaurant. I was also happy to eat her delicious mo-mos.

I kept an eye on the time, as I would need to be back with Kyabjé Düd'jom Rinpoche by six o'clock, and that would entail walking around the chörten in a clockwise direction when I was actually quite close to his house. I enjoyed the inconvenience of that – and, not being inconvenienced by it. In some ways being partially Tibetan was rewarding in terms of making me feel natural. It was harder to feel natural in England – although, at some point, I would have to make a transition. I would eventually have to learn how to be a ngakpa in England – no matter what I was wearing. I bade farewell to Tséring Drölma and performed another three 'khora before going to Düd'jom Rinpoche's door. As always, the door was opened before I knocked.

Once I was seated before Düd'jom Rinpoche and I'd been served with a glass of Sprite – he said *"Chögyam inner doubt of nondual view resolving – so, meditation simply continuity of the view sustaining."*

That was surprising. I had no doubt, yes—of that I had no doubt—but sustaining continuity of the view was something beyond me. I put that to Düd'jom Rinpoche and he smiled *"O yah – Chögyam, natural. Nondual view, natural. Natural condition simply remaining."*

---

7   *lags so* / ལགས་སོ་ – yes, agreement.

I couldn't contest it. Somehow it was true when I was with Düd'jom Rinpoche. There seemed to be a version of 'me' who seemed to rest in the natural state when with Düd'jom Rinpoche. It was as if I rested in his ambience – whenever I was with him.

"All other meditations reference points having. Conceptual meditations fabricated by the mind only to artificiality leading. That is not how we should meditate. One should all senses within natural state releasing – then at ease, resting. Do not lose this view."

Some people I have met meditate to arrive at the conclusion that 'this is it – I have arrived'. If one meditates in this way, it is merely intellectualisation. There must be no object of meditation and no distraction. Distraction from resting in awareness is delusion. If one is distracted from the present moment nothing is accomplished.

Whatever thoughts arise, one should let them arise. One should neither follow after them nor suppress them. Whatever phenomena arise, whatever appears, one should not grasp at the appearance of phenomena as one rests in the natural state. With a natural mind one is like a child looking into a Lhakhang. When all phenomena are simply left as they are – they are luminous. When appearances are not modified, their colours do not fade – and their brilliance does not lessen. If one does not spoil phenomena with obsessive conceptualisation – appearances and awareness will nakedly manifest as wisdom.

Düd'jom Rinpoche asked me if I understood. I replied that I had understood.

"But Chögyam 'not intelligent' saying. If this teaching understanding, then much intelligent. How answering?"

"Well, Rinpoche, I would say that I don't 'understand' by 'using intelligence'… If I understand – then I 'understand through the experience' of the practices you have given. It's as if you had given me mo-mos for dinner. I eat the mo-mos and therefore know what they are. Then later I go to visit some Tibetan friends—and they serve mo-mos—I will recognise them as mo-mos. I wouldn't have to examine the mo-mos and intellectualise about how they were made. I'd just know they were mo-mos – and tell them I was so glad they cooked mo-mos."

Kyabjé Düd'jom Rinpoche roared with laughter at that *"O yah! Now I know Chögyam in West, well teaching. Chögyam no difficulty having. You are teachings explaining and everyone understanding."*

No sooner had Düd'jom Rinpoche said this than I reflected on what I'd said and the way I'd expressed it. It occurred to me that I'd been too informal and too familiar in my expression. He looked at me with a slight tilt of his head *"Now doubt arising. What doubt arising?"*

I explained my thoughts and Düd'jom Rinpoche shook his head. He told me that I was more natural than I had been on previous occasions and this was due to what I had been taught by Künzang Dorje Rinpoche. I had a tendency to be formal. This was good but I need not be excessively respectful – or mannerly to the degree that it robbed me of humour and spontaneity. My 'mo-mo example' had been good – and showed no trace of over-familiarity.

"Anyway" Düd'jom Rinpoche recommenced *"many extremely vast teachings, are peoples mystified making. Maybe these peoples more intelligence than Chögyam having. Some peoples translation making and book writing – but still mystified becoming. When finding, then maybe 'mo-mo answer' giving. This is concise essential meaning. When gap between last-thought-cessation and next-thought-arising – there is knowingness presence* [8]. *This not even slightest modified. This luminous, naked awareness. This—in itself—is nondual awareness."*

Unfortunately, one doesn't permanently find oneself congruent with the nature of reality. A thought arises – and that is none other than the natural display of awareness. But if one does not recognise thoughts as soon as they arise, they will proliferate and mask their source. So simply recognising what arises—in the moment it arises—disrupts the tendency to conceptual proliferation. Release thoughts within the moment of recognition.

"When state remaining, arising thoughts all equally liberated. This trek-chod [9]. *From within nature of original space, awareness suddenly manifesting. This not fabricated nor created. Just persevering – then nonduality is never mere intellectual understanding."*

Vividness of presence[10] is beyond the intellectual appropriation of signs.

---

8 Present wakefulness – da-ta'i shépa (*da lTa'i shes pa* / ད་ལྟའི་ཤེས་པ).
9 *khregs chod* / ཁྲེགས་ཆོད – cutting through rigidity, exploding the horizon of conventional meaning, or penetrating solidity. Together with thod rGal these two are the main sections of rDzogs chen.
10 Vividness of presence – sèl-nang sharwa (*gSal sNang shar ba* / གསལ་སྣང་ཤར་བ).

It is not swayed by concepts – or the biases of monism, dualism, nihilism, or eternalism[11]. Eternalism is denied because reality is not permanent – yet reality is not created by anything. Nihilism is denied because reality is not mere nothingness—or annihilation—it is lucidly present. Monism is denied because reality does not exist as a single entity, because it is present and clear in terms of being multiplistic. Dualism is denied because multiplicity is indivisible in terms of its one taste.

This realisation is the space of unconditioned reality. In terms of meditation, vivid presence is the perception of arising phenomena from the absolute space in which phenomena arise.

This is ultimate reality. There is no division of 'khor and 'das—samsara and nirvana—because one recognises the arising and dissolution of phenomena as pervasive displays of the luminous awareness. Primordial awareness is beyond time and space. It is unwavering in recognition of the nature of the luminosity of vivid presence.

Phenomena as arising appearances are naturally self-luminous and empty of dualistic constructs. Phenomena are not apprehended by an intellect. Phenomena are not manipulated by conceptual mind, nor are they nullified by awareness. Phenomena are simply non-separate from pervasive space.

"No distinction between luminosity and emptiness coming. No ambivalence. In this manner, Chögyam naturally in primordial awareness resting."

And it was momentarily possible. When Düd'jom Rinpoche spoke in this way it was as if he was the conductor of an orchestra. I found myself being what he described. This was transmission. If I didn't find myself being what was described I couldn't imagine I'd received transmission.

"O yah" Düd'jom Rinpoche answered when I put this to him. *"This always nature of transmission."* PAUSE *"First Tsawa'i Lama relying and firm understanding establishing. Then teachings carefully investigating."*

---

11 The four denials are found in Guru Rinpoche's Rigpa Ngo-trö gÇér-thong Rangdröl (*rig pa ngo sProd gCer mThong rang grol* / རིག་པ་ངོ་སྤྲོད་གཅེར་མཐོང་རང་གྲོལ་) 'Self Liberation through Seeing with Rigpa – a Direct Introduction to Intrinsic Awareness' from 'Self-Liberation in the Primordial State of the Peaceful and Wrathful Yidams.' The four denials are also found in the Theravadin Tradition in the Lokayatika Sutta and in the Aro gTér Song of the Owl Headed Dakini (*'ug gDong mKha' 'gro sNying thig mDo* / ཨུག་གདོང་མཁའ་འགྲོ་སྙིང་ཐིག་མདོ་).

"Then all arising experiences in mind penetrating. You must students telling: this realisation – gained through reflection, devotion, and practice of shi-nè, lhatong, nyi'mèd, and lhundrüp. Liberation not recognised by intellectual knowledge acquiring. Liberation not from fleeting glimpses of rigpa. Solitary retreat requiring or nothing achieving."

Having abandoned purposeless distractions and banal pastimes – gain confidence from the power of the wisdom of meditation. This is achieved just as darkness is banished by the dawn. With the dawning of panoramic awareness wisdom, the need of referentiality is fragmented – and confidence arises in awareness. Such confidence however, of itself, will not provide recognition of the nondual state. One must continue practising until appearances are identical with the nature of reality. The root of cyclic experience will then be cut – and dualistic fixations will immediately be released. The apparently polarised appearances of 'this and that' will dissolve into the space of phenomena.

"Then grasping at phenomena dissolving. Through cutting fixation with self-identity – dualism extinguished. With dualism extinction there is only pure equality of samsara and nirvana. This Dzogchen culmination."

We talked for a while about the fact that some people became arrogant. Düd'jom Rinpoche had heard of this arrogance in people and detected it in their demeanour. He said that this only arose from intellectual understanding which had no basis in direct experience.

"The important point—always—is not 'courage' losing. When nonduality tasting— even one moment— then uplifted becoming. Chögyam not fearing that this is arrogance causing – because courage in 'presence of rigpa' having. Also, Chögyam always kind remaining – with natural outer demeanour." PAUSE *"Yah – tomorrow 'Three Points Hitting Essence' discussing. Then Chögyam leaving Bodhanath – and long journey home travelling."*

21

hitting the essence

I woke up feeling fresh, as I viewed the room through the mosquito netting. This was my penultimate day in Nepal. There'd be the long overland haul to Delhi to obtain my Afghani visa – and then the overland journey home. I'd decided for reasons which now seemed obscure, that it would be good for me to travel overland at least once. It would be interesting and I'd gain some real sense of the distance from Britain to Nepal. It seemed that without travelling overland once, I'd have no real sense of where I'd been. The question as to why the *Magic Bus* from Kabul was any more real than an international flight from Delhi suddenly seemed amusing. If I'd really wanted to experience the reality of the distance, I should have walked home. Maybe this stage of the journey would cure me of romanticism.

My time in India and Nepal had altered me – in addition to the alterations wrought by Kyabjé Düd'jom Rinpoche and Künzang Dorje Rinpoche. I was entirely at ease in the East. This was not to say that I'd lost my preference for western sanitaryware – but that I'd grown accustomed to the East and no longer felt that I belonged somewhere else. I met western people and was able to be helpful to them. I was able to be helpful in ways which no-one western had been to me. I felt no sense of superiority merely because I had enough experience to feel relaxed and at home wherever I was. I recognised that people could well feel anxious and insecure – and so I did my best to offer support to people whenever support seemed to be needed.

My sojourn in Bodhanath had been shorter than usual because I was running low on funds – but I had been extremely fortunate inasmuch as Düd'jom Rinpoche had a series of relatively free days. He knew my time was running out and wanted to make sure that I saw as much of him as was possible during that time. I would have liked to have stayed on in Nepal after Düd'jom Rinpoche's availability had ended – it would have been an excellent opportunity to undertake a solitary retreat. It was always good to go into retreat after receiving teachings in order to attempt to actualise what had been taught.

This had always been my policy wherever possible. I was moving steadily in the direction of completing three years of retreat. I would probably never have the finances to undertake anything over three months, but Kyabjé Düd'jom Rinpoche had told me that this was perfectly acceptable – or even smaller increments. In terms of Dzogchen, it was not necessary to complete three years of retreat in one stretch. It was more important to incorporate retreat into the flow of everyday life.

Kyabjé Düd'jom Rinpoche then began a discussion of 'Hitting the Essence'.

"First essential point – method of view introducing."

View is established through reasoning. According to Vajrayana – one is introduced to the knowledge of primal awareness in the fourth empowerment. There are many systems but essentially the most important point is to directly introduce the *nature of Mind* by dissolving namthogs.

When dualistic derangement becomes overwhelming, the actual presence of the *nature of Mind* may seem inaccessible – so even though one has been introduced to the *nature of Mind*, one will not recognise it. Because of that, one must allow concept consciousness to settle. Then dissolve namthogs into space and sem[1] will self-clarify. Having abandoned all attempts to modify anything, sem settles and becomes, *in-itself*, the knowledge of primordial awareness.

"Second essential point: meditation settling like continuously flowing river – and simply remaining." Rinpoche stressed that I should not be attempting either to instigate or curtail anything that arose.

This is chö-ku. If namthogs proliferate, simply continue in the presence of inherently creative energy – because this energy is potentiality which is nonother than primordial awareness. Whether namthogs proliferate or dissipate has no significance. Creative energy can develop into dualistic neuroses such as obsession or aggression – but if there is awareness that the inherent nature of these neuroses is simply chö-ku, then they will self-liberate as chö-ku.

---

1 *sems* / སེམས་ / *chitta* – conceptual mind.

"Third essential point. Irrespective of what in mind arising – everything freely arising allowed. No suppression attempting."

Whatever arises enters into its own natural condition. All arising phenomena are allowed to dissolve into the space from which they originally arose. There is no disjuncture between the self-arising and self-liberation. In this way, sem becomes what it actually is – through the creative energy of chö-ku. That being the case – whenever namthogs arise, they arise as inherently self-perfected due to the inherent potentiality-presence of intrinsic nondual awareness. The more gross the namthogs are, the stronger and clearer the nature of their liberation. Thus, it says in the text: *"Whatever arises in the mind becomes the food for naked empty Awareness."*

"So, Aro Tulku Chögyam – When discovering continuity of da-ta'i rigpa [2]*, don't spoil it with concepts of what meditation should be. Simply settle – and relax. Then openness of the natural state finding. This is direct knowingness – free from referentiality."*

When you are settled, recognise namthogs – as they arise from awareness. Don't try to prolong them. Simply gaze directly into the essence of namthogs and they dissolve into what they are – leaving no trace of anything other than what they are. Relax in the freedom of non-compulsion. In this there is pervasive appreciation without the need to grasp at anything. Whatever arises is naturally liberated directly into the nature of the ku-sum. This is Trek-chöd.

Some people employ physical postures which engage body, speech, and mind in order to stabilise perception of phenomena – but they do so with ambition. That is useless. The radiance of awareness dawns as an expanse of outer clarity and chains of luminous spheres, which appear directly within the sense fields. This is Thögal.

"So, directly dwell. 'This is it!' must never thinking." Rinpoche stressed that as we were Dzogchen practitioners – there was no need of meditation or distraction. When I could cut through samsara and nirvana with a single strike – I would find the sun of happiness in my heart. With these pith instructions I would liberate everything and duality would be self-exhausted.

---

2   da lTa'i rig pa / ད་ལྟའི་རིག་པ – uncontrived presence.

Düd'jom Rinpoche observed me. *"Now useful everyday advice coming."*

Composed self-control is to have heard the teachings. Having few strong negative emotions is to have engaged in meditation. Harmony with others is the sign of practice. Joyousness of heart attests to accomplishment. The root of Vajrayana is your mind. If you avoid unkindness – you will be better than many monks. If you take care of others when you can - you will be better than many who think they have bodhicitta. If you master pure perception, you will know the meaning of Vajrayana. Once illusion collapses – realisation will manifest. If you cease opting for one side or another – that is *View*. Having no ambition in mind is meditation. Lacking contrivance is perfect action.

"Abandoned hope and fear is fruition. If natural dignity having – then, how acting in each circumstance immediately knowing. If self-possessed, then always careful vows and pledges keeping. This, accomplishment leading."

22

Johnny Gurkha

The day before I was due to leave Nepal—and wend my way back to Jolly Old Blighty[1]—I decided I may as well check the *poste restante* [2] box in Kathmandu. I'd booked into the Johnny Gurkha Hotel in order to make an early start. I knew that I had to hitch a ride on a vegetable truck – so, booking one night in a hotel was a necessary expense.

Lucky for me that I *did* decide to check poste restante at the Kathmandu post office – because there was an ærogramme from Penelope Cholmondeley[3]. I was delighted to hear from her. The first part of her letter conveyed the most exceptionally magnificent tidings. Penelope had been able to sell a dozen of my etchings at a local Art gallery. Her mother —a well-known watercolour artist with excellent contacts—had introduced various well-to-do persons to my work. My naturalistic woodland etchings appeared to be far more popular than my '*Speaking with Ravens*' oil paintings. It turned out that people were prepared to part with surprising sums of money for them. Mrs Cholmondeley was evidently a highly respected figure in art-buying circles – and the respectability she leant my work was almost alarming.

Penelope asked if I'd received the *registered letter* she'd sent to the poste restante in McLeod Ganj – because she'd never received a reply. The letter must have come after I'd left for Nepal and I'd intended to travel home from Nepal. I'd be travelling over land – through Pakistan, Afghanistan—et cetera—and had no idea of going back to McLeod Ganj again.

---

1 Blighty—or Jolly Old Blighty—is an affectionate name for Britain. The word derives from the Bengali word bileti. The Bengali word is a loan of Indian Persian vilayati from vilayat meaning Iran – and later, Britain.
2 Poste restante is a service designed for travellers, who do not have a permanent address in the location where they wish to receive mail, enabling them to collect their mail free of charge at any participating Post Office.
3 Pronounced 'Chumley'. First recorded spelling of Cholmondeley was Sir Hugh Cholmondeley – circa 1250, Baron of Cholmondeley, Cheshire, during the reign of King Henry III.

There were however postal orders[4] to the tune of £1,540 [5] in that registered envelope – and so, returning to McLeod Ganj was marvellously necessary. This was a vast sum in view of the value of the pound in the East – and it changed my plans completely. I could take a flight to Delhi rather than hitching vegetable trucks – and it would take me two days to get to McLeod Ganj rather than ten to twelve days. From Delhi I'd get the overnight express to Pathankot and then grab a taxi to take me to McLeod Ganj. I'd previously had money enough to take me home to Britain—*if* I was careful—but now I could travel in a civilised manner. I was a fairly hardened traveller – but I had no taste for discomfort where it could be sensibly avoided. I left Penelope's letter unfinished – I could read the rest at my leisure once I'd secured my flight out of Nepal. I walked directly to the nearest travel agent singing:

As I walk along the old Durbar Marg[6] with an independent air / I can here'em all declare / "He must be a Millionaire!" / I can hear'em sigh—say "My-oh-my" / I can see'em widenin' their eyes / At the man whose dosh had just arrived from Bligh —ty. [7]

I was not unpleased by my spontaneous composition; as it scanned with the correct metre. I booked a ticket with no difficulty. There were plenty of empty seats. No bribe was required. I'd leave at high noon the next day. How life changed on the roll-of-the-dice. From relative poverty to relative affluence on the receipt of an ærogramme. *"Welcome to the world of illusion"* I whispered.

---

4   A postal order is a money order for sending money by post. It is purchased at a post office and payable at another post office to the named recipient. In the USA it is known as a postal money order. Postal orders are not legal tender, but a promissory note. They were established by a private company in 1792.
5   Effectively £8,000 in 2023 – but worth a great deal more in India in 1975 as the standard of living was much lower then, especially in Nepal and the Himalayan areas of India.
6   The Durbar Marg is a long wide avenue in Kathmandu, leading to the Royal Palace of Narayanhiti. It is lined with luxury hotels restaurants; global shopping outlets; expensive boutiques; travel agencies, embassies; commercial banking premises; and international airline offices.
7   Author's parody of *'The Man Who Broke the Bank at Monte Carlo'* by Fred Gilbert – 1892. Popularised by Charles Coborn (1852–1945) a British music hall performer from Stepney, London.

Let thoughts of past and future settle in the present moment – and, in that moment, simply experience what is naturally there. Kyabjé Düd'jom Rinpoche Jig'drèl Yeshé Dorje

I purchased an ærogramme before leaving the post office in order to put Penelope's mind at ease as soon as possible, vis-à-vis the reason I'd not replied to her registered letter. It had been so wonderfully kind of her to wing that money to me. I had asked her to send me any money gleaned from sales – but hadn't really expected anything. The sale of one etching would have been delightful – but to have sold them all, was little short of miraculous. In those days British postal orders could be cashed in Indian banks—on production of a British passport—and it was a relatively safe way of getting money out East. Penelope had always been kind – and I was glad she'd stayed in touch with me.

After booking my flight to Delhi, I breezed into the *Tibet Antiques Emporium* to say goodbye to Karma Lama. He'd translated for me with Kyabjé Düd'jom Rinpoche and Kyabjé Dilgo Khyentsé Rinpoche and had been massively obliging. Although he claimed to be entirely uneducated with regard to Dharma, we did just fine – because I was familiar with Vajrayana technical vocabulary and understood everything fairly easily when he left those words untranslated. Karma Lama had refused payment. He told me that I'd more than reimbursed him by the many hours we spent discussing Blues. He was a great enthusiast and even borrowed a guitar in order that I could play him a few numbers. The guitar was an Indian model – a *'Givson'*. This name—which rang the changes on 'Gibson'—caused me to chuckle as did the *'Live's Strauss'* jeans I'd seen around town. The Givson[8] wasn't a *bad* guitar – and, lucky for me, it had a high action and heavy gauge strings which perfectly facilitated lap-slide playing. Karma Lama was entranced by lap-slide and I taught him the rudiments whilst I was there.

I was highly tempted by various things in the Tibet Antiques Emporium – but decided that they would have to wait 'til some point in the future when my finances were more certain. There was one phurba however, which I was loath to leave. It was a Dorje Tröllö phurba, made of human bone.

---

8 If 'Givson' is researched – it receives mainly unjustified negative feedback. It is not a high-quality instrument – but neither is it as anything near as bad as it is said to be.

There were many items which caught my attention for various reasons. That anyone is attracted by particular æsthetics is not unusual – but with this phurba, there was a sense of unaccountable familiarity. The idea that I might have owned it in my previous life did not occur to me – because I was not used to thinking along those lines. The feeling however was similar to returning to my hometown – and knowing the streets and lanes. The face of Dorje Tröllö was a face which I knew in terms of shape, line, colour, and texture. How that could be I could not explain. I was not given to taking every fancy as an intuition – and so I built no story out of it. I simply liked it a great deal and felt an unusual urge to purchase it. The meaning of Dorje Tröllö and his *primordial wisdom chaos* [9] was vivid in my mind. I kept telling myself however, that it would be a huge extravagance. I couldn't afford it. Eventually I asked *"Karma la… if I were to put a deposit on this… would you keep it by for me 'til I come out to Nepal next year?"*

"No, Chögyam la – you now taking and later paying" he smiled. *"You are disciple of Kyabjé Düd'jom Rinpoche – so no problem."* PAUSE *"You also very much good Blues teaching! Where would I such teachings in Nepal receiving without you?"*

That was an experience of cultural cross-weaving which has remained with me as a description of the two people I've always been – and continue to be. I say two people – but I'm only two people in terms of how people see me. There aren't many people who will comfortably tolerate both passions in the same person. Buddhism makes western artists suspicious.

---

9   Primordial Wisdom Chaos – yeshé cholwa (*ye shes 'chol ba* / ཡེ་ཤེས་འཆོལ་བ་). 'Ye' means 'primordial', and 'shes' means 'knowing' – therefore yeshé means primordial wisdom or uncreated knowingness. 'Cholwa means chaotic but it also signifies a broad variety of ideas including: actualisation, irregularity, thrown together at random, eccentricity, raving, and deviating from the norm. The syllable 'chol / འཆོལ་ expands the meaning and gives subtleties with regard to the word 'chaotic': 'chol bar 'gro / འཆོལ་བར་འགྲོ་ – intermixing; 'chol bar byed / འཆོལ་བར་བྱེད་ – contrivances; 'chol bar byed pa / འཆོལ་བར་བྱེད་པ་ – thrown into disorder; 'chol med / འཆོལ་མེད་ – randomness; 'chol ma / འཆོལ་མ་ – sly sensual woman; *'chol ba pa* / འཆོལ་བ་ – crafty libidinous man; gLags 'chol / གླགས་འཆོལ་ – seeking opportunities; 'chol gTam / འཆོལ་གཏམ་ – brazen speech; 'chol pa / འཆོལ་པ་ – disorderly; 'chol sPyod kyi mDzad pa / འཆོལ་སྤྱོད་ཀྱི་མཛད་པ་ – wild actions. When considering the breadth of meaning supplied by these words, it can be seen that there is a precise application of language – in terms of Vajrayana. 'chol bar byed pa—thrown into disorder—means that duality is thrown into disorder. gLags 'chol means that primordial wisdom is seeking opportunities to undermine duality.

The Blues and the Arts make western Buddhists suspicious. In the East however, there seem to be no such problems.

I chatted with Karma Lama for an hour or so—in between customers—but eventually had to make my departure. There were the fine fellows from the Lhasa and Kathmandu Trading Company of whom I needed to take my leave. They'd also been of immense help to me as a budget pilgrim. They'd given me some fine advice and they wished me well on my journey back to Britain. I left the shop with the Dorje Tröllö phurba in my satchel – feeling as if I had taken possession of the crown jewels. I did not take it out to look at it in the street—as that seemed inappropriate—but occasionally I delved into my satchel simply to assure myself of its presence. It seemed possible to see it by feeling it.

Eventually I sat down to read the rest of Penelope's letter – an act which unexpectedly dampened my glee. I read a name. Gerald Crosby. I was happy—for Penelope—on reading the remainder of her letter. She'd found a gentleman friend. His name was Gerald Crosby – and he sounded like a fine fellow. He played piano extremely well. He liked Boogie Woogie – and even knew how to pronounce it. Penelope confided this with delight – knowing that I would be pleased she'd not taken up with an ignoramus.

Penelope *had* turned her lights on me, full beam. That had been in the final days of our time together at the house in Hotwells – and, I'd regretfully admitted to the impossibility of our situation. I regretfully acknowledged the same to Meryl and Rebecca—and they to me—because… well – it was too horrible to think about it.

Let thoughts of past and future settle in the present moment – and, in that moment, simply experience what is naturally there. Kyabjé Düd'jom Rinpoche Jig'drèl Yeshé Dorje

I'd have joyfully accepted any one of the three lovely ladies. They were each wonderful, witty, intelligent, and culturally perspicacious – but I'd assured 'dette that I was *not* leaving her for either one of the three. Why had I done *that?* Well, 'dette had accused me directly of being already enamoured of one of them – and she with me. I'd therefore sworn on the graves of Ron, Steve, and Robert Johnson that this was absolutely not the case. And—at *that* moment in time—it was… absolutely *not* the case.

I'd concluded my relationship with 'dette in relative calm – consequent to a few tears. She left the house in Hotwells – and that was the end. I never saw her again. I was sorry about that – because we could have remained friends. I was not, however, the kind of person she would want as a friend. I was too plebeian. I was too *laissez faire / laisser aller / laisser passer* where she was trenchant – and I was too trenchant where she was *com ci com ca / ça va, ça vient*. She liked me because I could say things like that – but unlike her, I couldn't actually speak French. I could say *laissez le bon temps rouler* – but she found that both *gauche* and *invraisemblable*. My French and Latin had all been learned on the Foundation Year at Farnham Art School, where every other student seemed to be upper-middle class. I'd always loved language and so I'd imbibed it with relish.

Shortly after 'dette had departed, Penelope, Rebecca, and Meryl had each found a private moment to reveal their long-standing romantic interest in me. There's an expression which involves being hit with a shovel – but I've never found the appropriate expression for having that happen three times, unexpectedly in rapid succession. Somehow – the fact that I was with 'dette had prevented me thinking of her three friends vis-à-vis romance. Once I knew how they felt toward me however – I found myself to be in love with each of them. How had—*that*—happened?

Penelope, Rebecca, and Meryl had each known just how impossible it was —both for themselves and for me—but each felt obliged to tell her story, knowing that I could not choose one of them thereby rejecting the other two. They, for their part, felt the same. None could bear to be chosen and have their best friends declined – and they were dear friends, who resolutely wished to remain friends. For anything to have happened between me and one of them would have spelt betrayal all 'round. So... I'd sat together with each. Each cried – and, with each, I cried. By the end of the day, I could have sung *Tied to the Whipping Post* [10]. It was simultaneously a glorious honour and a merciless tragedy – worthy, at least, of Shakespeare's pen.

Let thoughts of past and future settle in the present moment – and, in that moment, simply experience what is naturally there. Kyabjé Düd'jom Rinpoche Jig'drèl Yeshé Dorje

---

10 *Tied to the Whipping Post*—written by Gregg Allman (Gregory LeNoir Allman) of the Allman Brothers—released in 1969.

On that baleful note, I'd left Bristol. Then—after a stint of factory work during which time my father died—I'd left for Nepal, to study with Kyabjé Düd'jom Rinpoche. He'd sent me to Künzang Dorje Rinpoche and I'd studied with him intensely for several months. Everything had been redeemed, renewed, and revitalised by my time with Künzang Dorje Rinpoche in Tso Pema – and now I was heading home.

What a point for Penelope's letter to arrive – revealing as it did, that not only was she enfolded in romance, but so also, were Meryl and Rebecca. It had all happened as a result of a series of concerts, musical recitals, and consequent soirées. No one need know the details. I didn't need to know the details either – it simply spelt 'The End'. The curtain fell. The music of the finale faded into the rickety demands of Nepalese street-vendors *"Tiger Balm* [11] *sir – you are Tiger Balm needing?"*

"No—my good man—I have no need of Tiger Balm… thank you very much indeed."

If any one of the three ladies had been left unattached, I'd… But why? Why would I have assumed that any one of the three ladies would have been interested in Vajrayana to the extent of embracing the life of a sangyum? We'd discussed Vajrayana, certainly, and they'd all been interested – but only in terms of conversation. They weren't Christian but they weren't looking for religion – they simply had a kindly interest in what interested me. It was the same for me in terms of talking about what interested them. They'd each wanted a relationship with me – but, if I was realistic, they would not have realised that Vajrayana took precedence over everything else in my life. I was lucky therefore that they were all unavailable. I realised that the possibility of making mistakes vis-à-vis relationships was still very much on the cards for me. When would I cease to be the self-appointed romantic victim of inadvisable involvements?

---

11 *Tiger Balm*—used by hikers in Nepal for pain relief—is manufactured by Haw Par Healthcare in Singapore. It was developed in the 1870s by Aw Chu Kin, a Burmese herbalist in Rangoon – and perfected by his sons Aw Boon Haw and Aw Boon Par. Originally containing tiger-bone it now consists of menthol, camphor, mint oil, cajuput oil, clove bud oil, cassia oil, and paraffin wax.

Goodbye Forever

All *any* lady had to do was grin at me and I'd amorously reciprocate. A parody passed through my mind *'When for no reason I feel / I'm bitten, head over heels / That's a moray* [12].' I was lucky in almost always seeming to find humour in such situations.

This was a piece of hard-wired patterning which I was going to have to dissolve – or I'd never accomplish what Düd'jom Rinpoche and Künzang Dorje Rinpoche wanted me to accomplish.

I decided to sit in the shade of the trees. The trees were those within the King's Palace grounds. I gazed up at the fruit-bats enjoying their daytime dangle. I'd see them again in the evening as I sat in the garden of the Johnny Gurkha Restaurant. They'd fly from the palace—across Thamel —in the direction of the Rang-jung Chörten at Swayambhunath. They flew low and their wing-beats were slow. I loved watching them— thousands of them—as they passed through the sky.

I wrote Penelope a generously long account of my time in the smallest handwriting I could command. I'd congratulated Penelope on her new romance – and asked her to pass on my good wishes to Rebecca and Meryl to the same effect. To have written *'I wish it had been me'* would have been honest – but it would also have been disgustingly self-indulgent.

The evening arrived. I sat at the Johnny Gurkha listening to the Hindustani Classical music ensemble. I always applauded the musicians – and they always smiled at me in acknowledgement of the applause. I was always the one to ignite the applause and they'd come to recognise the white skirted European who loved their music. After one round of applause a singularly bellicose hippie leaned over from his table *'Hey man! Ain't cool to clap! Ain't cool!"*

I looked at him with some puzzlement *"Really... I was unaware of that."*

He turned away shaking his head in derision and saying something about *bourgeois cretins*. The musicians commenced playing another raga. The bellicose hippie and coterie on the next table talked loudly throughout it.

---

12 *That's Amore* by Harry Warren and Jack Brooks (1953) became the signature song for Dean Martin. *Amore* means love in Italian. *A moray* is an eel with a notoriously painful bite that causes extensive bleeding. They have teeth which face backwards, which inhibits escape – and a second set of pharyngeal jaws which enable them to hold on to their prey.

They were evidently uninterested in listening – and unconcerned that anyone else might be attempting to listen. It occurred to me to tell them they didn't know how lucky they were to hear this music. Hindustani Classical music is quite an elite cultural form in India and it can be as difficult and expensive to hear it as it would be to attend a concert at Glyndebourne [13]. It also occurred to me that it was, after all, a restaurant – and not a concert hall. Who was I to pass judgement merely because I had a penchant for Hindustani and Carnatic Classical Music[14].

The piece which the ensemble played was their concluding performance for that evening. It was a long raga which featured the bass sitar—surbdahar—and it was utterly marvellous. At its conclusion—forgetting that it wasn't cool to clap—I applauded.

"Didn't you—hear—*me* man!" the hippie barked with unveiled hostility. "*I said! It*—ain't—cool—*craaaagh...*" Before the last word attempted to leave his mouth, he was hit by a stream of bat guano. His companions rocked backwards in their chairs to avoid it. One of them toppled backward onto the ground banging his head. The bat guano raked the table like machinegun fire – and sprayed the hippie-belligerent's shirt and face, some evidently entering his mouth. This confused his diction somewhat and his final utterance was *'It—ain't—cool—craaaagh!"*

He leapt out of his seat and ran to the lavatory. *'The bat'* I mused *'said it far better than I could've done.'* I was content that I'd kept the thought to myself. Three years previously I could not have resisted the urge. I was glad at least that I had greater self-governance.

His companions looked bewildered. The fallen companion of the fellow splattered with bat guano picked himself up off the ground and resumed his seat. It was evident that the group of friends couldn't quite understand what had happened.

---

13 Glyndebourne festival held at Glyndebourne near Lewes, East Sussex—inaugurated by the Christie family in celebration of Mozart—dates back to 1934. The primary orchestras are the *London Philharmonic* and the *Orchestra of the Age of Enlightenment*.
14 Indian classical music has two major traditions. Hindustani, Northern Indian and Carnatic, Southern Indian. They were not distinct traditions before the 15th century. Hindustani emphasises improvisation and Carnatic tends to be more compositionally based.

"Your friend..." I offered "... was strafed by bat guano – and, I fear, he may have got some of it in his mouth. Being fruit bat excrement, it's likely to be quite acidic due to the diet – and... he's probably going to be in some pain. You—may—need to order him something to take the taste away – I'd recommend banana lassi [15] ... as it will, with any luck, neutralise the acid..."

They thanked me for my advice, still in a state of bewilderment – but staring at me as if I was an alien being. I therefore continued *"If I were you... I'd order the banana lassi now, as it'll take some time to arrive and the insides of his mouth will be painful – unless he was able to get to a tap in seconds."*

"Yeah man... like cool – er... yeah... like thanks for the help... er... yeah man... thanks, cool."

It seemed as if I was *cool* after all – in spite of my applause. I said nothing to that effect – but sauntered back to my room. I thought it better. The hippie-belligerent wouldn't wish to meet me subsequent to what must have been something of a humiliating experience. I didn't want him to have to thank me for my advice vis-à-vis the banana lassi – and... in any case... I had other thoughts on my mind.

The music had been fabulous... and, I'd found myself drifting back in time to the evenings I'd spent improvising on my sitar with the three ladies. I'd so enjoyed my time in Hotwells with Penelope, Meryl, and Rebecca – that it would be peevish in the extreme to get maudlin at this point in time. I'd had my opportunity – but... some kind of need to be honourable had chained, manacled, and gagged me. I still occasionally wondered who the evil genius had been who'd worked out that diabolical scenario. Could any human being—ever in the entire history of romance —have been so vilely abused by circumstances? But who was I attempting to hoodwink? What would Penelope, Rebecca, and Meryl want with an itinerant Vajrayanist anyway?

What space had I allowed in my plan for a relationship with *any* lady – apart from a *companion itinerant*? I was planning to spend most of my life engaged in Summer manual-work in order to spend the rest of the year in India and Nepal.

---

15 Lassi is a traditional dahi (yogurt) based drink originally from the Punjab, India. Lassi is a blend of yogurt, water, spices, and fruit – often banana. Bhang Lassi is infused with cannabis and a popular drink with hippies before the turn of the century.

I'd somehow never quite seen the major difficulty with the plan – I'd doomed myself to celibacy unless I met someone with an equal commitment to Vajrayana. I had no interest in casual affairs on-the-road, so I'd be alone until such time as I met . . . who? But who was I—as a ngakpa—to be seeking the joys of a normal life? I'd chosen the abnormal —from a western point of view—and I'd have to roll with the punches. As these thoughts progressed a feeling of the slightest gloom stole over me. Ruminating thus, I suddenly caught myself in mid-foolishness – and smiled faintly at my insipidity. Life was simply *what it was*. I was simply *where I was*—doing *what I was doing*—and there was *no more to say*. I had a great deal of money waiting for me in McLeod Ganj. Anyone else would have been unreservedly ecstatic about it – and, after a while, I found myself to be so. I never indulged *too* much in regret. Regret was for 'thom yors. Künzang Dorje Rinpoche had told me that – and I knew it to be absolutely true. I sat in silence until I'd blown a hole through ridiculousness.

23

homeward bound

I'm sittin' in the railway station / Got a ticket to my destination / On a tour of one-night stands / My suitcase and guitar in hand / And every stop is neatly planned / For a poet and a one-man band. Homeward Bound—Paul Simon and Art Garfunkel—released in 1966.[1]

So sang Simon and Garfunkel. It occurred to me that I could have been that *poet and one-man band*. I could have been sitting in some railway station other than Old Delhi. If Ron and Steve had not died, I might have been a poet and a four-man band – waiting with them in some airport transit lounge, en route for some grandiosely gargantuan gig somewhere. Ron and Steve were world-class players and Ron, in particular, was a singular genius. He had a massive IQ and a photographic memory. He played his first piano concert at the age of four or five. He could musically notate any Blues he heard as if he was writing shorthand. He once found a few interesting 'errors' in Jimi Hendrix' playing[2]. Nothing escaped his notice. There would have been no stopping us—apart from death—and in 1970 *death* is what happened. Ron died of a heart attack. He had a weak heart. None of us had known. Then Steve died in a car crash – his father at the wheel. Musical heroes usually died of drug overdoses, but the Savage Cabbage Blues Band died by accident – leaving me as a musical orphan. Without that calamity however, I may never have met Kyabjé Düd'jom Rinpoche Jig'drèl Yeshé Dorje or Künzang Dorje Rinpoche.

It was uncomfortable to feel grateful in relation to tragedy. I was where I was, partially by accident – and partially by a visionary history that oscillated in terms of its tangibility and intangibility. Sometimes the visionary past of my previous incarnation seemed quite real – but that was mainly when I was with Düd'jom Rinpoche or Künzang Dorje Rinpoche. At other times I felt rather out of my depth in a world where *spatio-temporal transdimensionality* was regarded as quotidian normalcy.

---

1 Written by Paul Simon, while waiting for a train at Widnes Railway Station near Liverpool. *Homeward Bound* appears on the third studio album, *Parsley, Sage, Rosemary and Thyme*.
2 Jimi Hendrix said *"I've been imitated so well, I've heard people copy my mistakes."*

I remembered marvelling—at the age of four—at how my father drove a car through a town avoiding other cars and slowing to a halt exactly where he wanted to stop. He operated pedals with his feet – and moved a lever that came up from the floor. He had to do all this whilst operating other levers that came off the steering column – and he did it all whilst holding a conversation with my mother. How could a human being do all those things at once? All I had to do with respect to driving a car, however – was to grow older. I'd eventually reach the age when driving would be easy. The situation with Vajrayana however – was radically different. Nothing would happen merely as a result of getting older.

Tonight, I'll sing my songs again / I'll play the game and pretend / But all my words come back to me / In shades of mediocrity / Like emptiness in harmony / I need someone to comfort me.

Well, I needed no one to comfort me. I was more than comfortable in being precisely where I was. That was a step in the right direction. *Emptiness in harmony* rang true, when I was not indulging *in shades of mediocrity,* as I had been in my final day in Nepal. I certainly didn't need to play any game of pretend – although how *that* would be in Britain, I was not sure. I was sure that *enacting the rôle of Lama* would be something of a pretence. I knew I could teach in terms of giving explanations – but I knew I was not Künzang Dorje Rinpoche. I knew that I never would be – but I knew that I *could* be useful to people as a fractional reflection of what he was. I knew also that both Düd'jom Rinpoche and Künzang Dorje Rinpoche had told me I should teach and function as a Lama to people in the West. This was a conundrum with which I found myself wrestling periodically. There was never any answer apart from reliance on my Lamas.

Being on my way home to Britain—by gradual stages—seemed strange after so long in the East. It was an unexpected sensation. There was a question however that seemed to have surfaced – or had just begun to surface. What, or who, would 'I' *be* when 'I' returned to Bristol? I'd worn gö kar chang lo robes for nine months. I felt I knew who I was in those robes – but who would I be, back in Britain. Who would I be, dressed in Levi 501's and American Airforce polo boots? I'd still be the same person who'd spent the most stupendous time with Künzang Dorje Rinpoche – one of Tibet's greatest living yogis. He was a Dzogchen master, rTsa rLung master, and… master of all he surveyed – but, what was I? What would I be back in Bristol, should I decide to return to that city?

I'd promised Derek Crowe that I'd give a slide presentation for the Related Studies department – so I'd have to stand up in that lecture theatre – and... say what? I had no idea. I could talk for weeks about what had happened – but I couldn't... because I could not mention Künzang Dorje Rinpoche. I'd promised not to mention his name until I had permission. It was a slightly bewildering prospect – but in the end I decided that I'd simply slot back into whatever life appeared to be in relation *to whatever 'I' might be*. Life would undoubtedly explain who I was, when I got there. If one visits a greengrocer's shop, one is automatically defined as *a customer seeking to purchase vegetables*. If one takes a train ride one is *a passenger*. If I gave a lecture at an Art School as *a visiting lecturer* – that was who I would be; as long as it lasted. And so, *through one situation after another* I'd become a citizen of whatever country it happened to be. That seemed to be the meaning of quotidian normalcy. As *English eccentrics* were a known phenomenon, many different misfits—of whom I would be one—would be included. I'd heard of historic English eccentrics who were far more overtly eccentric than I was – so I probably had no need to be concerned.

I'd been a misfit since my first trip to India and Nepal in 1971 – and now... I might, perhaps, be even more so. I had no way of judging. I'd actually been a misfit all my life – and yet, life had worked out relatively normally. So, what concerned me about going home? I'd always found friends. At junior school there'd been Steve Bruce. Later there'd been Ron Larkin – and, even to some extent, Jack Hackman. Of course, there'd been Derek Crowe. I'd had lady friends who'd mainly appreciated me for what I was – and finally... Penelope, Meryl, and Rebecca. After a false start, there'd also been ladies on the Illustration degree course – although we'd never become as close friends as I was with Penelope, Rebecca, and Meryl.

This was all true of the past – but now I'd probably turned up the volume on alienation. Maybe I should plan to live in the East – if my intestines would stand it... In the end I decided to forget these ruminations. Life would simply be what it was – and I'd roll with the changes. I'd dive into whatever presented itself as a positive direction. In the meantime – I had a few unexpected days to spend in McLeod Ganj. I'd see Ngakpa Yeshé Dorje and Khandro Ten'dzin Drölkar. That was always a joyful prospect. On that note I fell asleep.

I awoke the next morning – and packed the few items I'd removed for the purposes of ablution. I'd asked the hotel to order me a taxi – and it turned up early. Delightful surprise. I was soon at Tribhuvan Airport and meandered through their convoluted protocols. It was strange to be flying out of the Kathmandu Valley rather than riding a vegetable truck and I smiled at the scenery knowing that I'd be in Delhi in time to catch the *overnight express* to Pathankot. The trick on that train was to book 2ND CLASS 2 TIER A.C. RESERVE. It was superior to 1st class as it was newer and had a fan: not quite A.C.—air conditioned—but it helped a great deal with the heat. I had some difficulty booking because I was informed that the train was fully booked. No problem. I was wise to that ploy. I'd been told that they always tried this number on western people. The answer was to slip a 100 rupee note into your passport and ask the assistant if he was absolutely sure there was not just one spare berth he'd overlooked. Sure enough, a place was available *"Oh yes sir – I am one place finding."*

"Thank you very much indeed, sir – I appreciate your diligence."

I spent the afternoon looking around the Red Fort in Old Delhi – because the train left from Old Delhi station. There were a few shops there that specialised in Tibetan antiques and so I perused their wares happily for some hours. I came away with an extremely moderately priced skull-drum—wrapped it carefully in cloth—and stowed it in my rucksack.

Soon it was time to find my train. It was easy and after standing in line for 20 minutes to confirm my booking – I made my way onto the platform. The train arrived and I boarded. I marvelled at the ease of it all – but when I found my compartment, I found my berth occupied. The Indian gentleman protested that he had purchased a ticket for the seat months before – and insisted that it was his seat. I left the train and found a railway official to whom I put the problem. He rolled his eyes on hearing the story and returned to the train with me. The Indian gentleman was ejected from the train with many angry words on both sides. The railway official apologised and reassured me that there were sadly always 'a few who tried this trick'. Some years later I was reliably informed that my bribe had actually bought the unfortunate Indian gentleman's seat from under him. I subsequently never employed bribery again on trains in India.

Glad to have that inconvenience out of the way – I clambered up onto the sleeping rack and stretched out.

It wasn't marvellously comfortable—by western standards—but I found it luxurious. The situation was safe because theft was unlikely – but nonetheless, I made sure my rucksack was strapped to the rail by both straps. After an hour the train pulled out and I settled down to sleep – but that didn't prove as easy as I'd anticipated. There was a high-volume snorer. I tried to ignore him – but to no avail. No problem – I knew the cure for that. Finger-snapping usually served to rouse a person to a lighter level of sleep – at which snoring would cease. I tried this a few times to no avail. I moved on to snapping fingers with both hands, as loudly as I was able – but was not rewarded with any abatement of snoring. Finally in desperation I started clapping my hands together as loudly as I could – at which an Indian passenger leapt from his berth with obvious indignation. He came toward me and I prepared myself for an unpleasant scene – but to my surprise he rushed past me. He went straight for the snorer—grabbed him by the nose—then shook his head violently from side to side. That stopped the snoring. I soon fell asleep in a state of vague amusement that my hand clapping had offended no one.

The journey from Kathmandu to Delhi had been swift in comparison to previous experience and I marvelled at the difference that money made to one's circumstances. I'd have to be careful with thoughts of this nature. I could see how a person could become the slave of money. I could cripple my freedom by imagining that certain comforts were necessary. I could fly home from Delhi if I so desired and still have money to spare – but… I decided against that. That would be to waste money. A flight to Delhi was one thing – but squandering a few hundred on a one-way inter-continental flight was another. A one-way flight to Britain would cost almost as much as a return flight – so that was clearly out of the question. I prepared myself for the overland adventure and the wonder of the giant Buddha statues in Afghanistan. It would be a pilgrimage, and to see those ancient Buddhas would be astounding – as it would be to be near the birthplace of Guru Rinpoche.

Many people hold Guru Rinpoche to have been born in the Swat Valley[3] – but Kyabjé Künzang Dorje Rinpoche placed his birthplace further west, in Afghanistan. He indicated various lakes[4] as the possible Dhanakosha Lake[5] in which Guru Rinpoche manifested.

The bus from Kabul to Iran and thence Turkey would take me through Ögyen – as Ögyen lay in the area that is now Uruzgan, Bamiyan, Daykundi, and Ghazni. I was intrigued by the similarity of the names Uruzgan[6] and Ögyen. This was a miraculous accident – because I had only thought to travel overland as a challenge to my timidity. It was not that I was *actually* timid – but I tended to insist on pushing against the tendency to avoid *grand adversity*. Some people, of course, almost relished hardship – and so it was sometimes not simple to decide whether I was being timid or sensible. When young, 'sensible' seemed to carry implications of suburban middle-class middle management – or parochial mediocrity.

So where *was* Lake Dhanakosha? Afghanistan has few lakes – but two important ones are Saberi in the southwest and Istadeh-ye Moqor, 60 miles south of Ghazni in the southeast. There are five small lakes in the Baba Mountains known as the Amir lakes. These are noted for their unusual shades of colour, from dark green to milky white, caused by the underlying bedrock.

---

3   The Swat Valley is the Malakand area of Khyber, Pakistan. It was a major centre in Gandhara, where Buddhism continued up to the 10th century. The Swat Valley lies at an altitude of roughly 3,500 feet. Its climate is cooler than Pakistan in general – and it has dense forests, luxuriant alpine meadows, and snow-covered mountain peaks. Lopön Ögyen Ten'dzin Rinpoche and others have suggested that Ögyen was actually in Bengal – so its location remains disputed.
4   **1.** Ab-i Istada is an endorheic salt lake in Ghazni, in the Chaman Fault in the southern foothills of the Hindu Kush. **2.** Chaqmaqtin Lake lies in the Wakhan region of Afghanistan at an elevation of about 12,000 feet. The Vaksu River flows east from the lake into Tajikistan at the eastern end of the valley. The Bozai Darya rises a short distance west of the lake and flows west to join the River Wakhjir. **3.** Zorkul is a lake in the Pamirs which runs along the border between Afghanistan and Tajikistan. Lake Zorkul extends east to west for about 15 miles.
5   *dha na ko sha* / ཛྙ་ན་ཀོ་ཤ
6   Uruzgan (also spelt Urozgan and Oruzgan), is one of the 34 provinces of Afghanistan. Uruzgan is located in the centre of the country and is still mostly a tribal society. In 2004, the new Daykundi Province was carved out of an area in the north. Uruzgan borders the provinces of Kandahar, Daykundi, Ghazni, Zabul, and Helmand.

One of the epithets of Dhanakosha is 'Ocean of Milk' – so Band-e Amir[7] was a distinct possibility. Band-e Amir lies at the heart of a radial complex of valleys and high mountain chains, a short distance west of Bamiyan, site of the gigantic standing Buddhas. In the relief map the lakes are a little north-east of the bend in the road west of Bamiyan. I would pass through this region on *The Magic Bus*, from Kabul to London. A joyful thought.

The journey from Bodhanath to Delhi had once been an ordeal. Now it was almost a jaunt. It was still a tiring jaunt – but there was no longer any sense of being in an alien environment. I knew how to keep an eye on my luggage. I knew how to safeguard my passport and money – without being unduly paranoid in the process. It was still a journey between two foreign countries – but they may as well have been Germany and Austria in terms of my knowing how to negotiate situations as they arose. It occurred to me that I could approach death in the same way—whenever it arrived—because, to some degree, I knew how to die. I had died so many times within the same life. I had—without using the words—said 'Goodbye Forever' so many times – and, having bade farewell, I'd simply headed out into the empty space of life. The words of Bob Dylan echoed through those ideas.

> *How does it feel to be on your own?*
> *With no direction home?*
> *Like a complete unknown?*
> *Like a rolling stone* [8]*?*

No direction home? Not quite. I knew where my mother lived. I knew people who would accommodate me for periods of time. Yes, I was *a complete unknown* on the road between here and there – but when I got *there*, McLeod Ganj, I'd be known fairly well. Who was I to romanticise myself? I was no rolling stone – but somehow the song was helpful to me. Bob Dylan had been part of my life and was still part of my life as a person born in 1950s England. It was useful to have the sense of shared experience – in being that mystery tramp.

---

7   Band-e Amir, Latitude 50° North – longitude 67–12° East.
8   *Like a Rolling Stone*—Bob Dylan—1965

> *You said you'd never compromise / With the mystery tramp, but now you realise / He ain't selling any alibis / As you stare into the vacuum of his eyes / And he says: "Do you want to make a deal?"*

Well, I had no deals to offer, and wanted no one to make any compromises for my sake – but I had no idea how others might perceive me.

> *You used to be so amused / At Napoleon in rags and the language that he used / Go to him now, he calls you, you can't refuse / When you ain't got nothing, you've got nothing to lose / You're invisible now, you got no secrets to conceal.*

I couldn't say I had nothing – but I felt as if I had nothing to lose, even though I had a growing inventory of Vajrayana shrine objects in Bristol. They grew every time I returned from the Himalayas – but in one way they weren't really mine. The items were all for a shrine room that would exist after I was gone. My hypothetical students would inherit it all and hopefully pass them down the generations. If I was to establish the gö kar chang lo'i dé in the West – there might one day be a Retreat Centre.

I was living through history – and the history was comprised of so many different factors. There were endless threads of connection that wove their ways in terms of the past – and on into the future. I'd been introduced to the idea of interdependent origination[9] by Geshé Ngawang Dhargyey[10] in 1971. I was aware that I was—along with everyone else—surfing the waves of infinite causes. The fact that I was in nominal control of the surfboard did not mean that I had much effect on the sea. Yet in all that there was a trajectory: I had been set a task – and was inspired by it. Whether I would ever establish the gö kar chang lo'i dé in the West, I did not know. I could not know.

---

9   Interdependent origination – ten'drèl du 'jungwa (*rTen 'brel du 'byung ba* / རྟེན་འབྲེལ་དུ་འབྱུང་བ་ / *pratityasamutpada*). Phenomena, outer and inner, do not appear without causes – nor are they caused by an uncreated creator i.e. 'God'. Phenomena arise through the coalescence of particular causes and conditions. Shakyamuni Buddha stated *'When this is, that is. From the arising of this comes the arising of that. When this is not, that is not. From the cessation of this comes the cessation of that.'*
10 Geshé Ngawang Dhargyey (1921–1995) born in Trehor, Kham. He studied at the local Dhargyey Gompa until he was 18, when he went to Sera, in Lhasa. In 1971 he was appointed teacher at the Library of Tibetan Works and Archives. He died in New Zealand in 1995.

All I could know was that Kyabjé Düd'jom Rinpoche and Künzang Dorje Rinpoche considered it possible.

I'd fallen asleep quite quickly after lying down on the wooden shelf that served as a bed on the overnight train to Pathankot. I was lucky in having blankets under me. I'd purchased them at a shop near the Red Fort – and they were quite sufficient for relative comfort. I fell into a dream. It was not a dream of clarity – but a strange dream in which I was already in Afghanistan. I had been thinking about this adventure with delight. I would be going through the land where—according to Künzang Dorje Rinpoche—Guru Rinpoche was born.

The dream placed me on the shore of a lake – a seemingly huge lake. At first, I wondered where I was and it occurred to me that I might be looking at one of the Great lakes on the Canadian / American border. Then it occurred to me that I had never been to America. Then it occurred to me that I was questioning the nature of my dream – and at that point I became lucid.

There was no lake. There was a track leading through a forest. High on the mountainside—glimpsed through the trees—was a cluster of buildings clinging to precipitous cliffs. I looked about me and at the two young ladies who accompanied me and realised that I was not myself. I was not Ngakpa Chögyam but neither was Ngakpa Chögyam absent. I had the sense that I was a merged identity and part of that merging was Aro Yeshé.

I attempted to be entirely Aro Yeshé – but that proved impossible. I then attempted to be Ngakpa Chögyam – but I was not capable of returning to him either. I knew this because I could call Ngakpa Chögyam 'him'. I wanted to speak with the two young women—Jomo A-yé Khandro and Jomo A-shé Khandro—but they were a part of a flow of imagery.

Then clarity vanished and the dream dominated again. I saw many different landscapes. Shallow fast-flowing rivers. An ancient suspension bridge. A building that I seemed to know to be the home of Thangtong Gyalpo. Then a valley, the higher reaches of which was littered with tents – one being a large yurt made of tiger hides. Then I was in the presence of Khyungchen Aro Lingma who had subsumed the landscape. There was simply the vastness of the sky from which she shone.

Then the smell of smoke – but not of a wood fire. It was the smell of the train that was 20 minutes or so away from Pathankot. I'd been awoken by the lurch of the train. I sat up and organised myself, so that I'd be ready to disembark.

The train pulled into Pathankot railway station and soon I was sitting in a taxi with the previous night's dreams of lakes and mountains far behind. I hoped that one day I would be able to explore within *dreams of clarity* without losing awareness before anything coherent could be discovered. Although the lack of coherence was disappointing – I became aware that I was entirely relaxed about my journey. I was at home on this route between Bodhanath and McLeod Ganj – and that was wonderfully encouraging. The nineteen-year-old who first set out for the Himalayas was someone else entirely, even though there was a connective thread of *empty form* – the visionary dimension of Aro Lingma.

There was a *moment*. It was a point-instant moment, that I knew as *Aro Lingma*. It was a hundred thousand million light years within the smallest fraction of recognisable time. It was eternity, whilst it lasted. That eternity would echo for some indefinable period and then dissolve into common temporal reality. Everything was known in that moment – not in terms of information but in terms of knowingness, the sensation of *there being nothing to know other than knowingness*. That was now an experience that was no longer unfamiliar. When I explained this to Kyabjé Düd'jom Rinpoche and to Künzang Dorje Rinpoche in later years – they both nodded and smiled.

Appendices

The following three appendices are not strictly appendices – but material that has been removed from previous chapters on the basis that they were too dense with information to be included in those chapters. I had not wanted to lose this material however – as I know there will be some people who will be able to digest such information. Even those who cannot immediately tackle dense tracts on Vajrayana, may find themselves able to do so at a later point in study and practice.

Finally, both as a writer and as a disciple – I find myself unable to omit anything my Lamas have imparted. I have not covered everything they taught – because some aspects require transmission and are only available to those with requisite experience. I have probably divulged more than some would consider proper – but it seems that much that was considered secret in the 1970s became available in the 1980s. This process has continued decade by decade – and now in the third decade of the 21st century there is little that cannot be accessed. From certain perspectives, Khandro Déchen and I could be regarded as conservative in what we still consider secret – but we do not regard ourselves as being subject to the dictates of laissez-faire fashion. We are obviously committed to being of service to those who are committed to Vajrayana – and to that end we have gone into as much depth as seemed appropriate.

We have drawn the line in various places – one being that we do not give transmission or empowerment via the internet. Our reason for this is that were a romantic couple to attempt making love via the internet – it would be masturbation rather than sexual intercourse. We see *human proximity* as being vital for transmission or empowerment.

Appendix I

gTértöns and gTérma

"Yah… now, today gTértöns and gTérma necessary speaking." PAUSE *"Düd'jom Rinpoche is telling. I must all things explaining."* Künzang Dorje Rinpoche looked somewhat solemn. *"All things explaining because you must precisely for future time understanding. Düd'jom Rinpoche better explaining – but no time having. Anyway, many—many—detail not necessary. Central forms explaining."*

Not that he did not have great devotion towards Düd'jom Rinpoche – but I had never heard him say that Düd'jom Rinpoche would be better at explaining a subject. I therefore gained the impression that this was a vast and fabulously complex subject. Düd'jom Rinpoche was known to be the encyclopædia to whom all other encyclopædics both deferred and referred.

Rinpoche had made no jests. This was now unusual – because his jests were part of how he now communicated with me. I wondered what this might portend. There was a soft diffuse light in the room. Outside it was raining – but it was barely discernible. It was more like a heavy mist which occasionally coalesced into drizzle. I'd become a little damp on my way from the Nyingma gompa and it made me feel a little cold. Rinpoche offered me a blanket. I thanked him but said I'd better dry out before wrapping it 'round my shoulders. I didn't want to seal in the damp. He thought this was sensible – but said nothing further on the subject.

"Yah… I am no text having. One text I am owning – but in Sikkim leaving. So all from memory must be saying. Not all gTértöns naming – but some must be telling." Rinpoche looked at me for a moment or two in silence – then smiled. He picked up his dorje and tapped it on the table, leant back and stroked his chin beard *'Rinchen Lingpa* [1]; *Sang-gyé Lingpa* [2]; *Lhatsün Namkha Jig'mèd* [3] – *all gTérma revealing. Ja'tsön Nyingpo* [4] *Könchog Chidü* [5] *revealing.*

---

1   *rin chen gLing pa* / རིན་ཆེན་གླིང་པ་ / 1295–1375
2   *sangs rGyas gLing pa* / སངས་རྒྱས་གླིང་པ་ / 1340–1396
3   1597–1660
4   1585–1656
5   *dKon mChog sPyi 'dus* / དཀོན་མཆོག་སྤྱི་འདུས་.

"Namchö Min'gyür Dorje [6], *Ögyen Chog'gyür Déchen Lingpa* [7] *and Tennyi Lingpa Padma Tséwang Gyalpo* [8] *also gTérma revealing."*

"Yah... gTérchen Künkyong Lingpa [9] *– family name, dPa'wo. This why also name dPa'wo gTértön having."* PAUSE *"gTérchen Kunkyong Lingpa born in Shang Lhaphu Bi-dzing* [10], *Tsang in Fire Rat year of the seventh cycle* [11]. *Father dPa'wo Gyaltsen Gön* [12] *– mother Demchog dPa'mo* [13]."

He began to reveal gTérma when he was fourteen years old. His first gTérma was the Bairo Nyingthig[14] inspired by Dorje Legpa, which he discovered at the White Chörten at Sam-yé[15]. He gathered many disciples. He was invited to many important religious occasions for the power of his presence. He entered parinirvana in 1489 at the age of 93.

"Then, Ten-nyi Lingpa Padma Tséwang Gyalpo[16] *– incarnation of Trisong Detsen's daughter Princess Lhaçam Nu'jin Salé* [17], *who also carried the blessing of the great master Vairochana."*

Following various predictions, Ten-nyi Lingpa Padma Tsewang Gyalpo found many treasures at various sites where Guru Rinpoche and his disciples had taught and lived. Among them are the Künzang Nyingthig[18], and the Shitrö Yeshé Thongdröl[19], found in Chung Riwoche[20] and Paro Taktsang in Bhutan.

6 gNam chos mi 'gyur rDo rJe / གནམ་ཆོས་མི་འགྱུར་རྡོ་རྗེ་ / 1645–1667.
7 o rGyan mChog gyur bDa chen gLing pa / ཨོ་རྒྱན་མཆོག་གྱུར་བདེ་ཆེན་གླིང་པ་ / 1829–1870.
8 bsTan gNyis gLing pa padma tshe dBang rGyal po / བསྟན་གཉིས་གླིང་པ་པདྨ་ཚེ་དབང་རྒྱལ་པོ་ / 1480–1535.
9 gTer chen kun skyong gLing pa / གཏེར་ཆེན་ཀུན་སྐྱོང་གླིང་པ་ / 1408–1489.
10 shangs lha phu bi rDzing / ཤངས་ལྷ་ཕུ་བི་རྫིང་
11 1396.
12 dPa' bo rGyal mTshan mGon / དཔའ་བོ་རྒྱལ་མཚན་མགོན་
13 bDe mChog dPa' mo / བདེ་མཆོག་དཔའ་མོ་
14 ba'i ro sNying thig / བའི་རོ་སྙིང་ཐིག་
15 bSam yas mChod rTen dKar po / བསམ་ཡས་མཆོད་རྟེན་དཀར་པོ་
16 bsTan gNyis gLing pa pad ma tshe dBang rGyal po / བསྟན་གཉིས་གླིང་པ་པདྨ་ཚེ་དབང་རྒྱལ་པོ་ / 1480–1535.
17 lha lCam nus 'byin sa le / ལྷ་ལྕམ་ནུས་འབྱིན་ས་ལེ་
18 kun bZang sNying thig / ཀུན་བཟང་སྙིང་ཐིག་
19 zhi khro ye shes mThong grol / ཞི་ཁྲོ་ཡེ་ཤེས་མཐོང་གྲོལ་
20 Chung Riwoche – the great compound associated with the Chang gTér which was built by Thangtong Gyalpo.

One important contribution to the Chang gTér was his revelation of a gTérma originally discovered by Rig'dzin Gö-dem who had re-hidden it in order that it could be found at a later time when it would be of greater value. This text on Dorje Phagmo was found before a multitude at Riwo Palbar. Ten-nyi Lingpa Padma Tsewang Gyalpo was one of the Eight Great Lingpas – and took incarnation as Namchak Tsa-sum Lingpa, Chö-jé Lingpa, and Rig'dzin Jig'mèd Lingpa.

Lhatsün Namkha' Jig'mèd[21] was an incarnation of Vimalamitra and Longchenpa, born in 1597 at Jaryül in southern Tibet. He spent many years practising in remote places in central and western Tibet. In central Tibet, he summoned the protectors to assist him in restoring Samyé. At Tsari, he stopped a huge avalanche simply by gazing at it while making the threatening mudra[22]. He revealed the Dorje Nyingpo Tringyi Tollü Chö'khor (The Spontaneous Song of the Clouds: the Indestructible Essence of Reality) – a condensed summation of the inner teachings of all gTérma lineages.

Through his practice of Riwo Sangchö, Lhatsün was able to remove all human and non-human obstacles in Sikkim, opening it as a 'secret land' of the teachings. He taught Dzogchen widely in Sikkim in the remaining years of his life – and founded the lineage of Sikkim Dzogchen that continues to the present. Over 200 of Lhatsün Namkha' Jig'mèd's writings survive. 'Accomplishing the Life-Force of the Rig'dzins' and 'The Spontaneous Song of the Clouds' are practised to the present day particularly in Sikkim.

"Yah… so… now nature of gTérma something saying." PAUSE *"gTérma is short transmission lineage. Disciple of Guru Rinpoche who transmission from him receiving can today transmission giving. If this gTértön is particular teaching in this life holding – then only second to Guru Rinpoche. This like Traktung Düd'jom Lingpa and Düd'jom Rinpoche Jig'drèl Yeshé Dorje."*

Kyabjé Künzang Dorje Rinpoche asked me whether I could name any gTértöns.

---

21 *lha bTsun nam mKha' jigs 'med* / ལྷ་བཙུན་ནམ་མཁའ་འཇིགས་མེད་ / 1597–1653.
22 Threatening mudra, scorpion gesture – dig-dzub (*sDigs mDzub* / སྡིགས་མཛུབ་).

"Yes Rinpoche..." I replied *"but I really only know the five gTértön Kings,*[23] *Nyang-ral Nyima 'ö-Zér, "Guru Chöwang, Dorje Lingpa, Pema Lingpa, and Jamyang Khyentsé Wangpo – and of course Düd'jom Lingpa and Kyabjé Düd'jom Rinpoche Jig'drèl Yeshé Dorje."*

"Ya... Guru Chöwang name also remembering" he exclaimed in humorous fervour. *"Maybe one time future there is some connection coming."*

"What kind of connection might that be Rinpoche?"

Künzang Dorje Rinpoche was silent for some moments *"Not knowing. Maybe some sign coming."* PAUSE *"Yah... maybe symbol – maybe nang yul*[24] *but I can no more saying."* PAUSE *"Yah, then consort of Guru Chöwang – Jomo Menmo remembering. She also gTértön. Always must be khandro remembering."* PAUSE *"Then Min'gyür Paldrön*[25]*, Sé-ra Khandro Künzang Dé-kyong Wangmo, Ayu Khandro, Tare Lhamo and Khyungchen Aro Lingma."* PAUSE *"Other gTértön also from 25 female disciples of Guru Rinpoche coming. One day all name all giving – but much researching necessary. Time now too short coming."* PAUSE *"You are other gTértön names knowing?"*

"I think I may know a few, Rinpoche." PAUSE *"Rig'dzin Gödem*[26] *who discovered the Chang gTér; Karma Lingpa*[27] *in whose gTérmas the Bardo Thödröl teachings are found; Thangtong Gyalpo*[28] *the astonishing polymath who built the first iron suspension bridges in Bhutan and Tibet.*

---

23 Five gTértön Kings: Nyang-ral Nyima 'ö-Zér (1124–1192); Guru Chöwang (1212–1270), also known as Guru Chökyi Wangchuk; Dorje Lingpa (1346–1405); Pema Lingpa (1445–1521); Jamyang Khyentsé Wangpo (1820–1892).
24 *sNang yul* / སྣང་ཡུལ་ – appearing object. In 1988 Ngak'chang Rinpoche was given an ancient nine-pronged dorje in Zürich, Switzerland. This was later identified by 'Khordong gTérchen Tulku Chhi'mèd Rig'dzin Rinpoche as the gTérma of Guru Chöwang.
25 *mi 'gyur dpal sgron* / མི་འགྱུར་དཔལ་ / 1699–1769.
26 Rig'dzin Gödem Ngödrup Gyaltsen (*rig 'dzin rGod lDem dNgos grub rGyal mTshan* / རིག་འཛིན་རྒོད་ལྡེམ་དངོས་གྲུབ་རྒྱལ་མཚན་ / 1307–1408). At the age of twelve, three vulture feathers spontaneously grew from the crown of his head. When he was 24, five more grew. 'Rig'dzin Gödem' means 'Rig'dzin Vulture Feathers'. He was an incarnation of Nanam Dorje Dud'jom (*sNa nam rDo rJe bDud 'joms* / སྣ་ནམ་རྡོ་རྗེ་བདུད་འཇོམས་) and a previous incarnation of gTértön Sogyal Lérab Lingpa.
27 Karma Lingpa (1326–1386).
28 *thang sTong rGyal po* / ཐང་སྟོང་རྒྱལ་པོ་ / 1361–1485.

"Then also Ratna Lingpa ; Jig'mèd Lingpa whose gTérma was the Longchen Nyingthig; Ögyen gTérdak Lingpa²⁹; and Kyabjé Khenchen Jig'mèd Phüntsog ³⁰."

"O yah, Rig'dzin Gödem's gTérma – I am holding ³¹. Also Chhi'mèd Rig'dzin Rinpoche is holding. His name also 'Khordong gTérchen Tulku' because he is 'Khordong gTér holding."

At this point Rinpoche mused for a moment with a strange expression. I wondered what this could portend – but it was merely a momentary question in my mind.

"O yah – now Chögyam thinking." PAUSE "but nothing thinking too much necessary." PAUSE "Yah… Kyabjé Khenchen Jig'mèd Phüntsog – this one—complete genuine incarnation—*of gTértön Sogyal. Other coming also. One in Bhutan – he is good Lama. "One other, name claiming – but this one just ordinary person from Lakar ³² family coming. May be good qualities coming. Maybe bad qualities coming. Otherwise nothing saying. Often like this in Tibet coming when wealthy people's son incarnation wanting."* PAUSE *"Then, Ratna Lingpa he is the Nyingma Gyüdbum³³ compiling—Collected Tantras of Nyingma—this you knowing. He also names Zhigpo Lingpa ³⁴ and Dro'dül Lingpa³⁵ having – because in one life, he is predicted gTérmas from three different future lives revealing. I am one friend having – Chökyi Wangchuk ³⁶. He is Ratna Lingpa lineage holding – also own gTérma receiving. One time you must be meeting. He is Bhutan living – but sometimes Nepal coming."*

Rinpoche explained that Ratna Lingpa was born in Drushul, Lhodrak.

---

29 gTér-dak Lingpa (1646–1714).
30 *'jigs 'med phun tshogs 'byung gNas* / འཇིགས་མེད་ཕུན་ཚོགས་འབྱུང་གནས། /1933–2004.
31 Künzang Dorje Rinpoche was a gTértön. He never mentioned it publicly – but he revealed a Dzogchen gTérma of Ling Gésar.
32 Sogyal Lakar (*bSod rGyal bLa dKar* / བསོད་རྒྱལ་ / 1947–2019) was claimed to be the incarnation the 19th century gTértön Sogyal Lérab Lingpa – but this was contested by 'Khordong gTérchen Tulku Chhi'mèd Rig'dzin Rinpoche and several other Nyingma Lamas.
33 *rNying ma rGyud 'bum* / རྙིང་མ་རྒྱུད་འབུམ། – a collection of Vajrayana texts of Mahayoga, Anuyoga, and Atiyoga.
34 *zhig po gLing pa* / ཞིག་པོ་གླིང་པ།
35 *'gro 'dul gLing pa* / འགྲོ་འདུལ་གླིང་པ།
36 Ngak'chang Rinpoche and Khandro Déchen met Chökyi Wangchuk in 1990 in Yang-lé-shöd, became friends – and remained close until Chökyi Wangchuk Rinpoche passed into parinirvana in 2013.

His father was mDo-dé Dar[37] and his mother was Sri-thar mèn[38]. He was an incarnation of Langdro Könchog Jung-né[39], one of the 25 disciples of Guru Rinpoche. Ratna Lingpa learned reading and writing effortlessly and had numerous visions from the age of nine. When he was 27, he had a vision of Guru Rinpoche as a ngakpa dressed in raw silk – who displayed to him three texts. They were white, red, and blue in colour. Guru Rinpoche asked Ratna Lingpa to choose one. Ratna Lingpa replied that he chose all three. Because of Ratna Lingpa's *auspicious audacity* Guru Rinpoche gave him the white, red, and blue collations. He was thus able to reveal gTérma which would have otherwise needed three lives to reveal. When he was 30 years old, he revealed gTérma in Southern Tibet, at Khyungchen Drak[40], Dritang Koro Drak[41], and Kharchu Palgyi Pug[42]. These added up to 25 gTérma which included wrathful yidam cycles, Dzogchen, the long-life Tsédrup Sang-dü[43] cycle, and the Phurba Yang-sang La'mèd[44]. Because sectarian factions had excluded the Nyingma tantras from the Kan'gyür[45], Ratna Lingpa gathered the Nyingma tantras into a Tantric anthology of 42 volumes. This collection is no longer extant – but it was the foundation for the Nyingma Gyüdbum which Jig'mèd Lingpa assembled in the 1770s. Ratna Lingpa's lineage continued through his own children, especially his son Rig'dzin Tséwang Dragpa[46] of whom Chökyi Wangchuk Rinpoche is an incarnation.

This was a wealth of information. I'd come to expect this from both Düd'jom Rinpoche and Künzang Dorje Rinpoche. They both had encyclopædic knowledge – and they were both generous in making it available to me. It stretched my memory beyond capacity – but I would not allow that. I kept reading and re-reading my notes in the hope that everything they told me would remain as part of my working knowledge. It was time for Künzang Dorje Rinpoche's afternoon tea – and my hot lemon and honey.

---

37 *mDo sDe dar* / མདོ་སྡེ་དར.
38 *sri thar sMan* / སྲི་ཐར་སྨན.
39 *lang gro dKon mChog 'byung gNas* / ལང་གྲོ་དཀོན་མཆོག་འབྱུང་གནས.
40 *khyung chen brag* / ཁྱུང་ཆེན་བྲག.
41 *'bri than ko ro brag* / འབྲི་ཐན་ཀོ་རོ་བྲག.
42 *mKhar chu dPal gyi phug* / མཁར་ཆུ་དཔལ་གྱི་ཕུག.
43 *tshe sGrub gSang 'dus* / ཚེ་སྒྲུབ་གསང་འདུས.
44 *phur pa yang gSang bLa 'med* / ཕུར་པ་ཡང་གསང་བླ་འམེད.
45 *bKa' 'gyur* / བཀའ་འགྱུར.
46 *rig 'dzin tshe dBang grags pa* / རིག་འཛིན་ཚེ་དབང་གྲགས་པ.

He found it amusing every time that I drank this and appeared to enjoy it. The fact that I disliked both Pö-ja and Ja-ngarmo[47] also caused him amusement, but he conceded that I was not nervous in terms of having strong preferences – and that was 'natural' rather than 'affected'. His main concern was that I presented naturally. He had heard that some Injis drank Pö-ja as an act of bravado – and persisted until some of them came to enjoy it.

Just when I thought I'd reached overload with names, Rinpoche said *"Yah – some days we much gTérma speaking necessary. So, more gTértöns telling. Maybe you are more gTértöns now knowing?"*

Suddenly names flooded in my mind *"Rinchen Lingpa, Sang-gyé Lingpa, Ten-nyi Lingpa Padma Tséwang Gyalpo, Lhatsün Namkha Jig'mèd, and, Ja'tsön Nyingpo."*

"O yah – Ja'tsön Nyingpo, Könchog Chidü revealing." PAUSE *"More telling?"*

"Yes... Namchö Min'gyür Dorje and Ögyen Chog'gyür Déchen Lingpa."

"Yah – good" in English.

Rinpoche explained that there were three Uncommon Transmissions: the Aspirational Empowerment, Prophetic Authorisation and Entrustment from Khandros.

"Aro gTér entrustment from Khandro Yeshé Tsogyel – and Khyungchen Aro Lingma revealing."

These modes of transmission are particular to the gTértöns of the Nyingma Tradition. The gTérmas are teachings and practices of the three Inner Tantras. A complete gTérma must contain teachings on Chenrézigs; Peaceful, Joyous and Wrathful drüpthabs; rTsa rLung practices; and, teachings on the three series of Dzogchen.

There are two types of concealment – the first being Earth gTérma. This is concealment and discovery via symbolic key scripts written on paper and concealed in rocks, lakes, and lhakhangs. The symbolic scripts are employed to awaken recollection of what has been concealed in the nature of Mind of each gTértön. Sometimes the entire text is discovered at the place of concealment.

---

47 *ja mNgar mo* / ཇ་མངར་མོ་ – Indian sweet tea with milk.

Earth gTérma include dorjes and other Tantric implements and symbols such as mélongs, faceted crystals, and crystal spheres.

The second category is Mind gTérma. gTértöns may first find symbolic scripts arising in mind. Such cyphers then become the key to revelation. Mostly there is no symbolic script – and the gTérmas are revealed directly. Whichever form it takes, Guru Rinpoche would have concealed the teachings in the nature of the Mind with respect to his disciples, through power of Mind-mandate[48]. This also occurs with teachings from Yeshé Tsogyel.

Nyingma gTérmas are not concealed in other dimensions as texts which are then retrieved and brought to this world as the same physical texts. They are revealed through the nature of the Minds of disciples of Guru Rinpoche and Yeshé Tsogyel.

"Yah… Pure Vision gTérmas – these from many sources coming. From Thangtong Gyalpo, Tashi Khyi'dren, or Mahasiddhas emanating. Aro gTérmas is like this coming – Düd'jom Rinpoche is telling."

There are four reasons for the concealment and discovery of gTérmas: that the teachings and practices will not disappear; that the instructions will not change or become distorted; that the power of the teachings and practices will not diminish; and, that the *transmission lineage* will remain direct rather than become attenuated.

Many ancient teachings have disappeared – but through gTérma their continual reappearance is guaranteed. Recently appearing gTérma are effulgent with the *warm breath of the khandros* – and their authenticity is palpable. Within each lineage there is no intermediary or interface between the current living gTértön and Guru Rinpoche or Yeshé Tsogyel.

"It is as if gTértöns, Guru Rinpoche and Yeshé Tsogyel meeting, day before gTérma teaching. This you experience with Kyabjé Düd'jom Rinpoche."

It wasn't a question – but I somehow felt impelled to answer *"Yes Rinpoche – I have no doubt of that. That is exactly what I experienced."*

---

48 Mind-mandate – Tèd-gya dzadpa (*gTad rGya mDzad pa* / གཏད་རྒྱ་མཛད་པ་): giving transmission directly mind to mind.

At that point we sang the Seven Line Song of Guru Rinpoche and sat in silence for some five minutes. Rinpoche then explained that it was valuable for multifarious gTérmas to be discovered in each generation in order to suit the propensities, inclinations, predispositions, and predilections of a wide variety of people. *"Western people also gTérma needing and so Düd'jom Rinpoche is gTérma revealing – and instruction Chögyam giving."*

Prophetic Authorisation and Empowerment means that Guru Rinpoche or Yeshé Tsogyel have prophesied that at specified times, specific disciples would take incarnation as gTértöns and discover what had been transmitted. These prophecies were not like most predictions – because Guru Rinpoche and Yeshé Tsogyel potentiate the future discovery.

Guru Rinpoche devised symbolic scripts for the gTérmas, placed them in treasuries, and concealed them in the phenomenal world. He then entrusted them to the khandros and protectors who were instructed to guard them and deliver them to the appropriate gTértöns.

The concealment of gTérmas has three aspects. Firstly Guru Rinpoche conferred numerous empowerments into the three Inner Tantras. He then concealed those teachings in the nature of Mind of particular disciples. Sometimes he concealed the same teachings in more than one disciple. This threefold process is *Aspirational Empowerment of Mind-mandate concealment*.

The place of concealment was not the 'ordinary mind' of the disciples but the *beginningless nondual nature* of the disciples – and therefore corruption due to inauspicious circumstances or maleficent occlusion would not be possible.

After transmission, Yeshé Tsogyel compiled the teachings with the assistance of other accomplished calligraphers. She wrote down the teachings in symbolic scripts and placed them in treasuries – concealing them in different places, so they would be discovered by future gTértöns.

Sometimes Guru Rinpoche and Yeshé Tsogyel visited and authenticated places when concealing gTérmas – but often they concealed teachings from a distance employing protectors who would then be entrusted with guarding the teachings.

"Guru Rinpoche not all gTérmas in Tibet and Bhutan in his time concealing. So, if need coming, then Guru Rinpoche also gTérma today providing."

The transmission continues because of Guru Rinpoche's nondual intentionality. At the time of concealment, Guru Rinpoche foretold the future discovery of the teachings, including where, when, and by whom, they would be discovered. He also foretold who the supporting consorts of the gTértöns would be.

There are two types of symbolic script, the khandro scripts and non-human scripts. All the various khandro scripts are illegible to people who have no realisation – or who have no connection with a particular gTérma. These scripts include Tibetan, Sanskrit, and Ögyen. Some cyphers are merely a word or phrase. Some give a mere indication of the purport of the teaching.

The symbolic scripts are transcribed by the disciples of Guru Rinpoche and sometimes by Yeshé Tsogyel and Guru Rinpoche. Although they are called yellow texts – gTérma have appeared on many colours of paper written in coloured inks or gold ink.

Sometimes gTérma were hidden in caskets made of gems. After the texts were placed in caskets they were entrusted to protectors such as Mamo Ékajati, Raksha gZa' Rahula, and Dorje Legpa. They controlled who had the right to discover them. Mamo Ékajati, Raksha gZa' Rahula, and Dorje Legpa then protected the gTértöns and the practitioners who were their disciples. There are many other such protectors amongst the eight classes of non-human entities such as lha, kLu, gNod sByin and srinpo. These are all beings who received transmission from Guru Rinpoche and Yeshé Tsogyel – and are oathbound to protect the gTérmas.

There are over a hundred Great gTértöns and hundreds of Minor gTértöns. If gTértöns reveal teachings of three types, they are known as Great gTértöns. These three categories are: teachings on Guru Rinpoche and Yeshé Tsogyel, Chenrézigs, and Dzogchen. A Great gTértön would need to have revealed a complete system of teaching – one which would enable people to attain nondual realisation without recourse to any other teaching or practice. If gTértöns only reveal practices they are known as Minor gTértöns.

There are 189 discoverers of Sa gTér and 41 of Gong-gTér[49] and Dag-nang gTér[50]. There are other gTértöns however, who are not named due to there being gTérma—arising from Guru Rinpoche and Yeshé Tsogyel—which are becoming available in this time. There have also been gTérmas which appeared consequent to Guru Rinpoche's departure from Tibet – and their gTértöns were not always predicted.

Many—but not all—gTértöns exhibit unusual capacities in childhood. They take birth with wondrous signs, and often learn with no effort. Many display miracles and have visions of past Lamas and yidams.

"But some gTértöns same like ordinary people until gTérma discovering" Rinpoche added with an indecipherable expression. *"Düd'jom Rinpoche saying 'Chögyam is gTérma revealing in future time.' So, what saying? Chögyam ordinary or not ordinary? Miracle coming or no miracle coming?"*

"Before I answer this Rinpoche, I must say that I am not going to speak with humility – false or otherwise."

"Good answer!" Rinpoche laughed. *"What next coming?"*

"Firstly, I'm not ordinary – but that doesn't mean I'm better or worse than others, just different. I was an Art student. Many Art students are individualistic or eccentric – so I was not unusual at Art School. I was a fairly average Art student. I did work hard – but so did others. I got a first-class honours degree – but that is not so unusual. Anyone can achieve that, simply by hard work. I don't have any great talent – but I do work hard."

Rinpoche nodded fairly expressionlessly – but with a gesture that suggested I should continue.

"As to miracles – no. None that would fit Vajrayana categories. I did have visions as a child." PAUSE *"I still have some extraordinary dreams – but I wouldn't describe them as miraculous. "They gave me no special powers other than determination and the ability to hold to any decisions I make."*

Rinpoche nodded and waited for my next exposition. He could detect that I had more to say.

---

49 dGongs gTer – Mind gTérma.
50 dag sNang gTer – Pure Vision gTérma.

"I suppose, there have been many things which I would—personally—regard as 'miraculous'. Meeting Kyabjé Düd'jom Rinpoche was miraculous. Being accepted as his student and given ngakpa ordination and robes was miraculous. When I first came to India, all I wanted was to—meet—ngakpas. I had no idea that it was remotely possible to become a ngakpa. Then there's coming here and being with you for this time – that is miraculous. It's all miraculous from the perspective of the average western person. I feel that I have had miraculous luck." Then I chuckled rather slightly *"I've also had bad luck."*

Rinpoche said nothing of my good luck – but asked me about the bad luck. I told him about Alice, Mr Love, Lindie Dale, and the deaths of Ron and Steve. I also told him about my having been rejected as an applicant for interview at the Royal College of Art in London – but that could have been good luck as easily as bad. Rinpoche listened patiently and then said *"O yah – much 'life experience' all at very young age coming."*

"Yes Rinpoche." PAUSE *"It has seemed like that to me. Other people I have known have commented that I have experienced more losses and bereavements than they have. They've been surprised that I survived it all – and remained a basically happy person who likes to laugh."* PAUSE *"Maybe that's a miracle."*

"Big miracle is like 'thom yor arriving – and now, 'thom yor empty becoming" he laughed. *"But maybe not ordinary 'thom yor. So no difficulty – and fast change coming."*

"I'm probably still capable of being a 'thom yor from time to time, Rinpoche – so I hope you will not be disappointed…"

"Yah… now 'thom yor style again speaking – but quickly changing."

"Certainly" I laughed. *"I've suddenly changed my mind. You will not be disappointed. I will accomplish everything I have been asked to accomplish."*

"O yah! This better!" he laughed. *"Now…"* he became grave again. *"Sometimes gTértöns prophetic guides from manifestations of Guru Rinpoche and Yeshé Tsogyel in vision receiving."*

gTértöns either discover prophetic guides in their places of concealment, or they may have to discover the instructions which explain how to find them. Many gTértöns have found gTérmas along with indications of consequent gTérma discoveries. When there is no prophetic guide, gTértöns find the gTérma through their own clarity.

"Khyungchen Aro Lingma's gTérma already revealed. Already Aro Yeshé from Aro Lingma receiving. So, this again from mindstream discovering. No guide needing. No cypher. No khandro script reading. This is Kyabjé Düd'jom Rinpoche in letter writing."

Künzang Dorje Rinpoche explained that mostly gTértöns had to perform preparatory practices before discovering gTérma. Such practices are revealed by the prophetic guides and consist of yidam drüpthabs. If gTértöns have previously discovered drüpthabs they use them as preparatory practices – or else they will use drüpthabs discovered by other gTértöns.

"This why Chögyam must all Düd'jom gTér ngöndros practising. These all completed. Then Tröma Nakmo completing. Then 'pho-wa next completing. Düd'jom Rinpoche writing – I must 'phowa all instruction giving and precisely guiding. Then Chögyam all preparations completing. Then gTérma revealing. This very simple coming – but first—before gTérma—must be khandro finding. Nothing finding without khandro first finding."

The practices to which Rinpoche had referred had not been easy – but neither had they been difficult. They had certainly not been onerous – but finding a khandro, a *sangyum*, seemed the most difficult and potentially problematic proposition. Naturally, success in this endeavour would be utterly delightful – but failure seemed only too likely. I put this to Künzang Dorje Rinpoche and he shook his head *"No difficulty coming – unless Kyabjé Künzang Dorje Rinpoche not believing."*

"If you say there will be no difficulty – then I believe it. I believe it even though I can't conceptualise it in terms of my history with lady friends. I am extremely happy to believe it. It would make a marvellously welcome change."

Rinpoche narrowed his eyes slightly *"No difficulty coming."* PAUSE *"You thinking Künzang Dorje not life in West knowing."*

"Yes, Rinpoche – that thought did occur in my mind but only briefly."

"Then what doing?"

"Then I thought that it was a narrow view – and that I had no way of knowing what you knew. It occurred to me that what you knew was probably entirely independent of experience of western culture."

Künzang Dorje Rinpoche gazed at me for some moments, then *"O yah. Now much carefully thinking."* He went on to say that there were things which could be known about the future due to what existed in the present. It was little different from seeing a storm coming across the plains of India toward the hills. Had I ever seen this? I said that I'd seen it several times when I was in retreat up above Triund – and knew I'd need to be back in my retreat hut within minutes. Hail could start falling. There could be hailstones the size of grapes or horse chestnuts. Some were like apples. An occasional grapefruit-sized ball which could kill a person if it struck them on the head.

"Yah – then future by sign in present telling." PAUSE *"But Düd'jom Rinpoche seeing far – and he is telling. He is one khandro seeing—'Chögyam sangyum' in future— so no doubt necessary having."* PAUSE *"What now saying?"*

"That I have no doubt of your vision, Rinpoche. I do not need the assurance that Düd'jom Rinpoche sees it too. If I have any doubt, the doubt concerns me – and whether I will be able to avoid making mistakes. I will naturally try to be careful. I'll naturally try to do my best not to cause obstacles to the prediction. Looking at my past however – I am conscious of patterns. I feel that it is now a great responsibility not to fall into previous patterns. I know that I can be observant of patterns – but I know that patterns can present themselves with such contrasting appearances that I might not see a pattern before I'm in the middle of it."

Künzang Dorje Rinpoche shrugged and said that he had no doubt I would do my best – and that if I made mistakes, they would be small mistakes which would not cause long term harm in terms of finding a sangyum. All I had to do was keep the idea in mind. He then returned to his discussion of gTérma.

"So, if gTérma casket finding – then practices must perform before casket opening."

Before decoding symbolic scripts, transcribing them, and disseminating it to others – there had to be practices. This would not concern me because the Aro gTér had already been revealed and disseminated. The result would therefore be auspicious and without disturbances. In some cases, due to perfect circumstances, there is no need for preparatory practices.

When the time of revelation draws close and the preparations are complete the gTértön goes to the place indicated and accesses the gTérma from rocks, earth, lakes, lhakhangs, statues, trees, sky, or the nature of Mind – wherever it has been hidden by Guru Rinpoche, Yeshé Tsogyel, or a gTértön who has re-concealed a gTérma. In the case of the Aro gTér it had not been re-concealed – and so there was no special place and no special time. The only factor necessary was the auspicious sangyum.

In the case of outer public discovery, people are invited to witness the event. If it is an inner discovery, only specifically chosen people are present. If it is a secret discovery – no one is present. If gTérma are concealed at specific locations, gTértöns perform tsog'khorlo with their vajra brothers and vajra sisters. Often the discovery takes place during the tsog'khorlo – but sometimes it occurs after the tsog'khorlo without visible signs of symbolic activity.

gTértöns however do not always go to concealment places – because the gTérma protectors may bring the gTérmas to them. Sometimes a portal in the rocks opens spontaneously when gTértöns arrive – or when they perform mudras, or even at a gesture.

"Sometimes gTérma revealing – much hardship coming. Very narrow path in rocky mountain climbing or great abyss descending. Sometimes cannot reaching. Great fear looking from great height. Sometimes the rocks with ladders climbing. gTérma reaching hammer and chisel needing. Pema Lingpa first gTérma in lake discovering." PAUSE *"Chögyam not this hardship having – but maybe hardship from mi-kha coming."*

"Mi-kha, Rinpoche? Do you know what that might be?"

"Mi-kha..." Rinpoche laughed *"subject not important. Mi-kha from all subjects coming. Mi-kha from green shirt wearing and peoples saying 'Why green shirt wearing when yellow shirt possible?' Mi-kha from blue shirt wearing and peoples saying 'Why blue shirt wearing when red shirt possible?' Mi-kha from black shirt wearing and peoples saying 'Why black shirt wearing when white shirt possible?' Mi-kha from fried mo-mo eating and peoples saying 'Why fried mo-mo eating when steam mo-mo possible?' Mi-kha from teaching and peoples saying 'Why teaching when silent possible?' Mi-kha from silent and peoples saying 'Why silent when teaching possible?'..."*

"Yah... where 'thom yor finding — there mi-kha also finding and peoples this and that saying." PAUSE "Mi-kha always coming for everyone — but when Inji gTérma coming" he laughed "then much much much mi-kha coming — too much mi-kha coming."

Right. Not a massively cheerful prospect. "Might it be better, Rinpoche — if this gTérma waited for some other incarnation when Aro Yeshé might be born in Bhutan?"

"No." Rinpoche smiled slightly and gave a shake of his head. "Düd'jom Rinpoche 'finding' saying. You must be finding. Chögyam no choice having."

"Well, if there's no choice — that makes it far easier."

Rinpoche laughed uproariously at that "O yah! Mighty warrior! This I am too much liking."

Mighty warrior... I was many things — but not that. I could be reckless, rash, heedless, or even wild inasmuch as an Englishman could ever be wild. Mad dogs and Englishmen went out in the midday sun[51] — so the song went. No sooner was this in my mind when Kyabjé Künzang Dorje Rinpoche said "Song now coming."

"Yes, Rinpoche... I was thinking that I was more of a mad dog than a warrior. It's from an amusing old song."

And then of course I had to sing.

"Mad dogs and Englishmen go out in the midday sun. The toughest Burmese bandit can never understand it. In Rangoon the heat of noon is just what the natives shun. They put their Scotch or Rye down and lie down. In a jungle town where the sun beats down to the rage of man and beast; the English garb, of the English sahib, merely gets a bit more creased. In Bangkok at twelve o'clock they foam at the mouth and run — but mad dogs and Englishmen go out in the midday sun."

---

51 *Mad Dogs and Englishmen* by Noël Coward 1931. The title refers to the saying '*Only mad dogs and Englishmen go out in the midday sun*' coined by Rudyard Kipling. The song was first performed in *The Third Little Show* at the Music Box Theatre, New York, in 1931, by Beatrice Lillie.

This of course—at Rinpoche's insistence—had to be translated. This involved me having to find alternative words. It caused great amusement – and I wondered why Rinpoche would wish to understand a song which was simply a humorous entertainment. Of course, it should have been obvious. He wanted to know about western culture – and more particularly western culture as it pertained to me as his student. Rinpoche was always curious about western culture – but it was never an 'idle curiosity'. I knew that he would remember everything I told him. I knew this, because he occasionally referred to something I'd explained weeks before[52].

"Great gTértöns, other gTértöns deputising to discover gTérmas. Jamyang Khyentsé Wangpo is doing."

During a symbolic enactment, a gTérma appeared in front of Jamyang Khyentsé Wangpo in the presence of an assembly of his disciples. It suddenly appeared on his çog-tsé. In such cases gTérmas are usually kept hidden until the precise time of revelation has arrived.

The discovery of Sa gTérma requires five certainties: time, place, support, companion, and physical appurtenances. If there is misalignment it renders discovery impossible. Sa gTér depend on external circumstances. Mind gTérma however are only marginally affected by circumstances and are thus not subject to as many obstacles.

gTértöns are very rarely monastics – and when they are, the presence of khandro and dPa'wo are still necessary, even though there is no sexual relationship. gTértöns are often householders with families, owning any possible possessions to which they have felt drawn.

"Kyabjé Düd'jom Rinpoche Jig'drèl Yeshé Dorje, such a gTértön. He is Great gTértön. Householder gTértöns every experience of life – method of nondual attainment becoming. Enjoyment of sensory objects also method of nondual attainment. Nothing excluded." PAUSE *"So Düd'jom Rinpoche is saying Chögyam must be sangyum finding. Künzang Dorje also saying Chögyam must be sangyum finding. Chögyam must be soon finding."*

---

52 This occurred over the course of many years – right up to Kyabjé Künzang Dorje Rinpoche's parinirvana.

Künzang Dorje Rinpoche explained that the encouragement of a sangyum actualises the union of wisdom and method in terms of female and male qualities. For the gTérma tradition a consort was vitally important for the discovery of gTérma. Through the union of ecstasy and emptiness the mind of the gTértön is opened to the discovery of gTérma. If the right consort cannot support the gTértön, the discovery might become impossible or extremely difficult. If the right consort cannot be found, then the gTértön's life may be at risk. The purpose of gTértöns' lives is to discover gTérma – and if gTérma cannot be revealed, then their life force can be seriously diminished.

"If authentic khandro cannot consort becoming… then sometimes gift, ornament, or dress of khandro can substitute using" PAUSE *"but this not for Chögyam possible. This not possible… because Kyabjé Düd'jom Rinpoche saying Chögyam must sangyum finding."*

After this, Rinpoche concluded and told me that we'd finished with lists for the day. He told me that what he'd taught would serve me as references for the future in terms of the Lamas I might meet. He said that some of the names might prove useful and some might not. It was then time for dinner – and as was often the case, Rinpoche had asked the lady of the house to prepare mo-mos.

We ate our mo-mos and tsé-cho—quaffed Eagle beer—and talked of British history. Rinpoche was interested in the succession of Kings and Queens – and I did my best. I had studied history and was able to provide a reasonable picture. Rinpoche never failed to amaze me in terms of his voracious ability to amass information about the world.

Appendix II

the inner tantras

My relationship with Künzang Dorje Rinpoche had shifted. I felt, not exactly *relaxed* – but free of burdensome anxiety. I now knew absolutely that I was *not* going to be told to go away. Even if I lapsed and spoke like a 'thom yor again, it would not betoken disaster. It would betoken remembering—immediately—that all I had to be was natural and present. I had to allow my innate intelligence to function. I knew I could *self-correct* if I caught a certain expression in Künzang Dorje Rinpoche's face. This moment was an opportunity and I now responded as if I'd suddenly awoken from a daydream at the wheel of a fast-moving car.

"O yah… so… Mahayoga." Rinpoche commenced *"Dorje Sempa is Mahayoga Tantras to King Ja of Zahor transmitting. King Ja also from Dri'mèd Dragpa* [1] *receiving. This because Dri'mèd Dragpa is from Chana Dorje* [2] *in Singhala* [3] *obtaining."*

The lineage of Mahayoga transmission is unbroken to the present day. It was Sang-gyé Sangwa [4] who passed the lineage to Dri'mèd Shényèn [5] and Guru Rinpoche – thence establishing their practice in Tibet. Mahayoga is sometimes known as the Father Tantra [6]. It is the generation phase of visualising the yidam as luminosity inseparable from emptiness. The View is to realise the inseparability of phenomena and emptiness [7]. The meditation is skilful means to attain the inseparability of emptiness and form through envisioning everything as the pure dKyil'khor of the yidams. In terms of action, 'pure' and 'impure' are not differentiated. The five meats and five nectars are accepted without judgement.

---

1 *dri 'med grags pa* / དྲི་འམེད་གྲགས་པ / *Virmalakirti*.
2 *phyag na rDo rJe* / ཕྱག་ན་རྡོ་རྗེ / *Vajrapani*.
3 Singhala – Srilanka (Ceylon / Brithanya Lamkava / Brithaniya Ilangai). It was a British colony between 1796 and 1948.
4 *sangs rGyas gSang ba* / སངས་རྒྱས་གསང་བ / *Buddhaguhya*.
5 *dri 'med bShes gNyen* / དྲི་མེད་བཤེས་གཉེན / *Vimalamitra*.
6 Father Tantra – pha gyüd (*pha rGyud* / ཕ་རྒྱུད).
7 Inseparability of phenomena and emptiness – nang-tong cher-mèd (*sNang sTong dByer 'med* / སྣང་སྟོང་དབྱེར་འམེད).

Dorje Sempa and Dri'mèd Dragpa transmitted the Anuyoga tantras to King Ja who passed them to Mahasiddha Kukuraja. Thereafter they passed to Nubchen Sang-gyé Yeshé [8] one of the 25 disciples of Guru Rinpoche. Nubchen Sang-gyé Yeshé taught Anuyoga throughout Tibet and the lineage of transmission remains unbroken. Twenty-two Anuyoga tantras exist in the Nyingma Gyüdbum.

In terms of the View there are three dKyil'khors: the dKyil'khor of Küntuzangmo[9] and her luminosity; the dKyil'khor of Küntuzangpo[10] and the indivisibility of Küntuzangmo and Küntuzangpo; and, the dKyil'khor of Dewa Chenpo[11]. In terms of action, the practice is the path of dröl-lam[12] visualising all phenomena and beings as the dKyil'khor of yidams. The method consists of actualising the rTsa, rLung, and thig-lé[13] – and the result is realisation achieved in one lifetime.

"Here" Künzang Dorje Rinpoche said as an aside *"many scholars mistake making. Thig-lé not 'drop'. Thig-lé is 'essence'. Two words coming – thigs and thig. So, essence is 'thig' spelling – and drop is 'thigs' spelling."*

Dzogchen was transmitted mind to mind from beginninglessness by Küntuzangpo to Dorje Sempa. Dorje Sempa then transmitted Dzogchen through symbols to the Rig'dzins – those who have realised the primordial state. Among the Rig'dzins was Garab Dorje. Garab Dorje miraculously appeared in Ögyen and transmitted these symbolic teachings to Jampal Shényèn, who transmitted them to Shri Simha. Shri Simha passed them on to Yeshé mDo[14], Dri'mèd Shényèn, Guru Rinpoche and Lotsa Nampar Nangdzèd[15], the translator.

---

8   *gNubs chen sangs rGyas ye shes* / གནུབས་ཆེན་སངས་རྒྱས་ཡེ་ཤེས་.
9   dKyil'khor of Küntuzangmo (*dByings sKye med kun tu bZang mo'i dKyil 'khor* / དབྱིངས་སྐྱེ་མེད་ཀུན་ཏུ་བཟང་མོའི་དཀྱིལ་འཁོར་) – unborn chö-ying (*chos dByings* / ཆོས་དབྱིངས་ / *Dharmadhatu*).
10 dKyil'khor of Küntuzangpo (*ye shes kun tu bZang po'i dKyil 'khor* / ཡེ་ཤེས་ཀུན་ཏུ་བཟང་པོའི་དཀྱིལ་འཁོར་).
11 dKyil'khor of Dewa Chenpo (*sras bDe ba chen po'i dKyil 'khor* / སྲས་བདེ་བ་ཆེན་པོའི་དཀྱིལ་འཁོར་ / *mahasukha mandala*) – cycle of great bliss.
12 *grol lam* / གྲོལ་ལམ་ – liberation path.
13 rTsa (*rTsa* / རྩ་ / *nadi*) – spatial channels; rLung (*rLung* / རླུང་ / *prana*) – spatial winds; thig-lé (*thig le* / ཐིག་ལེ་ / *bindu*) – spatial essences.
14 *ye shes mDo* / ཡེ་ཤེས་མདོ་ / *Jnanasutra*.
15 *lo tsa rNam par sNang mDzad* / ལོ་ཙ་རྣམ་པར་སྣང་མཛད་ / *Vairochana*.

"O yah – Gang-zag Nyèn-gyüd [16] *these are oral transmissions of Ati Yoga – three types: direct, symbolic, and oral. This Dzogchen – also shintu naljor thegpa* [17] *name using."*

Dzogchen has three series of teachings: Dzogchen sem-dé, Dzogchen long-dé and Dzogchen men-ngag-dé. The sem-dé and long-dé series came to the Himalayan countries from India in the 10th century. Neither however, has been widely taught or survived as living traditions in the major Nyingma lineages. Practice of Dzogchen sem-dé and Dzogchen long-dé declined after the 11th century. Men-ngak-dé was introduced later, from the 12th century, and flourished to the present day. Men-ngak-dé is now the main teaching and practice of Dzogchen taught in the major Nyingma lineages.

"This why Kyabjé Düd'jom Rinpoche saying Chögyam must Aro gTér teaching. Dzogchen sem-dé and Dzogchen long-dé both Aro gTér inside – so, value in future coming."

The three series of Dzogchen equate with the three testaments of Garab Dorje, the Tsig-sum nè-dek[18] - Hitting the essence in three points. These three points are: direct introduction, remaining without doubt, and continuing in the state. Sem-dé is related to direct introduction. Long-dé is related to remaining without doubt. Men-ngak-dé is related to continuing in the state.

Sem-dé means *the series of the nature of Mind*. It is the series of Dzogchen with the most detailed transmission through explanation. Sem-dé equates to direct introduction. It offers explanations as direct introduction and offers methods in terms of direct introduction.

"Yah – so Düd'jom Rinpoche is much from Dzogchen sem-dé teaching – and you are as transmission hearing. Düd'jom Rinpoche writing – from early age Chögyam shi-nè practising. Word not knowing – but practice knowing. Also lhatong—also nyi'mèd —also lhundrüp.

---

16 *gang zag sNyan brGyud* / གང་ཟག་སྙན་བརྒྱུད་ – hearing transmission; mouth to ear lineage; individual hearing lineage.
17 *shin tu rNal 'byor gyi theg pa* / ཤིན་ཏུ་རྣལ་འབྱོར་གྱི་ཐེག་པ་ / *ati-yoga yana* / *upadesha* / *mahasandhi*.
18 *tshig gSum gNad du brDeg* / ཚིག་གསུམ་གནད་དུ་བརྡེག་ – The Three Phrases which Strike the Vital Point; the final words of Garab Dorje (*dGa' rab rDo rJe* / དགའ་རབ་རྡོ་རྗེ་ / *Pramodavajra* / *Prahevajra* / *Surativajra*) to Jampal Shényèn (*'jam dPal bShes gNyen* / འཇམ་དཔལ་བཤེས་གཉེན་ / *Manjushrimitra*).

"This from Aro Lingma receiving – but no words. Only direct. Then Japanese Lama and powerful ship captain reading." PAUSE *"So now all things no difficulty understanding."*

The unique aspect of Dzogchen sem-dé is that it contains the ngöndro for Dzogchen as a whole. The ngöndro is called the Four Naljors and is a preparation for the Four Ting-ngé'dzin. Without Dzogchen sem-dé, Dzogchen can only be approached through the Tantric ngöndro – followed by kyé-rim and dzog-rim practices.

Dzogchen long-dé, relates to remaining without doubt. It has less explanation within it than Dzogchen sem-dé. It bases itself on the fact that one has already received direct introduction and concerns itself with *remaining without doubt* about what has been transmitted. If there is doubt – then transmission has not been received.

The methods of Dzogchen long-dé concern returning to rigpa through the 'felt texture of subtle sensation' – because doubt is a sensation, just as being without doubt is a sensation. The difference is that the doubt-free state has no adhering concepts. Doubt is an experience. Being free of doubt is also an experience; it is a state in itself. Long-dé is concerned with sensation, experiential sensation. Presence of awareness is found in the dimension of sensation. In many different teachings of the Long-dé there are particular postures using gom-tag[19] and gom-shing[20] and supports of various kinds which have the function of pressing on certain pressure points. These pressure points are used to cultivate sensation, in which one finds the presence of awareness. sKu-mNyé is another similar method. It utilises sensation by stimulating the tsa-lung system.

Dzogchen men-ngag-dé relates to continuing in the state. Very little explanation is included. There are simply directions for how to continue in the state. Dzogchen men-ngag-dé encompasses a great variety of methods but their character is very difficult to discuss outside the level of experience required to understand their significance.

There is some difference of view in the Nyingma Tradition in terms of whether Dzogchen belongs to the six tantras – or whether it exists within its own category.

---

19 *sGom thag* / སྒོམ་ཐག་ – meditation belt.
20 *sGom shing* / སྒོམ་ཤིང་ or gom-tén (*sGom brTan* / སྒོམ་བརྟན་) – meditation crutch, stick; meditation support.

Atiyoga—as it is taught in better known lineages as one of the inner tantras—lacks aspects of Dzogchen sem-dé and Dzogchen long-dé. It is the direct approach to the essential nature of the mind, which is *Buddha nature* [21] through the recognition of the naked awareness state of one's own mind. These teachings were transmitted by Dorje Sempa to Garab Dorje who in turn transmitted them to other human teachers – primarily Guru Rinpoche. These teachings have three divisions: those of Dzogchen sem-dé, Dzogchen long-dé, and Dzogchen men-ngag-dé.

The Nyingma Gyüd'bum has 21 texts of Dzogchen sem-dé and seven of Dzogchen men-ngag-dé. The Division of Dzogchen men-ngag-dé are contained in the 17 tantras also in the Nying ma Gyud'bum.

The view is established that all phenomena are spontaneously realised from the beginning.

The meditation is khregs chod – the natural revelation to realise chöku, longku, and trülku which cuts through all attempts to referentially appropriate phenomena. It employs the spontaneous iridescent wisdom of long-ku to achieve the rainbow body of trülku, through the practice of thod rGal.

The activity is that without acceptance or rejection you recognise phenomena as the display of the dharmakaya.

The result is that duality and nonduality are indivisible. The spontaneous state of Küntuzangpo is ever present.

Being Nyingma, is to be open to the whole stream of practice. Although the emphasis is on the three inner tantras, one is open to any or all of the yanas, and these are practised under one's Tsawa'i Lama. Tsawa'i Lamas might teach from the perspective of Dzogchen but even so, they may give teachings from any of the vehicles. They will give guidance according to the particular needs and experience of the practitioner at the time.

---

21 Buddha nature – dé-zhing sheg-pa'i nyingpo (*de bZhin gShegs pa'i sNying po* / དེ་བཞིན་ གཤེགས་པའི་སྙིང་པོ་).

Appendix III

A Descriptive History of the Rig'dzinpas and Rig'dzinmas of the Great Secret Mantra Vehicle

– they who are dignified in White Skirts and resplendent with Long Hair

– a brief oral commentary by Kyabjé Künzang Dorje Rinpoche

Two renowned sanghas arose in Tibet in the 8th Century, during the time of the three masters Khen Lob Chö Sum[1]. These two divisions are: the monastics with shaven-heads and saffron robes – the rabjung ngur-mig gi dé[2]; and, the sangha of white skirts and long plaited hair – the gö kar chang lo'i dé.

In the upper and lower regions of Kham[3] in Tibet, those of the gö kar chang lo'i dé are known as A-mé[4]. In Ngari[5], they are known as Jopa[6] and in the Ü-tsang[7] region, they are called Ngak'chang. In Bhutan, Sikkim and other bordering kingdoms, these practitioners are known as serkhyimpas[8], gomchens[9] or ordained householders.

Both sanghas—the rabjung ngur-mig gi dé and the gö kar chang lo'i dé— had equal sovereignty. Historically, this was clearly specified during the reign of Trisong Détsen.

---

1 *mKhen sLob chos gSum* / མཁན་སློབ་ཆོས་གསུམ. 'Khen' refers to Khenpo Shantarakshita, 'Lob' to the Tantric Buddha Lopön Padmasambhava, and 'Chö' to the Dharma King, Trisong Détsen.
2 *rab byung ngur sMrig gi sDe* / རབ་བྱུང་ངུར་སྨྲིག་གི་སྡེ
3 *khams* / ཁམས
4 *a mye* / ཨ་སྨྱེ
5 *mNga' ris* / མངའ་རིས), the far-western region of Tibet
6 *jo pa* / ཇོ་པ
7 *dBus gTsang* / དབུས་གཙང
8 *ser khyim pa* / སེར་ཁྱིམ་པ – refers to refers to practitioners who wear yellow (ser) monastic clothing but live as householders (khyimpa)
9 *sGom chen* / སྒོམ་ཆེན

In connection with that, there was an occasion when the powerful King Tri Ralpachen[10], who ruled central Tibet in the years of 866–896, weaved silk into the two ends of his hair. This was as an object of offering (to both sanghas) and he requested that both sanghas sit on top of his hair and walk upon it. This is clearly stated in reliable histories of the Tibetan monarchies.

In those histories, four jopas are described who, in service to the Dharma kings of Töd Gugé[11] and Gungthang[12], reversed harmful forces causing illness. Similarly, for the Dharma kings of Nangchen[13] and Dége[14], there were three groups consisting of four great lamas at the centre (of the region), four ministers in between, and four Amnyés in the low part of the valley. They were renowned for dispelling harmful forces of illness.

Moreover, ngakpas staying in three valleys performing the Do[15] created a triangle of earth and sky which is like a hamkhung[16]. If people in a region are being controlled by fearful mental experiences caused by the extremely great swirling agitation of gods and demons, etcetera (generated by hope and fear), then the presence of those who have sharpness and swiftness and other powerful energies of wrathful activity, is extremely beneficial.

Furthermore, in Central Tibet, at the time of Drogön Chögyal Phakpa[17] who lived from 1235–1280, there were said to be four great ngakpas in the four directions of Drogön Tsang[18].

10 *khri ral pa can* / ཁྲི་རལ་པ་ཅན
11 *sTod gu ge* / སྟོད་གུ་གེ
12 *gung thang* / གུང་ཐང
13 *nang chen* / ནང་ཆེན
14 *sDe dGe* / སྡེ་དགེ
15 *mDo* / མདོ – most important type of ransom ritual used to dispel harm and obstacles. These are the rituals of suppression, burning and throwing which are described further into the text.
16 *ham khung* / ཧམ་ཁུང. Any conjunction of lines of a triangle formed by earth, sky, valleys, rivers, etcetera, or established points on the ground, will accomplish the hamkhung, which is a HAM syllable in the shape of a triangle. It could be dangerous for anyone but ngakpas to do this practice. NB: Kyabjé Künzang Dorje Rinpoche
17 *'gro mGon chos rGyal 'phags pa* / འགྲོ་མགོན་ཆོས་རྒྱལ་འཕགས་པ
18 *'gro mGon tshang* / འགྲོ་མགོན་ཚང

A Descriptive History of the Rig'dzinpas and Rig'dzinmas of the Great Secret Mantra Vehicle

In the time of the Great 5th Dala'i Lama, the supreme protector who lived from 1617–1682, there were also four ngakpas in the four main directions in the secret mantra golden shrine room[19]. These ngakpas performed all the healing rituals, rituals to reverse adverse conditions, and long life rituals. These were performed by ngakpas only.

Furthermore, ngakpas, who are worthy of the most holy veneration, accomplish the activities of burying, burning, and throwing those possessed of the seven violations[20] including: those who contradict the words of the Buddha; those who allow samaya to degenerate and so forth; enemies of the Three Jewels and the Lopön and so forth; the ten obstructers and all of their enemies and harmful protectors. All of their (the samaya violators) forms without exception, are reduced to ashes so that merely their names remain and their consciousness' are liberated into dharmadhatu.

Those obstructing enemies who are violators, having been commanded by the power of the truth of the Three Jewels, are first summoned. Then, having been bound through mudra, they are suppressed many levels beneath the earth without the ability to re-emerge.

Similarly, having summoned the violators by (the power of) truth and bound them by mudra, employ the method of the 'me lha'[21] or alternatively, bind them by summoning and join the form (of the violators) with the ling-ga[22] and throw it.

The method of destroying the rampant diffusion and so forth of those dreadful enemies of the Buddhist doctrine, Dharma people in general, and the body of the Lama in particular, is the union of method and knowledge, the great compassion. This cuts the stream of negative karma. The visualisation of this should be possessed of the three points about which one should be clear[23].

---

19 sér khang (*gSer khang* / གསེར་ཁང་)
20 nyampa dün (*nyams pa bDun* / ཉམས་པ་བདུན་)
21 *me lha* / མེ་ལྷ་ – a yidam associated with the fire rituals.
22 *ling ga* / ལིང་ག་ – an effigy gTorma used in wrathful rituals.
23 sélwa sum (*gSal ba gSum* / གསལ་བ་) – the three aspects of clear visualisation related to generation stage meditation which include 1. the clear visualisation of the yidam's appearance; 2. maintaining the pride of being the yidam; 3. recalling the pure, insubstantial qualities of the yidam. NB: Lopön Péling Ögyen Ten'dzin Rinpoche (*slob dPon pad gLing o rGyan bsTan 'dzin rin po che*)

This wrathful activity placing violators in the state of permanent bliss is widely known as *the three activities of suppression, burning and throwing*. The primary activity of ngakpas is to accomplish this activity continuously.

Regarding the magical weapon activities

There are the divisions of the nine reversals, seven reversals, one reversal, and so forth. The nine reversals include: the magical weapon activity of mantra[24]; the magical weapon activity of stone[25]; the magical weapon activity of blood[26]; the magical weapon activity of corpse[27]; the magical weapon activity of thorn[28]; the magical weapon activity of mustard seed[29]; the magical weapon activity of arrow[30]; the magical weapon activity of gTorma[31]; and the magical weapon activity of poison[32].

Similarly, there is a magical weapon activity that is supreme and singular – the magical weapon activity of the horn of the revelry of wrath[33]. This horn should be the right horn of a wild yak[34] from the southern Tibetan jungle, Kyilgyi Srin[35]. If one cannot obtain such a horn, one should use the right horn of either a valuable or ordinary yak[36], of a dzo[37], or of an ox.

According to the teachings of the Inner Tantras, one fills the horn with poisons, blood, and a variety of other sorcery substances and then the substances are thrown.

---

24 thun zor (*thun zor* / བུན་ཟོར་)
25 do zor (*rDo zor* / རྡོ་ཟོར་)
26 trak zor (*khrak zor* / ཁྲག་ཟོར་)
27 pung zor (*phung zor* / ཕུང་ཟོར་)
28 tsér zor (*tsher zor* / ཚེར་ཟོར་)
29 yung zor (*yungs zor* / ཡུངས་ཟོར་)
30 da zor (*mDa zor* / མདའ་ཟོར་)
31 tor zor (*gTor zor* / གཏོར་ཟོར་)
32 dug zor (*dug zor* / དུག་ཟོར་)
33 trowo rolpa'i rwa zor *khro bo rol ba'i rwa zor* / ཁྲོ་བོ་རོལ་བའི་རྭ་ཟོར་)
34 drong (*drong* / འབྲོང་)
35 *dKyil gyi srin* / དཀྱིལ་གྱི་སྲིན་ – centre of the Rakshasas.
36 *g.yag* / གཡག
37 *mDzo* / མཛོ – a cross between a yak and a cow.

There are two types of blood: poisonous blood and mixed blood. Poisonous blood is a mixture of three black poisons: tsenduk nakpo[38], thar-nu nakpo[39] and bongwa chen nakpo[40]. It is best if one can obtain all three. If the three cannot be acquired, it is necessary to have at least one. These poisons grow in places where sunlight does not reach, such as rocky chasms or river gorges.

Regarding mixed blood

That which is called mixed blood must include the heartblood of an heroic warrior killed in hand-to-hand combat. If this cannot be acquired, it is necessary to have blood from the heart of a person who has been killed by an arrow, knife, or spear. That, mixed with the three black poisons is what is called mixed blood – poisonous blood. It is certain that these are the necessary substances for the magical weapon activities and the ling-ga liberating activities.

It is necessary that those who perform these activities practise as much as they can until they are able to demonstrate the signs of accomplishment of the activities of the sadhana practice (approach, accomplishment, and activity) of the Three Roots (Lama, Yidam and Dakini). To accomplish liberation (of obstructing forces) into the Ten Buddhafields, first, one needs the power to summon. In the middle, one needs the power to liberate. In the end, one needs the ability to guide (obstructing forces to the Buddhafields). One must be a master of Vajrayana.

Furthermore, there are two types of ngakpas – those of family lineage[41] and those of Dharma lineage[42]. Ngakpa family lineages are connected father to son—or mother to daughter—and passed down through generations. At present, there are family lineage holders such as, of the Nyingma lineage, Lachen Minling Trichen Rinpoche[43], and the Sakya lineage, Drölma Potrang-gyi Trichen Rinpoche[44]. These are called the family lineage of ngakpas who hold the succession.

---

38 *bTsan dug nag po* /
39 *tha nu nag po* /
40 *bong ba can nag po* /
41 rig gyüd (*rigs rGyud* /)
42 chö gyüd (*chos rGyud* /)
43 *bla chen sMin gLing khri chen rin po che* /
44 *sGrol ma pho brang gi khri chen rin po che* /

Ngakpas of the Dharma lineage exist in both the Nyingma and Sarma traditions. Furthermore, it is not necessary to possess the ngakpa lineage of family because one enters the kyil'khor of whatever class of tantric deity is appropriate, oneself. Through receiving empowerment, scriptural authorisation and practice instructions from the lama endowed with characteristics, one becomes an excellent vessel. Then, it is necessary to demonstrate that one has accomplished the mantra accumulations of the three activities of drüpthab practice (approach, accomplishment, and activity).

Ngakpas like that have heads with long hair of non-contrivance. Their bodies have the white skirts of non-contrivance. Their minds have the natural state of non-contrivance. This is called the three non-contrivances[45] of the ngakpa.

Further, in ordinary worldly language, there is a custom of calling ngakpas 'white,' 'black' and 'multi-coloured.' Those who practice Dzogchen, bCud lan (essence extraction), gTummo, wear white, and fully integrate their lives with rigpa are called 'white ngakpas'. Further, those who accomplish drüpthab practice in solitary mountain retreat each year and perform ceremonies for worldly people the rest of the year are called 'multi-coloured ngakpas.' Ngakpas holding family lineages who spend less than seven days a year in retreat and who perform exorcisms and act as healers or astrologers, are known as 'black ngakpas.' They are well known as 'village ngakpas' in the language of worldly people.

Further, in latter day Tibet, there were only three ngakpa gompas that were very well known. In Amdo[46], there is a ngakpa gompa called Repkong[47]. There, ordained ngakpas have long-flowing, matted hair and wear a multi-coloured zen of which the lower part has a red stripe. This is worn as a shawl. The clothing of the Dorje Lopöns of this gompa is the same as above, although there is also a custom of wearing a white shamthab.

---

45 ma chö nam sum gyi ngakpa (*ma bCos rNam gSum gyi sNgags pa* / མ་བཅོས་རྣམ་གསུམ་གྱི་སྔགས་པ་)
46 *a mDo* / ཨ་མདོ་
47 *reb kong* / རེབ་གོང་

In this way, at Chakri Phurdrak[48], where there is a self-arising letter 'A' on a rock cliff, the clothing of the ngakpas who are known as servants of the government of Chakri is like that of the ordained ngakpas described above.

On the border of Ü and Tsang, in Shangzab Phulung[49], there are ngakpas called zabphu[50] ngakpas. These ngakpas wear long, free-flowing hair, the zen-tra[51] (multi-colored zen), and the nambu karpo[52] (white woollen) shamthab. In this place, once one has completed the accumulations and purifications through general practice, and the preliminary practices, and has requested the three transmissions of empowerment, scriptural authorisation, and instructions for the Lama Gongdü[53], one is allowed to wear the white skirt and robes. I, myself, at the time when I was 27 and 28 years old, for some years, had the experience of staying at this ngakpa gompa.

Generally, in Tibet, there are many ngakpa gompas. One cannot speak in detail about each and every one of them in terms of number of residents, histories and so forth.

Previously, on one occasion in McLeod Ganj, Upper Dharamsala, India, the Tibetan government office of Dharma affairs organised a five-day Dharma event for the purpose of benefiting Tibetan politics and religion, general and specific. Many monks and nuns, together with ngakpas, were invited in order to accomplish 100,000 accumulations of Rig'dzin Dungdrup[54] from the Chang gTér of Rig'dzin Go-dem[55]. On that occasion, at first, the ngakpas were belittled by being called householders. Although all the participants were being offered five rupees apiece daily, the ngakpas did not receive any.

---

48 *chags ri'i phur brag* / ཆགས་རིའི་ཕུར་བྲག
49 *shangs zab phu lung* / ཤངས་ཟབ་ཕུ་ལུང
50 *zab phu* / ཟབ་ཕུ་
51 *gZan phra* / གཟན་ཕྲ
52 *gNam bu dKar po* / གནམ་བུ་དཀར་པོ
53 *bla ma dGongs 'dus* / བླ་མ་དགོངས་འདུས
54 *rig 'dzin gDung sGrub* / རིག་འཛིན་གདུང་སྒྲུབ
55 *rig 'dzin rGod lDem* / རིག་འཛིན་རྒོད་ལྡེམ

"How pitiful," I said to my friend. *"I will wear full ngakpa dress—and together with the other ngakpas—enter the assembly. If we do not receive offerings appropriate to us as members of the gö kar chang lo'i dé, I will compose a letter to Gyalwa'i Rinpoche[56] saying that we did not receive the full measure of offerings and so forth."*

The next day I went there in full ngakpa dress. At the door of the assembly hall for the dharma event, some attendants were sitting on chairs for the purpose of distributing offerings to those who entered. Immediately, they saw me and a second ngakpa. One attendant said, *"Look, some chakpo[57] who look like ngakpas have come."* Another said, *"No, they are ngakpas from Tso Pema."* Then the five rupees offered as an expression of respect, were given without argument.

So, it is our own fault if ngakpas are belittled. It is fine for a ngakpas and ngakmas to be fathers and mothers. Now however, they enter assembly halls and are afraid to sit in the assembly row. They shave their heads or wear monastic clothing as well as shave their heads. When they wear ordinary chubas and do not dress in the various accoutrements of ngakpa attire, this is what happens.

Moreover, in Bhutan, Sikkim, and bordering valleys and so forth, there are ngakpas of a different type. They do not wear their hair long or the white skirt, but monk's clothes. They have wives and are family lineage holders. They are called 'serkhyim' ngakpas (ordained 'monastic' householders). In Tibet, there was a gompa like that called Bonpo[58]. There are some gompas like this where they have round, shaven heads and loose chubas – yet they insist they are ngakpas. They spend their lives doing business and performing village ceremonies. Again, being that, they are called neither ngakpa nor monk. The loose, large chuba is the dress of the lay people.

Once, I received a request from the prince of Sikkim and was appointed to be the retreat master for retreatants entering the three-year retreat. Kyabjé Chatral Rinpoche[59] came when the retreat boundaries were released and said: *"Now that this retreat has been completed here in Sikkim, this is a special practice place of Guru Rinpoche.*

---

56 r*Gyal ba'i rin po che* / རྒྱལ་བའི་རིན་པོ་ཆེ་ – the Dalai Lama.
57 *chag po* / ཆག་པོ་ – vow breaker, literally 'broken vessel'.
58 *dBon po* / དབོན་པོ་
59 *bya bral sangs rGyas rDo rje rin po che* / བྱ་བྲལ་སངས་རྒྱས་རྡོ་རྗེ་རིན་པོ་ཆེ་

"Moreover, from now on, if hair remains uncut and ngakpa dress is worn, this country will acquire great merit and virtue. Prince, you yourself should not remain a bachelor. It is necessary for you to find a kind-hearted woman."

He gave clear advice in this way.

The great Rig'dzin Lamas of India; individuals who are the extraordinary holders of the doctrine of the practice lineage, the dharma lineage of the ultimate meaning, and the family lineage; and in the same way, all the holy Lamas of the kama and gTérma transmission in Tibet, in particular, the noble beings who have the three qualities of wisdom, love and power – cannot be written about here as this is beyond the power of expression.

Further, the seventh (samaya vow) procludes 'proclamation of secrets to sentient beings who are not completely ripened.' Thus, the secret mantra vehicle is called so because it is secret. The secret mantra teachings are without fault and must accordingly remain secret to beings that are unsuitable vessels or have distorted views. There are indeed many hidden yogis and yoginis who have mastered the practices of the Inner Tantra and have attained siddhis.

The secret mantra vehicle is faultless. Attaining mastery in the classes of Tantra in the superior secret mantra vehicle, hidden yogis and yoginis attain self-mastery through the two siddhis. It is possible that there are many of these practitioners.

Colophon: This brief account of the white-skirt, long-haired ngakpas was given at the request of a few Dharma friends who hold the name ngakpa, especially the ngakpa lineage holder Aro Tulku Chögyam. Based on the understanding, awareness, and experience of Kunzang Dorje, a ngakpa of the Horja family lineage[60], wrote this brief collection of accounts of the ngakpas, in his 70th year, the year of the earth-rabbit, at the base of the mountain in Tsogyel Gé'phel Jong[61], in Yang-lé-shöd[62], a sacred place of Nepal.

---

60 *hor bya* / ཧོར་བྱ – Family Ngakpa Lineage.
61 *mTsho rGyal dGe 'phel lJongs* / མཚོ་རྒྱལ་དགེ་འཕེལ་ལྗོངས
62 *yang le shod* / ཡང་ལེ་ཤོད

glossary

A tsi

A rTsis / ཨ་རྩིས་ – a sound betokening astonishment.

amulet

tag-chog (*bTags chog* / བཏགས་ཆོག).

anjali mudra

thal mo'i chag gya (*thal mo'i phyag rGya* / ཐལ་མོའི་ཕྱག་རྒྱ). This salutation or prayer mudra is performed with the hands pressed together with straight fingers pointing upwards and the thumbs facing you.

ar-jag göd

ar jag rGod / ཨར་ཇག་རྒོད་ – bandit.

a-ra

a rag / ཨ་རག་ – spirit liquor made from barley or other grains.

bag chag

bag chags / བག་ཆགས་ / *vasana* – karmic traces, dormant thought-habits.

bardo

bar do / བར་དོ་ – intermediate state.

bodhicitta

see: changchub sem.

bodhisattva

see: changchub sempa.

Buddha families, three

rig-sum dorje 'dzin pa'i sa (*rigs gSum rDo rJe 'dzin pa'i sa* / རིགས་གསུམ་རྡོ་རྗེ་འཛིན་པའི་ས་): Buddha-body family – ku-sum dé-zhin sheg pa'i rig (*sKu gSum de bZhin gShegs pa'i rigs* / སྐུ་གསུམ་དེ་བཞིན་གཤེགས་པའི་རིགས་); Lotus-speech family – sung padma'i rig (*gSung pad ma'i rigs* / གསུང་པདྨའི་རིགས་); Vajra-mind family – thug dorje rig (*thugs rDo rJe rigs* / ཐུགས་རྡོ་རྗེ་རིགས་).

Buddha nature

dé-zhing sheg-pa'i nyingpo (*de bZhin gShegs pa'i sNying po* / དེ་བཞིན་གཤེགས་པའི་སྙིང་པོ་).

bumpa

bum pa / བུམ་པ་ / *khumba* – vase.

chag drog

lCags sGrog / ལྕགས་སྒྲོག་ – shackles. One of the implements used by Ngakpa Yeshé Dorje for exorcism.

chagya

phyag rGya / ཕྱག་རྒྱ་ / *mudra* – awareness gesture, symbolic hand-ballet.

chang

chang / ཆང་ – barley beer.

Chang gTér

byang gTer / བྱང་གཏེར་ – Northern gTérmas, revealed by gTértön Rig'dzin Gödem (*gTer sTon rig 'dzin rGod kyi lDem 'phru can* / གཏེར་སྟོན་རིག་འཛིན་རྒོད་ཀྱི་ལྡེམ་འཕྲུ་ཅན་ / 1337–1408).

changchub sem

byang chub sems / བྱང་ཆུབ་སེམས་ / *bodhicitta* – awakened heart-mind of empathetic appreciation, active compassion.

changchub sempa

byang chub sems dPa' / བྱང་ཆུབ་སེམས་དཔའ་ / *bodhisattva* – awakened heart-mind warrior.

char-gÇodpa

char gCod pa / ཆར་གཅོད་པ་ – rain-stopping practitioner.

chatral

bya bral / བྱ་བྲལ་ – free of duties or occupations; effortlessness; free of any deliberate actions; free of anything that has to be done.

chir-log

phyir bzLog / ཕྱིར་བཟློག་ – exorcism.

chö trang'gyür

chos mKhrang 'gyur / ཆོས་མཁྲང་འགྱུར་ – Dharma hardened.

chö-ku

chos sKu / ཆོས་སྐུ་ / *dharmakaya* – the sphere of unconditioned potentiality.

chö-nyid ngön-sum

chos nyid mNgon sum / ཆོས་ཉིད་མངོན་སུམ་ / *manifest dharmata* – the appearance of actual reality; direct perception of essential nature of reality.

chod-gyüd

sPyod rGyud / སྤྱོད་རྒྱུད་ / *Upatantra* – activity tantra.

chom-pa

sPyom pa / སྤྱོམ་པ་ – chutzpah, splendour, lavishness, ebullience, or even ostentation.

chörten

mChod rTen / མཆོད་རྟེན་ / *stupa*.

chu tangmo

chu grang mo / ཆུ་གྲང་མོ་ – cold water.

gÇod damaru

gCod rNga / གཅོད་རྔ་ – a large, hand-held drum.

çog-tsé

cog tse / ཅོག་ཙེ་ – small practice table.

completion phase

dzog rim (*rDzogs rim* / རྫོགས་རིམ་).

conch shell earrings

see: dung-kyi a-long.

convivial

cham-po (*'cham po* / འཆམ་པོ་) – convivial agreeable, amiable, congenial, amicable, cordial, genial, affable.

çud-len

bCud len / བཅུད་ལེན་. Çud-len pa is the Tibetan equivalent to *rasayana* in Sanskrit – and means 'extracting the essences' and subsisting on the essences. Çud-len means vital essence, distilled essence, quintessence, taste, elixir, potency, nutritional substance, extraction, essential aspect. It also means the preparation of elixirs for the elderly to prolong life. Çud-len involves the extraction of essences from stones and mineral deposits (*rDo'i bCud len* / རྡོའི་བཅུད་ལེན་), earth (*sa'i bCud len* / སའི་བཅུད་ལེན་), roots (*rTsa ba'i bCud len* / རྩ་བའི་བཅུད་ལེན་), flower petals (*me tog gi bCud len* / མེ་ཏོག་གི་བཅུད་ལེན་), and breath (*rLung gi bCud len* / རླུང་གི་བཅུད་ལེན་). There is also nondual presence (*rig pa'i bCud len* / རིག་པའི་བཅུད་ལེན་), which requires nondual absorption. The practice is eating incrementally less until one can survive by sucking a special kind of stone.

culture

rig-né (*rig gNas* / རིག་གནས་).

cyclic experience and perception

see: 'Khor dé

cymbals

see: rolmo.

da'dung

mDa' mDung / མདའ་མདུང་ – arrow-spear. One of the implements used by Ngakpa Yeshé Dorje for exorcism.

da-ta'i rigpa

da lTa'i rig pa / ད་ལྟའི་རིག་པ་ – uncontrived presence.

dag-nang gTér

see: gTér.

dam-tsig sem-dPa'

gDam tshigs sems dPa' / གདམ་ཚིགས་སེམས་དཔའ་ – avowed mind hero.

damaru

nga (*rNga* / རྔ་) – drum.

damçan

dam can / དམ་ཅན་ – protector.

damtsig

dam tshig / དམ་ཚིག་ / *samaya* – vow.

gDang, rolpa, and rTsal

gDang / གདང་ / *rol pa* / རོལ་པ་ / *rTsal* / རྩལ་ – three aspects of energy: inner-outer undivided, internally manifesting, and externally manifesting.

development phase

kyèd rim (*bsKyed rim* / བསྐྱེད་རིམ་).

dig-dzub

sDigs mDzub / སྡིགས་མཛུབ་ – threatening mudra, scorpion gesture.

divination

tra-se-na (*pra se na* / པྲ་སེ་ན་).

dob-dob

lDob lDob / ལྡོབ་ལྡོབ་ – police monks who existed in large Gelug gompas such as Sera, Ganden, and Drepung. These monks were often keen on sport, fighting, and other secular pursuits.

dödma'i sang-gyé

gDod ma'i sangs rGyas / གདོད་མའི་སངས་རྒྱས་ – primordial Buddhahood.

dorje

rDo rJe / རྡོ་རྗེ་ / *vajra* – thunderbolt sceptre.

Dorje Jig-jèd Jampal Shin-jé

rDo rJe 'jigs byed 'jam dPal gShin rJe / རྡོ་རྗེ་འཇིགས་བྱེད་འཇམ་དཔལ་གཤིན་རྗེ་ / Yamantaka – wrathful Jampalyang (*'jam dPal dByangs* / འཇམ་དཔལ་དབྱངས་ / Manjushri) yidam of body.

Dorje Legpa

rDo rJe legs pa / རྡོ་རྗེ་ལེགས་པ་ / *vajra sadhu* – one of three main Nyingma protectors, who rides a goat or snow lion.

Dorje Zahorma

rDo rJe za hor ma / རྡོ་རྗེ་ཟ་ཧོར་མ་ / or rig'dzin chi-wa (*rig 'dzin sPyi zhwa* རིག་འཛིན་སྤྱི་ཞྭ་) – the general Nyingma Lama's hat. For empowerments the lotus hat of Ögyen is worn – Ögyen pé-zha (*o rGyan pad zhwa* / ཨོ་རྒྱན་པད་ཞྭ་).

'dré

'dre / འདྲེ – ghost; dön 'dré (*gDon 'dre* / གདོན་འདྲེ) – demonic ghost.

dri-dre

gri 'dre / གྲི་འདྲེ – demon knife. One of the implements used by Ngakpa Yeshé Dorje for exorcism.

drilbu

dril bu / དྲིལ་བུ / *ghanta* – bell.

drog dza'

grogs mDza' / གྲོགས་མཛའ – lover.

drokpa

'brog pa / འབྲོག་པ – nomad herdsman of either sheep or yak. Chang thang gi drokpa (*byang thang gi 'brog pa* / བྱང་ཐང་གི་འབྲོག་པ – yak herding nomads of the northern high-plains.

dröl-lam

grol lam / གྲོལ་ལམ – liberation path.

drub-dé ma

sGrub sDe ma / སྒྲུབ་སྡེ་མ – consort.

Drüpchen

grub thob chen po / གྲུབ་ཐོབ་ཆེན་པོ / *mahasiddha*.

dualistic derangements, five

nyon mongpa dug nga (*nyon mongs pa dug lNga* / ཉོན་མོངས་པ་དུག་ལྔ). 1. obduracy, arrogance, territorialism; 2. aversion, aggression, militancy; 3. obsession, fixation, fascination; 4. paranoia, envy, jealousy, protectiveness; and, 5. indifference, unresponsiveness, oblivious torpor.

bDüd

bDud / དུད་ – mara, demon, negative influence.

'dul-trim

'dul khrims / འདུལ་ཁྲིམས་ / *vinaya* – the monastic vows of discipline.

dung-kyi a-long

dung kyi A long / དུང་གྱི་ཨ་ལོང་ – conch shell earrings. The best have a spiral carved out of their centres – but most are simple hoops. The dung-kyi a-long are part of the gö kar chang lo dress. They were common in Tibet but rarely seen after the exodus.

dung-wa

rDung ba / རྡུང་བ་ – cudgel. One of the implements used by Ngakpa Yeshé Dorje for exorcism.

Dzogchen, three series

1. Dzogchen sem-dé (*rDzogs chen sems sDe* / རྫོགས་ཆེན་སེམས་སྡེ་ / *cittavarga*); 2. Dzogchen long-dé (*rDzogs chen kLong sDe* / རྫོགས་ཆེན་ཀློང་སྡེ་ / *abhyantaravarga*); 3. Dzogchen men-ngag-dé (*rDzogs chen man ngag sDe* / རྫོགས་ཆེན་མན་ངག་སྡེ་ / *upadesavarga*).

Dzogchen Thöd-gal

rDzogs chen thod rGal / རྫོགས་ཆེན་ཐོད་རྒལ་ – the rainbow body practice which involves dark retreat (Mun-tsam (*mun mTshams* / མུན་མཚམས་), having previously engaged in sky gazing Dark retreat is conducted in total darkness, in which vision is experienced beyond the limits of internal and external separation. The practice engages the subtle body of spatial channels, winds, and essences to generate a spontaneous flow of luminous rainbow-spheres which gradually expand in size and complexity – through which one recognizes the nature of Mind in the physical continuum. Thöd-gal (*thod rGal* / ཐོད་རྒལ་) means direct vision.

It is also translated as: direct crossing; simultaneous passing; instantaneous directness; crossing in one leap; and passing over the summit. Thöd-gal comprises four visions (thöd-gal gyi nangwa zhi / *thod rGal gyi sNang ba bZhi* / ཐོད་རྒལ་གྱི་སྣང་བ་བཞི་) – Manifest Chö-nyid, Heightened Experience, Summit Awareness, and Exhaustion of Limitations.

É hong

e hong / ཨེ་ཧོང་ – a colloquial Tibetan expression of disgust.

element Buddhas & consorts

Earth element: Rinchen Jungné (*rin chen 'byung gNas* / རིན་ཆེན་འབྱུང་གནས་ / *Ratnasambhava*) and Dorje Mamaki (rDo rJe ma ma ki / རྡོ་རྗེ་མ་མ་ཀི་ / *Vajra Mamaki*).

Water element: Mikyöpa (*mi bsKyod pa* / མི་བསྐྱོད་པ་ / *Akshobhya*) and Sanggye Chanma (*sangs rGyas sPyan ma* / སངས་རྒྱས་སྤྱན་མ་ / *Locana*).

Fire element: 'od Pa'mèd (*'od pags 'med* / འོད་པགས་འམེད་ / *Amitabha*) and Gö-kar mo (*gos dKar mo* / གོས་དཀར་མོ་ / *Pandara*).

Air element: Dön-yö Drüp-pa (*don yod grub pa* / དོན་ཡོད་གྲུབ་པ་ / *Amoghasiddhi*) and Damtsig Drölma (*dam tshig sGrol ma* / དམ་ཚིག་སྒྲོལ་མ་ / *Visvapani* / Green Tara).

Space element: Nampar Nangdzé (*nam par sNang mDzad* / རྣམ་པར་སྣང་མཛད་ / *Vairochana*) and Ying-chugma (*dByings phyug ma* / དབྱིངས་ཕྱུག་མ་ / *Dharmadhatvishvari*).

empowerments, four

bum wang (*bum pa* / བུམ་དབང་) – vase empowerment; tsig wang (*tshig dBang* / ཚིག་དབང་) – word empowerment; sang wang (*gSang dBang* / གསང་དབང་) – secret empowerment; shérab yeshé kyi wang (*shes rab ye shes kyi dBang* / ཤེས་རབ་ཡེ་ཤེས་ཀྱི་དབང་ / *prajna jnana abhiseka*) – knowledge-wisdom empowerment.

Esoteric Mahayana

nang-kor (*nang sKor* / ནང་སྐོར་).

exorcism

see: chir-log.

Exoteric Mahayana

chi-kor (*phyi sKor* / ཕྱི་སྐོར་).

Father Tantra

pha gyüd (*pha rGyud* / པ་རྒྱུད་).

Formless Mahamudra

chag chen nam 'mèd (*phyag chen rNam 'med* / ཕྱག་ཆེན་རྣམ་འམེད་) – comprises of the Najor Zhi (*rNal 'byor bZhi* / རྣལ་འབྱོར་བཞི་) – the four yogas: 1. Tsé gCig (*rTse gCig* / རྩེ་གཅིག་) one pointedness; 2. Trodral (*sPros bral* / སྤྲོས་བྲལ་) non-elaboration or lacking complexity; 3. Ro-gÇig (*ro gCig* / རོ་གཅིག་) one taste; and 4. Gom'mèd (*sGom 'med* / སྒོམ་འམེད་) non-meditation. Formless Mahamudra is also known as Naked Mahamudra (chag chen gÇér thong / *phyag chen gCer mThong* / ཕྱག་ཆེན་གཅེར་མཐོང་).

Gang-kar ti-sé

gangs dKar ti se / གངས་དཀར་ཏི་སེ་ – White Glacier, Mount Kailash.

gang-zag nyèn-gyüd

gang zag sNyan brGyud / གང་ཟག་སྙན་བརྒྱུད་ – hearing transmission; mouth to ear lineage; individual hearing lineage.

gar 'cham

gar 'cham / གར་འཆམ་ – ritual dance.

Garwa Nagpo

mGar ba nag po / མགར་བ་ནག་པོ་ – a Nyingma protector; the Vajra Blacksmith.

gé-nyèn

dGe bsNyen / དགེ་བསྙེན་ / *sravaka* – a monk with eight vows to observe. Celibacy is not enjoined upon gé-nyèns or gé-nyènmas, Buddhist lay adherents who maintain the five precepts.

Geshé

dGe bShes / དགེ་བཤེས་ – Gélug academic title; holder of a high academic degree in Buddhist philosophy.

gö kar chang lo'i dé

gos dKar lCang lo'i sDe / གོས་དཀར་ལྕང་ལོའི་སྡེ་ – white raiment and uncut hair series (category or class). Black gö kar chang lo: Nagpo'i Ngak'phang (*nag po'i sNgags 'phang* / ནག་པོའི་སྔགས་འཕང་); Multicoloured gö kar chang lo: Tra-chol lé'i Ngak'phang (*khra chol le'i sNgags 'phang* / ཁྲ་ཚོལ་ལེའི་སྔགས་འཕང་); White gö kar chang lo: Karpo'i Ngak'phang (*dKar po'i sNgags 'phang* / དཀར་པོའི་སྔགས་འཕང་).

gom-shing

sGom shing / སྒོམ་ཤིང་ or gom-tén (*sGom brTan* / སྒོམ་བརྟན་) – meditation crutch, stick; meditation support.

gom-tag

sGom thag / སྒོམ་ཐག་ – meditation belt.

gompa

dGon pa / དགོན་པ་ – meditation place, temple.

gompa drum

nga-chen (*rNga chen* / རྔ་ཆེན་) – a large drum on a stand.

grigug

    gri gug / གྲི་གུག – a hooked knife with a curved blade. One of the implements used by Ngakpa Yeshé Dorje for exorcism.

hagiography

    namthar *(rNam thar* / རྣམ་ཐར).

Hayagriva

    Tamdrin *(rTa mGrin* / རྟ་མགྲིན / *pad ma gSung* / པདྨ་གསུང / *Hayagriva)* – wrathful Chenrézigs, yidam of speech.

immeasurables, four

    Four Immeasurables: equanimity, loving kindness, compassion, and joy. *Equanimity* is the wish to be free from preference and prejudice; to know things simply as they are; to experience the world knowing one is simply existent; and, to perceive the nature of whatever arises. *Loving kindness* is the wish for all to be happy, well, and at peace; to be open to whatever presents itself; to experience the world—as one is encountered by it—to be what it actually is; and to welcome whatever arises. *Compassion* is the wish to free all from suffering, harm, and disturbance; to accept life circumstances as they are; to experience natural acceptance for all beings; and to serve whatever needs arise for others. *Joy* is to enjoy the activities of life; to enjoy phenomena simply as they are; to experience the joy of reality in terms of whatever is accomplished; and to know how to respond in relation to whatever arises.

inner yogas

    see: naro chö drug.

inseparability of phenomena and emptiness

    nang-tong cher-mèd *(sNang sTong dByer 'med* / སྣང་སྟོང་དབྱེར་འམེད).

interdependent origination

> ten'drèl du 'jungwa (*rTen 'brel du 'byung ba* / རྟེན་འབྲེལ་དུ་འབྱུང་བ་ / *pratityasamutpada*). Phenomena, outer and inner, do not appear without causes – nor are they caused by an uncreated creator i.e. 'God'. Phenomena arise through the coalescence of particular causes and conditions. Shakyamuni Buddha stated *When this is, that is. From the arising of this comes the arising of that. When this is not, that is not. From the cessation of this comes the cessation of that.*'

irony

> kün-né gôd-pa (*kun nas dGod pa* / ཀུན་ནས་དགོད་པ་) – irony.

'ja'lü

> *ja' lus* / འཇའ་ལུས་ – dissolution of the body at death into the essence of the elements, as coloured light.

ja ngarmo

> *ja mNgar mo* / ཇ་མངར་མོ་ – Indian sweet tea with milk.

ja wa'i gyud

> *bya ba'i rGyud* / བྱ་བའི་རྒྱུད་ / *Kriyatantra*.

Jampal Shin-jé

> *'jam dPal gShin rJe* / འཇམ་དཔལ་གཤིན་རྗེ་ ; Dorje Jig-jèd (*rDo rJe 'jigs byed* / རྡོ་རྗེ་འཇིགས་བྱེད་ / *Yamantaka*) – wrathful Jampalyang (*'jam dPal dByangs* / འཇམ་དཔལ་དབྱངས་ / *Manjushri*) – yidam of body.

Jétsunma

> *rJe bTsun ma* / རྗེ་བཙུན་མ་ – means 'Lady', as in the female of 'Lord'.

jig rTen drug

> *jig rTen drug* / འཇིག་རྟེན་དྲུག་ / *khams drug* / ཁམས་དྲུག་ – the Dzogchen practice of the Six Lokas or experiential domains of duality.

jig-ten-gyi tha-nyèd

'jig rTen gyi tha sNyad / འཇིག་རྟེན་གྱི་བ་སྙད་ / *lokavyavahara* – social conventions. Ma-chèd ma-tag pa'i jig-ten gyi tha-nyèd (*ma dPyad ma brTags pa'i 'jig rTen gyi tha sNyad* / མ་དཔྱད་མ་བརྟགས་པའི་འཇིག་རྟེན་གྱི་བ་སྙད་) – unanalysed social convention.

ka'bab

bKa' babs / བཀའ་བབས་ – transmission.

ka-jor

kha sByor / ཁ་སྦྱོར་ – sexual union, also kissing. Nyi'mèd ka-jor (*gNyis 'med kha sByor* / གཉིས་མེད་ཁ་སྦྱོར་) means nondual integration.

kangling

rKang gLing / རྐང་གླིང་ – trumpet made from a human femoral bone, mainly employed in the practice of gÇod (*gCod* / གཅོད་).

kar-sum

dKar gSum / དཀར་གསུམ་ – the three whites: milk, butter, and yoghurt.

karmamudra

lé-kyi chagya (*las kyi phyag rGya* / ལས་ཀྱི་ཕྱག་རྒྱ་) – Tantric sexual yoga.

kha chang

kha byang / ཁ་བྱང་ – prophetic guide.

khandro cypher

Khandro Da'yig (*mKha' 'gro'i brDa' yig* / མཁའ་འགྲོའི་བརྡའ་ཡིག་) – khandro cypher / dakini script. Also thiglé'i yi-ge (*thig le'i yi ge* / ཐིག་ལེའི་ཡི་གེ་) – essence cypher; pung-yig (*sPung yig* / སྤུང་ཡིག་) – amassed cypher; bé-yig (*sBas yig* / སྦས་ཡིག་) – hidden cypher; shur-yig (*bShur yig* / བཤུར་ཡིག་) – burning cypher.

khang ral-zhig

khang ral zhig / ཁང་རལ་ཞིག – ruined house.

khap-sé

kha zas / ཁ་ཟས – strips of plaited dough which are fried.

Khenpo

mKhan po / མཁན་པོ / *upadhyaya* – one who has completed the major course of studies in philosophy, logic, and vinaya.

'Khor'dé

'khor 'das / འཁོར་འདས – cyclic experience and its transcendence.

khorwa

'khor ba / འཁོར་བ / *samsara* – cyclic perception and cyclic experience.

dKyil'khor

dKyil 'khor / དཀྱིལ་འཁོར / *mandala* – centre and periphery.

ku sum

sKu gSum / སྐུ་གསུམ / *trikaya* – the three spheres of being: chö-ku (*chos sKu* / ཆོས་སྐུ / *dharmakaya*) – the sphere of unconditioned potentiality; long-ku (*longs sKu* / ལོངས་སྐུ / *sambhogakaya*) – the sphere of nondual appearances; and, trülku (*sPrul sKu* / སྤྲུལ་སྐུ / *nirmanakaya*) – the sphere of realised manifestation.

ku drag

sKu drag / སྐུ་དྲག – noble, aristocrat, gentry, high official.

ku zèn

sKu gZan / སྐུ་གཟན – shawl.

kün-né gôd-pa

kun nas dGod pa / ཀུན་ནས་དགོད་པ – irony.

kun-tag dag'dzin

kun brTags bDag 'dzin / ཀུན་བཏགས་བདག་འཛིན – conceptualised self-referencing; theoretical self-referencing habituation.

kya

sKya / སྐྱ – means grey, pale grey, light, colourless; yellowish-white, light-blue, light green, or light yellow. Kya-wo (*sKya bo* / སྐྱ་བོ) – means layman; a person clothed in the coarse grey serge.

kyé bu dampa

sKyes bu dam pa / སྐྱེས་བུ་དམ་པ / *satpurusha* – holy being, saint, virtuous, wise-man.

kyé ma hu

kye ma kyi hud / ཀྱེ་མ་ཀྱི་ཧུད – exclamation of deep distress.

Lama

bLa ma / བླ་མ / *guru*.

lé

las / ལས / *karma* – perception and response, more commonly known as cause and effect.

lha

lha / ལྷ – extra-dimensional beings.

lhatong

see: naljors, four.

liberation on…

Liberation on hearing – bardo (*bar do* / བར་དོ) is the intermediate phase between lives and the Bardro Thödröl (*bar do thos grol* / བར་དོ་ཐོས་གྲོལ) is liberation on hearing in the Bardo.

There are other means of liberation such as: Thongdrol (*mThong grol* / མཐོང་གྲོལ་) – liberation through seeing; Nyongdröl (*Nyong grol* / མྱོང་གྲོལ་) – liberation on tasting; Takdröl (*bTags grol* / བཏགས་གྲོལ་) – liberation on touching or wearing; and, Drèndröl (*dran grol* / དྲན་གྲོལ་) – liberation on recollection or ideation.

Lopön

sLob dPon / སློབ་དཔོན་ / *acarya* – preceptor.

ma-dzé da-gyüd

ma mDzes brDa brGyud / མ་མཛེས་བརྡ་བརྒྱུད་ – informal symbolic transmission or unconventional symbolic transmission.

madman

myönpa (*sMyon pa* / སྨྱོན་པ་).

merit

sônam (*bSod nams* / བསོད་ནམས་ / *punya*). It is translated as 'merit' but actually has a meaning closer to 'skill' or 'capacity'.

mi-kha

mi kha / མི་ཁ་ – slander, libel, defamation, vilification calumny, scandalising, gossip, character assassination criticism of the ignorant; literally 'bad mouth'.

mind-mandate

tèd-gya dzadpa (*gTad rGya mDzad pa* / གཏད་རྒྱ་མཛད་པ་) – giving transmission directly mind to mind.

mo-mo

mog mog / མོག་མོག་ – Tibetan fried or steamed pasties with a meat or (*modern*) vegetable filling.

mu-göd

dMu rGod / དམུ་རྒོད་ – unruly, savage, untamed, wild, incorrigible, barbaric.

myön Héruka

sMyon he ru ka / སྨྱོན་ཧེ་རུ་ཀ་ / *avadhuta*. There is no entirely good translation. Keith Dowman employed 'divine madman' others employ 'crazy saint' or 'crazy wisdom master'. Dung-sé Thrin-lé Norbu Rinpoche employs 'wisdom eccentric' and this is probably the best translation. sMyon means mad or crazy. Héruka is Sanskrit, and the Tibetan equivalent is trak'thung (*khrag 'thung* / ཁྲག་འཐུང་) which means *blood drinker* – one who drinks the hot blood of delusion and transforms it into wisdom. Trak'thung can also mean *one who drinks from a human skull bowl*.

naljor gyüd

rNal 'byor rGyud / རྣལ་འབྱོར་རྒྱུད་ / *Yogatantra*.

naljorpa/ma

rNal 'byor pa / རྣལ་འབྱོར་པ་ / *yogi or yogin* – practitioner of Vajrayana yogas such as the Six Yogas of Naropa and Niguma.

naljors, four

rNal 'byor / རྣལ་འབྱོར་ / *yoga*. The four naljors are the preliminary practices of Dzogchen: 1. shi-nè *zhi gNas* / ཞི་གནས་ / *samatha* – calm abiding; 2. lhathong (*lhag mThong* / ལྷག་མཐོང་ / *vipassana* – further vision; 3. nyi'mèd (*gNyis 'med* / གཉིས་མེད་ / *advaya*) – not two, nondual; 4. lhundrüp (*lhun grub* / ལྷུན་གྲུབ་ / *anabhoga*) – spontaneity.

nambu karpo

gNam bu dKar po / གནམ་བུ་དཀར་པོ་) – white woollen shamthab.

nang yul

>sNang yul / སྣང་ཡུལ་ – appearing object.

naro chö drug

>see: yogas, six.

natural mind

>rang bab kyi dranpa (rang babs kyi dran pa / རང་བབས་ཀྱི་དྲན་པ་).

nature of reality

>dé-kho na-nyid (de kho na nyid / དེ་ཁོ་ན་ཉིད་).

ngak

>sNgags / སྔགས་ / mantra – awareness spell.

ngakpa

>sNgags pa / སྔགས་པ་ / mantrin and ngakmas (sNgags ma / སྔགས་མ་ / mantrini) – the word 'ngakpa' can be used to mean both male and female mantrikas / tantrikas.

ngar-sum

>mNgar gSum / མངར་གསུམ་ – the three sweets: sugar, honey and molasses.

nöd-zhin

>gNod sByin / གནོད་སྦྱིན་ / yaksha – storm-bringer.

nyèn

>gNyan / གཉན་ – malevolent mountain entity.

nyi'mèd

>see: naljors, four.

Nyingma traktung, eight

1. Jampal Shin-jé (*jam dPal gShin rJe* / འཇམ་དཔལ་གཤིན་རྗེ་) ; Dorje Jig-jèd (*rDo rJe 'jigs byed* / རྡོ་རྗེ་འཇིགས་བྱེད་ / *Yamantaka*) – wrathful Jampalyang (*jam dPal dByangs* / འཇམ་དཔལ་དབྱངས་ / *Manjushri*) – yidam of body.
2. Tamdrin (*rTa mGrin* / རྟ་མགྲིན་ / *pad ma gSung* / པདྨ་གསུང་ / *Hayagriva*) – wrathful Chenrézigs, yidam of speech.
3. Yangdak Héruka (*yang dag thugs* / ཡང་དག་ཐུགས་ / *Vishuddha* / *Sri Samyak*) – wrathful Chana Dorje, yidam of mind.
4. Chemchog Héruka (*che mChog* / ཆེ་མཆོག་ / *Mahottara*) – wrathful Küntuzangpo, yidam of nondual qualities.
5. Dorje Phurba (*rDo rJe phur ba* / རྡོ་རྗེ་ཕུར་བ་) / Phurba Thinlé (*phur ba 'phrin las* / ཕུར་བ་འཕྲིན་ལས་) / Dorje Zhonu (*rDo rJe gZhon nu* / རྡོ་རྗེ་གཞོན་ནུ་ / *Vajrakilaya* / *Vajrakumara*) – wrathful Dorje Sempa (*rDo rJe sems dPa'* / རྡོ་རྗེ་སེམས་དཔའ་ / *Vajrasattva*) – yidam of purification.
6. Mamo Botong (*ma mo rBod gTong* / མ་མོ་རྦོད་གཏོང་ / *Matarah*) – wrathful Namkha'i Nyingpo (*nam mKha'i sNying po* / ནམ་མཁའི་སྙིང་པོ་ / *Akasagarbha*) – yidam of summoning and dispatching.
7. Jig-ten Chod-töd (*'jig rTen mChod bsTod* / འཇིག་རྟེན་མཆོད་བསྟོད་ / *Lokastotrapujanatha*) – wrathful Sa-yi Nyingpo (*sa yi sNying po* / ས་ཡི་སྙིང་པོ་ / *Ksitigarbha*) – yidam of secular presentation and admiration.
8. Mödpa Dra-ngak (*mod pa drag sNgags* / མོད་པ་དྲག་སྔགས་ / *Vajramantrabhiru*) – wrathful Jampa (*byams pa* / བྱམས་པ་ / *Maitreya*) – yidam of wrathful mantras.

nyingthig yabzhi

sNying thig ya bZhi / སྙིང་ཐིག་ཡ་བཞི་ – the Four Sections of Nying-thig, which consists of: Vima Nyingthig, Lama Yangthig, Khandro Nyingthig, and Khandro Yangthig. The Vima Nyingthig and Khandro Nyingthig are also known as the 'Mother Nying-thig' and the Lama Yangthig and Khandro Yangthig are known as the 'Child Nying-thig'. The two collections are therefore called 'The Four Sections of Mother and Child – Nyingthig ma-bu zhi (*sNying thig ma bu bZhi* / སྙིང་ཐིག་མ་བུ་བཞི་).

O yah

'ong yag / འོང་ཡག – an expression with multiple meanings depending on tone of voice, facial expression, and hand gestures: approbation, applause, surprise, ennui, mild exasperation, doubt, suspicion, perplexity, disgruntlement.

'og-lung

'og rLung / འོག་རླུང་ – lower wind; flatus, flatulence.

'og-rim

'og rim / འོག་རིམ – lower level, subordinate, inferior.

outer, inner and secret demons

see: chi dag ta'i rudra.

Palden Lhamo

dPal lDan lha mo / དཔལ་ལྡན་ལྷ་མོ / *Sri Devi* – the female consort of Nakpo Chenpo (Mahakala).

paleb

bag leb / པག་ལེབ – a Tibetan muffin.

dPa'wo chag

dPa' bo lCags / དཔའ་བོ་ལྕགས – hero's whip. One of the implements used by Ngakpa Yeshé Dorje for exorcism.

phat

phat / ཕཊ) – disperse into beginningless space! Combination of *pha* – beyond; and *t* (reversed) – cutting.

phurba

phur ba / ཕུར་བ / *kila or kilaya* – thunderbolt nail: the three bladed dagger of emptiness which stabs attraction, aversion, and indifference.

po-ja

bod ja / བོད་ཇ་ – Tibetan butter tea.

prediction

ma'ong lung tèn (*ma 'ongs lung bsTan* / མ་འོངས་ལུང་བསྟན་), lung tén (*lung bsTan* / ལུང་བསྟན་), or lung tön (*lung sTon* / ལུང་སྟོན་).

present wakefulness

da-ta'i shépa (*da lTa'i shes pa* / ད་ལྟའི་ཤེས་པ་).

Primordial Awareness

yeshé (*ye shes* / ཡེ་ཤེས་). Yeshé Nga (*ye shes lNga* / ཡེ་ཤེས་ལྔ་) – five aspects of primordial awareness: 1. Space Wisdom – chö-kyi ying-kyi yeshé (*chos kyi dByings kyi ye shes* / ཆོས་ཀྱི་དབྱིངས་ཀྱི་ཡེ་ཤེས་ / *dharmadhatujnana*); 2. Mirror wisdom – mélong tabu'i yeshé (*me long lTa bu'i ye shes* / མེ་ལོང་ལྟ་བུའི་ཡེ་ཤེས་ / *adarsajnana*); 3. Equality Wisdom – nyam-nyid yeshé (*mNyam nyid ye shes* / མཉམ་ཉིད་ཡེ་ཤེས་ / *samatajnana*); 4. Discerning Wisdom – so-sor thogpa'i yeshé (*so sor rTog pa'i ye shes* / སོ་སོར་རྟོག་པའི་ཡེ་ཤེས་ / *pratyaveksanajnana*); 5. All-accomplishing wisdom – ja-wa drup-pa'i yeshé (*bya ba grub pa'i ye shes* / བྱ་བ་གྲུབ་པའི་ཡེ་ཤེས་ / *krtyanusthanajnana*).

Primordial Wisdom Chaos

yeshé cholwa (*ye shes 'chol ba* / ཡེ་ཤེས་འཆོལ་བ་). 'Ye' means 'primordial', and 'shes' means 'knowing' – therefore yeshé means primordial wisdom or uncreated knowingness. 'Cholwa means chaotic but it also signifies a broad variety of ideas including: actualisation, irregularity, thrown together at random, eccentricity, raving, and deviating from the norm.

The syllable 'chol' when found in these words expands the sense of meaning and gives us subtleties of meaning with regard to the word 'chaotic'; words such as: 'chol bar gro – intermixing; 'chol bar byed – contrivances; 'chol bar byed pa – thrown into disorder; 'chol med – randomness; 'chol ma – sly sensual woman; 'chol ba pa – crafty libidinous man; 'gLags 'chol – seeking opportunities; 'chol gTam – brazen speech; 'chol pa – disorderly; 'chol sPyod kyi mDzad pa – wild actions. When considering the breadth of meaning supplied by these words, it can be seen that there is a precise application of language – in terms of Vajrayana. 'chol bar byed pa—thrown into disorder—means that duality is thrown into disorder. gLags 'chol means that primordial wisdom is seeking opportunities to undermine duality.

prophetic guide

kha chang (*kha byang* / ཁ་བྱང་).

protective tantric ritual

life-wheel, hail, and spells – srog-ser tad sum (*srog ser gTad gSum* / སྲོག་སེར་གཏད་གསུམ་): the three aspects of protective tantric ritual.

pun

tsig gyag (*tshig rGyag* / ཚིག་རྒྱག).

rain-stopping practitioner

see: char-gÇodpa.

rainbow body

see: 'ja'lü.

ral-dri

ral gri / རལ་གྲི – sword. One of the implements used by Ngakpa Yeshé Dorje for exorcism.

Rig'dzin

rig 'dzin / རིག་འཛིན་ / *vidyadhara* – means awareness holder. The Sanskrit term vidyadhara refers to either: 1. one who has gained siddhis through accomplishment (Vajrayana tantric literature); or 2. a magical winged being (Sutric literature).

rilbu

ril bu / རིལ་བུ་ – medical pills. Ngödrüp rilbu (*dNgos grub ril bu* / དངོས་གྲུབ་རིལ་བུ་) – siddhi pills; Chhi'mèd rilbu (*'chi 'med ril bu* / འཆི་འམེད་རིལ་བུ་) – long-life pills; and, 'ja'lü ril bu (*ja' lus ril bu* / འཇའ་ལུས་རིལ་བུ་) – rainbow light pills, prepared from Black Naga Devil lu-dud nagpo (*kLu bDud nag po* / ཀླུ་བདུད་ནག་པོ་ / codonopsis / bonnet bell-flower).

rolmo

rol mo / རོལ་མོ་ – large wrathful cymbals with hemispherical bosses. Rolmo bupchal (*rol mo sBub chal* / རོལ་མོ་སྦུབ་ཆལ་) – extremely large wrathful cymbals.

rudra

chi dag ta'i rudra (*phyi bDag lTa'i ru dra* / ཕྱི་བདག་ལྟའི་རུ་ད་) – the outer rudra of viewing in terms of gross self-referencing. Nang dag ta'i rudra (*nang bDag lTa'i ru dra* / ནང་བདག་ལྟའི་རུ་ད་) – inner rudra of viewing in terms of self-referencing. Sang-wa dag ta'i rudra (*gSang ba bDag lTa'i ru dra* / གསང་བ་བདག་ལྟའི་རུ་ད་) – innermost 'secret rudra' of viewing in terms of self-referencing.

sa dag

sa bDag / ས་བདག་ – Lord of the Earth. A local protective being.

saint

kyebu chenpo (*sKyes bu chen po* / སྐྱེས་བུ་ཆེན་པོ་ / satpurusha).

samsara

see: cyclic experience and perception.

samsara and nirvana

'Khor dé ('*khor 'das* / འཁོར་འདས་) – cyclic experience and its transcendence.

sang wang

see: empowerments, four.

sangyab

gSang yab / གསང་ཡབ་ – literally 'secret father', but meaning 'consort', 'religious husband'.

sangyum

gSang yum / གསང་ཡུམ་ / *guhyakalatrata* – literally 'secret mother', but meaning 'consort', 'religious wife'.

scholar

kun-khyen (*kun mKhyen* / ཀུན་མཁྱེན་).

sèl shing

gSal shing / གསལ་ཤིང་ – impalement stake. One of the implements used by Ngakpa Yeshé Dorje for exorcism.

sem

sems / སེམས་ / *chitta* – conceptual mind.

sem 'dzin

sems 'dzin / སེམས་འཛིན་.

sem tral'mèd pa

sems khral 'med pa / སེམས་ཁྲལ་འམེད་པ་ – unceremonious, at ease.

shamthab

sham thabs / ཤམ་ཐབས་ – a pleated skirt tied at the waist with a sash.

shérab yeshé kyi wang

>*see:* empowerments, four.

sherpa

>*shar pa* / འཤར་པ་ – Easterner.

Shin-jé

>*gShin rJe* / གཤིན་རྗེ་ – Lord of Death.

shintu naljor thegpa

>*shin tu rNal 'byor gyi theg pa* / ཤིན་ཏུ་རྣལ་འབྱོར་གྱི་ཐེག་པ་ / *ati-yoga yana* / *upadesha* / *mahasandhi*.

shurma

>*shur ma* / ཤུར་མ་ – pike. One of the implements used by Ngakpa Yeshé Dorje for exorcism.

skull damaru

>thöd nga (*thod rNga* / ཐོད་རྔ་) or go-ru nga (*mGo rus rNga* / མགོ་རུས་རྔ་). The skull damaru is made from a male and female human calvarium, cut above the ears. Internally they are inscribed with male and female yidam mantras. The skins are cured by burying them with copper; mineral salts, and herbal formulations for a few weeks. These are then stretched and applied to the two sides, giving the skins a mottled green or blue appearance. From the 1960s diaspora, they were made up to the late 1980s in India and Nepal. India and Nepal however, are no longer a source – export being banned, due to criminal acquisition of human bone.

sor

>*bSor* / བསོར་ – spear. One of the implements used by Ngakpa Yeshé Dorje for exorcism.

srinmo

srin mo / སྲིན་མོ་ / *rakshasi* – often translated as demoness, ogress or vampire, but there is no useful translation.

stick drum

lag nga (*lag rNga* / ལག་རྔ་).

ta-ri

sTa ri / སྟ་རི་ – hatchet. One of the implements used by Ngakpa Yeshé Dorje for exorcism.

Tamdrin

rTa mGrin / རྟ་མགྲིན་ / *pad ma gSung* / པད་མ་གསུང་ / *Hayagriva* – wrathful Chenrézigs, yidam of speech.

Tantra, classes, six

gyüd-dé drug (*rGyud sDe drug* / རྒྱུད་སྡེ་དྲུག་). In the Nyingma Tradition the tantras are divided into six classes: the three outer tantras *(common to Sarma and Nyingma):* are Kriya tantra; charya or upa tantra; and yoga tantra. The three inner tantras *(specific to Nyingma):* are Mahayoga, Anuyoga, and Atiyoga or Dzogchen.

gTér

gTer / གཏེར་ – teachings and practices hidden by Guru Rinpoche and Yeshé Tsogyel to be found in a later time. Sa gTér (*sa gTer* / ས་གཏེར་), earth gTér – physical religious objects.; gong gTér (*dGongs gTer* / དགོངས་གཏེར་); dag-nang gTér (*dag sNang gTer* / དག་སྣང་གཏེར་) – Pure Vision gTérma.

gTértön

gTer sTon / གཏེར་སྟོན་ – a discoverer of gTér.

gTorma

gTor ma / གཏོར་མ / *balingta* – three-dimensional strewing-oblation profferment, either edible or nonedible; sculpted objects ceremonially presented to yidams (awareness beings / meditational deities) or protectors for diverse purposes connected with rites of amenity and attainment.

rTsa, rLung, and thig-lé

rTsa (*rTsa* / རྩ / *nadi*) – spatial channels; rLung (*rLung* / རླུང་* / *prana*) – spatial winds; thig-lé (*thig le* / ཐིག་ལེ / *bindu*) – spatial essences.

te'ü dung

sTe'u mDung / སྟེའུ་མདུང་ – axe-lance. One of the implements used by Ngakpa Yeshé Dorje for exorcism.

thöd nga

see: skull damaru.

tholum

tho lum / ཐོ་ལུམ – iron ball. One of the implements used by Ngakpa Yeshé Dorje for exorcism.

'thom yor

'thom yor / འཐོམ་ཡོར – idiot.

mThu-gyé jèd

mThu rGyas byed / མཐུ་རྒྱས་བྱེད – performing black magic.

thu-tèd

mThu gTad / མཐུ་གཏད – power, strength, force. black magic, casting spell.

thu-wo

mThu bo / མཐུ་བོ་ — wizard, witch, magician, sorcerer, necromancer.

thug-jé-ché

thugs rJe che / ཐུགས་རྗེ་ཆེ་ — thank you.

to-nga

sTod sNgags / སྟོད་སྔགས་ or *sTod sNgags* / སྟོད་སྔགས་ — a ngakpa's upper garment.

tog tsé

tog tse / ཏོག་ཙེ་ — mattock. One of the implements used by Ngakpa Yeshé Dorje for exorcism.

towa

tho ba / ཐོ་བ་ — hammer. One of the implements used by Ngakpa Yeshé Dorje for exorcism.

trab-pa

bKrabs pa / བཀྲབས་པ་ — warrior.

trek-chod

khregs chod / ཁྲེགས་ཆོད་ — cutting through rigidity, exploding the horizon of conventional meaning, or penetrating solidity. Together with thod rGal these two are the main sections of rDzogs chen.

tri kang

kring kang / ཀྲིང་ཀང་ — forked spear. One of the implements used by Ngakpa Yeshé Dorje for exorcism.

tsampa

tsam pa / ཙམ་པ་ — barley that is roasted, crushed, and roasted again.

tsé cho

tshal cho / ཚལ་ཆོ་ – vegetable chow-mein (lo-mein in the USA).

tsé dreng wa

rTse sGreng ba / རྩེ་སྒྲེང་བ་ – scimitar. One of the implements used by Ngakpa Yeshé Dorje for exorcism.

tsèn

bTsan / བཙན་ – demon.

tsig wang

see: empowerments, four.

tsig-sum nè-dek

tshig gSum gNad du brDeg / ཚིག་གསུམ་གནད་དུ་བརྡེག་ – The Three Phrases which Strike the Vital Point; the final words of Garab Dorje (*dGa' rab rDo rJe* / དགའ་རབ་རྡོ་རྗེ་ / *Pramodavajra* / *Prahevajra* / *Surativajra*) to Jampal Shényèn (*'jam dPal bShes gNyen* / འཇམ་དཔལ་བཤེས་གཉེན་ / *Manjushrimitra*).

tsog'khorlo

tshogs kyi 'khor lo / ཚོགས་ཀྱི་འཁོར་ལོ་ / *ganachakra* / *gha na tsa kra* – vajra banquet cycle. This is a practice of generosity in terms of the sense fields.

gTummo

see: yogas, six.

vividness of presence

sèl-nang shar-wa (*gSal sNang shar ba* / གསལ་སྣང་ཤར་བ་).

wang

dBang sKur / དབང་བསྐུར་ / *abhisheka* – an empowerment.

wild

    shèd ngèn (*shed ngan* / ཤེད་ངན་).

ya-tsan

    ya mTshan / ཡ་མཚན་ – amazement.

yag-po 'dug

    yag po 'dug / ཡག་པོ་འདུག་ – this is good.

Yamantaka

    Jampal Shin-jé (*'jam dPal gShin rJe* / འཇམ་དཔལ་གཤིན་རྗེ་); Dorje Jig-jèd (*rDo rJe 'jigs byed* / རྡོ་རྗེ་འཇིགས་བྱེད་ / *Yamantaka*) – wrathful Jampalyang (*'jam dPal dByangs* / འཇམ་དཔལ་དབྱངས་ / *Manjushri*) yidam of body.

Yangchen-ma

    dByangs chen ma / དབྱངས་ཆེན་མ་ / *Sarasvati* – the Buddha of Knowledge and Eloquence. Yangchen-ma's manifestations are as follows: Rinchen Yangchen ma (*rin chen dByangs chan ma* / རིན་ཆེན་དབྱངས་ཆེན་མ་) – Melodious Ratna Buddha; Dorje Yangchen-ma (*rDo rJe dByangs chan ma* / རྡོ་རྗེ་དབྱངས་ཆེན་མ་) – Melodious Vajra Buddha; Padma'i Yangchen ma (*pad ma'i dByangs chan ma* / པདྨའི་དབྱངས་ཆེན་མ་) – Melodious Padma Buddha; Thrinlé-kyi Yangchen-ma (*'phrin las kyi dByangs chan ma* / འཕྲིན་ལས་ཀྱི་དབྱངས་ཆེན་མ་) – Melodious Karma Buddha; Sang-gyé Kün-ngö Yangchen-ma (*sang rGyas kun dNgos dByangs chan ma* / སངས་རྒྱས་ཀུན་དངོས་དབྱངས་ཆེན་མ་) – Melodious Embodiment of all Buddhas; and Ngawang Yangchen-ma (*ngag dBang dByangs chan ma* / ངག་དབང་དབྱངས་ཆེན་མ་) – Melodious Buddha of Powerful Speech.

Yangdag Héruka

yang dag thugs / ཡང་དག་ཐུགས / *Vishuddha* / *Sri Samyak* – wrathful Chana Dorje, yidam of mind.

yanpa tang

yan pa bTang / ཡན་པ་བཏང – running wild.

Yeshé sem dPa'

ye shes sems dPa' / ཡེ་ཤེས་སེམས་དཔའ / *jnana sattva*.

yidam

yi dam / ཡི་དམ – meditational deity: the nondual anthropomorphic form employed for self-identification in visualisation practices of Tantra.

yogas, six

The six Yogas of Naropa or Six Yogas of Niguma – the Naro or Nigu Chödrug (*na ro* / *ni gu chos drug* ན་རོ་ཆོས་དྲུག / ནི་གུ་ཆོས་དྲུག / *saddharma*).
These are:
1. gTummo (*gTum mo* / གཏུམ་མོ / *candali*) – spatial heat.
2. gyu-lü (*sGyu lus* / སྒྱུ་ལུས / *Smayakaya*) – illusory body.
3. mi-lam (*rMi lam* / རྨི་ལམ / *vapnadarsana*) – dream yoga, dream path.
4. 'ö-Sel (*'od gSal* / འོད་གསལ / *prabhasvara*) – clear light luminosity.
5. 'pho-wa (*'pho ba* / འཕོ་བ / *samkranti*) – transference of consciousness.
6. bardo (*bar do* / བར་དོ / *antarabhava*) – intermediate states.
There is also Drong'jug (*grongs 'jug* / གྲོངས་འཇུག) – transference of consciousness to someone or some animal who has just died. This however was lost when Marpa's son died. It is however held to exist in a few small gTérma lineages.

Zangdogpalri

zangs mDog dPal ri / ཟངས་མདོག་དཔལ་རི་ – the Copper-coloured Mountain is the dimension of Guru Rinpoche. Kyabjé Düd'jom Rinpoche said *"Guru Rinpoche manifested the inconceivable Palace of Lotus Light, and presides there with emanations in each of the eight continents of the rakshasas, giving teachings like the Eight Great Methods of Attainment of the Kagyèd."*

zen-tra

gZan phra / གཟན་ཕྲ་ – multi-coloured shawl.

zha-nak

zhwa nag / ཞྭ་ནག་ – Black Hat. The Black Hat dance is often performed on the eve of Losar (*lo gSar* / ལོ་གསར་), the Tibetan new year.

zhi

gZhi / གཞི་ / alaya.

zo-zhing

bZo zhing / བཟོ་ཞིང་ – working class, peasantry.

zorwa

zor ba / ཟོར་བ་ – sickle. One of the implements used by Ngakpa Yeshé Dorje for exorcism.

www.ingramcontent.com/pod-product-compliance
Lightning Source LLC
Chambersburg PA
CBHW050428240426
43661CB00055B/2305